# Grand Army of Labor

THE WORKING CLASS
IN AMERICAN HISTORY



*A list of books in the series appears at the end of this book.*

# Grand Army of Labor

## Workers, Veterans, and the Meaning of the Civil War

MATTHEW E. STANLEY

UNIVERSITY OF ILLINOIS PRESS
Urbana, Chicago, and Springfield

1 2 3 4 5 C P 5 4 3 2 1
♾ This book is printed on acid-free paper.

Library of Congress Cataloging-in-Publication Data
Names: Stanley, Matthew E., author.
Title: Grand army of labor: workers, veterans, and the meaning of the Civil War / Matthew E. Stanley.
Description: Urbana: University of Illinois Press, [2021] | Series: The working class in American history | Includes bibliographical references and index. |
Identifiers: LCCN 2020038243 (print) | LCCN 2020038244 (ebook) | ISBN 9780252043741 (cloth) | ISBN 9780252085734 (paperback) | ISBN 9780252052644 (ebook)
Subjects: LCSH: Labor movement—United States—History—19th century. | Working class—United States—History—19th century. | Radicalism—United States—History—19th century. | Right and left—United States—History—19th century. | United States—History—Civil War, 1861–1865.
Classification: LCC HD8072 .S783 2021 (print) | LCC HD8072 (ebook) | DDC 322/.2097309034—dc23
LC record available at https://lccn.loc.gov/2020038243
LC ebook record available at https://lccn.loc.gov/2020038244

# Contents

# Foreword

THIS BOOK CONCERNS how working people created, drew on, and seized popular understandings of history to confront corporate domination. Their challenge is the challenge of our own time as well. I wrote this book during a new and growing inequality regime. To borrow the parlance of nineteenth-century workers, fast-food chains, box stores, and white-collar offices of contingent employees are our "workhouses" and "plantations"; hedge fund managers, pharma executives, and tech behemoths are the neo-"masters" of today's "Money Power." In fact, I put the final touches on this book in the (likely) early stages of a global pandemic that has illuminated yet again the contradictions of democracy in a capitalist society. This battle against an inanimate but largely preventable enemy—like the next worldwide contagion or the coming climate catastrophe—is magnifying decades of bipartisan privatization, austerity, falling tax rates, financial deregulation, free trade, and undermining of unions. Though the context has changed, workers across national borders, and especially in the United States, continue to resist a power elite predicated on labor disempowerment, police militarization, mass surveillance, classed and raced incarceration, and staggering disparities according to wealth.

The ravages of neoliberalism, meanwhile, have led to a renewed mass interest in anti-capitalist politics. That politics is in many ways historically broad even as it is less sustained by working-class institutions than were earlier movements. Union membership remains conventionally low, but support for unions is at its greatest point in decades, as are the numbers of strikes and labor actions. A self-described "democratic socialist" is arguably the most popular politician in the country and a viable presidential candidate. Like earlier radicals, today's leftists deliberate and diverge on how to confront and shape popular historical memory. Such questions have taken on increased urgency in the context of Black Lives Matter and the spontaneous toppling of monuments that venerate white supremacist, slaveholding, segregationist, patriarchal, and settler-colonial projects. For protesters, and many of the rest of the "non-gilded," it is increasingly evident that meaningful antiracism and antisexism *must* flow through the shared struggle of the many in pursuit of class interests. However, like past radicals, adherents to the "new socialism" of Bernie Sanders, Alexandria Ocasio-Cortez, and the resurgent Democratic Socialists of America are working through how to effectively construct a class-based politics both inside and beyond capitalist parties. They are reckoning with how to build—and present—a movement that is broad enough to win power and defend itself institutionally *while also* foregrounding the specific oppressions of certain groups of workers.

Though culture derives from social conditions, and not the other way around, much of this work involves constructing identities, sifting through historical frameworks, structuring collective memories, and generating discourses so as to facilitate organization, strengthen institutions, and foster consciousness. In other words, it is cultural work, and we must take culture seriously. In this sense, *Grand Army of Labor* betrays the poverty of both economic justice that decenters antiracism and antisexism *and* single-axis identity politics and the "oppression gymnastics" they tend to engender. In reiterating the necessity of solidarity, this story reminds us that oppressions—sexism, homophobia, transphobia, ableism, and xenophobia, as well as racism and classism—mutually constitute one another and that to eliminate one form we must upend them all. It is my sincere hope that this study of how working people used the memory of the Civil War to resist exploitation and define social liberation might offer a point of contemplation or a sliver of instruction during our New Gilded Age.

# Acknowledgments

I AM INDEBTED to so many people in so many places that I cannot reasonably list them all. Chris Phillips, Mark Lause, Wayne Durrill, and Martin Francis kick-started my thinking about the nexus between identity, collective memory, cultural politics, and materiality as they relate to the Civil War era. I formulated this project slowly, presenting parts of it at conferences, debating it in workshops, and discussing it in bars over rounds of beer. David Roediger, Alice Kessler-Harris, Andrew Hartman, Matt Hulbert, Paul M. Renfro, Bob Hutton, and Jacob Lee all read and ruminated on parts of this work. To them I extend my gratitude. Robert J. Cook, Jeff Johnson, Keri Leigh Merritt, Rashauna Johnson, and A. J. Aiseraithe commented on smaller portions, namely conference papers, and provided helpful feedback. Robert Weir, Ernest Freeberg, Christopher Phelps, Tom Lorman, Worth Robert Miller, Dana Caldemeyer, Scott Huffard, Blake Renfro, Evan Hart, Mike Crane, Patrick Whitehead, Dan Breen, Nina Silber, and Frank Towers also assisted generously in different capacities. I am likewise duty-bound to thank the staffs of various libraries and archives, from Amsterdam to Ann Arbor, and from Chicago to Chapel Hill. Through both grants and award money, the National Endowment for the Humanities, Albany State University, and the Center for Civil War Research at the University of Mississippi provided financial assistance toward my research. Finally, I offer a special thanks to my editor, James G. Engelhardt, for believing in this project and seeing it through. It goes without saying that any mistakes are fully my own.

I have personal debts, too. To my numerous comrades, colleagues, friends, and family: your mark is on every page. However, none of my obligations are greater than those to my wife, Emily, and our daughter, Ruby. If there is any element of truth, allure, or value in this book, it is for them.

Grand Army of Labor

# Introduction

## A Second Great Emancipator

THEIR WORLD WAS ONE of widespread poverty amid unprecedented plenty—a society in which the richest 4,000 families amassed as much wealth as the remaining 11.6 million families combined. Countless workers viewed widening social stratification, vast gaps in opportunity, and their own powerlessness as permanent, propertyless wage earners as violations of what it should mean to be American. They did not feel like free citizens. Politically, working people battled over wealth inequality, state intervention in the economy, corporate money in politics, and how citizens should deal with the deficiencies of capitalism. The "wage slaves" who manned Cornelius Vanderbilt's freight yards and Andrew Carnegie's blast furnaces faced material disparities and economic volatility between Reconstruction and the early twentieth century, when bloodshed over slavery and civil rights in the postwar South were replaced by new battles—both political and literal—between capital and labor. Above all, they awaited a new "emancipation."

By 1894 the United States was attaining remarkable heights of machine-based production, shifting increasingly from an agrarian to an urban and industrial society. Globally, its economic growth was second to none. But despite its emergence as the most profitable nation on earth, and eventually its most powerful, social division was giving way to outright fracture. The factory system encouraged added exploitative processes of supervision, routinization, and labor discipline, resulting in profound levels of worker discontent, alienation, and, at times, mutiny. Capital aggregation led to the consolidation of whole manufacturing sectors: coal, oil, and steel. With the expansion of postwar federal might, the rejuvenation of the settler-colonial project, and the eventual "closing" of the American West, the United States was transitioning from a continental to a hemispheric and world economic-military force. Empire brought unrest abroad and at home. Neither rising xenophobia, anti-Indianism, and anti-Black racism nor the normalization of capitalist ideology could obscure spiraling inequality. Class conflict reached a violent frenzy, from the sugarcane fields of Louisiana to the rail depots of Chicago's South Side and from the steel mills of western Pennsylvania to the hard-rock mining towns of northern Idaho.

New York journalist and former abolitionist John Swinton was one of the multitudes who envisioned another "great emancipator." Late that summer he attended a speech at the city's Cooper Union, as he had many times before. But this occasion was different. The speaker was labor leader Eugene V. Debs, and his moral clarity drew Swinton immediately back to another orator he had seen grace that very stage in the winter of 1860: Abraham Lincoln. Both Lincoln and Debs were Westerners, from the windswept prairies of central Illinois and Indiana. Swinton thought both men gaunt yet rugged, shrill-voiced yet audibly commanding, common-looking yet unforgettable. Both Debs and Lincoln were humorous, empathic, and clear, and both had been demonized by plutocrats. Swinton saw Debs's vision as part of a "logical sequence" beginning with the early Republican Party. He left the grand hall that night convinced that he was witnessing the emergence of a "new western leader in the struggle for labor's emancipation." "As Lincoln, of Illinois, became an efficient agent for freedom, so, perchance might Debs, of Indiana, become in the impending conflict for the liberation of labor," he predicted.[1]

Swinton was right. Debs's star *was* ascending—as were the Lincoln comparisons. The labor captain's image as a "second Great Emancipator" began with his orchestration of the American Railway Union, and admirers persistently likened the "Hoosier Poet" to major antislavery figures.[2] In turn, this "Abraham Lincoln of the moment" often adopted emancipationist motifs in order to denounce "wage slavery."[3] Populists paired him with their producerist hero, labeling Debs "the Lincoln in the new struggle for freedom."[4] Socialists, too, insisted that both Midwesterners "stood for emancipation" as part of a political tradition of labor liberation.[5] Reverend Frank DeWitt Talmage confessed that no speaker in history came nearer to Lincoln than did Debs.[6] Indeed, countless contemporaries equated Debs with William Lloyd Garrison, Dred Scott, and Debs's personal hero, John Brown.[7] Speaking in eulogy, socialist editor James O'Neal asserted that in being "off to mingle with the great liberators of the past," the radical Hoosier proved an eternal emancipator. Another mourner announced simply, "Debs is dead. Not so. Debs lives."[8]

As leader of the Socialist Party of America, Debs made the connection between himself and the Middle Western "Rail-splitter" explicit when in the fall of 1906 he led a vigil at Lincoln's tomb in Springfield, Illinois. "Slave power," Debs pronounced from the mausoleum terrace, "which loathed and despised Lincoln, was no more heartless than the power of capitalism, which to-day holds the workingmen of the Nation in bondage." Spectators circulated the speech widely, and admirers insisted Debs was "the Abraham Lincoln of the times."[9] As Swinton observed in his final assessment, "Lincoln spoke for man; so spoke Debs. Lincoln spoke for right and progress; so spoke Debs. Lincoln spoke for freedom of labor; so spoke Debs. Lincoln was the foe of human slavery; so is Debs."[10]

Eugene Debs made Lincoln in death the antiracist and egalitarian he had not been in life, using the slain president to cultivate his own mythos as a latter-day abolitionist. Debs's conjuring of the Civil War canon befit his roots. The fiery five-time presidential candidate, who would become the most prominent American socialist of the early twentieth century, was born in 1855, northwest of the southern Indiana hills where Lincoln had spent his youth. The child of Alsatian immigrants, Debs's labor activism turned revolutionary socialism harmonized with Protestant millennialism, and he saw his message as the moral link between "the martyred Christ of the working class," Marxism, and the abolitionist tradition.[11] He consciously adopted—and morphed—Lincoln's idea that autonomous producers and politically independent citizens should be "neither *hirers* or *hired*."[12] It was hypocrisy, Debs thought, that the bourgeoisie, who "glorify all the revolutions of the past and shake their fists at all the revolutions of the future," would co-opt the war's radical legacy while suppressing radicalism in their own time. He linked that collective memory to class interests: "The capitalist class has been put in power by past revolution; therefore, they are glorious. The capitalists yearn to remain in perpetual power; therefore, there must be no more revolutions."[13]

Debs invoked not only Lincoln and Brown but also Thomas Paine, Thaddeus Stevens, and Wendell Phillips. He compared bygone antislavery militants to anti-capitalist apostles in his own time.[14] As one Debs supporter declared, "The Socialists today occupy the same position as did the Abolitionists. The Socialists are engaged in a new Abolition movement to liberate all workingmen from the bondage and oppression of concentrated wealth."[15] "Abraham Lincoln was a Socialist," another exclaimed. "He had every belief of a Socialist. . . . [I]f he were alive today, why he would be the first man to uphold Socialism."[16] As his politics evolved, Debs's "new abolition" grew increasingly sensitive to dynamics of race. His message also coincided with a generation of Black socialists who carried their own radical traditions into Euro-American–dominated movements yet endorsed a strategy of using the legacy of antislavery to widen socialism's appeal.

By 1915 Debs applied his "abolitionist" critique to the bloodletting in Europe. Fearing that conflict abroad would lead the federal government to violate civil liberties at home, he predicted that the United States would enter the war not in the pursuit of democracy but at the behest of moneyed interests.[17] Proclaiming himself a "proletariat revolutionist" who opposed every war but class war, the incendiary Hoosier was convicted of sedition under the Espionage Act of 1917 due to anti-war speech, using his final court statement to address antislavery politics and historical memory. Debs reminded the jurors that the subversives of one generation are the idols of the next, avowing that time and deliberation had transformed antislavery crusaders and women suffragists, who were censured as "infidels" and "monsters of depravity" in their own time, into veritable heroes. Just as abolitionists had fought to destroy chattel slavery, socialists now endeavored to eradicate "wage slavery." Once dismissed as utopians or denounced as revolutionaries, a changed nation, on the cusp of the Nineteenth Amendment, demanded that slavery's staunchest opponents be reconsidered. Now, Debs insisted, American citizens were rightly "teaching children to revere their memories."[18]

Workers sharply politicized and fiercely contested such memories because they regarded conceptualizations of the past as critically important. The labor movement's "invented traditions" of commemoration and identity may have belonged to the superstructure of ideas, but they situated groups and individuals in the material world.[19] Cultural politics might be derived primarily from social conditions, rather than serve as the sources of them, but memories were not mere perceptions. Rather, as either a conservative engine of consensus or a revolutionary and counterhegemonic apparatus, collective remembrance was a tool—one linked to specific political outcomes.[20] Representations of the Civil War in particular were crucial to the development of class consciousness in the United States. They revealed the relationship between how working people conceived the past, real-world political victories and defeats, and the capacity for, as well as barriers to, solidarity.

*Grand Army of Labor: Workers, Veterans, and the Meaning of the Civil War* explores the sweeping variety of Civil War memory within Gilded Age and Progressive Era labor unions, among political radicals, and in third party movements. Though it at times addresses sharecroppers and domestic laborers, including attempts by unions and parties to exclude or organize them, this study is primarily concerned not with the productive relations of class per se but with industrial workers and farmers who exhibited class consciousness through participation in coordinated worker movements. This analysis adopts what E. P. Thompson describes as the material positions of workers being "handled in cultural terms" and engendered through rituals, value systems, and stories.[21] The living memory of Civil War veterans saw a profusion of working-class cultural politics that created contradictions—contradictions that often gave rise to change, but also to schism and disintegration. Those cultural politics also exposed a palpable tension between modes of Civil War commemoration rooted in nationalism and reform and revolutionary memories centered more on internationalism and socialism that spawned from and coincided with surges in labor militancy. The demarcations between radicals and reformers, legislative and anti- or extra-parliamentary proponents, and disciples of the ballot and of the strike were fluid, situational, and often blurred. However, more conservative group memories, channeled largely through the American Federation of Labor and facilitated by the Red Scare, pushed socialist and revolutionary labor—and their concomitant collective memory—to the commemorative margins.

The revolutionary working-class interpretations of the Civil War that emanated from and well beyond the First and Second Internationals largely neglected to develop analyses of race and thus failed to integrate the racialization of capitalism into the meaning of the war and their politics of collective memory.[22] As Theodore W. Allen contends, so much of the American story involves "democratic departures" being "frustrated by *re*inventions of the 'white race.'"[23] The progressive toeholds, surges, and achievements of organized labor during the industrial era were no exception. The Third International and the Communist Party, however, *did* advance coherent historical ideas regarding the production of race, or what Karen E. Fields and Barbara J. Fields term "racecraft."[24] Such theories particularly concern how racism interacts with capitalism, sometimes to the benefit of white workers, but more critically how it adds systematic layers of exploitation onto nonwhite people. The more racially sophisticated Civil War memory within the Communist Party and the Popular Front was, quite understandably, more metaphorical in its character, further detached from the experiences of actual war participants, and more steeped in the politics of the domestic, including those of the color line. By the time such concepts were popularized among white radicals in the 1930s, pressed between two periods of far-reaching right-wing assault, the US labor movement had already run the gauntlet of the First Red Scare. Much of its revolutionary possibility had been negotiated into reform, ground into submission, or stamped out of existence. At the other end of the Popular Front came the Cold War's deradicalizing reaper. The Second Red Scare discredited or snuffed out a miscellany of leftists, as well as their revolutionary visions of the American past and the Civil War.

In other words, collective memories within the labor movement during the Long Gilded Age evinced revolution and reform, as two competing and sometimes coinciding narratives emerged between Reconstruction and World War I. The first depicted the Civil War's legacy as a precursor to a sweeping—even global and perhaps violent—liberation of *all* workers, or what Karl Marx termed a "new era of the emancipation of labor."[25] The second, meanwhile, emphasized the preservation of the Union, the imperatives of legalism and social order, and the fundamental loyalty of white workingmen to the reconstituted nation-state. The first worked largely in the service of industrial unionism; the second tended to further conciliatory labor strategies, as well as the leadership prerogatives of exclusionary craft unions. That the revolutionary memory of the war proved so tenacious is a testament to the persistence of oppression under industrial capitalism. Yet it was consistently thwarted—undermined from without and within—and ultimately ceded to a vision of the war (and of the future) based on compromise with capital and the sanctity of the state. The preeminence of reformist memory supplemented trade union bureaucratization, labor nationalism, and the propagation of antiradicalism on the American scene during and after the Great War. To the extent that capitalists and labor leadership exploited reform memory to blunt industrial unionism, this is a story of declension. In that it exposes how myriad obstacles to collective struggle were expressed through worker culture, this is a story of instruction. But to the degree that revolutionary memory, and thus revolutionary unity, persevered, this is a story of radical possibilities.

* * *

Labor during the age of industrial capitalism was refracted through the semantics, ideas, and personalities of the sectional conflict—an *antislavery vernacular*. As evidenced by Marx and Friedrich Engels's *Manifesto* for the "emancipation" (*Befreiung*) of labor and "abolition" (*Abschaffung*) of property, antebellum labor movements cribbed the cultural politics of abolitionism, using Black slavery to better convey the debasement of wage labor.[26] Worker self-activity involved ceaselessly reconstructing and contesting that vernacular, translating familiar concepts into radical political discourses and ushering common workingmen into alternative politics. The Lincoln-Debs analogy is but one example of how Gilded Age and Progressive Era workers, from members of the AFL's Grand Army of the Blue and Gray to those of the socialist Abraham Lincoln Liberty League, used war-era representations to craft conceptions of self, enlist the unorganized, strategize their movements, and envisage their futures.[27]

The labor movement's wielding of Civil War memory achieved at least five often overlapping principal functions: ideology, recruitment, nostalgia, assimilation, and nationalism. First, antislavery vernacular provided an ideological infrastructure for freedom and emancipation by invoking African American bondage and liberation as a precursor to a wider emancipatory project. War memories were harbingers of hard political ideas and action, and workingmen of all races and regions used the sectional contest to imagine and broaden equality claims and radical prospects. The key to the destruction of the wage system, as many workers saw it, was to learn from and prevail where abolitionists had failed. They devised direct action—strikes, boycotts, political pressure, and even targeted violence—as metaphorical if not literal extensions of war.

Memory was also an enrollment tool. Union veterans were for at least a generation the nation's largest and most influential voting bloc. In the decades following Appomattox, the words of war spoke directly to workingmen who had donned blue or gray, as well as to a postwar society shaped indelibly by the conflict. Eliciting the war was a galvanic organizational device. "Veteranspeak" proved critical to the cultural transition from debates over sectional issues to contests over the relationship between capital and labor. Antislavery vernacular spawned a cultural architecture for not only battle and division but also comradeship and notions of honor and manhood within male-dominated crafts.[28] "Union" as a double entendre fastened the struggle against the slaveholding aristocracy to the interests of organized labor.[29] The coupling of the Union cause with the union cause, of Union men with union men—bound through a similar esprit de corps and sense of moral destiny—furnished a powerful connective tissue for worker conscription and political mobilization.

Antislavery vernacular signified a form of political nostalgia despite the fact that most radicals were not anti-modernists. Although far more concerned with creation and innovation than with tradition, labor's representations of the Civil War regularly included a less than coherent longing for the preindustrial capitalist world that the war had ushered out. Those likenesses of artisan republicanism and small-scale capitalism—an era when laborers ostensibly controlled their own tools, their own time, and their own bodies—provided a salve for the striking material inequalities, horrid conditions, and antidemocratic realities of the modern workplace. Utilizing the past as a means toward change, workers and reformers sometimes harkened back to a mythic bygone, calling forth the "liberté, égalité, fraternité" of revolutionary France, Jeffersonian agrarianism, or the small producer ideal of the early Republicans. In doing so, they presented a vision of history that counteracted the anti-republican concentration of private power during the Gilded Age.

Depicting unions as the inheritance of either a global emancipation or a redemptive national story had the effect of assimilating the foreign-born and white ethnic labor force. The US population tripled in the half century following 1865. Urban workingmen, already heavily Irish, Scandinavian, and especially German and German-speaking, became further atomized as the quickening pace of industrialization mirrored the inflow of ethnically diverse peoples from Italy, Poland, Russia, Greece, Portugal, and Austria-Hungary. Organized labor came to combine Old World notions of community and loyalty with unmistakably American symbols and history.[30] War memory enabled labor leaders to cast first-generation workers with few cultural ties to the United States as being part of a comprehensible domestic tradition in which a distinctly national cast of players—Abraham Lincoln, John Brown, Thaddeus Stevens—had shaped an allegedly American struggle: one against slavery in *all* forms and for the emancipation of *all* workers. Despite the false dichotomy between "native" and "foreign" Jacobinism, workingmen did in fact use commemoration to make their cause appear especially indigenous. But this nationalization technique also acted in concert with a frequent acknowledgment that the War for the Union had been a conflict of world historical importance and part of a global process of revolutionary activity that shared a chronological bloodline with the French Revolution, the Revolutions of 1848, and even the Paris Commune.[31]

Finally, collective memories provided the labor left an Americanizing instrument. While Marx and Engels were perhaps correct to identify political liberalization (emancipation and Radical Reconstruction) in the world's fastest-growing industrial economy with the potential for accelerated class struggle, they failed to grasp the extent to which racial and ethnic animosities, entrenched ideas regarding merit and mobility, a dynamic bourgeoisie, and the success with which elites were able to paint socialism as a violent immigrant conspiracy would become roadblocks to the consciousness and institutional and political coherence of a self-defined working class. Nevertheless, antislavery vernacular proved a way to facilitate the class solution by bridging the tenets of European socialism with American history. As Paul Buhle notes, "textualist" Marxists, whose immigrant backgrounds, theoretical inclinations, and somewhat provincial ethnic institutions limited their exposure to wider US culture, needed a way to meld their revolution with native radicalism. Through "Americanization," the Civil War's lessons became a way for radicals to appeal to white veterans, African Americans, women's rights advocates, and homegrown reformers with backgrounds in abolitionism, transcendentalism, spiritualism, or anti-monopolism.[32]

* * *

The US labor movement was "abolitionized." Land reformers, socialists, anarchists, labor agitators, social democrats, and populists all elicited the Civil

War veteran and invoked what W. E. B. Du Bois termed the "abolition-democracy" vanguard as an organizing symbol.[33] As David R. Roediger maintains, "The popular working class consciousness that emerged during the latter stages of the Civil War, especially in the North, saw the liberation of Black slaves as a *model*, and not just a threat."[34] Indeed, workers who participated in the Union war partook in unprecedented collective action, construed slaveholders as class (as well as national) enemies, and came face-to-face with expropriation of the planter elite. This experience supplied a generation of young and would-be industrial laborers with what Alan Dawley terms "a memorable vision of class struggle."[35] Wielding war memories, worker movements used class as a paradigm through which to reconcile wager-earners across North-South lines. They did so in numerous ways, both inside and outside formal politics and with various levels of sincerity, pragmatism, and long-term strategy. However, sustained attempts at class-based sectional rapprochement were repeatedly torpedoed by social and political forces that proved inherently antithetical to class unity: nationalism, militarism, regionalism, religion, and partisanship, as well as manipulated divisions of ethnicity, gender, and, most especially, race.

This discourse of Civil War meaning and memory emanated not only from the top down, from labor leadership to the shop floor, but also from the bottom up, as workingmen in rural mills, urban docks, factory yards, campaign stumps, convention halls, and printing houses framed their struggle as a "new civil war" or a "third American revolution." As labor organizations opened across gender and racial lines, women and workers of color participated in this memory creation as well. Even as a white, non-ethnic middle-class political consensus developed around individualized merit, exclusive property rights, and liberal economics, radical workers felt personally connected to the most transformational event of the nineteenth century: the emancipation of roughly 4 million people. As Andrew Zimmerman points out, "The American Civil War had such important consequences for nineteenth-century revolutionary thought and politics at least in part because it appeared to be an extraordinarily successful instance of revolutionary political-economic change."[36]

The labor movement's "language of class" was drawn from American history, most conspicuously the War of the Rebellion.[37] Postwar labor "made striking use of the past," posits Leon Fink, and "dipped selectively into a popular storehouse of memory and myth to capture alternative images of human possibility."[38] Similarly, Mark A. Lause alleges that trade unionists "easily expropriated the terminology of the 'Irrepressible Conflict' to describe the relations of labor and capital."[39] Many workers expressed what John L.

Brooke labels a "new political history of language" through a vernacular that drew on the antislavery enterprise in order to challenge liberal understandings of property and reconfigure arrangements of power by expanding the body politic and reconsidering the role of the state.[40] Moreover, divergent memories of the Civil War *within* American labor reflected and reinforced broader strategic and ideological cleavages among workingmen and between socialism and liberalism, internationalism and nationalism, and revolution and reform. The subjects of this work espoused subaltern narratives—alternatives to the more conservative and white middle-class interpretations of the Grand Army of the Republic and United Confederate Veterans. They used language (newspapers, books, poems, speeches) and public space (political rallies, street processions, parades, public commemorations) to tie war memory to their bids for political change and social valence.

The notion of a "continued" Civil War was central to the identities of radical workers. In establishing the concept of "collective memory," sociologist Maurice Halbwachs recognized the variations in how different groups organize, preserve, and represent the past, including distinctions according to class. The eminent social historians E. P. Thompson, Herbert Gutman, and Eric Hobsbawm expounded this concept, alleging that peasants and proletarians typically construct aspirations and express political aims by repurposing traditional symbols. In delineating class not only as an outgrowth of productive relations but as a cultural formation, Thompson stressed that such an identity of interests was stimulated through shared customs.[41] Speaking on the relation between historical memory and the left, and connecting the Paris Commune with the June Days and French Revolution, Leon Trotsky confirmed that even Marxist revolutionaries "live in traditions."[42]

This relation between condition and consciousness—the former preceding the latter—illustrates that politics and culture are reciprocal but not equal. Collective memories, like culture itself, are primarily responses to and derivatives of, rather than sources of, social and material circumstances. As such, the process of class consciousness and the pursuit of a "class for itself" in the United States, though rooted in common worker experiences and common worker fates, were nonetheless filtered through what David Montgomery terms "a mythology of the war and emancipation."[43] The conditions of industry's "human jungle" led to increased battles between capital and labor and new imaginings of "slavery," often qualified with specific conceptions of whiteness.[44] Many industrial workers deemed the Union triumph a "disillusioning victory" (combining revolutionary potential as a social movement with capitalist consolidation) and maintained that the gains of the war were limited and that its legacy remained unfinished.[45] Others awaited a "third revolution," as workers of both races lamented what they viewed as the vacated promises of the Civil War.

Former soldiers manipulated wartime language to forge working-class narratives. Workers north and south, and veterans in particular, regenerated three sets of vernacular: that of the *abolitionist* ("slave," "master," "bondage"), the *battlefield* ("battalion," "campaign," "deserter"), and the *revolution* ("war," "rebellion," "emancipation"). As part of what one might think of as nineteenth-century "history wars" both *among* American political factions and *within* labor, working-class, and left-wing movements, these words took on assorted political meaning between 1865 and 1918. But they were rooted firmly in wartime understandings and experiences. Symbols mattered too, as workers employed wartime concepts (hierarchy, fraternity, and honor) as well as the physical objects of war (the canteen, the bayonet, and soldier encampments) in order to promote a host of various radical and reform impulses. The Knights of Labor had its Blue and Gray Association; the GAR its Grand Army of Labor; and the People's Party its "Blue and Gray ticket."[46]

Workers and farmers, both of whom painted themselves as neo-abolitionists fighting "economic enslavement," sometimes united through labor republicanism.[47] Generated in order to foster a more democratic economy, labor republicanism was an ideological weapon against antidemocratic elites.[48] It deviated from eighteenth-century liberal republicanism and Civil War–era laissez-faire republicanism in its philosophy of "non-domination," either social or economic, public or private, of the law or of the marketplace. The philosophy insisted that "dependence on another's will," whether it be the de jure privileges of an aristocrat or the de facto privileges of a capitalist, was the essence of unfreedom. Emphasizing what Joseph Gerteis terms a "common republican class framework," the cultural schemas of earlier dissenters served as vehicles for class solidarity.[49] To agrarians, this entailed emphasizing good land use tied to political independence and social egalitarianism (a connection the Republican Party abandoned as its radicalism waned).[50] As such, labor republicanism was simultaneously influenced by early Republican archetypes yet divorced from the party's postwar liberal economic credo.[51]

"Free labor" gave way to "wage slavery" as workers' expectations clashed with the realities of industrial capitalism. Once embraced by trade unionists, the Republican ideal, which viewed dependent labor solely as a stepping stone to small-scale proprietorship and self-ownership, could not survive the shift to permanent short-term contract labor after the Civil War.[52] As Leon Fink identifies, subsequent battles over the "language of freedom" produced a variety of dialects. "Free labor" was highly contested, with workers connecting it to democracy and the antislavery tradition and employers emphasizing a purely market definition, even as the public construction behind Adam Smith's "hidden hand" was, according to Eric Hobsbawm, "becoming visible in all sorts of ways." Though the Civil War amendments—themselves extensions of the free-labor movement—greatly enhanced civic rights, the emphasis on the individual alongside corporate-friendly court interpretations and capitalist culture steadily placed property rights above worker and community needs and reinforced new forms of unfreedom for working people. As such, agrarian radicals and trade unionists conceived of their organizations as fulfillments of the free-labor promise—the idea that independence lay with either landownership or workplace control and that no man should possess more land than he could cultivate nor dictate another man's labor.[53] Gradually, "free labor," like "free contract," or the obfuscatory "right to work" in our own time, became purely an abstraction: the "freedom" to sell one's labor at market and, in times of economic downturn, the "freedom" to starve.[54]

These civic identities often converged with militia culture, as the Civil War further linked popular understandings of citizenship, combat, and manhood. Nineteenth-century republicanism was not only gendered and raced but also deeply enmeshed with military service. Antebellum political clubs, from Democratic Red Shirts and Republican Wide Awakes to Turnverein socialists, trafficked in paramilitary symbolism and civic volunteerism. For laborers and mechanics, who made up 42 percent of the Union army, and subsistence farmers, who constituted much of the rest, soldiering sometimes guided radicalism.[55] Not only did the GAR, with its conservative nationalist foundation of native-born constituents, grow to half a million members by the 1890s, but from Chicago's Bohemian Rifles to Jacob Coxey's "Industrial Army of the Unemployed," radical, reformist, and dissenting veterans summoned, refitted, and utilized the masculinized republicanism of the war.

Labor's martial bent made "maleness" normal, and gendered corollaries impaired working-class organization. The Knights of Labor, the Industrial Workers of the World, and other gender- and skill-inclusive worker organizations no doubt challenged society's dominant masculinity. Some spoke straightforwardly to the distinct oppressions faced by working-class women, "the slaves of slaves." Although male workers were especially attracted to the language of war, women actively constructed war memories, sometimes geared toward gender-specific political goals. However, the widespread association of labor with military service, and worker conflict as an imagined battleground, also reinforced cross-class patriarchy and cast American labor as something intrinsically male. This working-class masculinity linked "manhood" with independent proprietorship, the absence of wage dependency, and, by the Gilded

Age, the presence of industrial or (more often) "skilled" production. Although female sewing machine operators, like Welsh miners or Black agricultural workers, did not lack skill, "skilled" and "unskilled" were used to define a "circle of labor" that gave prominence to native-born white men. It also connected "real" work with male spaces and specific modes of male-governed physical labor, segregating "manly" labor from domestic and unpaid work, and even from agricultural labor. In this sense, war memory masculinized the envisaged model worker. It rendered the prototypical union member, particularly within the AFL, as a white (and typically nonimmigrant) male breadwinner—a figure nearly as brawny, red-blooded, and racially homogeneous as the universal Union soldier type represented in popular commemoration.[56]

Black workers engaged in class-based coalitions also used memory in race-specific ways. They sought to vindicate emancipation, realize the promises of Reconstruction, and expand the boundaries of freedom. Some African Americans insisted that "slavery" be understood not as a vague form of oppression but as a historical condition unique to the Black experience in America. However, Black radicals perceived the material and labor management roots of racial construction and identified white supremacy as an asset to the ruling class. Black workers—and Black thinkers from Frederick Douglass to Angela Davis—also recognized the connection between chattel slavery and the "slavery of wages," or what Black Guerrilla Family cofounder George Jackson later termed "neoslavery" ("modern variety of chattel slavery updated to disguise itself"), as the product of the same coercive mechanism.[57]

To most white laborers, meanwhile, the primary legacy of the war was not African American liberation per se but the destruction of a uniquely oppressive labor system and the potential to extend an emancipatory program to other areas of the economy. Yet, the failure of this "neo-emancipation" to include racial analysis—or even simply to condemn white supremacy and construe racial difference (correctly) as a *byproduct of* capitalism that was not *identical to* capitalism—proved a colossal impediment to solidarity. More than conceding no audience, eschewing "purity" tests, or engaging those with disagreements so as to build and organize, left-wing anti-oppression politics—and the cultural drives that accompanied them—too often accommodated bigotry or were simply guided by white supremacy. The organized labor factions and individuals who *did* fight on antiracist terms, attempting to unify the class by challenging rather than promoting gender and racial discrimination, tended to be drowned out not merely by the interpersonal racism of white workers but by dominant ideas and influences regarding race and gender that were broadcast and stoked through every channel of the white capitalist power structure.

Scholars of Civil War memory have overlooked these labor-veterans. The rise of memory studies in the 1980s coincided with both the decline of Marxism as a framework of analysis and the weakening of unions in American life.[58] A testament to how neoliberalism structures academic approaches and practices, alarmingly few historians investigate with rigor the class dynamics of collective memory or the political economy of veterans' organizations; fewer still tie memory and veteran culture to radical or labor politics. Responding to David W. Blight's tripartite paradigm of emancipationist memory, white supremacist memory, and reconciliationist memory, academic works on remembrance tend to focus instead on competing or complementary modes of racially liberal or racist and reactionary remembrance, particularly degrees of white reconciliation. These examinations of Civil War commemoration in toto overemphasize elites, present veterans who are insufficiently political, and often overlook subaltern forms of remembering regarding proletarian culture.

Labor radicals, however, attempted to achieve *class reconciliation* by combining aspects of emancipationist memory, which insisted that slavery's destruction was the primary legacy of the war, and reconciliationist memory, rooted in sectional rapprochement. Organized workingmen across racial and ethnic lines looked to pivot from both the "waving the bloody shirt" politics of sectional antagonism *and* notions of North-South reconciliation based on white solidarity. They sometimes romanticized the West, where white opportunity depended on nonwhite removal and anti-Indian violence animated racial capitalism, as a third American section where farmer-labor alliance might overcome the long-entrenched class hierarchies of North and South. This pan-sectionalism was based far less on nationalism, regionalism, or even race than on materiality. Workers advocated a type of reconciliation predicated on mutual opposition to elites, to the conditions of industrial capitalism, or to the economic system altogether. From the perspective of the labor left, there were good and practical reasons to pursue reunion based on common trade, vocation, and social station. Indeed, class was the only self-sustaining way to mobilize a labor force that was highly atomized by trade, race, gender, ethnicity, language, religion, and region. Yet class solidarity only (rather than class as a foundation or point of intersection for organizing the diverse elements of the working class) also proved a hindrance. Many white radicals viewed class—and often class alone, with other social differences seemingly liquidated—as the solution to deep fears within postwar society of fratricidal social fragmentation. Disregard for or eschewal of non- or extra-class distinction also had the effect of normalizing and prioritizing whiteness. To be sure, the degree to which African Americans, women, and non-"white on arrival" European Americans were included or particularized within class reconciliation and the extent to which it emphasized revolution or reform proved points of tension and even conflict, with the memory-scape mirroring the political and social setting.

Labor's task of seizing the popular narrative of the Civil War proved gargantuan. Using tradition to fight tradition, workers struggled to unseat more powerful memory makers. Although done to remarkable, if transitory, effect in the Greenback, Knights of Labor, and Populist movements, courting African Americans and ethnic workers to achieve class alignment led to intense backlash within both the white supremacist Democratic Party and the xenophobic Republican Party. Attempts at class reconciliation were further complicated by the fact that industrialists disproportionately employed Union veterans as private guards, detectives, and police—the hit force of capital.[59] By the 1880s, reactionary politicians, publishers, businessmen, and civic groups and militias also intermittently embraced (white non-working-class) blue-gray reunion in order to suppress labor organization and third party insurgency. Even as socialists and anarchists "reddened" the memory of emancipation, gulfs widened between trade unions and veterans' organizations, which increasingly conformed to civic traditionalism and political conservatism. The swelling GAR, in whose ranks industrial workers and immigrants were strikingly underrepresented, became a vehicle for Anglo-Saxon militarism, xenophobia, social hierarchy, and scientific racism—a cause and condition of 1890s imperialism and "patriotic onslaught."[60] The white supremacist United Confederate Veterans, meanwhile, which mirrored and romanticized the class hierarchy of the Old South, perpetuated similar anti-worker smears concerning foreign "communism."[61]

As the century turned, pro-owner court decisions and the violent quashing of strike actions gave added force to labor incrementalism. Reformist union men, particularly within the AFL, employed antislavery vernacular as a demonstration of labor loyalty, economic nationalism, and industrial chauvinism as organized labor moved away from worker militancy and toward respectability politics. Such workers often conceded inequality, justifying hierarchy (and the systemic injustices that underwrite it) through meritocratic bywords like "equality of opportunity." This class-compromise model, in which capitalism was tamed through regulation rather than transcended through worker control, often worked hand-in-glove with broader trends of white reunion and white nationalism during the nadir of Jim Crow. Labor patriotism also served to enrich traditional party structures and reinforce the very bourgeois liberalism—sanctity of private property and faith in a competitive marketplace—that undergirded many workers' social and economic grievances. Socialists invoked a revolutionary memory of the war, grafting remembrance onto personalities and labor campaigns. Yet anti-Bolshevism and government repression of the labor left during World War I exploited nationalism and the predisposition of many labor leaders toward legalism, process, and social order. Labor patriotism drained left nationalism—the Americanization of left-wing dissent—of its subversive edge, marginalizing industrial unionists and their imaginings of international working-class revolution. Crushing radical labor and curbing the leftist potential of US politics buttressed more conservative and nationalist elements within popular Civil War memory—a memory of uncommon common men, white racial nostalgia, and the development and righteousness of the nation-state that matured—though was vigorously challenged—during the 1930s and 1940s.

Civil War stories and images were critical points of reference within the labor movement for decades after Appomattox and well into the twentieth century. As John Swinton had explained, "The 'War for the Union' grew out of the Labor Question, and was waged over it: Shall the working population of our country, or any part of it, be held in slavery?"[62] Antislavery vernacular, which involved reading postwar society into the war or projecting the war onto contemporary politics in order to shape the future, was integral to the construction of working-class identity. Adhered to causes neither "lost" nor "won" but to *causes not yet won*, radical worker-veterans and their comrades used the words and wounds of war to envision a left alternative even as other old soldiers employed a similar emotional vocabulary to reinforce systems of nationalism, empire, eugenics, segregation, patriarchy, bourgeois consumerism, and corporate capitalism. Continuously exploring the uses of cultural politics as a means of claiming rights and resources, workers employed the Civil War to foster class consciousness, organize trade and party alliances, negotiate shifting social and political terrain, and reify notions of race, gender, and region. At their most ambitious, they expanded the very conceptions of human freedom.

CHAPTER 1

# King Labor

## Workers Imagine Emancipation beyond Equality

SAMUEL FENTON CARY took the stage at New York City's Cooper Union on July 3, 1868, in defense of workingmen. A famed antislavery reformer and a lifelong resident of Cincinnati, Cary supposed the emancipation of over 4 million enslaved people would be a sea change in the historical destinies of the world's laboring classes. As many workers saw it, the "universal emancipation of labor" was the next logical step following chattel slavery's destruction. But Cary also feared that the war had facilitated undue capital aggregation, enchaining common people through class domination. Beginning his lecture by asking rhetorically, "Who are the workingmen?," his answer was steeped in labor republicanism. Real workers, those who "produce all the wealth of the nation," were the men who had "fought the battles of the late war, saved the Republic from destruction, made all the sacrifices, and are now toiling in the field and workshop to pay for the debt incurred by the war." The "producers" of Union victory were not, according to Cary, the contractors, bondholders, speculators, and financiers who sat out the fight, "making money out of their country's misfortunes." He renounced those "owners of labor" as tantamount to the "slaveocracy."

Cary was adamant that the solutions to postwar inequalities resided in the so-called liberation of labor. Echoing the Chicago Labor Congress's declaration of 1867, he insisted that such deliverance include trade union organization, progressive taxation, a national currency, and land reform. This final point did not entail "an equal distribution of property," he reiterated. Rather, Cary lobbied for decommodification in which public lands withdrawn from the market be granted to both native and foreign-born settlers. In staking his claims, Cary appealed directly to the memory of the Union soldier. Workingmen were the ultimate patriots, he reminded his audience, for it was disproportionately laborers who had been "ready to offer their lives to preserve the integrity of the Union." It was they who had sacrificed the comforts of home and hearth and whose blood still stained the Southern soil. It was they who had marched, been imprisoned, fought, struggled, bled, and died, leaving widows and orphans behind. "The capitalists made no sacrifices during the war," Cary stated bluntly. Northern owners and financial elites were shirkers turned masters, simultaneously cowards and oppressive masters.[1]

A wartime Republican, Cary would go on to join the Greenback-Labor movement, becoming the party's vice presidential nominee in 1876. But in 1868, with a disempowered wage-earning class in the industrial North and landless freedpeople exploited under contract work in the transitioning South, land and labor were the fundamental questions. For former slaves, emancipation and military service buttressed demands for economic and political rights. Trade unionists co-opted emancipationist memory, too. For workingmen white and Black, the sectional conflict offered a lodestone of political meaning, and its collective memory became a site of consciousness-building and a rallying point for labor's cause. From the Old South's "Slave Power" to the "rebel aristocracy" of the war years, laborers—both wage earners and small farmers—employed antislavery vernacular to attack slaveholders as class enemies. Nurtured during the antebellum era and honed during the War of the Rebellion, this association of the Confederacy with oligarchy—of consolidated economic power with a sort of civic "treason" against American ideals—proved transferable to labor's postwar battles.

The popular memory of the antislavery movement and of the calamitous war that had just occurred was central to Reconstruction era debates over political economy. Just as the Civil War had been part of a grand labor struggle—W. E. B. Du Bois's "general strike"—agitators framed postwar debates over land and labor as part of an antislavery tradition. Workers built on the praxis of antebellum activists who sought to expand the meaning of freedom—abolitionists, trade unionists, suffragists, land reformers, utopians, socialists, and cooperationists—as well as on those of rights-demanding freedpeople. In doing so they articulated a cultural template of liberation in which the ruination of chattel slavery was but a harbinger. Invoking emancipation and military service to claim economic rights, Black veterans and freedpeople of the "Great Tradition"—the abolitionist-integrationist belief in full equality—became the first and most vocal laboring people to employ war memories to appeal for large-scale material redistribution. Defining liberation on their own terms, former slaves *anticipated* the postwar period as one of revolutionary possibility, including the reorganization or decommodification of land property. Although adherents exhibited competing strategies (rebellion, civil disobedience, mass migration), agrarian reform emerged as a clear demand. Yet property confiscation pitted radicalism against liberalism. This challenge to the notion that civic equality and a capitalist marketplace would lead to deserved outcomes spoke to contested interpretations of deeply American ideals: democracy, justice, and liberty.

Although many viewed Black liberation as separate from, or even a hindrance to, the fuller "emancipation of [white] labor," countless white workers also saw the destruction of slavery—what Karl Marx termed the "movement of slaves" into the greatest slave rebellion in world history—as a blueprint for their own emancipation.[2] Influenced by local circumstances and distinct political cultures, workers increasingly appropriated the legacy of African American bondage and liberation in order to confront "wage slavery" and communicated designs for "labor emancipation" in which the liquidation of plantation slavery was but one step. This process was evident in the cultural politics of the National Labor Union and through agrarian radicalism in Virginia, where the Readjuster Party used the antislavery vernacular to propel its interracial movement, foretelling both the achievements and dilemmas of later populist struggles. From the vantage of radicalizing wage earners, emancipation was a labor movement, and the labor movement emancipatory. As Mark A. Lause contends, the Civil War created modern American labor organization in part through such competing definitions of "free labor," as workers rejected the notion of "freedom" as the mere absence of legal enslavement.[3] At their most transformational, these liberation scripts challenged property rights *beyond* property in man.

## The Rebel Aristocracy

The ways in which working people remembered the Civil War sprang from the language of antebellum reform. In the North, laborers only gradually conceived of slavery's destruction as portending universal emancipation. The initial weakness of labor abolitionism spoke to racial consciousness among white workers, the class inclinations of white abolitionists, and the hegemonic capacity of proslavery elites. Throughout the Jacksonian era, outsized numbers of workingmen viewed slavery's opponents as direct threats to both their livelihoods and their understandings of the United States as a white republic. As Alexander Saxton argues, questions of slavery and race often pitted "white egalitarians," who frequently exhibited harsh white supremacy, against "white elitists," who sometimes demonstrated more liberal racial sensibilities.[4] Incited by prevailing social institutions, notably the Democratic Party and the

Catholic Church, Irish American laborers in particular viewed antislavery politics as tantamount to nativism and elitism. Along slavery's border, white workers overwhelmingly accepted the messaging of powerful reactionaries who insisted that the destruction of slavery would lead to material scarcity, labor competition, lack of employment, wage reduction, or "race war."[5] This was so especially in the Lower Middle West, where heightened economic and racial anxieties owing to proximity to the slaveholding South combined to reinforce racial exclusion. Within this economic model of race production, the depth, pervasiveness, and derivatives of anti-Black racism were singular.[6] Other workers recognized the class limitations of the abolitionist movement, associating its upper-middle-class leadership with the exploitation of labor. Abolitionism's moralizing strategy also often undermined its capacity to connect antislavery with the self-interests of white wage earners.[7] Hermann Schlüter asserts that the demands of the labor movement and the elimination of "wage slavery" principally were "met with far less understanding among the Abolitionists than the question of the abolition of chattel slavery among workingmen."[8] This abolitionist "blind spot" toward labor impelled countless white workers, known popularly as "the Niggers of the North," to view the slave's cause as separate from their own subjugation.[9] The class and cultural distance between abolitionists and laborers created an expectational gap in which the latter presumed "free labor" to be not merely the absence of bondage but also the steady mobility of workingmen and the elevation of labor's interests above those of capital. In the words of one labor reformer, although "labor for wages" was a great improvement on systems of slavery and feudalism, it was nevertheless an "imperfect and defective system," certain to be superseded by an economic order that rewarded labor without subjecting it to "autocratic" control.[10]

The early antagonism between labor and abolition hindered both. While trade unionists and land, labor, and currency reformers responded to incipient industrial conditions with emancipationist language, naturally prioritizing *their* immediate material needs, abolitionists frequently dismissed both "white slavery" and "wage slavery" as the fiction of labor spokesmen or the spin of proslavery propagandists. Those abolitionists who did consider the condition of wage earners insisted that the emancipation of Black slaves precede the fight for wages and hours, to the dismay of many Northern workers.[11] But even from the white working-class perspective, there was an increasingly self-evident logic in placing antislavery at the top of the reform agenda. Although comparisons—albeit often hyperbolized ones—between Black slavery and wage labor accentuated the injustice and hyper-exploitation of emerging factory work, the very existence of Black slavery also limited the extent of any critique of the wage system.[12] As David R. Roediger posits, "As long as slavery thrived, any attempt to come to grips with wage labor tended to lapse into exaggerated metaphors or frantic denials of those metaphors."[13] This trend of chattel slavery simultaneously inspiring and limiting the power of the trade union movement presaged the complicated relationship between the Northern proletariat and Black agricultural workers in the South during the postwar period.

Even so, worker "emancipation" remained a bipartisan reference in the Second Party System, as various political and ideological camps feared the idea of "owned workers," and white ones specifically. The Whig Party held that laboring men were best served through its program of internal improvements and state intervention in the economy; Democrats countered that their opposition to tariffs would produce "the emancipation of labor from the bonds of capital."[14] The emerging free-labor ethos would link an individual brand of democracy with communalism, postulating the West as a reserve for free men and free homesteads—republican alternatives to the undemocratic and unmanly threat of fixed wage earning. Yet this notion of white male workers "on the make" and an impermanent laboring class remained chimerical, and its adherents identified slavery, rather than capitalism, as the greatest threat to the opportunities of non-owners.[15] Moreover, the language of labor enslavement and liberation was not relegated to one section. Exploiting ethnic and economic strains, gender anxiety, and the allure of whiteness among their constituents, Democratic leaders, the party press, and fearmongering planters claimed that the freedom of white workingmen rested on Black enslavement. They alleged that any disruption of the South's racial-labor hierarchy would "degrade" white labor by slicing wages and employment. Slavery's opponents, meanwhile, emphasized the ideals of mobility and merit in a free-labor system or affirmed that true emancipation for (presumably white) workingmen was possible only in the absence of Black slavery. Addressing white workers who supported formal racial restriction, some white abolitionists argued that emancipation would produce a sort of informal racial segregation to the benefit of the white race. In an avowal that was sometimes personal and sometimes political, they professed that wages, family ties, and the "suitability" of the climate and working conditions would induce former slaves to stay put (and even prompt Northern Blacks to return south). Such abolitionists swore that the destruction of slavery was in fact the best means of keeping Black people restricted to the South and away from Northern white workers.[16]

Others saw more clearly the interrelation between the dissolution of chattel bondage and wage work. Anticipating Marx's dictum that "labor in a white skin cannot emancipate itself where it is branded in a black skin," Ohio's *Anti-slavery Bugle* contended that emancipation was an essential precursor to free labor: "Free labor can never be organized . . . by the side of slave labor."[17] Similarly, *New York Tribune* editor and Fourierist convert Horace Greeley, whose reform socialism advanced free-labor principles, questioned market outcomes and called for a full "emancipation of labor" through the obliteration of "wage slavery."[18] William H. Seward maintained this point while canvassing Ohio's Western Reserve during the fall of 1848, asserting that there were two antagonistic forces in American society: freedom and slavery. More than a repudiation of bondage, "freedom," Seward clarified, "insists on the emancipation and elevation of labor. . . . Freedom seeks complete and universal emancipation."[19] Indeed, free-soil ideology helped reconcile labor-abolitionist tension, and it slowly became evident to most Northern workingmen that, rather than serving as a distraction from the interests of workers, the struggle against the slave system was essential to general worker advancement.[20] By the mid-1840s, leading abolitionists such as William Lloyd Garrison had become more sensitive to labor's demands and lecturers more frequently targeted working-class audiences (artisans in fact became the primary signers of antislavery petitions). Meanwhile, white workers learned how to carve out space within the antislavery movement without losing their independent class and trade programs. As Philip S. Foner argues, the participation of white labor ultimately made antislavery politics relevant, and battles against slaveholding prepared workingmen for future battles against capital.[21]

At the same time, women activists recognized the parallels between slavery, wage exploitation, and gender oppression. In fact, from the beginnings of industrial production, working women had helped formulate what Paul Buhle terms a "native historical materialism."[22] Because markets and contracts do not arise from or exist within power-neutral conditions, women perhaps especially understood wage work as a form of mandatory subjugation, the alternative to which was destitution, rooted in the theft of one's surplus labor (legitimized as "profit"). Although the term "wage slave" originated in Great Britain in the early nineteenth century, women were among the first groups of US workers to compare their station to that of enslaved Black people.[23] As early as the 1830s, women in mills and factories, as well as middle-class reformers, referenced "wage slavery" and, later, gender-specific "emancipation." In 1836, 1,500 members of the Factory Girls' Association in Lowell, Massachusetts, marched through the streets of the mill town declaring, "I am not a slave."[24] This use of what Barry Goldberg terms the "master metaphor" put working women in conversation with middle-class reformers of various stripes.[25] Women's rights advocates also adopted and expounded on abolitionist language to attack patriarchal dependence, tying such ideas not merely to bread-and-butter issues but also to gendered injustices regarding education, property, inheritance, and sexual rights. Many sought "liberation" from fathers, brothers, and husbands.[26] Notions of female self-ownership and women as "secondary slaves," common among both working women and within particular circles of the antislavery movement, fused through the agenda of the Seneca Falls Convention in 1848. By 1860, reform literature, including Caroline H. Dall's *Right to Labor*, had popularized theories of women's "economic emancipation" that linked workplace and gender inequality.[27]

This malleable definition of emancipation permeated the early Republican Party, with workers crafting an ever more comprehensive definition of "antislavery." The Republicans' most radical extension of free-labor ideology—its "semi-socialist idea"—centered not on equal outcomes but on equality of opportunity through public education, infrastructural improvements, and the redistribution of land in the form of homesteads. The party's slogan "Free Labor, Free Soil, Free Men" was both an attack on the slaveholding cabal and a recognition of rights, land, and dignity for the laborer.[28] In addition to moral screeds against servitude, Republicans agreed that the peculiar institution beleaguered white workers as well as Black slaves, avowing that wage labor offered superior mobility to middling whites.[29] Even conservative Republicans, many of whom detested abolitionism and espoused legal or de facto racial exclusion, summoned Jeffersonian and Jacksonian anti-aristocracy to claim that slavery replicated a hereditary ruling elite.[30] Comparing financial *bondsmen* to those who own *bonded men* by insisting that both bankers and slaveholders profited from the unrequited labor of others, Ohio senator Thomas Morris damned the planter class as the "Goliath of all monopolies."[31] The terms "Slave Power," "slaveholding aristocracy," and "slaveocracy," which dated to at least the origins of the Liberty Party, gained wider currency throughout the 1850s.

The radical European American wing of the Republican Party adopted "emancipation" in support of abolition and woman suffrage. Many regarded America's republican experiment, or what Lincoln called "the last best hope of earth," as part of a transatlantic ideological struggle.[32] German Forty-Eighters—those who had participated in Europe's 1848 revolutions and whose "red republicanism" was shaped by a range of concepts from Enlightenment liberalism to Jacobinism to Marxism—formed the left wing of the fledgling Republicans. Such émigrés included Joseph Weydemeyer, Alexander Schimmelfennig, and August Willich, who deemed John Brown's raid on the federal arsenal at Harpers Ferry "an exploit on the battlefield of human emancipation" and a model for transnational revolution.[33] Although many

Forty-Eighters would later abandon the pursuit of African American civil rights in the name of so-called national preservation and join the Liberal Republican movement in 1872, German American socialists discerned free-labor ideology as a precondition of bourgeois revolution, a triumph over feudal aristocracy, and a forerunner to worker emancipation.[34] Cities in the "German Triangle" of Cincinnati, Milwaukee, and St. Louis offered willing audiences for radical social philosophy due in part to their high literacy and multiculturalism. Newspapers, weekly journals, literary clubs, and private and public libraries abounded, and German Communist Clubs, first in New York's Kleindeutschland and later in the Middle West, proved reliable abolitionist mouthpieces.[35] Liberal and republican social and political organizations that had begun in Germany under Napoleonic occupation, German American Turnverein societies published the works of Marx and Friedrich Engels alongside the romantic and transcendentalist poetry of Ralph Waldo Emerson and John Keats.

The emancipation metaphor increased as constitutional crisis drove the republic toward war.[36] The workers' interpretation of the sectional conflict as the opening phase of a greater struggle from below began during the war itself. Though most white Northerners resisted social revolution, "walkouts" of enslaved people and slave seizures by Union soldiers on the ground set the tempo for emancipation.[37] Social transformation buoyed the idea that the deliverance of enslaved Black people heralded worker liberation. In the North, waves of strikes from Boston to the Illinois coalfields led to a new momentum of union organization and labor militancy. Labor and socialist leaders in Europe further united in opposition to the Confederacy and behind the moral force of a US government now committed to the destruction of slavery, even though many of them, like textile workers in Manchester, acknowledged how their livelihoods relied on Southern cotton. Meanwhile, conservatives defended what they perceived as "white" interests. Fearing competition for wages and residences from freed slaves, especially in the Lower Middle West, panicked Democrats and conservative Republicans, stoked by the partisan press and the pulpit, argued that the destruction of the slave system would "disturb the markets of the world" and devastate white labor.[38] While most border Republicans remained racially aversive, a minority deemed fears of a "Negro invasion" little more than Democratic race-baiting. As Kentucky abolitionist Cassius Clay warned European American workers in Brooklyn in October 1862, "Show me a man who would today oppress a man on account of his color, and I will show you a man who will oppress you tomorrow."[39]

Four years of bloodshed overturned the slave regime and permanently transformed the size and scope of the American state.[40] In addition to popular legislation such as the Homestead Act and the Land Grant College Act, the Republican-commanded Congress of 1861–65 also promoted industrial expansion through the war economy, as banking, currency, debt, and tax reform ushered in unprecedented federal economic activism. The subsequent Reconstruction Amendments—a "second US Constitution"—afforded the federal government a new role as a "custodian of freedom."[41] Debates over the limits of newfound governmental power came to dominate the postwar era. Conflict arose from the tension between the equalitarian professions of the antebellum Republicans and the harsh and impersonal realities of industrial capitalism in a white republic.

Putting the final touches on his masterwork, *Das Kapital*, Marx, who linked Black freedom to the memory of John Brown and the liberation of the serfs in Russia, now wrote to his compatriot Engels.[42] With Reconstruction, he argued, the United States was "only now really entering the revolutionary phase."[43] Witnessing the contact between German-speaking Union soldiers and African Americans as perhaps the earliest collaboration between socialists and a self-emancipating proletariat, Marx foresaw the possibility of an interracial, multiethnic movement among the world's most diverse working class arising from slavery's collapse.[44] Authoring a letter to Lincoln from the International Workingmen's Association in January 1865, he called the president a "single-minded son of the working class" and hoped that the postwar era might bring about "the rescue of an enchained race and the reconstruction of a social world."[45] Marx's radical counterparts across the Atlantic also sought to broaden democracy, agreeing that emancipation meant little without guaranteed political and economic rights for freedpeople and workers, including access to land, safer working conditions, and greater control over their own labor.

Civil War memory naturally framed the citizenship and political aspirations of Black workers. Emancipation Day celebrations and Black colleges and agricultural and mechanical institutes became repositories of Black memory; "Douglass," "Lincoln," and "John Brown" became metonyms for Black schools, craft unions, and local militias; and white Union leaders such as Charles Sumner, Thaddeus Stevens, and Ulysses S. Grant were remembered as antiracist partners, not racial superiors.[46] Heartened by the Union army's promise of "forty acres and a mule," many formerly enslaved people demanded the property of disloyal planters.[47] Viewing land reform as a logical extension of emancipation, they tied propertarianism to emancipation and Black military service in various commemorative settings: church activities, familial namings, militias, and picnics, parades, and public celebrations. Drawing on the collective memory of slaves turned soldiers, many Black veterans developed a "Jacobin political orientation," in which "equal rights" often came to include agrarian autonomy, industrial independence, cooperative governance, and the "right not to have a master at all."[48] They expected reimbursement in return for centuries of labor theft on a tremendous scale.[49] Land reform was among the most transformational outgrowths of the prewar Republican vision, and "rehearsals for Reconstruction" in places such as Davis Bend, Mississippi; St. Simon's Island, Georgia; and Port Royal, South Carolina, demonstrated beyond any doubt the African American desire for land ownership and economic autonomy.[50] Freedpeople warned that to seize their newly won land and homes—what the *Boston Commonwealth* labeled their "castles of liberty"—and return them to former Confederates was tantamount to the restoration of slavery.[51]

Indeed, the end of slavery saw countless propertyless Southerners question the form of free labor that Northerners had characterized as "wage slavery." Wendell Phillips announced in 1868 that the overriding problem of Reconstruction was that "the black man has no capital."[52] Louis Charles Roudanez's *New Orleans Tribune* argued that, lest slavery simply morph into serfdom, freedpeople should be not merely "laborers" but their own "planters" as well. In fact, this "new class of landholders" should guide the "whole management" of their farm economy, as workers would never be able to transcend a meager existence as long as they were wage employees beholden to another's acreage, implements, and capital.[53] Fearing a resurgent planter oligarchy, Joseph T. Wilson, Black veteran and editor of Norfolk's *True Southerner*, maintained that workingmen should own their own labor. He proposed political alliances between Blacks and poor whites in order to "vote down the old aristocratic party." These non-elites composed "the class of Confederate soldiers who never had any heart in the rebellion, but were compelled by circumstances to enter the army," including deserters, scalawags, and nonideological Confederates.[54] Wilson, like other Southern Blacks, hoped the Reconstruction program would extinguish racial and economic castes, predicting that "soon the capitalist will lose his power to grind to dust the unfortunate and helpless," while "the strong arm that wielded the hammer over the anvil will gather the fruit of his labor."[55]

The "peasant dream" of landed proprietorship represented a pointed break with Republican liberalism. Emphasizing civic equality, exclusive property relations, and individual self-ownership rather than state intervention advancing land reform, such liberalism would leave newly emancipated people to their own material devices.[56] Some Northern whites *did* support reforming or confiscating what Charles Sumner termed the "nurseries of the rebellion." These included Thaddeus Stevens, who alleged that democracy was impossible "where a few own manors and the masses are landless," and Benjamin Wade, whose diatribe against consolidated capital in July 1867 warranted him a mention in the first German edition of *Das Kapital*.[57] Their numbers were few, however, as even the most ardent white Radical Republicans viewed process, legalism, and constitutional writ as sufficient to ensure African Americans equal social opportunity and impartial competitiveness in a "self-correcting" market.[58] Few Radical Republicans, much less white abolitionists, would have seen themselves as fostering inequality and the interests of capital. Yet by eschewing land reform in favor of the property rights of planters and by insisting that former slaves compete as equals in a "race neutral" forum, they lent policy force and moral legitimacy to a new and increasingly extreme relationship between owner and producer.[59] Not recognizing that capitalist markets might reflect and reinforce rather than undermine the social prejudices directed at a propertyless and recently emancipated proletariat, as James Oakes maintains, "even the most radical abolitionists betrayed a blind faith in the magical healing powers of a free market in labor."[60]

Land redistribution converged with long-held understandings of freedom, or with beliefs that land ownership safeguarded one from coercive masters (or markets), enabling economic and democratic independence. Yet the very notion of "redistribution" violated deeply entrenched (capitalist) understandings of property, as even most well-meaning reformers believed that prosperity required only hard work and thrift.[61] This strain of free labor failed to account for historical exploitation or structural disadvantage, as well as the power imbalances and coercive possibilities within "freedom of contract." In reality, large-scale material redistribution was inimical to pervasive American attitudes toward *white* private property. Although requisitioned land was a supremely republican concept and what Noah Webster termed "the very *soul of a republic*," its logic had always been racialized, with land "redistributed" from red or brown people to white people.[62] As Richard White posits, "Southern redistribution," therefore, "was about whether Southern whites could be treated as Indians and Southern blacks could be treated like white men."[63]

In other words, an economically radical Reconstruction was ideologically antithetical to Northern Republicans because it was materially antithetical to the interests of Northern capital. Most pro-Reconstruction Northerners sought to stabilize the South and grow their party through Black voting, not support policy that might fundamentally alter class or race relations in their own states and communities. Meanwhile, moneyed policy makers, their fear of class conflict heightened by events in Europe (such as the Paris Commune of 1871), grew increasingly opposed to the era's leveling potential.

Redistribution became contested not only by white Southerners who violently sought to remake the status quo ante bellum but also by Northern whites who were eager to open Southern markets and revive cotton production, using freedpeople and poor whites as a cheap labor pool.[64] Ultimately, land redistribution failed in part because Black allies in the North did not support it and because other issues—currency, civil service reform, and eventually the Panic of 1873—came to predominate among reformers.[65] Nevertheless, calls for land justice put forth an interpretation of labor radicalism that went beyond liberalism and the idea that emancipation meant only the absence of bondage. Moreover, Black discourses of freedom and liberty in the pursuit of landownership overlapped with the republican rhetoric of antebellum white workers, influencing labor organization.[66] Taken together, these counterclaims carried the potential to force a transformational confrontation with capital.

## Economic Emancipation

Even as consolidating trade unions appropriated the language and legacy of the early Republicans, the party of Lincoln's antebellum egalitarianism and postwar commitments to civic equality grew increasingly subordinate to those who commanded the economy's heights. In fact, Reconstruction had become part of a larger program of nation-state "territorialization" involving expansionistic capitalism and the hyper-exploitation of a multiracial labor force within and eventually beyond US continental boundaries.[67] This development saw Republican-backed financiers use the state to consolidate power through the tariff, the monetary system, and the public debt.[68] Whereas the federal government balked at land redistribution for the Black dispossessed, it gifted free (Indigenous) lands to white homesteaders in the West and land discounts to poor whites in the South. Most especially, the state provided immense land giveaways to railroad corporations, which received roughly 180 million acres during the postwar period. Yet even as Jay Gould's plutocracy devoured Thaddeus Stevens's democratic ideal, the dream of agrarian justice did not die. Antislavery vernacular as a feature of rural reform resurfaced in the Readjuster, Populist, and farmer-labor movements of the post-Reconstruction South. However, despite significant political legacies, such interracial undertakings proved mostly transitory, as major parties in both sections used racial and ethnic fear to undermine potential class solidarity. Racism remained, as it often had, a "psychological wage" for non-elites of the dominant race, who, even when handicapped by empty purses, forged identity and found consciousness—if a false consciousness—on the basis of white skin.[69]

Members of the National Labor Union—a protraction of antebellum labor congresses and worker collectives—were among the first postwar labor organizers to frame their struggle as a symbolic if not literal continuation of the War for the Union. Tradesmen forged the NLU, the country's first national labor federation, in the summer of 1866. The union was highly decentralized and possessed only a vague social philosophy. Founder William H. Sylvis opposed both European "red Republicanism" and American "Black Republicanism." Yet like the burgeoning international labor organization of communists, anarchists, socialists, and radical trade unionists, the NLU was bitingly critical of monopoly, describing it as "the root and very essence of slavery" and contending that labor unification was a precondition for the "universal emancipation from the power of capital."[70] Although Sylvis personally believed in separate spheres for women, the NLU recognized women's right to unionize, and women and abolitionists alike identified the organization as a new site of intersectional struggle.[71] Susan B. Anthony, Elizabeth Cady Stanton, Frederick Douglass, and Wendell Phillips all joined.[72] The NLU ultimately initiated the first labor lobby in Washington, DC, pushing the Grant administration to implement an eight-hour workday for federal employees. Although its symbolic and intellectual foundation was chiefly middle-class republicanism, the NLU's very existence accentuated the contradictions of free labor, including its promise to eliminate barriers to mobility.[73]

NLU leaders linked their campaign to the Union cause.[74] "The war abolished the right of property in man," Sylvis maintained, "but it did not abolish slavery." Referring to the union as a "great anti-slavery movement," he urged members to "push on the work of emancipation" until servitude was abolished in all regions and in every industry.[75] Grandstanding at a Fourth of July celebration in 1866, Andrew C. Cameron, the Scottish-born and Chartist-influenced editor of Chicago's *Workingman's Advocate*, explained that while honest Union soldiers had been off fighting and dying for their country, opportunistic capitalists and substitute-hiring "$300 men" had exploited their suffering through the ill-gotten wealth of government contracts and Wall Street speculation. The post-conflict order would now pit virtuous workers against the "bloated monied aristocracy," and he urged interracial alliance.[76] Cameron's interpretation of the war—that veterans must fight a continuing contest of industrial emancipation—was widely repeated within and beyond the NLU. It was also part of a tactical effort to recruit Union veterans, now nearly 2 million in number, to the trade union crusade.

The NLU marketed its program as a philosophical extension of liberal wartime policy. Speaking in Chicago in January 1865, Sylvis insisted that although the ongoing "political revolution" was coming to a close, a "social revolution"—a "collision between classes"—was still taking place across

Northern cities, where wage labor had become tantamount to bondage. He distinguished between "slavery," which he thought a universal condition of the exploited, and "the right of property in man," or chattel slavery, and maintained that relations between owner and workers were, for the most part, "that of master and slave."[77] The conclusion of the slaveholder's rebellion and the end of the abolitionist movement had opened up new imaginative outlets for a republicanism centered on combating the inequalities of industrial capitalism. As Alex Gourevitch explains, "Labor republicans could now present themselves as the true torchbearers of the revolutionary republicanism that the Civil War and its ideology of free labor had revived."[78]

While some reformers hoped that aging abolitionists including Wendell Phillips might bridge the gap between antislavery and workers' rights, new leaders such as Sylvis, land reformer Ira Steward, who invested "the spirit of abolition" in the eight-hour movement, and editor George McNeill solicited veterans by pronouncing that the war's true goals had not yet been achieved.[79] For his part, Sylvis saw "toilworn and war-battled veterans" as essential to labor reform.[80] As workers perpetually pointed out, it was not capitalists or politicians but rather the "hardy sons of toil who garnered the musket, and who rallied to the rescue when the country was threatened," and whose bones now "bleached upon a hundred battlefields." In the words of one editor, the class of men who had defeated treason were those of the workshop: the iron pourers and the engine drivers. They were "the men who make the country—who saved it . . . not a bloated monied aristocracy."[81] Yet Sylvis also attacked what he perceived as the wastefulness of Reconstruction spending, which benefited "worthless, ignorant negroes." Racist messaging from labor leadership exacerbated the difficulty of white Northern workers connecting their fortunes to those of Black Southern peasants. At the same time, Sylvis combined emancipationism—the insistence that slavery was the war's cause and Black liberation its primary triumph—with a call for continued struggle, proposing a new form of emancipatory organization:

> Whatever our opinions may be as to the immediate causes of that war, we can all agree that human slavery (property in man) was the first great cause. No man in America rejoiced more than I did at the downfall of negro slavery. But when the shackles fell from the limbs of those four millions of blacks, it did not make them *free* men; it simply transferred them from one condition of slavery to another; it placed them upon the platform of the white workingmen, and made all slaves together.[82]

Both major political parties looked to capitalize on those symbolic ties between labor and war memory. Andrew Johnson Democrats painted their man as a "Great Emancipator," not of Blacks, but of poor whites, and as a foe of the planter aristocracy.[83] Writing Johnson from London following Lincoln's assassination, the International Workingmen's Association extolled the Union and rejoiced that in the "new era of the Emancipation of labor, the American people devolved the responsibilities of leadership upon *two men of labor*: the one, Abraham Lincoln, the other, Andrew Johnson" (the endorsement was quickly withdrawn).[84] The *Workingman's Advocate* reminded its readers that, as rail-splitter and tailor, both Lincoln and his successor were progeny of the working class.[85] Adhering to the party's antebellum themes of independent producers, Republicans imagined Union war hero Ulysses S. Grant as a "Galena tanner," replete with workman's apron and tools.[86] Radical Republicans, such as Indianan George W. Julian, explained that the "emancipation of labor" demanded an egalitarian land program and set to prove that the Republicans were still the antithesis of the "rebel slaveholding oligarchy." With hyper-emotional "bloody shirt" politics reverberating, Julian equated the Democracy with rebellion and slavery and compared sharecropping to slavery and serfdom, arguing that only the Lincolnian policy of Western homesteads could truly liberate workers.[87] Yet by 1870, the same year the Vandalia Railroad hired a fourteen-year-old Eugene Debs as a paint-scraper, kick-starting the Hoosier's lifelong involvement with railroad employees, the old free-labor ideal was withering before the realities of a permanent wage system.[88] Sensing their opening, Democrats appropriated emancipationist symbolism. Speaking on behalf of white workers, one Horatio Seymour supporter claimed that to defeat Grant in the 1868 presidential election was to "emancipate honest labor" from the Republican "money oligarchy."[89]

Black workers, meanwhile, continued to combine class demands with emancipationist memory. Although Sylvis, whom workers designated as "Our Lincoln," promised African Americans that the NLU represented a "second Emancipation Proclamation," his root motivation was protecting white labor by organizing Black workers who might otherwise "scab."[90] White labor leaders encouraged African Americans to coordinate separately not out of racial enlightenment but because they sought to limit marketplace competitors. At the same time, Black men, though disproportionately "unskilled" (as defined by white craft unions) and with far fewer resources, established a separate Colored National Labor Union, which served to allay white anxieties. Immersed in community politics, African American union leaders melded labor activism with commemoration of liberation through Emancipation Day fetes, as well as of civil rights achievements, including mass celebrations of the Fifteenth Amendment.[91] More radical CNLU leaders continued to pair working-class coordination with calls for property confiscation and redistribution to former slaves.[92] CNLU president Isaac Myers, who founded the Colored Caulkers Trade Union Society in 1868, made an organizing trip to Richmond and Norfolk in 1870 in which he termed organized labor "the safeguard of the colored man." Reiterating Black labor's support for the party of Lincoln and Grant, he rebuked labor's color line, deeming it harmful to both Black and white workers.[93]

Labor organization proved tenuous in the former slaveholding states, where entrenched racial division undercut class solidarity as white workers benefited disproportionately from the transition to free labor.[94] Myers regretted that reaching Black workers in the Deep South demanded that organizers be "steel-plated against Ku-Klux bullets."[95] Frederick Douglass replaced Myers as head of the CNLU in 1872, which many white Democrats read as its de facto marriage to the Republican Party, widening labor's apartheid. Additionally, efforts to encompass both white and Black workers in Dixie met with traditional obstacles (rurality, segregation, planter hegemony, reactionary politics) rooted in the desire of white elites to preserve the status quo. Although the labor movement eventually made better headway in Virginia's New South urban centers, by the early 1870s the NLU was everywhere in decline, and it foundered entirely in 1872.

Radical factions elsewhere, such as the International Workingmen's Association, also known as the First International, drew on revolutionary nationalist and abolitionist rhetoric to call for a transnational "economical emancipation" and the abolition of class.[96] Though even relatively conservative labor groups, such as Eugene Debs's Brotherhood of Locomotive Firemen, appropriated antislavery vernacular and martial republicanism, others combined trade unionist, socialist, and agrarian interests. The Detroit Labor League was formed in the fall of 1877 in response to the Great Railroad Strike, a national wave of work stoppages and protests that saw 500,000 workers across various industries walk off their jobs, resulting in bloody suppression by state authorities and the deaths of at least 100 workers. The Detroit Labor League comprised both Socialist Labor and Greenback campaigns and backed the International. Its members, including printers, carpenters, iron molders, cigar makers, bricklayers, and horseshoers, deemed persistent inequality a betrayal of republican ideals articulated by the Founders and contested during the war.[97] European ancestral (later termed "ethnic") factions, as well as racial and regional sects, limited this professed universalism. Native-born reformers echoed mainstream nativism by deriding Internationalists and foreign-born blocs, such as the heavily German American Socialist Labor Party, for preferring electoral politics over unions or for the seeming refusal of some members to assimilate to American customs.[98] Even white workers who did not embrace emancipationist memory or celebrate the Reconstruction era (which is to say the vast majority) often co-opted the landed republicanism of former slaves.[99]

This fractured meaning of the Civil War stemmed from divergent interpretations of "free labor." Workingmen noted that although the conflict began as a contest between "King Cotton" and "King Corn," "King Labor"—made up of the producing men of both sections who had bled at Shiloh, Gettysburg, Chickamauga, and Petersburg—should be most venerated.[100] While many radicals imagined a postwar political economy of small shopkeepers, farmers, and artisans who controlled either space (in the South) or time (in the North), the Republican postwar shift toward big business blunted the party's former potential as an electoral vehicle for workers.[101] Factionalism and debate over the scope of Reconstruction debilitated the party of Sumner and Stevens as violence against Southern Blacks and white Republicans by private militias of former Confederates eroded African American progress. In the North, responses to growing conflict between capital and labor wrought friction amid communist and socialist Internationalists, who supported racial equality and women's political rights, and trade unionists concerned with bread-and-butter issues. Although some African American aid societies continued to petition for reparations for former slaves, by the late 1870s Republicans proved, in the words of Robin Blackburn, "incapable of defending either the wages of Northern workers or the political gains of Southern freedmen."[102]

No event better demonstrated the unsettled nature of the "free labor" question or solidified the ongoing "counterrevolution of property" than the interracial and multiethnic strikes of 1877. The spontaneous, bottom-up disputes involved tens of thousands of Union veterans on both sides. These included street battles in Baltimore, Pittsburgh, and Chicago. On the Mississippi River, meanwhile, the short-lived St. Louis Commune was, according to Walter Johnson, "the era's most compelling example of interracial politics—a final, flash-lit image of the fading promise of abolition democracy."[103] The government's backlash, from the War Department's creation of "riot duty" to the professionalization of the National Guard, also signaled a definitive shift in federal priorities from protecting freedpeople in the former Confederacy to using and expanding the repressive capacity of the state to forcefully check worker uprisings in the name of "domestic security." Former president Grant noticed this incongruity. He found it strange that Democrats and conservative Republicans who had previously "thought it 'horrible' to employ Federal troops 'to protect the lives of negroes'" now lacked hesitation in "exhausting the whole power of the government to suppress a strike on the slightest intimation that danger threatened."[104] In the words of Eric Foner, the year 1877 both underscored how the war era "tied the new industrial bourgeoisie to the

Republican party and the national state" and "marked a decisive retreat from the idea, born during the Civil War, of a powerful nation state protecting the rights of American citizens."[105] However, this scaling back of the state only applied to the protection of Black rights. In fact, federal intervention markedly increased after 1877 in many arenas, including the continued pursuit of continental empire. As the last Reconstruction governments fell, federal soldiers led by former Union generals abducted Indian lands and committed genocide against Indian people across the American West.

The breakdown of the "first civil rights movement" proved both critical to the development of racial capitalism and an integral stage in the reproduction of racial difference indicative of the "modern labor problem." Few white workers lamented Reconstruction's collapse; fewer still viewed the decade following the war as an unrealized rights revolution or a botched precursor to an emancipatory internationalism.[106] Yet Reconstruction had seen former slaves make claims *as workers*; it also saw workers make claims *as Black people and former slaves*. Recognizing this, the great scholar-activist W. E. B. Du Bois later branded nemeses of Reconstruction—those who sanctioned the violent overthrow of African American political and social gains—not only foes of the Black race but class enemies.[107] In other words, emancipation and subsequent demands for political and economic equality had been part of a transnational and transhistorical labor struggle, and the war on freedpeople, whether directed by white paramilitaries in the South or political opponents in the North, *was* a war on labor. When freedpeople, especially Union veterans, cited their status as producers to solicit equitable labor contracts, public education, voting rights, or land reform, they were using the collective memory of the war in the pursuit of universalist politics, furthering the cause of *all* workingmen. As labor abolitionists had understood, Black emancipation was constitutive of labor's cause, and in the ensuing decades, labor's cause would draw on Black emancipation as a model, a symbol, a language, and part of an expressed historical destiny. Even when that cause dimmed, the spread of farmer-labor alliances throughout the South highlighted the region's continued capacity for interracial, if racially unequal, cooperation. Such reform would spring from—and build upon—the Readjuster Party's template of reconciling regions and sections by trade and class rather than by white nationalism.

## Scalawag Memory

Reconstruction, Du Bois lamented during the height of Jim Crow, "could have rebuilt the economic foundations of Southern society, confiscated and redistributed wealth, and built a real democracy."[108] Indeed, social fluidity, proletarianization, and class stratification presented discrete possibilities for interracial cooperation in the postwar South. By the early 1870s, however, with Redemption rising, emancipationist memory was increasingly expressed in segregated spaces. Emancipation Day celebrations came to mirror the racially separate observances of Independence Day, Decoration Day, and, eventually, Labor Day. With rights gains under attack, Black politics became ever more oriented toward street demonstrations and small-scale workplace organization.[109] Although Republicans continued to invoke the independent producerism of Grant's presidential campaigns, including "dignity of labor" concepts that had previously been used to attack the Slave Power, a new "harmony of interests" between capitalists and labor privileged the former.[110] Meanwhile, white supremacy pervaded much white working-class culture and Democratic anti-Reconstruction campaigns, which emphasized African American political and social incapacity and mirrored and reinforced the burgeoning Lost Cause.[111] Racial liberalism was slowly stripped from the liberal nationalism of the war era as white citizens steadily perceived sectionalism *and* emancipationism as obstacles to national unity, expediting what Du Bois termed a "new feudalism" in the North's "Empire of Industry."[112] Although many white Union veterans had explicitly supported Black rights and taxpayer-supported reform programs, the Long Depression of the 1870s, as well as time and distance from the war's immediacy, changed collective attitudes. Anxious over political marginalization, demographic fluctuation, and the impersonal forces of a new industrial order, many "boys in blue" grew to reconcile with former enemies and linked both African American rights *and* labor organization across races to "anarchy" and the destruction of property rights. The intensification of sectional reunion among white veterans signaled a broader shift in the American public consciousness away from the war's emancipationist legacy.

But there was more to Civil War memory as it related to "the other South." New interracial agrarian movements co-opted, reshaped, and brandished old free-labor rhetoric, laying the symbolic and institutional groundwork for later labor and populist struggles. In Virginia, the cynicism of Reconstruction's end and strained relations between African Americans and the Republican Party opened the door for a radical though short-lived political insurgency. Founded at Richmond's Mozart Hall in February 1879 after the splintering of the anti-Reconstruction Conservative Party, the Readjusters (so called for their motion to "readjust" the state debt to unburden farmers) were a coalition of Republicans, Greenbackers, and racially moderate Conservatives who organized across the color line.[113] Anti-elite and anti-urban, the Readjusters had formed largely as a response to economic downturn in the 1870s. Unlike their conservative and white supremacist Funder opponents, Readjusters appealed directly to white Republicans and, after initial reluctance, African Americans, with several Black stalwarts winning party offices. In splitting the white vote, Readjusterism provided African American voters newfound political leverage. Assailing railroad rates, head tax disenfranchisement, and the slashing of public education budgets, by 1881 Readjusters held the governorship and both senate seats and won a majority in both houses of the General Assembly.

The upstart reformers were led by former Confederate general William Mahone, who had been a member of Robert E. Lee's staff and a hero of the Battle of the Crater. A Conservative and a railroad executive after the war, Mahone originally opposed Reconstruction. But the Panic of 1873 changed his fortunes and his politics. He became involved in state education, playing a key role in the creation of Virginia State University and eventually riding Readjuster politics all the way to the US Senate. There his sterling war record shielded him from charges of sectional disloyalty by anti-Reconstruction Bourbon Democrats.[114] The Mahone-supported Readjuster William E. Cameron, the popular mayor of Petersburg, Virginia's largest Black majority city, was also a Confederate veteran. Like Mahone, Cameron used interracial coalition to widen his statewide appeal and was elected governor in 1881. The scope of that Readjuster federation depended on linking the destiny of the state to veterans and the meaning of the late war, with an emphasis on the common soldier.[115] Converts centered class-based policy interests and the symbolism of shared veteranhood, even if such unity meant attempting to transcend sectional rifts. One Cameron supporter explained his party fidelity in reconciliationist terms. He "wanted the time to come when northern and southern maidens would together scatter flowers over the graves of the blue and the gray."[116]

Part of a far-reaching movement of "independent" and "reform" parties that swept across the country in response to the crash of 1873 and the fallout of Reconstruction, Mahoneism imperiled the sectional, economic, and racial status quos despite its opportunistic streak and racially imbalanced leadership. Mahone repudiated vengeance-driven "bloody shirt" politics and sought to eradicate the idea of "a Solid South against a Solid North."[117] His movement claimed to represent veterans, the dignity of labor, and "the rights of man against the privileges of an aristocracy of office-holding families."[118] Admirers branded him the "emancipator of the South from the slavery of prejudice, caste, and partisan bigotry."[119] Adversaries, meanwhile, castigated the former rebel as a more dangerous leveler than John Brown.[120] In an address in January

FIGURE 1. "Virginia.—The Readjuster State Convention at Richmond," *Frank Leslie's Illustrated Newspaper*, June 25, 1881. Artist Walter Goater's engraving of the interracial gallery during the nomination of Confederate veteran William E. Cameron reflects the Readjuster Party's repudiation of the Lost Cause and its relatively egalitarian aspirations. (Library of Virginia)

1881, Mahone himself declared that the party hoped to both remove "sectional contention" and "overthrow race prejudices."[121] Most white Readjusters agreed that the best means of undercutting sectional and racial obstacles was through class programs—not only schools, debt adjustment, and civic rights but also public farming and manufacturing aid, free vaccinations, public food distribution during crop failures, and state-funded hospitals, asylums, and penitentiaries.[122] Readjusters sought to refashion political identity through a new discourse of equality in order to recruit Black voters, who, while deeply attached to the party of Lincoln, also criticized Republicans' racially skewed patronage system, the party's aversion to material redistribution, and the feudalistic attitude of party leadership toward African Americans.[123]

Guided by initial anti-Readjuster sentiments from national Republicans including Ulysses S. Grant and Frederick Douglass, many Black Virginians remained leery. Suspicious of political cooperation or rightly viewing it as a recipe for white retaliation, Black citizens increasingly saw white-led interracialism as an attempt to control Black votes and property in the face of retrograde labor conditions throughout the South, including convict leasing. They protected their public commemorations accordingly. Reasserting the politics of self-help, most African American leaders insisted that building Black community and solidarity precede any interracial politics, which must also explicitly serve Black interests.[124] Emancipation Days proved vital not only to resisting the Lost Cause but also to promoting racial uplift. Lamenting a convict labor system little removed from slavery, and with Black workers crushed beneath employers and owners, race men encouraged Black emigration to the Northwest. These included Douglass, who now firmly believed that political rights could not be preserved without a propertarian basis on which to use and protect them.[125] Ostracized from formal politics, African American veterans used workingmen's societies and labor organizations to highlight themes of cultural independence and autonomous achievement.[126]

One such skeptic, Joseph T. Wilson, had by the 1880s become a fixture at Emancipation Day events, linking war memory to changing conceptions of Black politics. Writing against not only the nascent Lost Cause but also former white comrades who devalued the magnitude of emancipation, Wilson's *The Black Phalanx* (1882) was the first comprehensive study of the role of Black soldiers throughout US history. It underscored the legacy of liberation in the service of growing self-help politics. Like much of Virginia's Black middle class, Wilson stood firm with the Republicans, and most Black voters strongly preferred the nomination of Grant for an unprecedented third term in 1880. But as African American leverage proved decisive, white Readjusters became more receptive to race-specific demands, including anti-lynching and anti–poll tax positions, legalizing interracial marriage, the integration of restaurants, petty larceny reform, and the abolition of the whipping post. National Republican and state-level Black support for the party grew, especially among the rural and working classes, leading to a wave of Black labor activism in 1881.[127] The party's state convention that June boasted over 100 African American delegates who reiterated their faith in a movement that both cultivated "respect and attachment for the Union and observes the spirit of Reconstruction" and attempted to "permanently settle the antagonism of races."[128] Readjusters captured the governorship that fall, lowering taxes on small farms and businesses while raising corporate rates and abolishing the poll tax and the whipping post. By 1883, enrollment in Black schools had tripled.[129] In response, wider swaths of Black activists, including the Wendell Phillips Club of Boston, deemed white Readjusters sincere allies and proclaimed "a new era dawning for the colored people of the South."[130] Even Wilson would later call Mahone "the Lincoln of Virginia" and urge Black men to stand by him.[131]

The tropology of the Civil War and the notion that emancipation was both a Black historical experience and an ongoing project was critical to an interracial political alliance that built consensus through veteranhood. Readjusters commemorated "private soldiers," and Mahone courted political allies at Confederate reunions and Memorial Day celebrations.[132] Black Readjusters, meanwhile, named their clubs and union lodges after emancipationist figures, including Lincoln and Charles Sumner.[133] Although the Readjuster discourse drew on a phraseological mélange, from Thomas Paine through the early Republicans, it centered on the same appeals to Black manhood that had underwritten African American military service, as well as on emancipationist memory.[134] As explained by Readjuster George F. Bragg Jr., the white editor of the *Petersburg Lancet*, slaves had been "mere chattel . . . a thing," and emancipation turned them into free men and citizens.[135] Nationally, devotees applauded Grant's endorsement of the Republican-Readjuster fusion as working toward the "emancipation" of all citizens, Black and white.[136]

In the meantime, Democrats employed the same race-baiting they had used to discredit emancipation, Black enlistment, and Reconstruction. As Readjusters "carried the war into Africa" in order to harness disgruntled Black Republicans, their opponents excoriated the reformers' cause as one of "negro rule," certain to incite a "second civil war."[137] Virginia Democrats, under the leadership of railroad tycoon John S. Barbour, judged Mahoneism as "revolution," "socialism," "anarchy," and the "mongrelization of the races," linking its leader to carpetbagger "misrule."[138] Warning that Readjusterism was a "return to Radical rule," Barbour men charged Mahone with being a new type of slave master, intent on shackling *white* men.[139] One Democratic editor termed the insurgency a "motley mixture of antipodal elements . . . black spirits and white, blue spirits and gray, especially the *black*." The Readjusters' "farcical combination" threatened to upset the Solid South, both its Democratic rule and "natural" racial order.[140] The party's success also spurred a rash of Bourbon-Funder "nigger killings" as white-on-Black violence erupted across the state, most notably in Danville, where African American Readjusters had won the city government.[141] Pronouncing that the Ku Klux Klan had been resurrected, Black residents perceived the bloodshed as a continuation of wartime and Reconstruction atrocities, including Fort Pillow and Hamburg.[142] In a paper titled "The Danville Massacre," Black Readjuster R. A. Paul spoke to the necessity of defiance, linking the memory of slavery to the current political violence:

Better to dwell in Freedom's hall,
With a cold, damp floor and mouldering wall,
Than to bow the head and bend the knee,
In the proudest palace of Slaverie.[143]

When it came to a white man in Virginia leading an integrated insurgency against the racial and economic interests of the ruling elite, one analogy loomed above all others: that of John Brown. Complaining of the patronage positions of so-called Sambos, one Democrat implied that Readjusters would perpetuate violence: "Mahoneism is 'progressive' and John Brown's soul is marching on!"[144] Conservatives maintained that Mahone had tricked "ignorant negroes" by telling them that the public debt they were being asked to pay down was a result of Virginia having executed Brown and returned runaway slaves prior to the war.[145] Other anti-Readjusters avowed that Mahone had won Black supporters only by warning them that Democrats would return Black people to slavery.[146] Insisting that white Readjusters were "enslaving" gullible Blacks, one media opponent charged that "there was never a more groveling slavery than obedience to Mahone."[147] Of course, such allegations of coercion and scare lingo reinforced white prejudices that African American voters were easily duped and incapable of independent political action. As the specter of Black equality increasingly alienated white voters, Bourbon and Funder counterrevolutionaries combined to form a new Democratic Party in 1883. Readjusters, now retreating from Black issues, officially merged with Republicans the following year. Ultimately, Virginia's rejection of interracial politics was so thorough that the overthrow of Readjusterism corresponded with an African American exodus from the state—the beginnings of the Great Migration.[148]

Although Mahone would occasionally serve as a symbol of white reconciliationist politics through the 1880s, with his exploits at the Crater acted out in sham battles at grand bivouacs and blue-gray reunions, Readjusterism facilitated a wave of Black-white Decoration Day celebrations, fostering interracial remembrance within and beyond Virginia.[149] It also cultivated a commemorative subculture within the Republican Party of now-loyal former Confederates. In April 1888, at a banquet in honor of the recently departed General Grant's birthday, Mahone himself stood before a Northern audience and, along with letters from fellow "scalawags" James Longstreet and John Singleton Mosby, recounted Yankee magnanimity at Appomattox and reflected positively on his former foe and companion Republican.[150] Mahone's conversion to the party of emancipation led one speaker to marvel during the 1892 party convention in Minneapolis, where the aging Virginian was in attendance, at the splendor of "white men and black men, many who wore the blue, some who wore the gray," now rallying around the cause of John C. Frémont and Abraham Lincoln.[151]

Despite its transience, Readjusterism proved a direct repudiation of the Lost Cause and the fiction of a solid white South. Mahone historicized class oppression within a Black-white story, recalling slavery as a burden on laborers of all races. Whereas the South's white producers had been, according to one Readjuster, "oppressed by degrading competition with slave labor," which drove down wages and employment, economic protectionism and equality of opportunity would provide meaningful dignity for wage earners and downtrodden farmers.[152] In 1882 Mahone had urged another Confederate veteran to "live for the future . . . and not the dead past . . . while cherishing honorable memories of its glories."[153] His call to move beyond not merely sectionalism but also growing Democrat-Confederate nostalgia and white solidarity represented a different kind of New South. This agrarian, republican South rejected the manufacturing free-for-all, dire working conditions and white reaction of Henry W. Grady and Thomas Nelson Paige in favor of public investment, regulation of industries, and class-based coalition building.

Ultimately, Mahone's movement both paved the way for the Populist vision a decade later and provided the South's ruling class a template for how to stave Populism off.[154] Despite the national marginalization of emancipationist remembrance, Readjusterism had created a blueprint for how the cultural memory of the Civil War might herald Samuel Fenton Cary's "emancipation of labor," with workingmen repurposing liberation themes. As the *Wilmington Daily Gazette*, Delaware's "Democratic Bible," claimed in 1874, it was up to veterans to save the country once again, not from secession but from corruption and robber barons. "If the Union men are not active in their work of restoring the Union," one old soldier insisted, "then dishonest villains will succeed in engendering further civil strife."[155] Reasoning that the emancipation of slaves had preceded a general freedom of labor, Wendell Phillips hoped that the Republican Party would "turn its forces, well-drilled ranks, buoyant with success, to the elevation and protection of all labor, white and black."[156] To many workers, especially those who had fought for the Union, true national preservation meant not political restoration *only* or the protection of civil rights in the South but also organizing against an insidious Money Power—the progeny of the Slave Power. Alas, the success of white and Black farmer-laborers mobilizing in unison against that Money Power was proportional to the willingness of whites to meaningfully address race-specific grievances, as well as to accommodate Black memory and Black history. Interracial class solidarity—the notion of shared interests, bound fates, and psychological unity—meant effectively expressing that just as the oppression of small white farmers and laborers adversely impacted freedpeople, the singular terror inflicted on former slaves hindered the advancement of all laborers. Despite the Readjusters' backslide, moments of Black-white possibility were far from extinguished. Memories of slave resistance, abolitionists, and soldiering had vindicated a distinct—if fleeting—body politic centered on the language of liberation, paving the way for interracial farmer-labor politics and providing a model for labor's conception of worker emancipation.

CHAPTER 2

# Southern Palm, Northern Pine

## Greenbackers and the Reconciliation of Class

IN THE SUMMER OF 1880, a Union veteran returned to the Deep South. James Baird Weaver of Iowa was armed not with a sword but with a sweeping political program. He was attacking not former Confederates but presidential nominees and Union war heroes James A. Garfield and Winfield Scott Hancock. His aim was not to animate old battle lines but to construct new ones. Weaver was the presidential candidate of the Greenback-Labor Party, and he carried his class message through the heart of Dixie—Chattanooga, Birmingham, Montgomery, and Huntsville—where he was greeted by African American party activists. Addressing a crowd in Prescott, Arkansas, in the mid-August heat, the candidate turned his attention to a physically disabled supporter who explained that he had lost his leg fighting at Shiloh. Weaver, whose 2nd Iowa Volunteer Infantry endured some of the war's most horrific combat in the battle's infamous "Hornet's Nest," grew fully engaged as the tenor shifted from stump speech to personal dialogue between old soldiers. The Confederate veteran now addressed the Iowan: "You were here in the service of the United States, fighting for the stars and stripes. I was in the Confederate service. Here, in the presence of this vast audience, I extend to you my hand and heart. The boys in gray are with you. . . . We understand that you, as a Northern soldier, are willing to join hands with us and forget the past." Weaver responded that he hoped his new party would "dig a grave" across the Mason-Dixon Line and bury sectional animosities. "The blue and the gray," he assured, "were blended together" in the service of the common man.[1]

The poetry of the moment was undeniable, and it made for grand political theater. Weaver in fact recalled the Yankee-rebel "ceasefire" to a Northern audience a few days later at a rally in Terre Haute, Indiana, the home of twenty-four-year-old Eugene Debs. The Iowan retold how the venerable amputee "got up before the vast audience, displaying his stump of a leg," and decreed a new dawn of blue-gray unity.[2] Such unity meant eliciting the memory of the late war to facilitate a midway strategy between owner-friendly Republicans and Democratic white supremacy. Speaking to the upstart party as an alternative to race-baiting *and* the bloody shirt, one Greenback editor maintained that Weaver's party "has no wounds to heal, no bloody chasms to clasp hands across, but are a band of brothers made up of federals and confederates, yankees and cow-boys."[3]

This would not be the last reconciliatory act on the campaign trail—far from it. But it *was* one of both tactical utility and ideological sincerity. The ability of ex-Confederates and Unionists, including African Americans, to bridge wartime divides along class lines became the centerpiece of Weaver's 1880 campaign and proved a model for how insurgent politics would broach sectional reconciliation. Indeed, farmer-labor radicalism during the Gilded Age centered on the idea that although emancipation had negated one form of worker persecution by toppling chattel slavery, the War for the Union had failed in its aim of free labor and the democratic administration of economic power. Wage earners both industrial and agricultural remained beleaguered and largely immobile as oligopoly swayed the democratic process, corrupting traditional party politics. As one labor editor explained, while war had thankfully crushed the rebellion, it had also expedited capitalist domination and malfeasance. Much of the "Grand Army" had retreated into poverty, the South was left destitute, and "the toiling millions of the North had no special reason to rejoice."[4] During the late 1870s and 1880s both reformers, preaching the Social Gospel, and newly empowered trade unions and third parties challenged the industrial Goliath, drawing on antislavery vernacular to remember an unfinished emancipation.

Civil War memories—events, leaders, and ideas—anchored this farmer-labor progression. The Greenback-Labor, Knights of Labor, Farmers' Alliance, Agricultural Wheel, and Union Labor movements were part of an ideological and institutional succession running from the National Labor Union through the Populist Party. Their politics offered discrete opportunities for interracial remembrance after the decline of Reconstruction, with veterans bridging out of major parties and toward reformist and revolutionary politics.[5] Propelled by militant labor organization following the Great Railroad Strike, these mutually reinforcing and frequently overlapping labor and agrarian reform fronts included anti-monopolism, Greenbackism, socialism, anarchism, and left agrarianism. Their corresponding parties—Equal Rights, Reform,

Greenback, Socialist Labor, and Union Labor—organized in response to what workers perceived as the perversion of free labor.[6]

The cultural residue of the Civil War, including conceptions of loyalty, race, section, and veteranhood, was crucial to this challenge. Greenbackers in particular used wartime tropes to submit that the popular commemoration of the war, as either a North-South or a Black-white axis, was fatal to class and trade organization. Unlike liberal reformers and politicians, who avowed that equal civic rights would lead naturally to just outcomes, Greenbackers linked war memory to economic democracy. They insisted that social structures, market whimsy, and political policy, rather than individualized notions of uplift and failure, were responsible for soaring inequality, and hence demanded greater state intervention in the economy.[7] Suggesting that elites were exploiting loyalty politics and racial animosity as hegemonic tools, Greenbackers proposed a "new antislavery movement" rooted in the material interests—and the cultural identities—of workers and small-scale farmers. Yet in challenging the sectional and racial determinism of mainstream memory, the Greenbacker "producerist emancipation" betrayed persistent difficulties and core paradoxes. An effective class-based interracial coalition meant courting understandably skeptical Black voters loyal to the party of Lincoln and recently spurned by the betrayal of Reconstruction, as well as white laborers whose entrenched racial, ethnic, and trade identities often undercut the potential for solidarity. Greenback appeals to interracial politics would influence later farmer-labor campaigns, and the party's social and leadership networks would prove integral to the Populist moment of the 1890s.[8] However, conjuring slavery, emancipation, and military service—even in the name of a region-connecting and race-spanning class unity—sometimes proved as likely to inflame sectional passions as surmount them.

## The Soldier as Good as the Bondholder

The Greenback-Labor Party strategically placed veterans at the top of its party structure and used antislavery vernacular to endear old soldiers, quell internal discord, and craft patriotic narratives. Aligning with industrial organizations including the Knights of Labor, the GLP emerged from local and state Greenback and Labor tickets in industrial areas of northern Ohio, eastern Pennsylvania, and upstate New York following the Panic of 1873.[9] In Eugene Debs's Indiana, Greenbackers were loosely affiliated with anti-monopoly Democrats and made inroads among poor farmers in the southern portions of the state.[10] In all such hotbeds, the party marked a key moment in the postwar challenge to corporate capitalism. Reformers opposed a return to the gold standard and the reduction in national "greenback" dollars, promoting a number of progressive reforms, including the eight-hour workday, an end to child labor, and increased workplace safety regulations. Greenbackers connected monetary policy both to issues of racial equality and the symbolism of the Union soldier. GLP publicity so frequently melded the greenback and "the scarred veteran" that paper money advocacy became an extension of wartime loyalty. Massachusetts congressman Benjamin F. Butler, for one, insisted that greenback money had "saved our country" and was now "a just equivalent for the blood of our soldiers." Other Greenbackers, meanwhile, maintained that only the currency that had redeemed the nation possessed the potential to make citizens of former slaves.[11] Combining the fates of the freedman and the veteran, the party's statement of principles borrowed from Lincoln's vision of a government "of, by, and for the people." It assailed the current regime of "vicious, speculating, usury-sucking, prosperity-destroying, crime-breeding, tramp-creating aristocracies—a government of outrageous inequalities among its people—a government of *Money* as *King* and *Labor* as *Slaves*."[12]

The Greenback national committee denounced what it deemed the racial and sectional dog whistles of the Democratic and Republican Parties. Alternatively, by urging a farmer-labor scheme of "equal interest" for workingmen, Greenbackers looked to a material reconciliation involving both white and Black producers.[13] This class-based arrangement complicated prevailing commemorative discourses, undercutting Lost Cause, Yankee triumphalist, and white supremacist modes of remembrance. Even in the South, the GLP ran Confederate veterans such as Alabaman James Madison Pickens, who reached out to all the "oppressed and downtrodden sons of toil" and decried the Democratic Party's "bulldozing" of Black voters. Yet interracialism did not necessarily entail racial integration. Despite efforts—sincere or opportunistic—to unite workers across the color line, Greenback-Labor clubs remained segregated in Birmingham and other parts of the former Confederacy.[14]

Greenbackers publicized their program by inventing, appropriating, and refashioning war language while simultaneously downplaying North-South animus. Members underscored the plight of veterans to support inflationary or anti-gold monetary policy and jockeyed the "irrepressible conflict" over currency into a defense of pensions.[15] Old soldiers including Alabaman James M. Whitehead, a Greenback newspaper editor who had lost a leg at Cold Harbor and whose opponents labeled him "an unconfessed Republican" for being insufficiently white supremacist, saw wartime sacrifice as justifying postwar political independence.[16] At the National Convention of the Independent Greenback Party in Indianapolis's Grand Hotel in May 1876, delegates tactically appointed a trans-sectional committee, with representatives from California to Louisiana and from Rhode Island to Missouri. The party nominated New York inventor and philanthropist Peter Cooper and strategized how best to court disaffected Democrats.[17] Members posited class tension and wealth disparities as the new "conflict between freedom and slavery"—a civil struggle not between North and South but between "banks and the people."[18]

Greenbackers felt subjugated by this alliance between the nation-state and big finance, or what Martin J. Sklar terms the "corporate restructuring of American capitalism."[19] Claiming that the Emancipation Proclamation had "given to the slave a nominal freedom . . . but not emancipated labor," currency reformers drew on politics emblematic of African American liberation to check predatory moneylenders. Illinois congressman and Greenback theorist Alexander Campbell explained that capitalists did not seek to protect freedmen so much as transition to a form a serfdom and drive down the power of workers such as to "practically nationalize slavery—not African, but human slavery." True Greenbackism, then, was an interracial and modernizing phenomenon that nevertheless featured the cultural trappings of Republican tradition. According to one promoter, the movement sought to resist this new mutation of "ancient [not raced-based] slavery" and solve the imbalance between capital and labor under which "laborers in all sections and in all industries are still suffering from a system of oppression more subtle and refined [than chattel slavery]." Campbell warned that "the old pro-slavery serpent, beaten at the South, has crawled up North, and put on anti-slavery clothes, and established himself in Wall Street."[20]

Galvanized by the Great Railroad Strike, the party increasingly blended labor positions into its economic agenda by yoking its identity to early Republicanism *and* distancing itself from current Republicans.[21] At the founding convention of the GLP at Toledo in early 1878, members called for the abolition of the national banking system. They also sought the establishment of state and national labor bureaus; the preservation of public lands for settlers rather than corporations; progressive taxation; a one-term limit on the president; opposition to specie resumption; a regulated hourly workday; and the prohibition of child and prison labor. Reflecting society-wide xenophobia, especially against East Asians, Greenbackers denounced imported "servile" labor from China. Despite attacking Republican administrations as agents of big business—one Chicagoan maintained that Grant's "Let Us Have Peace" should be changed to "Let Us Have a Piece"—members venerated early Republican ideals, viewing themselves as the "defenders of the rights of labor."[22] The party platform appropriated Lincoln, echoing his first annual message to Congress, in which he affirmed the superiority of labor over capital. Yet it also reiterated the "patriotic devotion" of the worker and excoriated the "class of monopolists" who would conflate labor rights with European-style communism. With their triangulating platform, framers also tempted old soldiers by proffering an improved homestead law that might place the poor and middling though "brave defenders of the Union . . . upon an equality with his rich and affluent comrade."[23]

Despite attempts to breach North-South divides, Greenbackers sometimes defended Reconstruction's legacy, citing the betrayal of democracy in the South as evidence of elite chicanery. Greenbacker and 1878 Michigan gubernatorial candidate David Woodman, who equated temperance opponents with proslavery forces, spoke against anti-Reconstruction elements in the South: "If slavery really is dead, it takes but a very small circle and a very short séance to bring back its spirit."[24] Yet with the region in the midst of what Steven Hahn classifies as "a counterrevolution by landed capital and its allies," Greenbackers struggled to make inroads within the Southern peasantry that emancipation had created.[25] As the party's power base moved steadily westward, Greenback emphasis shifted away from currency reform, and the party's optics became more reconciliatory.[26] In the fall of 1878, GLP congressional candidates polled over 1 million votes and fourteen representatives were elected, including veterans Albert P. Forsythe of Illinois, Indianan Gilbert De La Matyr, Alabaman William Manning Lowe, Texan George Washington Jones, North Carolinian Daniel Lindsay Russell, and Weaver in Iowa.[27] The organization's national assembly in Washington, DC, in January 1880 drew a united front of farmers, laborers, socialists, women suffragists, and anti-monopolists of every variety. Recalling how the miscellany of reformers that composed the Free Soil Party eventually coalesced into the Republicans of Frémont and Lincoln, the *Washington Post* maintained that the Greenback league might prove "as broad as that of the old anti-slavery party." Its veteran-friendly positions ranged from a graduated income tax to the creation of a federal labor bureau to support for Charles Stewart Parnell and Irish home rule.[28]

These broad dimensions made considerable political space for women, who became cocreators of a Civil War memory adorned in working clothes. Although some reformers, including Susan B. Anthony, remained skeptical of third parties, Greenbackers won over scores of women by placing them in more visible positions of party leadership, notably as convention delegates.[29] Sara J. Spencer and Marietta Stow, who would become the first woman to run for vice president of the United States as a member of the Equal Rights Party, supported the Greenbackers.[30] Other women who would become prominent Populists, including Sarah E. Van De Vort Emery and Marion Todd, who served on California's platform committee and was nominated for attorney general in 1882, cut their political teeth in the party. In some states, the GLP became the first political party to nominate women for statewide office. Pressure from women even drove several state Greenback platforms to include woman suffrage planks.[31] Opponents, meanwhile, took note of the party's influx of suffragettes and relentlessly smeared them as mannish and unwomanly.

A kaleidoscopic bevy of reform, the National Greenback-Labor Convention met in the summer of 1880 at Chicago's Glass Palace and nominated Weaver and Barzalai J. Chambers to the top of the ticket. The delegation was racially integrated as well as geographically diverse. Attendees extolled the Glass Palace's assorted cast, many of them veterans of the late war, with some comparing the event to Philadelphia's Constitutional Convention or the National Assembly of Revolutionary France.[32] While the ideologically plural convention, which included forty-four delegates from the Socialist Labor Party, saw heated debate over issues ranging from woman suffrage to Chinese immigration, the pairing of Weaver and ex-Confederate Chambers was part of a wider strategy to link Southern plebeians to the party's base of small farmers in the Midwest. This reconciliatory design presaged the People's Party's blue-gray ticket of 1892.

Weaver in particular already possessed a reputation as an ally of the old soldier. Although he had become a Radical Republican during the war, Weaver's inability to rise in party leadership and the Republicans' conservative turn compelled him to leave the party of Lincoln, whose positions on railroads and finance he termed "a gigantic wrong." By 1877 Weaver's radicalizing views led him toward Greenbackism, which he identified as a "third way" with regard to veterans' politics.[33] As one of thirteen Greenbackers elected to Congress in 1878, Weaver drafted a "Soldiers and Sailors Bill" that improved the interest rates of veterans' benefits relative to those of bondholders.[34] Support for the "Weaver Bill" had led to blue-gray meetings in the West and in border states such as Missouri, with veterans attempting to transcend lingering sectional differences for the sake of economic self-empowerment.[35]

Weaver combined these economic policies with a modified form of the bloody shirt politics he had once endorsed, censuring any attempt to "revive fratricidal strife" while directing loyalty politics at class, not sectional, enemies. One observer extolled Weaver and his Chicago speech for continuing to attack "traitors" and throw "hot shot into the camps of our enemies."[36] He also sought to suspend race-baiting and North-South partisanship. Avowing "it is all quiet except on the Potomac," Weaver condemned any further discus-

FIGURE 2. James B. Weaver. As a Union veteran and the Greenback-Labor and People's Party presidential candidate, Weaver became a spokesman for pan-sectional alliance between dispossessed farmers and industrial workers. However, Weaver's tactical use of Civil War commemoration could not curtail—and in fact sometimes exacerbated—racial and sectional divisions within his parties. (Library of Congress)

sion of Anthony Burns, John Brown's raid, or the New York City Draft Riots on the House floor.[37] Nevertheless, he expressed an anti-concentrationist critique infused with Christian morality that militant abolitionists would have found familiar. This concomitant rejection of sectionalism and use of free-soil language to attack corporate capital would become trademarks of the Greenbackers and subsequent third party and labor insurgencies.

Chambers, meanwhile, was sixty-three years old at the time of the Chicago convention. A Kentucky-born surveyor, farmer, and veteran of the Texas Revolution, Chambers served in a Texas state militia during the War of the Rebellion, seeing limited service. Yet he had made a name for himself during the war by offending Confederate leadership through protests against Jefferson Davis's Twenty Negro Law. Opposition to the statute, which exempted any man who owned twenty or more slaves from military conscription, marginalized Chambers from the New South ruling class but bolstered his populist credentials. After the war he founded the town of Cleburne, Texas, named after his close friend Major General Patrick Cleburne, a rebel martyr who had endorsed freeing and arming slaves. Sponsoring inflationist economics in Reconstruction Texas, Chambers's politics evolved from concerns over national debt and opposition to the Specie Payment Resumption Act to include the more radical, independent planks of Marcus M. "Brick" Pomeroy's Union Greenback-Labor Party faction.[38] In Chicago, onlookers cheered as the convention's white and Black delegates endorsed the former Confederate.[39]

Those delegates crafted a national platform that combined mass democracy with the bread-and-butter labor initiatives that grew out of postwar economic instability.[40] The document chastised "economic feudalism" and an unjust distribution of wealth, lambasting industrial conditions that reduced workers to a "bare animal existence" and a state of "slavery."[41] Declaring that "capital should be the servant of labor, rather than its master," Weaver saw racial coexistence—political if not social cooperation—and sectional peace as prerequisites for an economically leveling coalition.[42] Although Bourbon Democrats charged the insurgents with communism and anarchism, or with being Thad Stevens Republicans in disguise, the platform mocked the notion that Republicans were the soldiers' party, claiming that the party of Lincoln, while "professing great gratitude to the soldier, has most unjustly discriminated against him in favor of the bondholder."[43]

Conversely, Greenbackers rendered their candidate as the embodiment of the citizen-soldier. The *Boston Commoner* defended Weaver's war record against that of Republican James A. Garfield, whom the editor deemed a political soldier more interested in running for elected office than in fighting. The author also vilified Democrat Winfield Scott Hancock, one of the Union luminaries of Gettysburg. Weaver, he explained, was a capable and honorable soldier who, unlike Hancock, possessed both the courage and the wherewithal to raise the bloody shirt when necessary in order to "arouse the patriotism of the North." Now, however, with sectional animus waning, Weaver was once again playing the part of the patriot, this time as a unifier of laboring men north and south.[44] Reuniting veterans also adopted Weaver into their cultural framework. An early fall reunion of the Army of West Virginia in Parkersburg, in which 6,000 packed a makeshift "wigwam," featured a life-size portrait of Weaver alongside Garfield and Hancock, all together with worn battle flags and other patriotic decorations.[45]

At a speech in Boston's Faneuil Hall in late August, Weaver explained how he hoped to convert both disgruntled Republicans and Democrats to the Greenback cause. Maintaining that partisan rancor prohibited men of either party from being swayed to the other, he argued that laboring voters might instead be induced to join a third party. The Iowan contended that the party of emancipation in particular had violated its founding egalitarian mission and "forfeited the love and confidence of the boys in blue" owing to corporate influence. Perhaps underestimating the degree of resistance to political interracialism among white workers, who were conditioned to fear any form of Black advancement as exacerbating their own economic precarity, Weaver also viewed his soldiers' coalition as race-spanning. Forwarding the emancipationist cause as one of *all* non-elites, he declared that "the revolution which began in public sentiment and culminated in the Rebellion" was "a grand effort to restore the dignity of labor."[46] The farmer-labor crusade was liberationist, and the Civil War had been, at its essence, a mass and ongoing labor movement.

Weaver-Chambers campaign songs aped these themes of class and trade over section and of the common soldier over the moneyed shirker. Often repurposed soldier and slave songs, and, as always, "La Marseillaise," Greenback tunes underscored martialism, sectional reconciliation through class, the protection of womanhood, workingmen as "slaves," and Eastern financiers as "shylocks." The notion of the Emancipation Proclamation as an unfinished venture reverberated. The song "Poll Your Vote" promised workers a path "out of bondage and into freedom"; "Reform Is Now Wanted" imagined a "workingmen's army" that might "martyr for freedom."[47] T. W. Taylor's "The Bankers and I Are Out" proffered ailing war widows as a reason to tax the "Money Kings," rather than the common men who had done the war's fighting and dying, and encouraged workers that "East and West, North and South" might unite against the bondholding syndicate.[48] Set to the tune of "Tramp, Tramp, Tramp," "Hope for the Toiling" alleged that while the "sable bondmen" had been set free, the work of emancipation was not complete until "the toilers all have land and liberty."[49] With "liberty" defined as not merely political rights but productive ownership (most often land), Greenback songs employed a soldierly language of marching, fighting, battles, army organization, and mourning for the fallen as metaphors for political conflict. "Sleeping on the Damp Cold Ground" used the tune of "Massa's in the Cold, Cold Ground" to urge workingmen to break their symbolic chains and march as a "mighty army"; others proposed to "sever every woman's chains," too.[50]

Like emancipation itself, all were part of a holy crusade. Songs including "God's Army" and "In the Army" described a struggle of republican commoners—an "army of the poor"—striding shoulder to shoulder in pursuit of a society in which working people were "no longer slaves to wicked knaves." Similarly, "The Dawn of Freedom" argued that workers sought a true expression of "free soil" yet remained "slaves to an aristocracy" not unlike that of the Old South plantocracy. "We Will Be Free!" envisioned the Greenback electorate as a phalanx of chain-breaking self-liberators, and "Up and Do" specifically imagined "women unchained." Depicting a conflict not of North against South but of workers against banks, "The People's War," "A New Yankee Doodle," and "The Workingmen's Marseillaise" suggested that real nobility lay not in inherited privilege but in those who toiled and tilled.[51] Yet these civic anthems also revealed the ideological gap between Greenbackers and anarchists and revolutionary socialists. "The Greenback Boys Are Waking," for instance, targeted the "money power" for inciting anti-red hysteria by raising the cry of "Commune!" every time monetary reformers made a demand.[52] Indeed, the Greenback ideal looked decidedly more like early Republican principles, or at least Greenbackers' conception of those principles, than it did the left anarchist and libertarian socialist elements of the Paris Commune.

The linking of the late war to calls for a bold new political economy through reunions, banners, and songs required that Greenbackers seize the title of "the soldiers' party" from Garfield Republicans. Greenbacker and Connecticut veteran J. H. Randall bemoaned that the party of Lincoln reveled in "Grant and the Empire! . . . Sherman and the Syndicate . . . Blaine and the 'bloody shirt.'" Republicans had saved the Union, he admitted, but through Grant's "imperialism" and the "legalized robbery of the toiling millions," it was now destroying the republic. Greenbackers made sociological claims for better workplace conditions, alleging that cast-off veterans were being "pauperized" at the expense of a "non-producing class." Proponents also maintained that theirs was *not* a radical program. The real "communists," they contended, were national banking associations, railroad and telegraph associations, and boards of trade: closed, secretive, and illegal. Randall explained that whereas for workers true "patriotism" is dying for one's country, for rich men it is the "enslavement" of working men.[53]

Banners, posters, and leaflets at party conventions, meetings, and parades reinforced such themes, including the "enslavement" of Union veterans. Promoting the party's electoral strategy in 1878 by swearing that corporations had resumed the "irrepressible conflict" against former soldiers, New York Greenbacker George W. Dacunha viewed William H. Seward's maxim as part of an ongoing class struggle within which Union veterans were centrally affected. He declared it a crime that "the boy in blue," whom foes had slandered as "greasy mechanics and mudsills," had saved the nation and liberated the slave, only to be reduced from the status of warrior to that of impoverished dependent. Lamenting that Lincoln's grand armies had destroyed a landed aristocracy in the South only to create a moneyed aristocracy in the North, Dacunha repurposed the sectional vocabulary of "slavery," "free labor," and "emancipation" toward an audience of potential voters who were both proud veterans and aggrieved workingmen.[54]

Weaver's 1880 campaign rejuvenated the early Greenback emphasis on wartime tropes. At a 5,000-person meeting and torchlight procession led by Union veterans in Creston, Iowa, partisans carried anti-Garfield placards that read "No Corporate Rags," "The Soldier as Good as the Bondholder," and "The Collective Man—No Individual . . . Weaver and Chambers."[55] For Greenbackers, this meant employing a new type of bloody shirt that invoked Union memory against corporate influence within the Republican Party. "The greenback," explained one Garfield-turned-Weaver-Republican newspaper, "was the only money found in the dead Union soldier's pocket."[56] Weaver himself charged Northern banking cronies with practicing a British system of finance and tax burden. Meanwhile, Democrats in Dixie, who had manipulated vote counts in several states, were an antidemocratic Slave Power reborn. In Alabama, where election returns were nakedly rigged, Greenbackers likened Bourbon leaders to the Russian autocracy.

A second wave of Greenback campaign songs accentuated the threat of plutocrats across both sections. Chorales such as "March from Maine to Texas," by John M. Todd, used military themes to describe a consortium of Southerners and "Yankee boys." Others, including Will S. Lurton and J. H. Randall's "They Shall Never Deceive Us Again," projected a recomposed meaning of "free men" related to class rather than race. Proclaiming that "the bloody shirt shall wave no longer," "A Campaign Song," written in 1880 by Josiah Pettybone of Indiana, was more overt in its connection of party ideals to veterans' issues. Emphasizing sectional reunion, Pettybone reminded, "When cruel war held sway, / Hard money passed away." This vision of what he deemed "Greenbacker's America" contrasted the brutality of the "cruel war" with the desire for peace, prosperity, and currency inflation:

> The Southern palm and the North pine,
> Their branches firm shall intertwine,

When the gallant Gray and loyal Blue,
Shall rally for Weaver and Chambers too.[57]

Yet other campaign anthems were less explicit in their call to white unity, underscoring emancipationist and interracial themes, even at the risk of alienating Confederate veterans. T. A. Bland's "General Weaver at Corinth" cohered Weaver's wartime bravery and honor to his current status as a "glorious leader of the people's cause" and a "foe of monopoly, injustice, and unequal laws." The song was also patently antislavery, likening Greenbackers to the Free-Soil Party's insurgency against major party acquiescence. Likewise, "As We Go Marching On," sung to the tune of "John Brown's Body" (and shared its chorus), lionized the abolitionist spirit.

We have sworn by the Eternal on the green and sodden graves,
Of our martyred soldiers who were bravest of the brave,
That we'll have the money weapons which emancipated slaves,
As we go marching on.

We'll rally to the ballot box proclaim that we are free,
Disperse the proud usurpers upon the land and sea,
We'll burst the chains of bondage, proclaim that we are free,
As we go marching on.[58]

"As We Go Marching On" was a plea to Union veterans to honor the legacy of fallen comrades by campaigning with the same resolve that had achieved emancipation; it also asserted with tragic irony that old soldiers *themselves* were now "enslaved" and must self-emancipate through a masculinized Greenback-Labor program. Missouri veteran and Greenbacker William Quayle believed that economically pinched laborers were becoming "the slaves of organized capital" and that the ensuing political battles would be, like combat itself, a "test of true manhood." He urged fellow veterans to "stand as the picket line of a grand army, true to our trust until we hear the cry."[59] Similarly, writing to old soldiers in the *National View*, one Arkansan claimed that Greenbackers had successfully "buried the past" in the name of ousting monarchy and monopoly. "Let the old soldiers North and South unite to save the country" by subduing "sectional hatred," he pleaded. Employing the veterans' mother tongue, he beseeched, "Will you join the coming campaign—the army of the national banks and bondholders, or the army of the people under the Greenback banner?"[60]

Republicans, meanwhile, combined song and bloody shirt in order to paint their Greenback challengers as traitors. Michigan Greenbacker George L. Yaple, elected to Congress in 1882 as a fusionist, termed his the "Union ticket."

Endorsed by the Union Labor Party and local Knights of Labor during his failed gubernatorial campaign in 1886, Yaple declared that, by prostituting themselves to corporations for the purpose of private gain, Republicans stood guilty of secession-like treason.[61] The GOP shot back, slandering Yaple as a "copperhead" who had supposedly rejoiced at Lincoln's assassination.[62] One Republican tune rebuked Yaple for backing Democrat and Union general Fitz John Porter and thus betraying the legacy of Ulysses S. Grant—someone whom any *truly* loyal veteran would "die to save." Michigan Greenbackers crafted counter-songs set to familiar war tunes and rife with battle cries and broken shackles, with Yaple as the small producerist "calling to arms . . . brave soldiers from our shops and farms."[63] Their candidate, whose nomination was "just as inevitable as Fort Sumter was after Harpers Ferry," was to the cause of reform "as Wendell Phillips was with the abolitionist movement," standing for the Union cause of "human rights and a united country." Yaple's struggle against the "money kings," his backers alleged, was just like that of Grant and Philip H. Sheridan against the rebels during the war. Likewise, Yaple rendered himself as the ally of "every man who fired a shot for liberty, every man who enlisted in the war, [every man] who may have left a leg at Shiloh, or lost an arm while planting a flag on Lookout Mountain."[64]

Greenback convention-goers framed their undertaking as the uncorrupted heir of free labor. The 1880 campaign sought to combine, in Weaver's words, "the old-time Democracy of Jefferson and Jackson and the pure Republicanism of Abraham Lincoln and Thaddeus Stevens." Greenbackers expressed their ideology through Republican figures, allegories, and iconography. Indeed, the delegates who met in Chicago's Glass Palace, recently vacated by Republicans nominating Garfield for president, had done so beneath banners of Lincoln and Stevens. Believing that the party of Union victory had, according to Mark Lause, "abandoned more than its symbols," some Greenbackers lauded Stevens as the true Great Emancipator. Socialists in particular stretched Lincoln's ties to labor to include an endorsement of worker militancy. Confederate veteran Albert Parsons even carried the red flag of revolution into the convention hall despite the fact that state Greenback parties had banned it due to its associations with so-called foreign radicalism. Abolitionist, Native American rights activist, and National Woman Suffrage Association leader Matilda Joslyn Gage, who had backed Grant in 1872 after first supporting Victoria Woodhull's Equal Rights ticket, alleged that the Republicans had "ceased to be a party of principles." The Greenbackers were, in contrast, "the party of the future."[65]

That future was dependent on some measure of reconciliatory symmetry. One editor deemed the Chicago convention an apex of "fraternal union of the Blue and the Gray" in which "hates of the past war" were intentionally suppressed.[66] Recalling being flanked by Union blue and Confederate gray at the Glass Palace, Weaver poeticized, "The first thing we did at our Chicago convention was to dig a grave across Mason and Dixon's line, and in that grave we put the bloody shirt." Liberation required a reunion ticket, Weaver and Chambers, blue and gray in "clasped hands, across this grave."[67] Greenback leadership deemed it intuitive that broader "emancipation" necessitated rapprochement along class lines, pledging to obliterate "sectional feeling" as a prerequisite for economic radicalism. Addressing a group of socialists and communists in St. Louis in July, Chambers framed the issues not as sectional but as "a battle for human rights."[68]

It was a winning message for workers who considered sectional politics a hindrance to class unity. Socialist, Knight of Labor, and Detroit's 1878 Greenback-Labor mayoral candidate—and future anarchist—Jo Labadie believed a "grand army of labor" that might overturn "wage slavery" would be best achieved through Greenback sectional armistice.[69] Socialist Labor Party national secretary Philip Van Patten explained that his decision to back the Weaver-Chambers ticket was similar to that of the diverse bloc of antislavery men who had defeated chattel slavery. Only this time, Van Patten pointed out, the new "abolitionists" sought to destroy the bondage of wages.[70] They needed all laboring hands on board, and enticing the broadest possible coalition of workers meant linking the GLP to both the self-interests and identities of veterans, especially in border states where old soldiers might march to the ballot box in unison. One Missouri newspaper marveled at two maimed soldiers, one Union and one Confederate, who supposedly stood side by side on their crutches at the Chicago convention "in rebuke to the men who are trying to stir up strife between the northern and southern soldiers."[71]

While there was necessary urgency to class reconciliation, as democratic movements from below and all popular fronts must prove broad enough to self-preserve, a sustainable reform alliance also required a conscious devaluation of whiteness. Yet because reconciliation demanded a deliberate "forgetting" of sectional issues, rather than simply framing the Confederate project as one that disadvantaged both Black slaves and laboring whites, the Greenback "truce" also often involved ignoring the opposite roles that Union and Confederate armies had played with regard to slavery. Invariably, this softening of the Confederate cause went hand in hand with the construction of patriotic narratives that affirmed hierarchies of whiteness. Though such prejudices, far from being unique to the GLP, mirrored society at large, Greenbackers widely embraced Sinophobia and anti-Semitism. Many local branches eschewed even limited interracialism. Red-baiting was also common, as local platforms denounced the "red flag of Communism imported from Europe."[72] This first American "Red Scare," which matured in response to the Great Railroad Strike and peaked nationally following the Haymarket affair, reinforced "natural" conceptions of whiteness, the sanctity of corporate property, and conservative notions of "Americanness." Anti-communism also undermined worker organization by attacking immigrants, women suffragists, Indians ("the communists of the Plains"), and reform of nearly any type. Ultimately, the contradictions between employing sectional vernacular to win veterans while simultaneously selling a North-South reconciliation based on class no doubt alienated many irreconcilable white partisans, as well as Black laborers, especially when combined with white identity.

Democrats, meanwhile, tapped into mounting transnational fears of worker radicalism let loose by the Paris Commune and the 1877 strikes, painting Weaver as a race-leveling extremist. This belligerent analogue was not limited to the Democrats. The Republican press, including Radicals such as Thomas Nast, who believed the nascent labor movement a communist plot, charged union delegates with being predatory "bummers," a moniker once reserved for the soldiers of William Tecumseh Sherman's March to the Sea.[73] Wartime language remained paramount to this representation of the thieving, traitorous worker, as newspapers cast the strikers of 1877's worker "insurrection" as "ruffians," "looters," and even "secessionists."[74] In particular, Weaver's views on agrarian reform and endorsement of the Socialist Labor Party's "free land" plank spurred a wave of anti-collectivist denunciations.[75] Fusing these anxieties toward labor mobilization with old-fashioned sectional dog-whistling, both major parties portrayed Greenbackers as the *real* sect of the bloody shirt. Labeling his cohorts "scalawags," "carpetbaggers," and Radical Republicans in disguise, Southern newspapers warned their white Democratic constituents that Weaver would usher in a new "mule and forty acres."[76] Concerned Bourbons, fresh off of Redemption in the South, insisted that this redistribution of wealth and its "land for the landless" smacked of the "pure republicanism of Thad Stevens."[77]

Nevertheless, the "Weaver battalions" used wartime tropes to defy the standard relationship between section and veteran.[78] War records predominated the back-and-forth. Greenbackers painted Weaver's Democratic opponent, Hancock, as both an aloof Easterner and a "corseted, aristocratic army officer," evoking both corrupt Northern financiers and the privileged slaveocracy.[79] For their part, Democrats, crying, "They rally in blue for Hancock, / For Hancock they rally in gray," curated their nominee's image as a reconciliationist, painting him as a highly decorated Union man now reaching out to white Southerners.[80] Breaking with the Republican model, the GLP envisioned a national electoral strategy—one more removed from the various baiting of race, region, and red politics. Speaking to a principally socialist audience, Chambers explained that the new party knew "no South, no North, no East and no West."[81] Despite downplaying white identity, this attempt to circumscribe the politics of section, which would culminate in the Populist campaign of 1892, also anticipated the blue-gray reunion movement of the 1890s that was often driven by the party elites and corporate entities that Greenbackers so despised.

Alas, Weaver's "reconciliation" of class proved an electoral failure. Even as Republicans cheered Garfield's victory behind a "Solid North," Democrats could at least take heart in the downfall of a far more radical, if improbable, threat.[82] Although the Greenbackers improved over their 1876 vote totals, winning over 300,000 votes and a smattering of counties in Missouri, Texas, Mississippi, and Iowa, party stalwarts had expected far better. With Bourbons entrenched and African Americans either disenfranchised or committed to the Republicans where they appeared on the ballot, and with the national economic situation improving, Greenbackers were beaten soundly in Arkansas and throughout the former Confederacy. The party's burst of momentum following the Great Railroad Strike had dissipated.[83] Despite a relatively egalitarian platform, a North-South ticket, and new style of campaigning, reconciliationist appeals tied to material interests were not enough to bridge either racial or sectional divisions in 1880. Upon defeat, Weaver compared the state of GLP politics to the Union in April 1861, arguing that, like Lincoln's call for 75,000 volunteers, the party must pick itself up and "retake the forts now in the hands of the rebels."[84]

## Patriotic Tillers

Despite a diluted platform and an opportunistic successor to Weaver, the Greenback Party retained aspirations of sectional *and* racial détente. By 1884 Greenbackers were still using loyalty dynamics to frame their presidential candidate, Union major general Benjamin F. Butler.[85] Both Democratic nominee Grover Cleveland and Republican James G. Blaine (whose running mate was Memorial Day founder and GAR leader John A. Logan) had sidestepped military service, and Butler men painted them as "substitute men."[86] Greenback newspapers, including the *Washington World and Citizen Soldier*, billed as the paper of old soldiers and anti-monopoly, arose during the election, wedding Butler to the veterans' cause.[87] In an 1878 currency reform speech in Terre Haute, Indiana, where Eugene Debs was serving as a Democratic city councilman, Butler praised the "true-hearted patriot" Thaddeus Stevens and suggested that current Republicans brazenly touted their abolitionist roots in order to mask the reality that they were "enslaving" laborers to emergent "money kings." As such, Butler avowed, the "money question" and the "industrial and financial question" must take precedence over the "southern question."[88] To add to this assessment of party, race, and section, Butler recommended a program of using both a new tax on liquor and tobacco and an appropriation of the internal revenue tax to pension Confederate veterans. Proponents likened this plan to the expansion of Revolutionary War pensions in 1826 and 1832 to cover all veterans regardless of when, where, or how long they served.[89] "Beast" Butler had been profoundly unpopular among white Southerners as wartime military governor of New Orleans. Now, in a most ironic turn, Republicans quickly suggested that Butler harbored Confederate sympathies, citing the "Butler resolution" as one of concord with Jefferson Davis and other traitors.[90]

Butler opened his campaign by speaking to a delegation of workingmen in Rhode Island in the summer of 1884. The multitude included the Central Labor Union, as well as trade organizations of typographers, tailors, cigar makers, shoemakers, bricklayers, stucco makers, plasterers, and painters. Before this crowd of at least 3,000 working people, the Massachusetts man looked to shed his well-earned reputation as a rag of the Democratic machine by trumpeting his anti-partisan and labor bona fides. He also regarded himself a paladin of the Union cause and an antagonist of privilege. Claiming "the greatest good for the greatest number," Butler spoke of a new set of practical economic rights. Espousing a break from sectionalism, he encouraged, "Let the history take care of itself. Let the dead bury the dead. Let us go forward to new life, new work in behalf of the living."[91]

This emphasis on the irredeemable corruption of the two major parties manifested in Greenback campaign literature. "A few hundred millionaires, a few hundred great corporations hold a chattel mortgage on the Republican Party," Edward H. G. Clark's campaign biography explained, "and they hold another chattel mortgage on the Republican Party's second fiddle, the Democratic Party." The antidote, Clark insisted, resided in the "organization of industry . . . the new dawn of political economy." This encompassed regulating banks, railroads, Wall Street, and various manufacturing and mercantile conglomerates while also minimizing the radicalism inherent to such a program or conveying that radicalism as indisputably nationalistic. "Americans are no communists," Clark swore, intimating Greenback wholesomeness. Indeed, much of that singular nativism was born out of the nation's baptismal conflict. Calling him "the most practical abolitionist in the United States" during the war, Clark painted Butler as an interracial defender and prophet. "It was the alert and audacious 'Massa Butler' who freed the slaves, long before the good, cautious 'Massa Lincoln' dared to take the grave responsibility." Clark's depiction of Butler as a friend of the veteran, and his pairing of slave emancipation with worker emancipation, reinforced the resolve that Butler should lead the "new antislavery movement" of trade unionism, Grange societies, and the Knights of Labor.[92]

At the vanguard of this neo-abolitionism, factory workers increasingly responded to the exigencies of the industrial workplace—low wages, fixed hours, subdivided labor, continuous supervision, locked facilities, the threat of speed-up, and the prohibition of movement—by summoning chattel bondage. They explained wages as a reconfigured "system of slavery" and antidemocratic threat.[93] In the countryside, meanwhile, dissidents critiqued discriminatory freight rates and the lack of competition in farming and commodity transport, with anti-monopolists tying war imagery to their critiques of the Money Power. Unionist memory in the West entailed US armies exterminating Native peoples and expropriating their lands as federal officials and white settler colonials named towns, counties, and landmarks after Union leaders. In the Dakota Territory, where such memory advanced alongside "Anglo-Saxon" conquest, veteran Melvin Grigsby declared the aggregation of capital "a danger greater than the danger of African slavery."[94]

Though Butler's disappointing election returns stalled the anti-monopoly crusade, the Agricultural Wheel and the Farmers' Alliance acted as institutional pivots for agrarian discontent between the decline of the GLP and the Populist moment of 1892.[95] The Alliance campaign organized along both separate sectional and racial lines (the Southern Alliance, Northern Alliance, Colored Alliance, Women's Alliance), seeking to "obliterate the Mason-Dixon line" and "join the hands of the Blue and Gray" in order to secure white reunion as one of shared material interests. To white Alliancemen, "clasping hands across the bloody chasm" was "predicated on recognizing that blacks had their place in the commonwealth of reform—a separate place several paces to the rear." Alliance members staged "bloody shirt" burying ceremonies (with red pokeberry juice as a stand-in for red blood) as Civil War veterans looked to pacify Southern fears of Northern racial reform.[96]

Veterans were well represented among the former Confederacy's agrarian reform leadership. Due to age and economic background—being young and poor at the time of the war—they had disproportionately served as enlisted men rather than as officers. In fact, Farmers' Alliances expanded in part because they functioned as substitutes for state services for veterans. White Southern farmers fumed at what they perceived as the "paternalistic government" of Northern Republicans imparting advantages on former Union soldiers, particularly through political influence in the massive GAR. This anger led Confederate veterans to seek aid and organization through institutions that further aggrandized the Lost Cause. Even so, romanticizing the Confederacy could prove politically treacherous for Alliancemen, who desired to court wartime Unionists in places like East Tennessee. Throughout the Upper and Border South, firebrands were forced to tread lightly when it came to sectionalism, lest they reopen wartime wounds. According to Connie L. Lester, attempts by Southern agriculturalists to affiliate with "like-minded northern farmers"—solidarity across sections along class lines—probably cost Alliancemen recruits in their own communities. Whether eschewing or embracing blue-gray reconciliation, war experiences and the identities of farmers as veterans fully impacted how agrarian movements recruited and self-defined.[97]

Founded in 1886 in Winston, North Carolina, Leonidas L. Polk's *Progressive Farmer* exemplified the racial and regional tensions of this Alliance-to-Populist trajectory. A distant relative of James K. Polk, Leonidas Lafayette Polk was born to slaveholders in Anson County in 1837. An anti-secessionist Whig, Polk nonetheless enlisted in the Confederate army and was wounded at Gettysburg. He entered North Carolina politics after the war, serving in the state legislature and the constitutional convention of 1865–66 before becoming the first commissioner of agriculture in 1877. Polk also grew active in agricultural fraternalism through the Grange movement, which, in addition to leaning heavily on white solidarity and leveraging influence against Reconstruction, housed so many former Confederates that Republicans branded it "an offspring of Copperheadism."[98] In 1873 Polk founded the hamlet of Polkton. The model community soon had a dozen stores, a hotel, two sawmills, two brickyards, a post office, a Methodist church, and a newspaper, *The Ansonian*. A committed Baptist and educational reformer, Polk helped establish North Carolina Agricultural and Mechanical College (now North Carolina State University) and Baptist Female University (now Meredith College). As organizer of the North Carolina Farmers' Alliance, he advocated for a state railroad commission, greater investment in public schools, the subtreasury plan, lower maximum interest rates, and convict-lease reform. He then rose to national prominence, elected as Alliance national vice president in 1887 and national president in 1889.[99]

Created to chronicle planting and livestock practices, the *Progressive Farmer* reflected Polk's reform economics and myriad interests, quickly becoming the most widely circulated newspaper in the state. Polk saw his publication—"serving no master, ruled by no faction"—as meeting a public need for agricultural and industrial knowledge.[100] Incorporating neoteric agricultural science, the *Progressive Farmer* encouraged "modern agrarianism" by promoting political populism without the outlandish partisanship and polemic typical of similar agricultural newspapers. Simply, Polk viewed himself as a producer who sought to upend "the old order of things before the war" through a combination of science, dignified toil, and governmental economic leveling.[101] This involved fulfilling the nostalgic sensibilities of old soldiers through wartime songs and poems.[102] By 1892 the *Progressive Farmer* stood squarely with the insurgent People's Party and its planks of nationalization, a graduated income tax, banking reform, and the eight-hour workday. Polk himself was even deemed a frontrunner for what eventually became the party's "blue-gray" presidential ticket, a prospect that was cut short by his death in the summer of 1892, just weeks before the party convention. By drawing on a cultural framework rooted in wartime understandings of class, loyalty, and region, Polk's publication was able to foster both a fierce regionalism that rallied veterans like himself to the Populist banner and the broader reconciled nationalism that came to define the decade and expedite the United States' imperial moment of 1898.

Alliancemen accentuated the native and traditionalist origins of their project. Even as cooperative agrarian programs often obscured steep disparities of property and influence *among* farmers, Polk hoped that disavowing the "aristocracy of wealth" might result in a "rejuvenated, self-made South" and a cooling of sectional passions.[103] This entailed a bourgeois fusion of progressivism and reaction, combining prototypes as varied as Jefferson's opinion on banks, John C. Calhoun's philosophy of credit, James Blaine's position on debt, and Lincoln's views on the dangerous "money power" and "centralized capital, allied to corporate power."[104] As part of this Cincinnatus persona of virtuous and masterless agriculturalists, Polk initially promoted himself not as a mutineer to the laissez-faire order but as a civic traditionalist.[105] Stressing land ownership as a means of independence, and independence as a barrier to political corruption, the editors assaulted Gilded Age materialism and conceptions of leisure. "Every man his own master" became their rallying cry.[106] Banks fail and fortunes are subject to manipulation, they admonished. The safest investment lay in the soil, with the tiller being "the only real producer."[107] Workingmen "literally earn their bread in the sweat of their faces," Polk explained, lamenting that proletarianization, or the process by which independent or semi-dependent workers became wage-dependent employees, had turned formerly independent men into "wage slaves" necessitating economic emancipation.[108]

White supremacy often attended this republican traditionalism, and Polk's newspaper aimed to stay true to the "instincts, traditions, and history of the

Anglo-Saxon race."[109] The editors also initially denounced "communistic, revolutionary" labor organizations, hoping that the "sturdy, patriotic tillers" might serve as a "break water" between violent strikers and "greedy capitalists."[110] Addressing the Farmers' Institute at Concord in 1887, J. D. Hodges explained that while labor's grievances were legitimate, he protested any interference with "individual liberty or the absolute right to freedom of contract." Adhering to the free-labor mobility ideal and the myth that success in a capitalist system rested with the individual rather than with society, Hodges instead preached frugality and industry so that today's worker might become tomorrow's capitalist.[111] Although cooperation between Alliancemen and the Knights of Labor became routine, leading Polk to proclaim a "New Revolution" in late 1889, anti-union conservatism, in part a backlash against the perceived anarchy of the Haymarket bombing the previous year, remained commonplace among Southern agrarians.[112]

In short, Polk sought African American political support even while attempting to preserve white authority. Like many white agrarian reformers, he regarded Black people as second-rate citizens, even endorsing their colonization in the West. As president of the Southern Alliance in the fall of 1891, the same year Alliance legislatures in Alabama and Georgia passed Jim Crow bills with Populist backing, Polk chose political expediency over interracialism, censuring striking Black cotton pickers who were assisted by the Colored Farmers' Alliance.[113] Employing Polk's jurisdiction in the movement to both vindicate white paternalism and sustain racial barriers within the Alliance, the *Progressive Farmer* issued dire warnings about the consequences of rural exodus.[114] Imploring readers to "stick to the farm," the editors tallied urban mortality rates, especially among African Americans, and underscored the health benefits of rural living in order to discourage land abandonment and emigration to cities.[115] Such arguments betrayed fears among the white Southern bourgeoisie that the South was irreparably behind the North in what one editor termed the "race of industrial progress."[116] Despite concerns about a shrinking labor pool and maintaining racial control over a disproportionately landless Black population, by denouncing cotton production in favor of small, diverse farmsteads, Alliancemen nevertheless threatened Jim Crow's sharecropping order.[117]

As national president, Polk traveled to Los Angeles to speak to the state convention of the California Farmers' Alliance in October 1891.[118] The event metamorphosed into a jamboree of class-based reconciliation and sectional reorientation. Hosted by Union veterans at the Nadean Hotel, Polk distinguished between Confederate veterans on the one hand and their "evil and designing" political leaders of 1861–65 on the other. Although most old soldiers had been "unwilling guests" at a "high carnival of blood and death," he explained that the cause of slavery was an erroneous one and abolition a blessing. Advocating reconciliation across North-South boundaries based on vocation, Polk pegged fiery sectionalists as men who "never smelled gunpowder . . . never heard the whistle of a mini ball." He deemed the struggle to combat a refurbished Slave Power not "for the freedom of the colored man, but for the upraising of virtuous labor from a slavery more degrading than the negro ever knew." Polk's display spawned musical pieces underscoring "passions quelled" and "sectionalism buried."[119] Populist newspapers endorsed his appeal to a relatively racially inclusive but white dominant "antislavery" politics and termed his appearance a "reunion of the blue and the gray."[120] However, the sectional regeneration and veteranspeak of the California convention proved a mere dress rehearsal for the presidential campaign the following year.

Using the Civil War as a prop, the Alliance and Union Labor societies provided the institutional and cultural framework for the forthcoming People's Party. The Union Labor Party's 1888 nominating convention in Cincinnati featured racially integrated delegates, as one-legged Confederate veteran and Union Labor Party gubernatorial candidate Charles M. Norwood of Arkansas demanded the party "strike decisive blows for the emancipation of enslaved labor."[121] Alliancemen, too, built on the GLP's material model of bridging North-South divisions, explaining that their organization was "a grand work for unity, fraternity, reconciliation and peace between the sections." Although white Alliance members hoped that the "unfortunate war" might be "buried and forgotten forever," even some Confederate veterans, including Polk, were willing to acknowledge the centrality of emancipation. Like the Greenbackers, they deemed wartime liberation incomplete in that it was not extended to the economic and industrial spheres—or to white farmers and workingmen. The Alliance made its position clear in 1891: "Not the war of twenty-five years ago which resulted in the emancipation of chattel slavery, but the gigantic struggle of to-day, between the classes and the masses, involving the stupendous issue of freedom, of honest labor from the degradation and slavery of plutocratic power, is the supreme incentive and object of this great political revolution."[122]

The palm and the pine proved difficult to root in common soil, as Civil War memory in the service of progressive reform was beset by external enemies and internal contradictions. The Weaver and Butler campaigns never surmounted the problem of circumventing sectionalism in order to underscore class unity while simultaneously using their own military experiences and war metaphors to sponsor the Greenback cause. Summoning the words of war—slavery, emancipation, masterhood, and soldiering—in the service of class solidarity won over consequential blocs of labor voters, especially in the South, West, and Middle West. Rejecting both whiteness and the bloody shirt, producerist "emancipation" alienated others by failing to attend to their racial or sectional prerequisites. However, in upholding economic freedom for the underclass while largely ignoring African American economic and civil rights struggles, Greenbackers too often proved unable or unwilling to abide race-specifics within their class and vocational platform. This policy defect mirrored the party's cultural shortcomings in failing to articulate how Black politics, and thus Black memory, could liberate even white workers. Greenbackers were correct in that class and trade were the optimal vehicles—the *only* sustainable vehicles, in fact—toward building a progressive coalition to challenge corporate capitalism. However, in-house factions, the strength of the two-party system, and the persistence of sectional animus and white supremacy undercut the latitude and efficacy of such an alliance. The Greenback model of 1880 prefigured the blue-gray Populism of 1892, setting the stage for a more sweeping if less progressive attempt at class-based reconciliation through the largest third party insurgency in US history. At the same time, antislavery vernacular was also permeating the culture of industrial unionists and their struggle for a "third revolution" against the slavery of wages.

CHAPTER 3

# Against Masters and Money Power

## The Knights of Labor and Wage Slavery

DECORATION DAY 1883 evinced triumph as well as solemnity. Just six days after the opening of the Brooklyn Bridge, engineering marvel of the industrial order, Americans recessed at ceremonies at Arlington National Cemetery, in baseball park grandstands, and through mourning rituals in public squares and country churchyards across the nation. All the same, Clarke Irvine, a worker from Oregon, Missouri, challenged the event's hypernationalism. Writing amid increasing white reconciliation at home and a growing transatlantic dialogue on workers' rights, Irvine denounced the occasion's imperial tinge.[1] He explained that the primary function of the military was not to free slaves or secure rights but to perpetuate the interests and safeguard the property of the fabulously wealthy. The army of emancipation had become the army of capital, and the army of continental empire as well. Yet it was toilers who shouldered the inglorious burdens of far-off conquest, and they now found themselves in far more physical danger than active duty soldiers. "Labor is a mighty warfare," Irvine avowed. Modern work was a status in which wage earners were "slain . . . in the service and line of duty." Human bodies were ravaged by explosions, falls, cave-ins, fires, derailments, and collisions, "picked off like advancing skirmishers." Yet unlike old soldiers, injured workers saw no pension and no popular glory. Irvine endorsed "desertion" as a possible recourse. This posture, in which "whole regiments" of laborers were "mowed down" by the hazards of capitalism, constituted "the great warfare of labor."[2]

The Great Railroad Strike initiated a new phase of this industrial war. According to Jeremy Brecher, the strikes had been "the first event in U.S. history to bring to the country's attention the vast new class of workers who possessed neither workshops nor farms, and thus had to work for those who did, the new class of industrial capitalists."[3] Bosses calling on "a grand army" to put down "communist" strikers from Baltimore to San Francisco greatly expanded ownership's labor management arsenal through the deployment of private militias, municipal law enforcement, and US soldiers against workers. Overall, the strikes marked a watershed from debates over freedpeople to those between labor and capital in the urban North, from the ideals of Reconstruction to the ignominy of robber baron capitalism, reinforced by the elevated role of police as protectors of property in a new aristocracy of magnates and financiers.[4]

The worker defeats of 1877 nevertheless provided ingredients for new working-class coalitions.[5] Writing in London, Karl Marx praised the strike actions as the first nationwide movement against "the associated capital oligarchy" since the Civil War.[6] He also anticipated that the aftermath would finally result in the formation of a viable labor party in America. Though Marx's hope for a truly national workers' party went unrealized (a testament to the depth of American racism and the entrenched power of the two-party system), the strikes had indeed portended great change for America's working people. Although at no point, Philip S. Foner reiterates, "did the workers have either the power or the leadership to have transformed the strikes into a revolutionary seizure of the economy or the state," the stoppages contributed to the proliferation of class consciousness.[7] Strikers and working-class crowds had spontaneously and independently seized control of major industrial centers and increasingly perceived themselves not as producers in the antebellum sense (as extensions of their employers) but as a separate and exploited class.[8] By presenting workers primarily as agents in an impersonal economic system and products of social environments rather than undeserving stock types whose precarity owed to individual moral failing, this consciousness also represented a crushing blow to the American exceptionalist falsehood that capitalism could exist without class conflict. Further, it became evident to more workers that labor unions, unprecedented in size, influence, and inclusivity, constituted the most salient defiance of the class pyramid if not the capitalist order. From the perspective of the ruling class, it all looked like social leveling. Just as white reactionaries had linked Reconstruction programs, from the state house of South Carolina to the blood-soaked streets of Colfax, Louisiana, to Communard Paris, fears of an "American Commune" took on new urgency in the face of labor mobilization.

The most prominent organization to rise from the ashes of 1877 was the Noble and Holy Order of the Knights of Labor. Rather than directly repudiating capitalism through revolutionary socialism, the Knights of Labor largely promoted a moral vision of the economy centered on a cooperative commonwealth and the virtue of producers. These adherents to labor republicanism believed that the issue of "slavery" (economic domination and market coercions) was yet unsettled and viewed themselves as the rightful heirs of the abolitionists and Radical Republicans.[9] Their "civil war" was not between Black and white or North and South but between "honest toilers" and those who reduced wage workers to unfree and "unmanly" states of dependency. Chattel slavery and Black emancipation proved models for how Black and white Knights imagined, dialogued, and strategized about "labor emancipation." Members weaponized war commemoration in favor of the eight-hour workday, as an indictment of liberalism, and as a means of promoting interracial organization. Indeed, leader Terence V. Powderly's "army of the discontented" furnished a case study of where veteran and labor commemoration overlapped and how workingmen administered Civil War memory in the New South.[10] Performing the arduous task of attempting—at least in theory—to overcome sectional and racial divisions while continuously summoning war memories in order to appeal to veterans within an industrial "army," Knights established affiliate groups for worker-veterans, including the Blue and Gray Association of the Knights of Labor. Even though it involved familiar terms and deeply American concepts, the Knights' labor republicanism and the turn by some members toward radicalism alienated labor-veteran auxiliaries from mainstream veterans' organizations, notably the Grand Army of the Republic. The ramifications of this break from a mass base of organized workers surely furthered the labor movement's disinclination toward the Republican Party and hastened the GAR's development toward a civic cult of militarism, ethnic nationalism, and conservative patriotism. Yet notions of bondage, freedom, combat, and military organization remained central to the organization's self-understanding, as identity and collective memory bound institutions and workaday politics. As they understood themselves, the Knights of Labor were republican emancipators—abolitionist soldiers of a righteous crusade—battling "industrial masters" so as to dismantle the "slavery" of the wage system.

## The Present Slavery—The Coming Freedom

Immigrants, especially from southern and eastern Europe, repeopled America's industrializing cities during the age of empire. Others, including the family of Eugene Debs, now a leader of the Brotherhood of Locomotive Firemen and soon to be radicalized by the Burlington railroad strike of 1888, settled in emerging rail and coal towns. Many found the dream of a better life vacated. Debs and other workers confronted owners who devised labor surpluses to drive down wages, exploit racial consciousness, and fragment workforces into nationality groups so as to undermine union organizing.[11] Management exercised "*extra*-market coercions": wage theft, company scrip and stores, short-weighting and short-counting, and the use of private police forces to surveil and control access to company property.[12] At the same time, unprecedented financial and industrial consolidation rendered the political system unresponsive, and tumultuous markets and lack of workplace regulation left masses pitiable or destitute.[13]

Some abolitionists turned labor reformers, including Wendell Phillips, who had rejected the phrase "wage slavery" prior to the Civil War, now declared "war" on a wage system that "enslaved" its workers.[14] From the perspective of most organized workingmen, wage-earning servitude had replaced chattel slavery as the nation's economic backbone, and the postwar resolution to eradicate "wage slavery" was a continuation of the wartime effort to abolish plantation slavery. To them, only the concept of *bondage* could fully embody the state of dependency to which workers felt subjected. Accordingly, the Civil War years provided new prototypes not only for social struggle and literal battle but also for human enslavement and liberation. Yet turns of phrase such as "white slavery" and "the emancipation of white men" spoke not only to the callousness of industrial work, but also the primacy of white identity. These slavery allegories and their emancipation corollaries came to serve a variety of functions, empowering workingmen and both challenging and at times reinforcing racial caste.

The use of "slavery" to signify arbitrary hierarchy had a long life in neo-European and especially American civil discourse, owing to its direct racial implications and stark contrast with political "liberty." American revolutionaries once reckoned themselves "enslaved" by a tyrannical King George III. Southern planters feared becoming "slaves" to an antislavery federal government. Articulated by trade unionists, reformers, and even romantic poets, including William Cullen Bryant, the notion of wage earning as a status of enslavement, as well as concomitant "emancipation," predated the sectional crisis.[15] The title of Warren Burton's *White Slavery: A New Emancipation Cause*, published in 1839, inverted the "peculiar" racialization of Western Hemispheric slavery by pairing two seemingly unnatural, oxymoronic words—"white" and "slave"—for the sake of provocation, introducing a new language of racialized class grievance.[16] Fighting for higher wages and the ten-hour workday, budding labor unions naturally likened the "lords of the loom" to the "lords of the lash." "Wage slavery" gained increased currency in the mid-1860s through the writings of socialist theorists and labor reformers ranging from Karl Marx to Ira Steward.[17] Discerning the classist origins of racial construction, Marx reiterated that the "indirect slavery" of white Englishmen depended on the "direct slavery" of Black people across the Atlantic World.[18] This diction was indeed transnational, as US labor brotherhoods, British Chartists, and French socialists alike spoke frankly of American "wage slavery."[19]

Descriptions of white workers relative to Black slaves date to eighteenth-century Britain. Popularized by British evangelist Hannah More in order to illustrate the subordination of middle-class women to early nineteenth-century consumer culture, the phrase "white slavery" was highly varied in the decades prior to the Civil War.[20] Although "white slave" was also sometimes used to refer to legally enslaved people who were racially mixed or light-skinned or to people of European descent who were enslaved illicitly, it existed most often in the realm of metaphor.[21] As Eric Foner contends, the vocabulary of so-called white slaves "took on special power in America, where slavery was an immediate reality, not a distant symbol, the small producer still a powerful element in the social order, and the idea widespread that the wage earner was somehow less than fully free."[22] Perhaps the commonest insinuation behind "white slavery," as either a call for labor reform or a criticism of the Northern industrial system, was that white industrial laborers and Black slaves were exploited similarly. Many white reformers argued that white workers in fact toiled harder, longer, and with fewer occupational protections than Black slaves and that Yankee factories lacked the paternalistic underpinnings of Dixie plantations.

Northern arguments about the productivity of free labor inadvertently reinforced the "white slavery" analogy. Free labor advocacy, especially when combined with the need for discontented workers to organize by trade, became, according to David R. Roediger, "grist for the 'white slavery' mill."[23] For slaveholding critics of Yankee factories, and for many of the wage earners who manned them, the efficiencies of free labor were evidence of its exploitation. Criticizing the alleged class blindness of the abolitionist movement, and with an eye toward the liberation of wage labor, American Fourierists cited the nation's "many forms of slavery."[24] German members of the National Industrial Congress, who commonly addressed one another as "fellow slaves" and whose origins lay in the revolutionary Befreiungsbund of émigré Wilhelm Weitling, assumed as much in their 1850 report that described all US workers, Southern agricultural and Northern industrial, as "ultimately coerced and representing different layers of slavery."[25] Metamorphizing slavery led to the appearance of phrases such as "white nigger," "work like a nigger," and "slaving like a nigger" during the 1830s and 1840s, coinciding with small-scale industrial production and the budding trade union movement.[26] Part of long-standing European-on-European racism, the "Irishization" of white labor in the urban North victimized non-Black yet "not fully white" members of the working class.[27]

Wage earners first used "wage slavery" to describe the myriad constraints and coercions of the capitalist marketplace.[28] A compelling rhetorical device, the very comparison of wage exploitation to Black slavery was not merely a conflation of two oppressions (white workers typically understood that their conditions were different and better than those of Black slaves in that they possessed some capacity to organize). "Wage slavery" was also an implicit critique of the peculiar institution (and later the Republican Party's free labor/slave labor binary). It is therefore an oversimplification to argue, as some scholars have, that Northern laborers merely adopted the concept of "wage slavery" from planter elites and thereby became proslavery apologists. The workers' use of "wage slavery" was logical and in fact preceded its use by slaveholders, who embraced the term in part to weaken the antislavery movement.[29] Nevertheless, the concept soon became a fixture of the antebellum slave debates, with planters maintaining that the oppression of Southern Blacks was relative to (and more benevolent than) that of Northern or English industrial workers. Proslavery polemicists George Fitzhugh and James Henry Hammond branded the North's factory system the "white slave trade."[30] To the disciples of bondage, who derided Northern factory employees as ethnically mongrelized "mudsills" and "greasy mechanics," "white slavery" was an evil far worse than chattel slavery. "Wage slavery" was not only a workingman's exploitation but a *white man's* exploitation. These "wage slavery" imaginings fed sectional tropes. Envisaging "Pittsburgh slaveholders" and "New England slavery," carried out by the "stony-hearted, immensely rich, exacting masters" of Yankeeland, alleviated regional guilt over chattel bondage and, later, sharecropping.[31]

Notions of "wage slavery" proved central to antebellum party formation. Deflecting the moral critique at the center of abolitionism, slaveholder overtures to the hardships of *white* industrial work helped grow the proslavery but anti-nativist Democratic Party in the North. Such appeals were especially effective among newly arrived Irish laborers, for whom the middle-class Protestant "free soil" vision and start-up capital of independent farming held little allure or possibility. As Noel Ignatiev explains, "The truth is not, as some historians would have it, that slavery made it possible to extend to the Irish the privileges of citizenship, by providing another group for them to stand on, but the reverse, that the assimilation of the Irish into the white race made it possible to maintain slavery." Though Protestant elites stamped them as "niggers turned inside out," the subhuman "Black Irish" worked to adjust to a new society in which rulership was based not only on class but also on white skin privilege.[32]

To most abolitionists, however, many of whom downplayed white workers' claims of subjugation, "wage slavery" was overly simplistic. They demanded to know why the Underground Railroad was a one-way route.[33] The "wage slavery" metaphor was an almost exclusively material one, and, from the perspective of antislavery reformers, it ignored both the breadth of anti-Black prejudice and the singularity of chattel slavery as a system of terror and control.[34] From the perspective of white workers, meanwhile, discrediting "wage slavery" undermined their direct interests as browbeaten and propertyless producers. This divergence between aggrieved laborers and dismissive reformers reflects in part the class gap between wage workers and bourgeois abolitionists, who were roundly capitalistic in both ideology and leadership.[35] Despite rejecting the notion that the plight of (mostly white) factory workers was the same as that of Black slaves, other antislavery thinkers nevertheless saw a type of "white slavery" in the South's poor whites, whose material interests lay in slavery's destruction. They posited that destitute whites were also slavery's casualties because the existence of the plantation system kept them locked out of jobs, livable wages, and access to land and credit. As such, slavery's critics argued that no form of labor in the South was "free" and that all Southern workers—Black slaves and propertyless whites alike—were thus "victims of slavery." Hence, to be a landless white in the South was to be what Hinton Rowan Helper termed a "second degree slave."[36] Frederick Douglass agreed, avowing in *My Bondage and My Freedom* that by fomenting prejudice against poor whites, slaveholders had rendered "white mechanics and laborers of the south . . . almost as much a slave as the black slave himself."[37]

The use of Black people as a "negative reference group" vis-à-vis white workers continued within the cultural politics of organized labor, particularly at the point where white workers recast "wage slavery" into "white slavery."[38] Machine stitcher Clara Brown roused the "girls of Lynn" during their 1860 shoemakers' strike in Massachusetts by urging her coworkers, "Don't let them make niggers of you!" When another white worker shamed Brown because some of the striking women were in fact Black, she clarified, "I meant Southern niggers."[39] Espousing a racist-paternalistic outlook toward chattel bondage, the editor of Chicago's *Workingman's Advocate* argued that slavery in the antebellum South was worse "in some respects" than "the present system of slavery, in which labor is subjected to capital." However, he reminded readers that Black slaves, despite their "ignorance," were afforded certain necessities, including shelter, food, and medicine, that proved inaccessible to many Northern white workers. Overstating the base comforts of plantation slaves *and* the employment options of white workers, the editor, who referred to capitalists as "slave traders," maintained that the only significant difference between a Black slave and a white slave was that the latter was able to seek job opportunities elsewhere.[40] Indeed, though economic "slavery" made perfect sense within the worldview of nineteenth-century workers, "white slavery" served to reinforce racial hierarchy because it underscored the unorthodoxy of reducing white workers to a status that, throughout the Atlantic World, had been reserved for Black people.[41]

The use of "white slavery" expanded conceptually during the Gilded Age and Progressive Era as a euphemism not only for white workers in the North and poor whites in the South but also for the effects of liquor and the forced prostitution of white women. "New abolitionist" reformers and crusading exposé authors, who often downplayed the realities of antebellum chattel slavery in order to accentuate the horrors of this other, whiter flesh trade, stated that "the white slave of Chicago is a slave as much as the negro was before the Civil War, as the African is in the Belgian districts of the Congo." Like workingmen, Hull House activists and other anti-vicers employed antislavery imagery, especially that of Abraham Lincoln, to legitimate their own cause as one in a long sequence of human liberation.[42] Many reformers, including members of the Woman's Christian Temperance Union, viewed "white slavery" rhetoric as a practical means of reconciling North and South. Framing their multisided agenda of temperance and suffrage as part of an American emancipationist tradition, WCTU leaders including Frances Willard viewed intemperance, or "liquor bondage," as a "new slavery" that disproportionately impacted white women. In doing so they often urged sectional détente in ways that marginalized Black people and assailed racial equality.[43]

Workers also used "wage slavery" to suggest that the Civil War remained unfinished. Ira Steward questioned the use of "the antislavery idea" so long as workers did not possess "the power to exercise it."[44] Poet George Eddy explained in "Onward Freedom" that, even though "Afric's slavery" had been banished, other forms of bondage remained as "thousands bound in chains . . . more galling [than] chattel slavery" implored for deliverance.[45] Because "wage slavery" was often suggestive of white oppression, emancipation from such slavery was interpreted through white lenses. As Carol A. Horton explains, to most white workingmen, "the primary significance of Emancipation was not that it extended existing rights to a disfranchised group. Rather, it was that it destroyed an exploitative system of labor-capital relations that had formed an important part of the socioeconomic structure of the nation."[46] Consumerist qualifiers largely replaced the racialization of "wage slavery." Even so, workers and journalists continued to deploy the metaphor to heighten divisions between so-called skilled and unskilled workers, strikers and scabs, industrial and agriculture laborers, and Black and white workingmen.[47]

Knights, eight-hour advocates, and other reformers unceasingly invoked "slavery" and "masterhood" to describe their oppression. Slavery was poverty, Steward resolved in 1879, and poverty an outgrowth of slavery. Emancipation demanded that workers move "out of the slavery of poverty and into the freedom of wealth."[48] It grieved one Union veteran to see the American flag reduced to what Wendell Phillips once called "a flaunting lie!" through monopolization. "*Slave labor* is degrading," the old soldier protested, "and wage labor *is* slave labor," brought on by new opponents of free labor, the "enslavers of the Caucasian race."[49] As one socialist clarified, whereas "slave labor" meant direct, legal ownership, "wage slavery" entailed indirect ownership, with scarcity on the part of the "slave" and the "master" mentality principally unchanged.[50] This acknowledged discrepancy between the legal ownership of individual persons and the exploitation of social classes distinguished the "wage slavery" of capitalism's critics from those who, building on the arguments of antebellum slaveholders, would continue to use the "white slavery" metaphor to endorse the subjugation of so-called inferior races. Indeed, allegorical "white slavery" continued to serve as an endorsement of racial hierarchy. Even within ostensible attempts at racial inclusion, white-laborer-as-slave symbolism might convey how the irregularity of industrial capitalism upset the "natural" racial order, as "slavery" was, in the context of the Atlantic history, to be part of an exploited and racialized caste. "Republican racism" suggested that there were more and less deserving "slaves," with "white slavery" being a most unnatural form. This phenomenon also saw white workers accept the idea that Black oppression, unlike white oppression, was "the result of 'slavishness' rather than slavery."[51]

Nevertheless, such denotations were far from standard among the Knights of Labor's racially and ideologically diverse rank and file. To be sure, industrial unionization breathed new life and meaning into the "wage slavery" concept. Interracial organizing helped strip the phrase of not only its antebellum connotation as a defense of chattel slavery but also its frequent "white slavery" synonymity and associations with white worker preservation. In the hands of the Knights, by the 1880s "wage slavery" more clearly entailed a material (rather than racial) condition and a general and progressive indictment of the industrial milieu. Looking to carve out autonomy within the labor movement, Black publications also encouraged greater cross-class alliance through the adoption of various "wage slavery" metaphors. As the *New York Freeman* explained in 1886, it was obvious "that chattel slavery would certainly be followed by industrial slavery, no less galling and degrading to the enfranchised class and far more profitable to the employers of labor." Although the organization did not include a national antidiscrimination standard, that year recorded perhaps 95,000 Black members of the Knights of Labor, and in the South nearly half of all Knights were African American.[52]

The growing emphasis on "emancipation" within the Knights coincided with dedication to interracialism and the inclusion of women. As Lawrence B. Glickman argues, "While deemphasizing the slavery aspect of the slavery/freedom dichotomy, more and more workers pointed to the model of emancipation and suggested that with the end of chattel slavery 'all kinds of slavery' should be 'buried . . . forever.'"[53] This model often encompassed fuller intersections of race and gender. Knight Justus O. Woods protested that the "slavery of the present," a by-product of despotic markets and Social Darwinism, in fact created climates that were especially burdensome toward women, who were paid "half men's wages, even for the same work." Yet, like feudalism and chattel slavery, women "wage slaves" might also be "emancipated." "Negro slavery, hoary with age and panoplied by legality, went down with a crash before enlightened public conscience," Woods explained. To contest wage "slavery" was to champion enlightened values through inclusion and voluntary cooperation.[54]

Labor's notion of deepening "wage slavery" spurned popular slavery-to-freedom narratives, or what Robert Penn Warren later referred to as the North's "Treasury of Virtue." The Southern-born novelist explained that the aftermath of the conflict engendered two socially corrosive, deeply cherished historical misconceptions. Countered against the South's "Great Alibi," the idea of Southern victimhood that downplays slavery as the sectional conflict's root cause, the "Treasury of Virtue" was, according to Warren, the North's "psychological heritage" wrought by the war. That sanctimonious "Treasury" shifted the locus of troubled "race relations" southward, indicting the former slave states and exonerating the more liberal North through moral geography, thus speaking to the heart of Northern—and therefore American—pathos and identity. According to Warren, if the white Southerner felt trapped by history, the white Northerner felt redeemed.[55] However, proletarianization and "wage slavery" defied this Yankee myth and shattered the sharp contrast between free and slave labor that had been established by the early Republican Party. To countless workers, the Civil War could not have ended slavery if "slavery" persevered. As Amy Dru Stanley observes, "Postbellum images of the wage slave called into question not only free market doctrine, but also triumphant narratives of emancipation." Explaining this loss of independent production and transition "from freedom to dependence," one trade unionist lamented in 1871 that most former artisans were now "in the factories of the capitalists working as their wage-slaves. From being their own masters . . . they work for other masters."[56]

"Emancipation" from such conditions required abolitionists. Forward-looking labor leaders viewed themselves in the vein of William Lloyd Garrison and Frederick Douglass, and their organizations, newspapers, and workplace tactics featured the cultural trappings of a new antislavery movement. "Wage slavery" was frequently regionalized, if not fitted directly within the war's memory. One stalwart Knight recalled the guerrilla violence of Bleeding Kansas following a strike in Kansas City, proclaiming that the state militia and the so-called Law and Order movement (which had originated in Chicago in response to the Great Railroad Strike) "are occupying the same position to enslave whites as the 'Border Ruffians' did to enslave blacks."[57] Knights equated fixed hours, supervised shop floors, locked workplaces, physical immobility, and the tyranny of the clock with slavery in general, but especially with the peculiar institution. To be constantly monitored by a "driver" was, in the words of one machinist, "getting down to slavery."[58] Avowing that monopoly was rooted in undemocratic Old World values, Knights insisted that landlords, cattle barons, and railroad corporations had produced "modern serfdom."[59] They understood themselves as part of a historic progression of freedom that linked the eight-hour day with the destruction of bondage.[60] With the deliverance of enslaved Blacks as a model, "emancipation" became an increasingly mutable concept associated with economic independence. Meanwhile, workers cast opponents of their liberatory movement as "secessionists."[61] This revamped free labor critique spread as, according to Roediger, Marxists, socialists, and anarchists "turned it into an appeal to the revolutionary consciousness of the working class."[62] Although some professions of "wage slavery" were no more than "fanciful fictions" intended by labor spokesmen to highlight the glaring injustices of the industrial work house, as Bernard Mandel asserts, "the very fact that such comparisons could be seriously made indicates what laborers thought about their status."[63]

## Rebellion against Class Rule

The Knights of Labor embodied the worker-veteran refashioning of "antislavery." Founded in 1869 in Philadelphia by Uriah Smith Stephens, the Knights expanded from their tailors' union roots to become one of the most ideologically diverse labor organizations in US history. Having abandoned much of their early institutional secrecy by the early 1880s, the slogan "an injury to one is a concern to all" underscored inclusivity and the virtue of toil. While Knights viciously racialized certain "competitors," notably the Chinese, they nonetheless attempted—albeit sometimes half-heartedly—to organize a more comprehensive "House of Labor," regardless of race, gender, skill, or nationality.[64] Knights often infused Christian moralism into the concept of the "producer," which most preferred to "worker."[65] Blending republicanism, nationalism, and millennialism with active opposition to exploitation, corruption, and consolidated capital, many Knights understood their condition as part of a historical-material development from feudalism to chattel slavery to wages and now toward the "emancipation of labor." Hopeful foreign radicals viewed this "emancipation" as part of a grand historic cause. Friedrich Engels, who warned European socialists not to dismiss the movement but to assist it in being "revolutionized from within," saw great promise in the Knights as "the first national organization created by the American working class as a whole."[66]

The Knights' program reflected the diversity of its membership. Promoting what Henry Demarest Lloyd termed "industrial liberty" toward securing "political liberty," the Knights of Labor endorsed National Labor Union holdovers, including cooperatives, the prohibition of child labor, gender pay equity, and land and currency reform. Many even sought the eventual nationalization of railroads and other industries.[67] Members opposed "class legislation" of laws and policies that favored corporate interests, as well as "special privileges" provided by the government to private firms. While owners appealed to the "dignity of labor" as a means of maximizing production, Knights demanded economic rights because civic rights alone were insufficient to alleviate "the social problem."[68] In doing so, Knights repackaged antebellum value systems regarding virtuous labor into a working-class version of the predominant middle-class (and factory owner–approved) work ethic, thus expanding the horizon of worker rights.

The organization crested with the wave of labor upheaval in 1886. At its peak, roughly 20 percent of all US industrial workers were affiliated with the Knights, and the body may have boasted 1 million members.[69] Despite the Knights of Labor's advocacy of sweeping economic transformation, leadership repudiated anarchism and socialism (though some rank and file embraced it), and their clandestineness, which aped antebellum secret societies, was an incessant point of suspicion. Although many members communicated Marxian conceptions, few were self-identified Marxists. Their rejection of the wage-labor system was nevertheless predicated on cooperative theory—one that was often masculinized. Whereas not organizing the workplace was indicative of an "inactive and unmanly attitude," unionization was part of the same "manhood to act" that had driven soldiering. "Slavery," conversely, was a condition produced by an absence of such masculinity.[70] The national organization was ostensibly nonpartisan, and its leaders mostly eschewed electoral politics. Even so, between 1885 and 1888 the Knights ran their own electoral campaigns in hundreds of cities and towns and dozens of states and territories under various banners, including Union Labor, Workingmen, Independent, and United Labor.[71]

The Knights were unique in their efforts to incorporate women, who in turn contributed to the Order's cultural memory. Influenced by socialistic and radical literature, including Edward Bellamy's *Looking Backward*, working women shaped the Knights' industrial critique by building on their earlier work in abolitionism, women's agitation, spiritualism, transcendentalism, and anti-monopolism. Future Populist luminaries, including Mary Elizabeth Lease, served as delegates and became Master Workmen. Socialists Leonora O'Reilly and Mary Harris "Mother" Jones also first entered labor politics through the Knights of Labor. Like their male comrades, who were often situational allies, women members "Americanized" the labor struggle through the Civil War's ideas, lessons, and leaders. This memory became a way to link trade unionism, and women's role specifically, with other homegrown reform elements, including the Grange and the WCTU.[72] Although misogyny was commonplace, and both male and female Knights often accepted cross-class Victorian understandings of gendered "spheres," the Knights of Labor organized roughly 60,000 women between 1882 and 1890 in dozens of women's locals. While women never composed more than 10 percent of national membership, in certain cities they made up as high as 20 percent of all the Knights, often leaving a disproportionate cultural imprint through poetry and other media.[73] Some male Knights openly resisted women who defied patriarchal norms; others did not. Despite their admittedly groundbreaking rhetorical commitment to sexual equality, most Knights, including many women, remained ambivalent toward direct issues of gender, mirroring other inclusive labor organizations on questions of whether women should be viewed primarily as comrades or as domestics.[74]

Knights who were Civil War veterans also viewed themselves as the inheritors of the midcentury antislavery mission and framed their struggle as a continuation of the slave's cause.[75] Early Knights of Labor leaders, including cofounder Robert W. Keen, belonged to the GAR, and they stripped concepts such as "slavery" and "emancipation" of their sectional and racial moorings.[76] This de-sectionalization often involved the development of a patchwork social philosophy regarding how Union victory impacted the political economy. Uriah Stephens, for one, described Knights of Labor district assemblies as organizations that might "emancipate of the world's workers from Corporate Tyranny and Wages Slavery."[77] Knights insisted that, because "class legislation" had allowed the rich to avoid conscription and military service, workingmen did a disproportionate amount of the fighting and dying during the War of the Rebellion.[78] At the same time, the conflict ushered in a "mushroom aristocracy" rooted in government contracts, growing private control over the public treasury, and the rising power of Wall Street. Resisting this tyranny was a patriotic duty; it was also a continuation by worker-soldiers of the anti-aristocratic battles they had waged during the war against either a despotic federal government or, more commonly, the oppressive planter class. As one New York Knight explained in 1887, "It becomes our duty as citizens of the Republic to insist that the government shall no longer cater to the avarice of a few remorseless speculators at the expense to the masses of the people of poverty."[79]

Knights of Labor songs and sloganeering incorporated wartime themes, as illustrated by land reformer Henry George's Knights-backed New York City mayoral barnstorm of 1886. Written to the tune of the Knights of Labor's "Storm the Fort," the George movement's most famous song melded "campaigns" both political and military as advocates used reconciliationist phrases, including "let the past bury its dead," in order to champion their candidate and the creation of an independent labor party.[80] Free labor had been formative to George's worldview. The ideal of small-scale entrepreneurial capitalism—an ideal now undermined by monopoly and permanent wage labor—reinforced his notions of civic virtue, opportunity, and thrift and belief that no single person should amass too much wealth or power.[81] Although, as a writer for the *Daily Alta California*, George had penned a eulogy for Lincoln in April 1865, by the 1880s he reiterated how far the Republicans had strayed from their free-labor roots. "Were Lincoln living Lincoln would be with us," he avowed.[82]

Yet George's producerism was decidedly *not* revolutionary. His utopian capitalism rested on the ideal—but never the reality—of non-state intervention in the economy while letting supposedly unbiased markets determine the price of goods and labor. As Richard White maintains, George's movement also occurred as the fantasy of laissez-faire was at the tail end of its transition from "a doctrine of radicals and democrats to a doctrine of conservatives fearful of popular politics." Like antebellum laissez-faire radicals, George assumed that markets were impartial, rather than legal constructions that often reflect entrenched social inequalities, and that government intervention would necessarily benefit the wealthy. As such, he upheld the liberal anti-monopolist values of honest competition, contract freedom, and the "right to rise."[83] Yet witnessing George's free-labor utopianism undermined before their very eyes by industrial hierarchy and a fixed wage–earning class, many workers remained unconvinced. While conservatives mocked

George's "Grand Army," socialists critiqued the Union Labor Party from within, leading to the movement's expulsion of the "wild-eyed" faction for "un-American" ideas.[84]

Terence V. Powderly, leader of the Knights after 1879, was the son of an abolitionist mother and was weaned on antislavery. A dyed-in-the-wool Republican, young Powderly formed a local U. S. Grant club and came to possess an uncommon appreciation for sexual double standards in the workplace.[85] Yet as Republican radicalism dissipated, Powderly grew inspired by the labor unrest of 1877 and soon entered Greenback politics, serving as mayor of Scranton, Pennsylvania, and chairman of the Central Greenback Club of Lackawanna County. While the pro-Powderly *Scranton Daily Times* denounced the coercion of the lash in all forms, local "harmony of interest" Republicans likened worker strikes to the Reign of Terror and the Commune's Bloody Week, accusing Powderly of "treason" and "Molly Maguireism."[86] For his part, Powderly modified the emerging national reconciliation culture that eschewed bloody shirt politics in favor of white reunion, simultaneously condemning sectionalism and racial reaction. "No Mason and Dixon's line, no color-tests divide North, South, East and West," he explained to workers in Richmond in 1885. "Wherever laborers congregate . . . one chord of sympathy unites them all."[87] This shunning of sectional division through a vocabulary common to workingmen north and south became a fixture of the maturing labor movement.

Under Powderly's direction, the Knights of Labor ranks flourished alongside its monthly, the *Journal of United Labor*, which co-opted early Republican imagery as part of its industrial critique. Union army veteran and Greenbacker Sanford Kirkpatrick, for instance, aroused "that sterling old patriot, Ben Wade," and "the fires that were kindled by the immortal Lincoln" to urge workingmen to break from their current "bondage" and consolidate as one union of "FREE MEN."[88] Powderly, meanwhile, took "free land" to mean the rejection of limitless private property. Chided as a "communist," he deemed large-scale land ownership a "robbery of the peoples' heritage" and, like Thomas Paine, believed land to be "an inheritance ordained by God," with no individual having a right to monopolize it.[89] Although labor activism was "informed and tempered" by slavery and emancipation, Powderly only reluctantly backed strikes, which he viewed as unnecessarily destructive and equated with both the recent carnage of the Great Strike and that all-encompassing template for how Gilded Age Americans interpreted devastation, the War of the Rebellion.[90]

Powderly also solicited veterans, applying deliberately incendiary language to underscore the plight of laborers. Using his regular "Address of the General

Master Workman" as a pulpit, he consistently urged "industrial emancipation," branding "wage slavery" antithetical to modernity and basic humanity.[91] Asking, "Is labor emancipated?," Powderly warned against "disunion" in favor of a regiment-like solidarity among worker-veterans.[92] This free-slave dichotomy and appeal to martialism extended to nearly every issue within the labor movement. Writing on child labor and the importance of public education, Powderly explained, "The sword may strike the shackles from the limbs of a slave, but it is education and organization that make him a free man. He is still a slave whose limbs alone have been freed."[93] Foreshadowing May Day and Labor Day, he compared the Knights to Union soldiers in that both had "taken up the lance in defense of humanity."[94]

Whether such language was more rhetorical or real is less important than *why* Powderly imagined himself heading a battalion of working-class emancipators. Stemming from the practical need to recruit former soldiers, Powderly routinely defended his organization as the veteran's friend, insisting that the interests of common soldiers and workers were one and the same. He evoked soldiers' homes in order to deflect attention away from his cooperation with the Home Club of Lassalleans and anarchist dissidents within the Knights. As such, Powderly professed that old soldiers' homes were social models for retired workmen—the Knights of Labor's "soldiers of construction"—and alleged that proud yet aged workingmen needed housing security rather than an asylum, a poorhouse, or a workhouse.[95] In 1890 he attacked Solicitor of the Treasury William P. Hepburn for purportedly steering veterans away from the Knights of Labor. "If another civil war does occur," he predicted, "you will find the Knights of Labor fighting against the enemies of the Republic," infused with the same principles of righteousness that drove Lincoln's columns. Powderly at once lambasted "demagogues" who would prate before soldiers' organizations in order to win votes "until we had begun to believe that being an old soldier was next to being a god" but would then "rob the old soldier through his poverty" after Election Day. Imploring the "soldiers of the Grand Army" to "join hands with the Farmers Alliance and the Knights of Labor in driving every speculator off our soil," he urged Union veterans to be front and center in "the party of the future"—one aligned with militant workingmen.[96]

## A Third Revolution

The Knights of Labor forged Black-white alliances throughout the South. Though perhaps the most famed interracial association resulted in the Thibodaux Massacre in Louisiana in November 1887, in which white paramilitaries killed some sixty Black sugarcane workers who were attempting to unionize, the most successful organizing occurred in Richmond, Virginia. While class alliances in the city had traditionally been undermined by trade, racial, and gender divisions, labor leaders Black and white began to breach the color line through shared Civil War veteranhood following a series of failed ironworkers' and bricklayers' strikes in the late 1870s and early 1880s. Richmond's District Assembly No. 84 scored victory with the Haxall Mills boycott in the spring of 1885, which compelled one of the nation's largest flour producers to cease using convict labor, and again the following spring when it demanded the city quarry local stone and employ organized labor in the construction of a new city hall.[97] Tying this newfound trade organization to race pride and emancipationist memory, African American Knights formed the Lincoln Union Shoemakers, the Union Liberty Protective Society, and the Sumner Lodge No. 3 of Black ironworkers.[98] As with the Colored National Labor Union, the Knights of Labor often fused with support for the Republican Party and autonomous Black social, fraternal, and religious institutions.[99]

White labor leaders, meanwhile, looked to allay African American misgivings about the level of their interracial sincerity. In a dramatic gesture at the Knights of Labor General Assembly in Hamilton, Ontario, in October 1885, Powderly took Black delegate Joseph Brown Johnson by the hand and assured him that the Knights were committed to "complete enfranchisement." Printer and *Labor Herald* editor William H. Mullen then presented Powderly with an honorary gavel. It was made of wood from the Battle of Yorktown surrender site, the old St. John's Church, and Libby Prison, where, according to Mullen, Union soldiers had been imprisoned for struggling "to liberate a race of people from the galling yoke of slavery." Peter Rachleff notes that such gesture politics were part of the Knights' looking to assume the mantle of both 1776 and "the liberating forces of the Civil War."[100] Mullen's response focused on emancipation, reminding his audience that Union veterans were willing to sacrifice all life's comforts in order to "wipe out forever the blot and blight of slavery from the future history of America." Now, he insisted, old soldiers were part of a "grand army" that would commence a "third revolution . . . in which no single race is to be set free, but in which all the nations of the earth are to be liberated."[101]

The idea that Knights were engaged in a "third revolution" that was an extension of the first two speaks to what workers of both races perceived as the war era's unfinished ideals and vacated promises. The specifics of this revolution were characterized by Richmond's leading labor press, the *Labor Herald*. *Herald* editorials spotlighted the eight-hour workday, opposition to vagrancy laws and child labor, support for free silver, and the publication of blacklists of companies for targeted boycotting.[102] Regional idiosyncrasies shaped the city's labor activist culture, as Knights employed slavery-centered language within an interracial, urban wage-earning setting in a society where notions of "aristocracy" and allusions to "free men" held particular resonance. Proclaiming that there was "dignity in toil," its editors surmised that "true nobility" lay not in the idleness of planters or the cupidity of New South capitalists but in the physical and mental industry of common people. Capitalists, meanwhile, were tyrannical "masters" and industrial workers their "white slaves" or their "wage slaves."[103] To Black and many white workers, plantation resistance lent a symbolic or literal antecedent to factory resistance. Speaking to both systemic and individualized problems of the industrial economy, the publishers insisted that the "evil of aggregated wealth" had given rise to new urban patricians who neither labored nor loved their fellow man, creating inequities that might be righted through the wide-ranging organization of workers.[104] Altering a familiar class-race vernacular, editors insisted that "king monopoly" now looked to "make slaves of freemen."[105] While this lexis combined with anti-monopoly and pro-worker stances, it also accommodated the idea that labor and capital could coexist peacefully—it was not a socialist critique.

Knights likewise equated their subservience and "loss of independence" with that of antebellum bondmen.[106] Asking whether or not slavery had truly been abolished, workers charged that there was scant difference between an enslaved plantation hand and a "free" wage earner. "Are these men freemen, or are they slaves?" one editor questioned. "You might say they are freemen because they have the right to quit if not satisfied. It is not so. They are *forced* to work in order to get the necessities of life. . . . They are forced by surrounding circumstances." In other words, although "battle, with powder, ball, and bayonet," had shattered "the auctioneer selling human flesh," countless laborers presumed industrial "slavery" comparable to bondage owing to its national scope and lack of paternalism.[107] Even as Mullen praised Union veterans as vanguard emancipators, he questioned whether the current "slaves of monopoly" might be so easily liberated, ultimately determining that there remained "a battle to be fought for universal freedom."[108]

Meanwhile, "masterhood" as derived from the apprentice system could imply a particular attainment of craft or leadership position, such as "General Master Workman Powderly" or "Master Builders Association." In a political or racial sense, it might also entail the undue authority of man over man. Just as masters of the lash had directed antebellum plantations, masters of the clock and the wage now governed factory "plantations."[109] This parallel between "lords of the lash" and "lords of the loom," a connection made by reformers since the 1830s, was both rhetorical and real.[110] Many Black workers accepted the analogy as valid, if figurative. Indeed, white and Black workers—George Lippard's "slaves of the cities"—argued that both "lords" occupied coincident positions within labor's hierarchies. Both also zealously sought to control bodies, spaces, and time—to drive human flesh.[111] In another incident of clever wordplay, "master" was sometimes paired with "pastor" to describe the dual control of workplace and domestic life and the inclination of both toward "honor and obey." The more "American" term, one worker maintained, was simply "boss."[112]

Knights mockingly referred to wage earners who opposed unions and identified with capitalists—those who had committed "treason" against their class—as "aristocratic workingmen." "Such a man is an insolent traitor," the *Labor Herald* explained.

> He is not a capitalist and cannot rank with the capitalists. He is not an aristocrat, since he believes "a man ought to work all he is able to get work," whereas aristocrats pride themselves on their idleness. Even his sycophancy to the ruling class—his fondness for pandering to the spirit of capitalism, does not make him one of them. He is not a workingman for he is a traitor to the workingman's interests. He considers himself better than a brakesman, a switchman or section hand; he scorns their unions, denounces their strikes, and says boycotting is a crime. Why, such a man is worse than Jay Gould.[113]

This fastening of anti-labor sentiment to the same type of aristocratic interests that directed the Old South was part of the Knights' attempt to reconfigure the relationship between work, dignity, and power in the New South.

Anti-aristocracy also shone through in how the Knights of Labor used the war to frame the organization's struggle as a preservationist defense of American republicanism. Demanding a "*truly* republican . . . *genuinely* democratic" government, one Knight excoriated the "privileged gentry" classes.[114] Yet this philosophy of self-sufficiency was not equality of outcome but Lincolnian equality of opportunity, and it relied on both "progress" and protest.[115] Although "shyster newspapers" and "paid tools of the Money Power" cried for citizens to "Beware of Agitators!," another tradesman pointed out that all of US history was owed to the dissent tradition. "If it hadn't been for agitation, negro slavery, that blistering curse and foul blot on the country's past record, would never have been abolished." In fact, he explained, "all the progress that the world has made . . . has been brought about by means of aggressive and practical agitation."[116]

Americanism also sometimes meant disassociation from European revolutionaries, with some members emphatic in their antiradicalism. Drawing on the French Revolution as a portent of social violence, worker-veterans maintained that only labor rights would prevent a Great Terror redux.[117] Primary change, which signified a "complete alteration of the laws and statutes relating to the relative positions of labor and capital," should come about through peaceful means.[118] "We need no revolution, no bombs, no anarchists, no destruction of life and property," the *Labor Herald* asserted.[119] Another worker protested that "although the Knights of Labor are called dynamiters, communists, socialists . . . they conduct their business without coming to blows." This brand of nativism merged with traditionalism and business conservatism in espousing boycotts but hoping to avoid work stoppages so as not to "drive away capital."[120] Strikes were a last resort that some Knight leadership linked to the "barbarism" of 1877. In an instance of "respectable" self-policing, "mobs" and "riots" were to be summarily suppressed by the working classes themselves.[121] Editors denounced the Haymarket bombing as a "wicked affair," the result of too many foreign workers carrying the red flag.[122] Citing Russian anarchists and German socialists as examples of oligarchs strong-arming wage earners toward political subversion, ranking Knights warned businessmen that the steeper the class order and the more intransigent the owner class, the greater the impetus of workers to resist through violence.[123] Yet most rank-and-file members held little faith in the capacity of either moral suasion or appeals to profitability to convince capitalists to self-moderate. Owners often repeated the sanguine motto that "Labor and capital should go hand in hand." "So they do," one editor carped, "but we generally find the big hand of capital firmly clinching the little hand of labor."[124]

Advancing the "hand of labor" meant strategizing around "antislavery" interracialism. The haphazard Knights of Labor enforced no national antidiscrimination standard, allowed racial policy to be determined by local assemblies, and was riven by Sinophobia. Nevertheless, Knights did not restrict membership on the basis of race, and enemies regularly accused them of inciting "Negro insurrection."[125] They also backed women's rights—"equal pay for equal work"—and decreed women eligible for membership in 1881.[126] Given the agrarian orientation of the vast majority of Southern Blacks, as well as the enduring hegemony of the South's white ruling class, the degree to which the Knights were able to organize Black workers in the Upper South was exceptional.[127] More competent than abolitionists had been in convincing white workers that cross-race alliance was in their material self-interest, Knights exploited fears that capitalists might use Black workers and women as strikebreakers to the impairment of white men. This resulted in the enlistment of so-called unskilled laborers and buttressed the organization's ranks with African Americans who were condemned to menial jobs. While

Philip S. Foner insists that the Knights "did not wage a constant, determined campaign to eliminate racism from its ranks," Black and white workingmen frequently struck and boycotted in unison and marched together throughout the South: in Louisville, Birmingham, and Dallas.[128] In Virginia, Black workers constituted half of the state's Knights. Richmond, which featured an autonomous Black district assembly, had over 3,125 African American Knights in twenty-one local assemblies, some heavily composed of Black female domestic servants and tobacco hands. The city boasted perhaps the best organized Black labor force in the United States.[129] Altogether, as many as 60,000 African Americans were members of the Knights of Labor at its peak in 1886, and they blended labor and civic organization with emancipationist memory. In Richmond that meant Black Knights using labor networks to foster race pride and advancing public commemoration, including Emancipation Days, to engender working-class activism.[130]

Knights employed the designation "old soldier" widely, imparting a dual meaning as one who was both a war veteran and a veteran of the labor movement.[131] In Chicago, Confederate veteran, Knight, and Workingmen's Party leader Albert Parsons called on GAR members to join the "Grand Army of Labor."[132] Knights in Virginia appealed explicitly to disenfranchised veterans north and south, often citing the pension system as a model for the viability of social welfare. Demanding "*Let us be just before we are liberal*," honorary Knights of Labor member John Swinton condemned the notion of private charity as a substitute for public works. Failing to separate Black chattel bondage from wage exploitation, he decried the cruel irony that soldiers who had "marched and fought to emancipate the black man from the bondage of a century" should now be subject to "a tyranny more hateful than negro slavery ever was."[133] Though he was no Knight insider, Swinton's incapacity to speak to race-specific issues betrayed the limitations of even racially inclusive short-lived surges. His rejection of liberalism—civic equality and private alms—as the only precondition for social fairness had been echoed two decades earlier by many of the very freedpeople whose former social circumstances Swinton now trivialized.

By the mid-1880s interracialism was coursing through electoral politics. While the national Knights of Labor eschewed formal politics (though both Stephens and Powderly were elected to political office), local parties appropriated the Knight brand.[134] Although the *Labor Herald* prided itself on having "elected men from both parties" and claimed to back any "would-be champion of the workingmen," its leaders increasingly aligned with the Democracy.[135] In Richmond, where labor spokesmen filled Democratic ward committees and the district assembly formally nominated reform candidates,

Knights were so influential that the city hosted the union's annual convention. Yet the color line marred its procedural from the start. Hotelkeepers refused African American representatives, forcing them to stay in the Black section of town. Local authorities barred Black labor leader Frank Ferrell of New York from introducing Virginia's governor, Fitzhugh Lee, as a violation of local Jim Crow ordinances. Ferrell introduced Powderly instead, but not before reiterating that the Knights were committed to the abolition of distinctions based on creed, nationality, and color. Once onstage, the Pennsylvanian used the opportunity to castigate racial discrimination in the city and the organization, estranging many white Southerners. Lee, a former Confederate general and the nephew of Robert E. Lee, was visibly discomposed.[136] Southern delegates admonished that the political crisis had "done a great injury" to the Knights of Labor slate of candidates.[137] Though the Knights faded in the late 1880s, the emerging American Federation of Labor and its leader, Samuel Gompers, would learn the "lesson" of African American agitation in the Upper South, as they shunned "unskilled" workers and eluded wider social reforms in favor of the sole mission of unionization.[138]

## The Blue and the Gray of Labor and Capital

If the Civil War provided a model of worker resistance, its aftermath offered various frameworks by which old soldiers might reconcile to eradicate the "new slavery." As one organizer explained at an 1886 meeting of the Blue and Gray Association of the Knights of Labor, "War gave one kind of master for another, and wealth once owned by the masters of the South has been transferred to the monopolists of the North and multiplied a hundred-fold in power, and is now enslaving more than the war liberated."[139] Affiliate groups of the blue and the gray within larger bodies of organized labor looked to quash North-South differences by reifying "slavery," "emancipation," and "masterhood." Seeking to expand into the former Confederacy, Knights of Labor leaders performed the thorny task of attempting to overcome sectionalism while continuously summoning war memories in order to court veterans and build a type of solidarity ostensibly last seen in the army ranks. Printed in Marblehead, Massachusetts, between 1880 and 1889, the *Journal of United Labor* included war stories and anecdotes to placate its "grand army" of veterans.[140] Editors frequently quoted abolitionists, as well as Lincoln, often invoking his first annual message to Congress that labor was "prior to, and independent of capital."[141] One of the publication's primary—and sometimes contradictory—functions was to bridge the North-South divide by defying the bloody shirt while simultaneously engaging veterans through a potent antislavery vocabulary. Once again, war memories, even those based on universal principles, made war era venom difficult to suppress.

On October 10, 1885, a group of Union and Confederate veterans met at the St. Nicholas Hotel in Hamilton, Ontario. There they formed the Gray and Blue of the Knights of Labor, which aspired to promote both sectional and working-class harmony pursuant of a "toiler's emancipation." The meeting was attended by old soldiers from Connecticut to Missouri and from Louisiana to Iowa, including Richmond Knight Frank J. Reilly, previously of the 13th Virginia Infantry. Led by Arkansas veteran Thomas Green and Henry G. Taylor, a former New York Volunteers Zouave, members suggested that the path to industrial freedom ran through worker militancy. Pronouncing "Capital Divided, Labor Unites Us," and again minimizing the degree to which "sectional" issues were often sites of genuine ideological struggle with tangible consequences, especially for African Americans, Green and others insisted that the bloody shirt was also a tool by which the ruling class cynically pitted workingmen against one another. They explained, "We have organized this association to reunite those who were arrayed against each other on the field of battle, but now enrolled in the great army of peace, whose mission is to abolish poverty and establish the universal brotherhood of men."[142]

By the time the Knights of Labor Special Assembly met at Cleveland's Forest City House in May 1886, the Gray and Blue had burgeoned to a 300-man auxiliary.[143] In a message that presaged the Populist wave of 1892, Green, now the group's president, weighed his Confederate background against those of the organization's president pro tempore and secretary, who were Union veterans from Illinois and Louisiana.[144] Rejecting the secrecy of the Masons and the Pythians, the Gray and Blue Knights of Labor declared as public information all of its business and stood ready to receive every Knight, North or South, who fought in the late war. Another similar congress, the Veteran Labor Men, assembled that week, too.[145] For those within living memory of Gettysburg and Chickamauga, labor "warfare" was a much-preferred proxy for actual fighting, as worker federations sought to, in the words of one electoral-minded member, "prevent universal slaughter by universal suffrage; to make ballots prevent bullets, and hence organize voters to prevent the organization of soldiers."[146] Although the club was presumably short-lived, its utilization of trade unity and class consciousness among veterans to exorcise sectional animus portended the Populist insurgency the following decade.

Richmond's 1886 convention saw the Gray and Blue organization revitalized through the largely symbolic Blue and Gray Association of the Knights of Labor.[147] It is no coincidence that the group—"fraternal in its aims and helpful in its spirit, and kindly in its labors, and loyal to humanity"—arose on the

FIGURE 3. "The Blue and the Gray, All Knights of Labor" (circa 1880s). This unidentified image is indicative of the overlap between Civil War veteranhood and working-class culture, as well as of the sheer variety of associations of Union and Confederate veterans within Gilded Age trade unions, workingmen's fraternities, and labor organizations. Several of the Knights are displaying their GAR medals. (Catholic University of America)

border between North and South at the dawning of a national reconciliation movement.[148] Looking to craft a sense of brotherhood among old soldiers in support of the eight-hour movement, the Blue and Gray Association held annual encampments for old soldiers in both the North and the Deep South, with Reilly initially serving as one of its directors.[149] Association bivouacs took place in Washington, DC, Atlanta, and North Carolina well into the twentieth century, eventually incorporating Sons of Union Veterans and Sons of Confederate Veterans into their ranks.[150]

These small units of veteran men within broader labor organizations mirrored labor groups within the GAR. Their minority statuses revealed discrete irreconcilabilities within the labor-veteran convergence that typically broke along class or ideological lines. For instance, a fissure between the GAR and local labor leadership spoiled a Fourth of July barbecue in Debs's Terre Haute in 1887. The stir began when Knights of Labor officials invited Robert Schilling of Milwaukee to speak at the city's Alpha Union. A Knight leader and militant eight-hour advocate, Schilling had been indicted the previous year along with fifty-one others for conspiracy to boycott. GAR men, whose disproportionately middle-class veterans self-identified as protectors of law and order and suppressers of rebellion, dubbed him a "Milwaukee Anarchist" and countered the "socialist boycotter" with their own embargo. Schilling delivered his address anyhow, alluding to labor's expressly American values.[151]

Nevertheless, veteran and labor groups continued to share commemorative and political, if not physical, space. The GAR and the Knights participated alongside one another in parades, political rallies, and mourning and funerary culture throughout the late 1880s and early 1890s, particularly during Memorial Day, Fourth of July, and Labor Day festivities.[152] At a "Meeting of the Grand Army—The Lecture to Workingmen," hosted by Springfield, Ohio's Mitchell Post No. 45 GAR in the spring of 1887, attendees were listed by both their wartime military unit and their trade. The crowd included butchers, printers, molders, tinners, manufacturers, and farmers.[153] In September of that year, Knights and GAR posts staged a joint parade to commemorate the anniversary of the battle of North Point, featuring a handful of living War of 1812 veterans.[154] Old soldiers' groups also continued to meet in union and Knights of Labor halls.[155] When Grover Cleveland visited Chicago for the first time in the fall of 1887, roughly 30,000 citizens lined his parade route along Michigan Avenue. GAR posts were backdropped by emancipationist scenes from the late war, including General Grant on horseback, flanked by Union soldiers, and Lincoln holding the Emancipation Proclamation. These Grand Army men stood alongside the Knights of Labor, the Ancient Order of United Workmen, the Legion of Giuseppe Garibaldi, and the Thirteenth Ward Colored Democratic Club.[156]

Workers also combined wartime language with patriotic fetes as means of recruitment. Knight leadership paired their organization with the "booming of cannon" and "beating of drums" through an increased symbolic presence on Independence Day, the true legacies of which were "a peoples' government" and "one—and only one—flag." At the same time, Powderly dismissed critics as anti-American and defended the patriotism of the Knights of Labor. "Let those who are so disposed call our demonstrations 'spread eagleism' or 'Yankee Doodleism,'" he fired in 1887, arguing that jingoism drives a patriotic urgency against both "alien landlords" and "native rogues."[157] Local leaders often felt similarly despite the ethnic pluralism of the rank and file. Promising a "Grand Army of Labor," Knights in Omaha, Nebraska, invited all nonunion workers to join their lines during the city's 1894 Fourth of July celebrations.[158]

Established as a federal holiday in 1894, Labor Day proved an optimal outlet for the worker-veteran approach and a salve amid yet another crippling economic depression. Festivities in Washington, DC, the following year saw a potpourri of war era imagery, including a rebranding of loyalty politics. A stonecutters union likened strikebreakers to wartime "copperhead" traitors and unfurled a massive banner that read "Scabs Cannot Be Depended Upon Either in Peace or War." Proclaiming "Free Government, Free People, Free Books," Knight assemblies roused early Republican egalitarianism. The steam engineers union demanded justice for American Railway Union leader Eugene Debs, who had been imprisoned for his role in the Pullman Strike the previous year for upholding American constitutionality against a "moneyed power" bent on worker servitude. Yet in the wake of Coxey's Army's march on Washington and brutally suppressed strikes at Coeur d'Alene, Idaho, and Homestead, Pennsylvania, labor leadership and the civil authorities often quickly snuffed out what they viewed as subversive conduct. Following the arrest of Italian worker Witis Calvo for bolting to the front of a Labor Day procession and waving the red flag of the International, a second worker, Angelo Pieozzi, pulled a red banner from his pocket and flaunted it in front of the city police guard before being dragged off.[159]

Labor Day also proved a common outing for GAR encampments and reunions, including blue-gray reunions, such as the one in Cincinnati on Labor Day 1898, just months after the beginning of the Spanish-American War.[160] Workers in Duluth, Minnesota, heeded Boston labor leader George E. McNeill's call for a new kind of militia on Labor Day 1900. Promoting a "Grand Army of Toilers" to seek "labor's emancipation," they insisted that tools were the new guns and saw their "Grand Army of Peace" as one in a transhistorical procession of workers self-delivering first from serfdom, then chattel slavery, and now "wage slavery." McNeill's Grand Army of Labor would stand "shoulder to shoulder, the white man and the black man, the native born and the foreign born, men of all creeds and of no creed, of all political parties and of no political parties."[161]

Even as some Knights demanded racial and ethnic inclusion, the traditionalism that undergirded labor's appeal to veteranhood often intersected with and reinforced far-reaching patterns of white reunion in American society. By the 1890s, as sectional reconciliation became a genuinely national phenomenon, trade unions increasingly emphasized resolutionist and racially euphemistic themes of brotherhood and healing. Offering a "logical discourse on fraternity" to a meeting of veterans and workingmen in Montana in 1895, Reverend Jeremiah Turner of Butte urged labor and capital to "clasp hands as the old soldiers do." When "brothers fight," he maintained, repeating an old Knights of Labor maxim, the twins evils of anarchy and monopoly win. Explaining that reunion with the South was the last and greatest triumph of the Civil War, Turner sought "reconciliation without condescension." "It is a bright day in America when the hearts and the hands of the blue and the gray of our civil war are united," he relished. "It will be another bright day when the blue and the gray of labor and capital meet around one common campfire."[162]

Other attempts to distinguish between the legitimate language of Union veterans and illegitimacy of labor protest were more conspicuous. The coupling of labor rights (and federal spending associated with civil rights) with socialism and anarchism coursed during Reconstruction, exacerbated by upheaval in France. The Great Railroad Strike and the sensationalized media coverage of the Molly Maguires in the 1870s Pennsylvania countryside led veterans' organizations to additionally distance themselves from radical labor, with the anti-labor press characterizing the Knights of Labor as a "communist" group leading a "grand army of tramps."[163] Each violent response to a labor action and every renegade worker who made national news headlines drove the wedge further still. Branded as "insurrectionists" by bourgeois proponents of Victorian order, the Knights began a freefall in the aftermath of the Haymarket bombing. Massive opposition from employers; hostility between workers and administration; institutional infighting over issues such as trade and the role leadership should play in condemning attacks on Black Knights in the South; and competition between the Knights and the newly formed AFL all contributed to the organization's swift decline.[164]

Moreover, efforts to integrate labor and veterans' societies proved increasingly volatile. The connotation of "radicalism" had changed from sectional to material as workplace confrontations highlighted the contrast between workers and soldiers. Beginning with the professionalization of the National Guard following the railroad strikes of 1877, the frequent mobilization of soldiers by capitalist politicians against striking workers alienated workingmen who might have been responsive to the martial, if conservative, culture of old soldiers. Although military service had heightened class consciousness for countless veterans, according to David Montgomery, the army of the late nineteenth century "provided both the most formidable instrument for compelling people to conform to its wishes and an effective agency for reducing the possibility that government would need to resort to compulsion."[165] When seventy-five workers of the Nelson Mill in Cloquet, Minnesota, struck in the summer of 1890, the local press welcomed in the form of the state militia a new army of "boys in blue" who would "protect life and property."[166] This was Clarke Irvine's prognostication come true: the army of emancipation becoming the army of capital.

Irvine and other workers within and beyond the Knights continued to insist that war and emancipation had not constituted true liberation and that the brawls of the previous generation over section and slavery were but one chapter in a larger struggle against class oppression. With no income tax, inheritance tax, or checks on corporate earnings, and with effectively no federally protected workers' rights, the gap between haves and have-nots increased as never before. Wealth concentration led to corporate influence in politics and the establishment of an immensely powerful owner class in a society devoid of a formal aristocracy. Elite consumption—mansions, leisure, and baubles—confirmed social status and legitimacy, even as the moral dubiousness of vulgar wealth sometimes clashed with Victorian mores. "Before the War of the Rebellion we had two millionaires and no tramps," one Knight avowed. "Now, as the effect of nearly thirty years of class legislation, we have 31,000 millionaires and 2,000,000 tramps."[167] As countless workers saw it, not only did the Civil War leave freedom from wage labor unfulfilled, but workplace conditions were actually worsening. As J. L. Perryman, a Knight from Belleville, Illinois, explained, "The Civil War came in 1861, and after four years of terrific fighting, after the smoke of the battlefield had cleared, and when the deep boom of the cannon and the rapid roll of rifle had died away in the valleys, looking over the plain of the quick and the dead, the generals on both sides found out that not less than millions of American citizens had been swept away by the hurricane of civil war, and over ten billions of dollars had been sunk, and the end is not yet . . ."[168]

CHAPTER 4

# The Red Flag of Emancipation

## Socialism and Revolutionary Memory

GUSTAVE PAUL CLUSERET was a soldier of fortune shaped by the Civil War. Although he had led government troops in suppressing the June Days uprising in his native France in 1848, Cluseret later joined Giuseppe Garibaldi's Italian nationalists before coming to the United States and entering the Union army. He rose quickly within the Army of the Potomac as a member of John C. Frémont's staff and was promoted to brigadier general. Yet Cluseret grew impatient with the Lincoln administration, openly condemning its gradualist approach toward emancipation.[1] The ambitious Frenchman corresponded with leading Radical Republicans, including Charles Sumner, and rebuked the Union high command as overly aristocratic. Cluseret even co-established a weekly journal in New York City, the *New Nation*, which challenged Lincoln from the left in 1864 by backing Frémont for president and the short-lived Radical Democracy Party. Reckoning himself the political reincarnation of the Marquis de Lafayette, Cluseret drew inspiration from the legacies of the French Revolution and 1848's "springtime of nations."[2] For such radical democrats, experience in the slaveholders' rebellion reinforced their belief in international worker solidarity.[3] Red republicanism and even the communism of the International were extensions of militant abolitionism; African American liberation was harbinger of transnational industrial emancipation.[4]

In the winter of 1870 Cluseret attended a banquet at New York's Union Assembly Rooms honoring the anniversary of the June Days, during which the despotic Orléanist Louis-Philippe was ousted from power. The hall accommodated nearly 700 French nationals, including Charles Villa; the editors of the *Franco-American*; commissioner from Lyon and future Communard

M. C. Pelletier; and the brother of Italian revolutionary Felice Orsini, Louis Napoleon's would-be assassin. Celebrants paid tribute to Victor Noir, a recently slain republican journalist, and Henri Rochefort, owner of the anti–Second Empire newspaper *La Marseillaise*.[5] In addition to commemorating and mourning, the event also served two subtextual purposes: to denounce the tyrannical Napoleon III and to affix the hope for transformation in France to revolutionary success in the United States. These fomenters, many of them Union veterans, saw possible revolution in their homeland as a continuation of the War for the Union. Seeking "the institution of a Republic in France on the model of the great Republic of the Western World" with support from their "American brethren," the comrades of Cluseret, who had also organized for the Fenian Brotherhood and the Reform League, boldly deemed themselves "the advance guard of the grand republican army which was destined to sweep personal government from France and inaugurate a universal Republic."[6] They would soon get their chance. The following year, Cluseret, whom Union veteran and famed author Edward L. Pierce labeled "the Frenchman always in search of a revolution," served as minister of war during the Paris Commune.[7] Looking to build a worker-orientated democracy following Napoleon III's military debacle during the Franco-Prussian War, Communards sought "the reappropriation of the state by society," offering socialists everywhere a blueprint for radical democracy.[8]

The specter of revolution in France provided an anti-labor foil for US capitalists who perceived socialism and abolitionism as cut from the same subversive cloth. Dating to the antebellum period, such fearmongering was grounded in concrete interests of elites. One Texas editor had warned that "the socialist is an abolitionist everywhere" in that socialists hoped to "destroy individual rights in property."[9] The nascent secessionists of the Palmetto State's *Sumter Banner* agreed. Alleging that "wage slavery" was a form of involuntary servitude worse than Black slavery in the South, the editor excoriated the socialist agenda yet acknowledged its ideological consistency. He maintained that socialists were "the only abolitionists who understood [their] mission."[10] Proslavery Democrats had censured "the socialist and abolitionist parties" as one and the same, asserting that "every socialist is an abolitionist, and though every abolitionist is not a socialist, he is on the way to become one." Avowing that socialists were responsible for the rise of abolitionism in New England, the *New York Herald* had predicted that such a threat to the racial hierarchy would "convert every Yankee into as thoroughgoing red republican and socialist as any to be found in France or Germany."[11]

Emancipation and Reconstruction—proletariat liberation and mass democratization—only augmented the bugbear of property confiscation. Just as opponents of Radical Republicanism had accused Wendell Phillips, Thaddeus Stevens, and Benjamin Wade of perpetuating so-called French socialism during Reconstruction, the fearmongering Money Power, like the Slave Power before it, now painted working-class mobilization as an "American Commune." This was especially true in the aftermath of the Haymarket bombing. By the 1880s, according to editor Patrick Ford, the term "communism" had "for a long time served as a bludgeon in the hands of the enemies of Labor with which they have attempted to kill every reform movement that had any tendency to benefit the American workingman." Ford's *Irish World and American Industrial Liberator* linked Irish independence to the condition of international workers, comparing exploited US factory and farm laborers to the Irish peasantry. He posited that just as slaveholders had made the word "abolitionist" synonymous with criminality and disorder, capitalists now hoped to convert "communism" into an epithet for chaos and violence.[12]

The ruling class was right to be panicky. Socialists and anarchists *did* build on the redistributionist claims of abolitionists and freedpeople and exceeded those of trade unionists by challenging the legitimacy not only of slave property or plantations but also of the mechanisms of production and property rights altogether. Rather than recalling the abolitionist movement as many antebellum workers had, as being altogether bourgeois, or viewing abolitionists as mere pragmatic allies whose aim of free labor converged with their own, late nineteenth-century socialists came to see themselves as a postscript to abolitionism. This "red memory" operated through anarchist networks, militias, and workers' parties. Like their radical predecessors in farmer-labor movements, Gilded Age socialists pressed to end the "bloody shirt," as partisan debates over loyalty and section hindered working-class organization. Yet even while urging to "let the past bury its dead," red radicals drew on the past, as trade union halls, third party campaigns, printing houses, and shop floors became critical sites of memory production. Socialist Laborites, who ultimately used antislavery vernacular in the service of a flawed electoral and overly sectarian strategy, insisted they were the progeny of the Lincolnian small producer; anarchists modeled their militancy on the social leveling and antiauthoritarianism of John Brown. Both generally dismissed or downplayed racial analysis, often out of self-preservation. Many socialists saw the liquidation of nonclass difference, including racial difference, which they conflated with social division, as the only way to self-protect. The notion that the only distinction between chattel slavery and "white slavery" was the distinction between slaves sold *at* the market and slaves sold *in* the market was both personal *and* political. Nevertheless, in appropriating the antislavery enterprise, these "socialist armies" engaging in the "war for social emancipation" prefigured the Socialist Party of America and the Industrial Workers of the World. They constructed "red Abe Lincolns," "red Nat Turners," and "red John Browns" as threats to exclusive property rights and harbingers of a greater social upheaval—not only a third American revolution but a worldwide uprising.

## Socialism or Slavery

A Marxist network heralded what would become the "red memory" of the Civil War. Founded in the summer of 1876 and inspirited by the Paris Commune and the International, what became the Socialist Labor Party emerged from the convergence of various Marxist organizations, including the Workingmen's Party of Illinois and the Social Political Workingmen's Society of Cincinnati. The Workingmen's Party of the United States, the forerunner of the SLP, then rose in influence among German craft workers during the St. Louis General Strike of 1877.[13] By the early 1880s the SLP sometimes rallied around bourgeois reform, such as the Henry George campaign, but it largely followed a fundamentalist approach to electoral politics that included an impractical if somewhat noble refusal to adopt Anglophonic governance.[14] The party's platform advocated direct elections, universal suffrage, broad social welfare, and a progressive income tax. It also proposed wage equalization according to race and gender, the abolition of capital punishment and convict labor, the scientific management of natural resources, and the nationalization of land, railroads, telegraphs, canals, and machinery to be controlled by trade union cooperatives. Socialist Laborites understood capitalism "scientifically," as an emergent process, rather than as a conspiracy of greedy individuals, and felt it must be checked by structural political-economic changes rather by than moral appeals to sympathy for the poor. Employing US history in pursuit of what they termed "the emancipation of the working class," their left nationalism had an Americanizing effect on what was a predominantly ethnic and non-English-speaking contingent, putting what Theodore Draper describes as "an American head on an immigrant body."[15] Socialists harangued a plutocratic system that reduced workers to a state of human enslavement through an "industrial war" in which capitalists owned the means of production and stole surplus labor.[16] That conflict was predicated on capitalism being unfixed—merely one form in a succession of various modes of economic production. As Marx had noted, "like slave labour, like serf labour, hired labour is but a transitory and inferior form," undermined by its inequalities and internal contradictions.[17] But waging war also meant building an army. Pursuing this end, the SLP championed solidarity across racial and ethnic lines, at least in theory, and often overlapped with extant anarchist and labor organizations, including the Knights of Labor. Yet party members divided over electoral approach, with proponents of German socialist Ferdinand Lassalle (who became known as Lassalleans) envisioning a party insurgency based on the Republican insurgency of the 1850s. Marxists, conversely, hoped to achieve revolution through a strategy of industrial unions, strikes, and boycotts.[18]

Of Dutch Jewish and Spanish Portuguese ancestry, SLP leader Daniel De Leon had lived in Curaçao, Venezuela, and the Netherlands and studied at the University of Leiden in Germany before emigrating to New York in the early 1870s. He became a Georgist in 1886 and soon evolved into a full-throated Marxist. An advocate of Lassalle's parliamentary path, De Leon promoted the measured overthrow of capitalism through what he hoped would be a bloodless struggle, or what Antonio Gramsci subsequently termed a "passive revolution."[19] Adherents to De Leonist "emancipation" from "capitalist wage slavery" regarded trade union tactics—any goal short of capital's dismantling—as a betrayal of the working class.[20] After becoming head of the SLP in 1890, the inflexible De Leon railed against reformism, nationalism, and anti-immigration within trade unionism, especially the American Federation of Labor. He judged the Populists as bourgeois and reactionary and eventually saw much of his own party, including Civil War veterans such as Richard J. Hinton, defect for the Social Democratic Party and the Socialist Party of America.

De Leon's faction remained deeply influenced by the Union war, consistently referencing it as a metaphor, watershed, or counterpoint. Although he advocated political engagement through the SLP, De Leon nevertheless criticized politicians as faux "emancipators."[21] He censured mutual aid and colonizing socialists, mocking the idea that Job Harriman was, as some admirers applauded, "the Abe Lincoln of his day."[22] SLP affiliates generally viewed the recent war as class conflict between free and slave labor, the outgrowth of which saw increased wealth consolidation. Appropriating William H. Seward, the SLP publication the *Weekly People* described the industrial contest as "the irrepressible conflict between wage slaves and their masters." As proven at Homestead and Hazelton in Pennsylvania, this "second civil war" was a total war, complete with soldiers and shirkers, casualties and corpses. "Whether the wage worker likes it or not, he is forced to play a part in this war, either as sheep or soldier," provoked the editor, compelling workingmen to "take up the arms of a class conscious rebel."[23] As one member explained, "The abolition of wage slavery is the first and greatest aim for man; freed from that he will develop and extend . . . but bound by shackles he sinks below the brute."[24] In addition to drawing on the ideological legacies of past bourgeois revolutions, as well as on both French and Marxian socialism, socialists viewed the contest between capital and labor as more protracted in struggle and broad in scope than did their trade union forebears. Exclaiming "Liberté, Egalité, Fraternité!" and "No Masters, No Slaves!," they breathed international revolutionary meaning into concepts such as "slavery," "equality," "freedom," and "comradeship."[25]

If slave plantations represented "factories in the field," then industrial work constituted "slavery in the shops." Socialists detailed factory conditions as "American slave pens," replete with lightless rooms, unbearable odors, and flint-hearted overseers, all amid the deafening roar of machinery.[26] Working-class neighborhoods, meanwhile, were "slave markets," and labor agents the drivers of a new "plantation" system. Expressing a theme that would be repeated by radicals and reformers, freethinkers and firebrands from Ira Steward to socialist literati-activists Jack London and Upton Sinclair, Socialist Laborites described the shop as a workhouse and its workers as bondmen.[27] Terming industrial managers "slave-whackers," one labor reformer described machine shops as sties of "young girls, small boys, and half dead women [who] work like slaves." He invoked Lincoln's second inaugural reference to "every drop of blood drawn by the lash" by avowing that every cent earned in the "dirty, dark slave pens" came at the cost of a drop of blood.[28] This linkage of slavery's environs with those of the mine, the mill, and the yard was reiterated by workers from the International Cigar Makers' Union to striking textile workers in Lawrence, Massachusetts. Such symbolism would come to permeate both the Socialist Party of America and the IWW, who afterward claimed that the mills of Lowell, Clinton, Fitchburg, and Lancaster were not mere towns but slave societies operated by thousands of unfree laborers within the "slave bondage of capitalism."[29]

Socialists coupled the description of the industrial workplace as a plantation with accounts of the intensity of factory labor and the separation of employees from families and with comparisons of workers to livestock—all of which mirrored illustrations of chattel bondage. Together, such motifs suggested that exploitable labor combined with filthy conditions to create a "slave factory . . . more intense in its horrors than the famous slave pen."[30] Socialists argued that the threat of starvation and the threat of the lash—the tyranny of scarcity and of the whip—were equally oppressive forces, likening industrial managers to mechanical slave drivers who disciplined workers through the much-hated "speed-up."[31] Speaking to a form of "wage slavery" just as vicious as chattel slavery in West Virginia's Kelly Axe Manufacturing Company, one editor claimed it was the aim of "slave drivers" to abrade each

FIGURE 4. "New York City—The Great Labor Parade of September 1," *Frank Leslie's Illustrated Newspaper*, September 13, 1884. The banner comparing chattel slavery ("past slavery") with the wage system ("present slavery") was typical of socialist and anarchist rhetoric against "wage slavery." (Collection of the author)

worker into a "servile, humble slave, to jump at his master's bidding."[32] This notion of factory conditions, and especially that of child labor, as tantamount to a slave coop, with its pitiable want of space and light, was adopted by a panoply of trade unionists.[33] Asking, "What is the difference between the black industrial slavery of the '60s and the white industrial slavery of today?" one member of the Commercial Telegraphers' Union insisted that Western Union offices in Memphis, Atlanta, and New Orleans "might be compared with the slave pens of sixty years ago."[34]

Like antebellum slave pens, industrial factories were not only landscapes of human detainment but also settings of resistance.[35] Socialists linked the expansion of these "sites of slavery" with the acquisition of territory, "pauper labor," and new commercial markets. The *Weekly People* exposed Western influence on China's Boxer Rebellion and incursions in the Philippines, where tycoons and policy makers guided US imperialism at the expense of the American working class, who served as "food for bullets."[36] Although foreign demand had reduced the so-called army of the unemployed, domestic workers and unprotected industrial workers remained highly exploitable classes, resigned to either work or starve. SLP songs transmitted this martial solidarity across skill levels. Published in socialist weeklies, Stanislaus Cullen's "The War Song of the Fighting S.L.P.," sung to the tune of "John Brown's Body," depicted shackled slaves, lashing masters, the mustering of an army of workers, war cries, and pitched battles. Adducing Marx, Cullen reminded his audience that they had an entire world to gain and nothing to lose but their chains. He issued a "call to arms" and cautioned against the machinations of "labor-fleecers" who duped workers through the toxin of nationalism.[37]

Metaphors concerning slave estates and plantations, masters and pens, and bondage and liberation accented the SLP's lamentation of the downfall of the small producer. Like Greenbackers and Knights, socialists mythologized early Republicans, imagining themselves as natural heirs.[38] Yet Socialist Laborites went beyond reform and the romanticization of small-scale capitalism, maintaining instead that capital aggregation and profound shifts in economic relations required revolutionary solutions. Mass production had concentrated ever-growing industrial tools among a smaller number of owners, resulting in a more uniquely exploitative system. The general solution entailed cooperative ownership of production, even as they debated whether or not the transfer of large-scale property from the individual to the collective would involve compensation.[39] Socialists termed this process "confiscation," sometimes citing emancipation and the arguments for property seizure during Reconstruction. Following Marx and echoing socialist E. Belfort Bax's *Short History of the Paris Commune*, which praised Communard egalitarianism while lambasting the "murderous orgies of the capitalist [Versailles] troops," many socialists saw the Commune as both a lesson and a template for this type of redistributive and radical democracy.[40]

The SLP largely ignored the extent to which Marxist theory applied especially to the most disproportionately working-class and most organizationally isolated population: Black workers. Socialist Labor did attract African American supporters including Cincinnatian Peter H. Clark, a former abolitionist and leader of the 1877 railroad strikes who became a socialist congressional candidate the following year. Furthermore, as Ahmed Shawki notes, some prominent white SLP members were exceptional in their antiracism. These included the Frenchman Victor Drury, a Forty-Eighter and member of the First International, and the Irish American Thomas Maguire.[41] Nevertheless, the SLP's official line was race neutrality: neither discrimination toward nor specific provisions for nonwhite people. There *were* practical considerations behind this obfuscation of race, namely self-preservation. As Cedric J. Robinson explains, because early socialism was so fragile and atomized in terms of ethnicity, nationality, and religion, class solidarity *alone* (rather than class as the common point of intersection) "provided a category of political activity through which the diverse social elements of the revolutionary movement could be reconciled."[42] So although even paternalistic socialists backed universal political rights regardless of race, sex, and color, they made no particularist demands for women or African Americans; many insisted that racism and misogyny were entirely reducible to capitalism. Some did in fact view the commercially dynamic New South as a place ripe for industrial organization and socialist recruitment. This was not the same South that had rebelled in order to preserve its monolithic system of slaves and cotton, one socialist alleged, but instead a place of factories and pig iron, where low wages and currency deflation facilitated a new class consciousness.[43] However, the party did not meaningfully address race-specific grievances such as lynching, convict leasing, racial banishment, or the mass deprivation of civil liberties, all of which were heightened in the former Confederacy.[44] Gendered concerns were similarly neglected. Arguing that "the so-called Women's Rights question will be solved with the Labor question," the Workingmen's Party of the United States refused to conceive the "emancipation of women" as an issue rooted in *but that also exceeded* the problem of work and wages. The "great end," they insisted, was "economical emancipation" for the entire human race.[45]

Underscoring internationalism rather than sectionalism or nationalism, the SLP contained a pronounced—and in most cities a majority—ethnic element. Exiled by the Anti-Socialist Laws of 1878, which passed after two failed assassination attempts on Kaiser Wilhelm I, German subversives left Europe and funneled into revolutionary networks in New York, Philadelphia, Milwaukee, and especially Chicago, which they termed the "Paris of America," owing to its radical potential.[46] According to the Workingmen's Party's Declaration of Principles, "the emancipation of labor" was neither local nor national but a social problem across all nations.[47] Socialists endorsed the big-tent organization and global resolutions of the First and Second Internationals and the formation of a permanent international federation as the best strategy for undermining "industrial enslavement."[48] Not only were there dozens of German-language socialist publications between the 1870s and 1890s, but there were also nineteenth-century party newspapers printed in Polish, Swedish, Norwegian, Czech, Danish, Yiddish, and Hungarian. The emergence in the early 1890s of De Leon and the English-language the *Weekly People* further Anglicized what had been, in many places, a principally

German-speaking organization.[49] Identification with the figures, language, and symbols of the nation's epic bloodletting was both part and parcel of this Americanization.

Socialists both within and beyond the SLP embraced antislavery vernacular. Editors of one of the first socialist periodicals in the United States, *The Emancipator*, published in Cincinnati and Milwaukee, were keenly aware that their paper's title paralleled the sectional era. German socialists in Boston and elsewhere hosted abolitionist orators, including Wendell Phillips and John Synton.[50] At the SLP's twenty-fifth anniversary celebration in Indianapolis's Arbeiter Hall, Martin Hanley of New Jersey, who was also a Knights of Labor delegate, reminded his audience of "enslaved workingmen" that "John Brown became a martyr in the interest of freedom, but, after the slaves had been freed at the point of a bayonet, it was shown that they were not free men, but, with three millions of whites, were still slaves."[51] They interpreted what Marx referred to as the socialist "war against the system" (as opposed to the capitalist struggle of "man against man") through Brown's vanguardism.[52] The SLP rank and file viewed themselves as rightful inheritors of this cause, extended to mean the eradication of classes and wages and dedicated to "the emancipation of the proletariat . . . the last remnant of slavery in existence."[53]

Aided by radicalization following the Great Railroad Strike, Socialist Laborites made a strong electoral impression in the fall of 1877, with notable tallies in Cincinnati, Chicago, Louisville, Buffalo, Milwaukee, New York, and Brooklyn. Retaining their martial theme, the party's slogan became "Science the Arsenal, Reason the Weapon, the Ballot the Missile." The SLP made even greater gains the following year, especially in Chicago and St. Louis, where anti-electoral Marxists begrudgingly backed socialist candidates, winning multiple seats in the state legislatures and city assemblies.[54] De Leon, who would later turn against the voting strategy, favorably compared SLP electoral success with that of political antislavery in the 1840s, insisting that the socialists were in a much stronger political position than the abolitionists had been twenty years before their program (the abolition of chattel slavery) was fully enacted.[55] Yet by 1880, with votes falling and the breach between the Marxist and Lassallean factions widening, the party split. The majority opted to fuse with the Greenback nominee. A body of socialists represented the party at the Greenback convention as fusionists looked to use James B. Weaver's candidacy to ameliorate internal schism.

To some Socialist Laborites, the coming emancipation required a force of arms, including networks of outfitted workingmen tied to the trainband legacies of the bourgeois revolutions. Often formed in order to counter the privatized violence of armed guards and corporate hires, socialist militias won the support of both party hardliners, including Albert Parsons and August Spies, and ethnic Germans who linked militia participation to turnverein traditions. One foreign observer marveled at the organized drilling of not only America's numerous ethnic societies and fraternal organizations, including the Freemasons, the Knights of Pythias, and the GAR, but also its socialist clubs in New York, Cincinnati, San Francisco, and Chicago.[56] Led by the city's Fifth Ward, German socialists in the rapidly industrialized metropolis on Lake Michigan formed the armed "Lehr und Wehr Verein," and others organized the Bohemian Rifles as a part of the Illinois National Guard.[57] In St. Louis, meanwhile, perhaps 200 members of the Socialist Workingmen's Protective Association drilled regularly by 1878.[58] Yet these masculinized "workers' militias" soon proved controversial among both nonsocialist workers, who were reluctant to welcome the red flag of international revolution, as well as rank-and-file SLP members, especially the English-speaking contingent.[59] Proletariat militiamen were eventually shunned within the party and banned by Illinois courts. Despite the radicals' defense on Second Amendment grounds, the 1886 US Supreme Court case *Presser v. Illinois* determined that states had the right to regulate the organization, drilling, and parading of civilian military bodies.

## Soldiers of Social Emancipation

Richard Josiah Hinton's 1894 biography of John Brown superimposed the most incendiary abolitionist renegade onto a new army of liberation. Born in London in 1830, Hinton immigrated to New York City in 1851 and became a committed antislavery journalist and ardent Republican. He sojourned to Bleeding Kansas with other free-state emigrants in the summer of 1856. There he lobbied president-elect Lincoln for the recognition of Haiti as an independent nation, joined the Union army with the outbreak of war, and recruited Black soldiers as an officer in the 2nd Kansas Colored Infantry. Hinton eventually rose to inspector general of the Freedmen's Bureau, serving as a Grant administration appointee during Reconstruction.[60] His politics radicalized further. An SLP delegate in the 1880s, Hinton published extensively on topics ranging from agriculture to Civil War history to radical politics in his native England.[61] When the Social Democratic Party of America, a progenitor of the Socialist Party of America, was founded in 1898, he tried to persuade SLP exiles to join and planned a socialist colony near Cripple Creek, Colorado.[62]

Prior to his study of Brown, the Union veteran had conveyed his views on worker assembly in an 1885 treatise. Claiming that it was difficult for native-born non-wage-earners to comprehend the magnitude of workplace injustice,

Hinton looked to expose the "deep-seated causes" of the "social problem." He believed worker militancy arose in direct proportion to suffering and transgression, urging sympathy with organized labor. Moreover, Hinton insisted that the Knights of Labor possessed a fundamentally American "republican spirit," emphasizing its rejection of strikes, its nonpartisanship, and what he presented as its philosophy of cooperation over agitation. Hinton's attempt at a coherent academic argument for mass labor organization sought to bring trade unionism "out of the twilight of separatism into the daylight of united action and public discussion."[63] This effort to win over the unaligned general public was evident in his Civil War histories.

Published in 1894, *John Brown and His Men* divulged Hinton's historical didacticism. The author confessed to linking the past to the "nobler lines of the American endeavor . . . loftier purposes and higher impulses" in order to advocate a "true democracy." To fail at this, he reasoned, was to enthrone oligarchy and betray the Union cause. "Why should we have fought for the Union," he asked, "if freedom was not our blessed reward?"[64] Just as Marx viewed Lincoln as a "plebian" and model for democratic possibility, Hinton saw in Brown hope for the common classes.[65] He wrote in a class- and race-based dialectic of "slaveocrats," "plutocrats," and the antidemocratic slave and money kings whose obsession with "property rights" masked an unrestrained lust for mastery. Through Hinton, Brown seemed to be motivated by free labor and social democratic impulses, believing, for instance, that slaves were "entitled to all the proceeds of their labor."[66] Chattel slavery simultaneously "enthralled labor" and, through the concentration of wealth and political power, threatened the nation's democratic fabric.[67] Just weeks before his death, Brown wrote that slavery was evil because it perpetuated "uncheered labor" and cruelty toward workers.[68]

To Hinton, if not to Brown, these concepts of moral antislavery and economic egalitarianism were one and inseparable, not only to the free-labor vision but beyond it to a socialist future. As such, Hinton's work was critical of George Washington Brown, Eli Thayer, Charles L. Robinson, and other biographers whom he viewed as assailants of Brown's memory.[69] Although, as governor of Kansas, Robinson had declared Brown the primary inspiration of Union armies, he later became a pointed critic.[70] Likewise, in the aftermath of 1886's Haymarket bombing, Thayer painted Brown as an anti-constitutionalist and nihilistic Garrisonian, tying his legacy to that of a new radicalism in the Middle West: Chicago anarchism. Brown's defenders, and many of William Lloyd Garrison's, insisted correctly that he was no anarchist and no Garrisonian.[71] Hinton avowed that Brown was neither crazy nor unnecessarily fanatical. Rather, he posited that his subject was a man of "clear mentality and spiritual insight" and "lucidity of purpose."[72] Brown was a rational agent, he argued, if a racially leveling, proto-socialist prophet. Brown's assault on Harpers Ferry had been an attack on "the entrenched Slave Power," as well as on the complicit Northern states, "with all their compromising tendencies and commercial needs."[73] The demonization of the martyred abolitionist was the work of "hierarchical forms [of] class and privilege," Hinton explained, suggesting that law and order were the methods of so-called practical men who possessed the luxury of addressing conflicts through conservative and discriminatory bureaucracy.[74] Above all, Hinton's biography served as a vindication of Brown, countering a predominance of white literature during Jim Crow that would downplay Black liberation and portray Brown himself as an irrational actor and a bloodthirsty, crazed militant whose willingness to die on behalf of antislavery principles surely precluded his sanity.

Socialists consistently evoked Brown's radical memory, likening themselves to Wendell Phillips, Elijah P. Lovejoy, and other "agents for the negroes in the fight against chattel slavery," as well as to the union men who "struck for abolition."[75] The United Brotherhood of Carpenters and Joiners of America self-described as a "noble army of mechanics" and part of the "grand army of labor" who sought, like the Union army, to preserve the republic, or at least their version of what it should represent.[76] All socialists were naturally emancipationists, members insisted, and for this second salvation of the Union they quoted slavery's opponents. Heavily German, the United Brotherhood of Carpenters and Joiners of America was founded by SLP spokesman Gustav Luebkert and Lassallean socialist Peter J. McGuire. The purpose of the organization was, according to General Secretary Hugh McGregor, to "throw up an impassable barrier to the return of slavery while it marches forward toward the emancipation of the human race from poverty."[77] The editors of its organ, *The Carpenter*, which ran in both English and German, described laboring people as "armies" of "drilled soldiers," akin to those of Grant and Sherman, whose struggles were nothing short of "battles." They censured both the "industrial slavery" of wage workers and the "modern slavery" of vagrancy laws targeting African Americans.[78] Although *The Carpenter* recounted the War of the Rebellion as "a war against black slavery," editors claimed that "the late war did not abolish slavery; it simply changed its form."[79] They imagined themselves new "slaves," part of a "grand army" of minimum investment, maximum efficiency wage workers—"slaves without the advantages of slavery."[80]

Carpenters memorialized Brown and Lincoln as part of a pro-worker continuation: the outlaw for the working class and the "the son of a poor farmer."[81] Their journals cited Lincoln as not merely a friend of workingmen but a *product of the working class*; in him they found an "agitator" and "leveler" constitutive of the working class.[82] Although (or perhaps because) Lincoln had idealized artisanship republicanism and small capitalist enterprise, workingmen jolted by the transition to heavy machinery, the subdivision of labor, and perpetual wage earning force-fitted the Great Emancipator as their champion. Socialist editors also talked of restoring Lincoln's "dignity of labor"—that of the "village blacksmith" who had owned his own tools of production.[83] Denoting Lincoln's "House Divided" speech, *The Carpenter* republished Henry Demarest Lloyd's avowal that, similarly, the nation cannot survive when only some possess economic freedom, a dilemma remedied by trade unionism and the labor federation.[84] Indeed, carpenters alleged that there were "degrees of slavery" ranging from chattel slavery to "wage slavery" to industrial independence and that, in the vein of the sixteenth president, the organization of craft labor was the most effective remedy against "enslavement."[85]

The key to upending the wage system was to learn and succeed where abolitionists had failed. Urging direct action in the form of boycott, more sanguine carpenters maintained that chattel slavery would have been extirpated without violence had its opponents simply organized to refuse its cash crop yields of cotton, rice, and sugar.[86] Other leaders insisted that the point of an "army of labor" was tactical aggression and emphasized the importance of cohesion within the rank and file: "We cannot all be generals, colonels, or even corporals in the grand army of labor."[87] One Union veteran feared that the "labor question" (that of legal and peaceable organization) would have to be "settled with bullets." "I served three years in the Army of the Potomac to rid the country of the curse of slavery," he explained, avowing that monopolists were the new "slave drivers" and that the conditions of wage labor were approaching those of antebellum bondage.[88] One California union member noted that while Lincoln's Republicans had initially been the "reform party," they had become, through currency legislation and the movement toward trusts, the party that "made us bond slaves instead of chattel slaves" and that only a new "phalanx of reform" could prevent a second civil war.[89]

Yet socialist carpenters also largely urged détente on sectional matters. Knotty issues of slavery, Democratic loyalty, Reconstruction, and the contested presidential election of 1876 should all be halted, one editor contended. Agreeing with Populist senator from Kansas and Union veteran John James Ingalls, he affirmed, "The dead past has buried its dead. Social and economic questions are at front and center."[90] For many workers, this implicit endorsement of class or trade-based North-South rapprochement was an extension of the efforts of previous reformers to remove the bloody shirt as a barrier to worker solidarity. Others foresaw potential pitfalls in attempting to unify labor across regions and races through sectional fence-mending. Some feared that the nostalgia of blue-gray reunion might lead white workers and labor institutions to both absorb and perpetuate the growing trend of sectional reconciliation based on shared whiteness—a trend antithetical to the John Brown of the socialist imagination. In the hands of both radical provocateurs and their adversaries, Brown would become *the* rhetorical device and political symbol of either social disorder or militant antiauthoritarianism.

## Red Rebels

Anarchists and revolutionary socialists further "reddened" the memory of slavery and emancipation. Influenced by the writings of Pierre-Joseph Proudhon, Mikhail Bakunin, and Peter Kropotkin, most American anarchists believed that the domineering capacity of capital derived from the coercive power of the state and its "legal monopolies." This was especially true of communist anarchists and anarcho-syndicalists, who emphasized worker self-activity and advocated replacing the state, which constructed and defended private property, with worker cooperatives based on direct democracy. Some abolitionists, including individualist anarchists Ezra Heywood and Benjamin Tucker, used their experience in the antislavery movement to facilitate their shift toward anarchism.[91] They exploited inflammatory language to back autonomous workers' federations and criticize nonrevolutionary electoralism, sometimes accepting the tactical use of violence and often opposing the eight-hour movement because they deemed trade unions overly gradualist.[92] Many broke with the Federation of Organized Trades and Labor Unions (later the AFL), the SLP, and the Knights of Labor over the establishment and goals of the first May Day and its corresponding wave of strikes in 1886.

Anarchists also supported radical sexual equality. In fact, the International Working People's Association devoted two of its six points to educational equality between the sexes and equal rights without distinction to sex. Formed in London in 1881 in order to succeed the First International, and soon known as the "Black International," the International Working People's Association thrived in Chicago by calling for a "new American revolution."[93] Its women's leadership included Lucy Parsons and Lizzie Swank, assistant editor of *The Alarm* who later founded the Ladies' Federal Labor Union and the Illinois Women's Alliance.[94] A member of the SLP, Swank and others applied revolutionary socialist principles through gender-specific institutions, such as the Chicago Working Women's Union. Portraying both the workplace and the traditional domestic sphere as sites of domination, they mined the slave metaphor, emphasizing the additional oppression that women faced as either lesser paid and under-unionized factory workers, particularly in the garment industry, or paid or unpaid domestic laborers who were at all times subject to arbitrary dismissal.[95] Although anarchists debated ideas as broad as free love and Victorian concepts of marital union, they nevertheless shared with more conservative reformers a common cultural framework germane to the sectional conflict.[96]

Civil War commemoration enabled revolutionaries to Americanize what opponents saw as Old World political fanaticism. As Leon Fink explains, the American anarchist tradition "successfully married itself to a native Garrisonian and John Brown–derived tradition of political terrorism and moral action."[97] Gilded Age anarchism was most affiliated with émigrés from central and eastern Europe, including August Spies, Johann Most, and Alexander Berkman. However, the immediacy of the War for the Union and the presence of military veterans in the anarchist ranks fostered the movement's "native" character in ways that highlighted specifics of slavery and soldiering. While anarchists tapped into an extant militia culture of German *schutzengesellschaften* (shooting clubs) and turnverein (physical fitness) organizations, they also built on associations of uniform-donning old soldiers who met in flag-adorned clubs and fraternal halls, often with their wartime leadership intact.[98] Internationalist in network, anarchists nevertheless appropriated the great domestic agitators, particularly Paine and Jefferson, as well as radical abolitionists, and none more so than John Brown.[99] Even so, and despite Frederick Douglass's warning that "the Negro will become a chemist [bomb maker]" in the face of Jim Crow domination, anarchism remained uncoupled from Black radicalism, making little headway among African Americans owing to the personal racism of some anarchist leaders and, more critically, the movement's near-total failure to address anti-Black racism.[100]

Regardless, these neo-liberators possessed a keen strategic interest in the histories of slavery and emancipation. Albert R. Parsons, who was a teenager when he served in the Confederate military, viewed the fight for control of production as one of "slavery" (the proletariat condition within property-based economic relations) versus "liberty" (the absence of private ownership).[101] Freedom, or the idea of "each his own master," meant flouting a new aristocracy that wielded political control through economic power.[102] This Slave Power to Money Power continuum—the difference between slaves sold *at* the market and slaves sold *in* the market—necessitated "industrial emancipation," or the liberation of economic functions from the capitalist state.[103] Writing on the relative benefit of ballots and bullets in *The Alarm*, Parsons's English-language and Chicago-based publication, one workingman explained that economic royalists supported suffrage and democracy only insomuch as they did not threaten property.[104] In fact, voting was democratic, and thus a radical act, only in the event that voters shared roughly equal economic conditions, as low wages and high hours effectively disenfranchised working people. As such, elections represented a narrow countervailing power. In particular, electoral politics possessed only limited utility as a means of expropriating land, and according to *The Alarm*, capitalists were no more open to the rule of land reformers "than the South to the rule of abolitionists in 1861."[105] "The ballot," one anarchist explained, "cannot strike deeper." Summoning the spirit of 1789, he called on the "Red Flag of Emancipation" to strike off working-class shackles.[106]

Revolutionaries deemed themselves the "New Abolition." Witnessing what they characterized "as real a system of slavery as anything ever endured in the Southern states," *The Alarm* called for "a renewed war against bondage."[107] Old abolitionists turned labor activists compared antislavery with labor tactics.[108] Resistance to "wage slavery" was an antislavery tradition, and militant agitation constituted a "slave revolt" in the vein of antebellum slave uprisings.[109] In addition to the creation of red Nat Turners and red John Browns, the revolutionary veteran-labor coalition grounded its worker cooperation in military terms. Communist anarchists and anarcho-syndicalists explained that social cooperation, more "scientific" than the utopianism of Robert Owen or Charles Fourier and beyond the reformism of Louis Blanc, was worker-controlled production based on meeting human needs. For some, the ultimate model of organization was military service, or what one worker described as the "duty of a soldier to obey orders" and the willingness of armies to "kill and mutilate other men, against whom, individually, they have no grudge."[110] Revolutionaries acknowledged that coordination meant little without the willingness to bring it to bear through mass action. In the case of the "new abolitionists," this meant emancipation from the "master thief" and his monopoly over land and law. "We have fought the battle for liberty," one veteran explained, referring to the War of the Rebellion, "but only in economic emancipation will [workingmen] attain full realization."[111]

To some revolutionary socialist veterans, the labor-industrial struggle was a literal war over property.[112] Chicago radicals insisted that private property was a form of "slavery" because it deprived the propertyless of their "natural birthright" and rendered them dependent on a capricious wage system.[113] According to editors of *The Alarm*, who refrained from denigrating nationalism per se and instead harnessed American patriotism, this conflict between labor and capital was a continuation of the antebellum "property question" and a protraction of "the abolition movement which Phillips and Garrison and John Brown began."[114] Emphasizing the constructedness and injustice of property, these neo-abolitionists, many of them castaway Knights of Labor, posited a novel definition of patriotism that obliterated "arbitrarily defined" national borders to create an international brotherhood dedicated to the destruction of Black *and* white "slavery."[115] Like human bondage in the Old South, revolutionaries deemed legalized property a "ravenous beast" that trampled human rights. As one anarchist explained, "For it jails are built, scaffolds erected, and governments formed."[116]

Veterans turned revolutionaries debated the use of force as a means toward "emancipation." Facing a ruling class with the disposal to arrest and even kill indiscriminately and beyond the law, anarchists, like the Black Power and militant anti-war movements eight decades later, carefully considered the efficacy of violence. Many sanctioned terror tactics, which they deemed self-defense, against especially rapacious owners and politicians and compared factionalism on the issue of force to the tactical differences that arose within immediatist and militant antislavery agitation.[117] Maintaining that a genuine revolutionist must sometimes countenance bloodshed, many anarchists asserted that he who did not resist was "fit only to be a slave."[118] Betraying intra-movement disagreements, future Haymarket defendant Samuel Fielden denounced the eight-hour workday crusade because "slavery" was not a matter of hours worked but of relation to the means of production.[119] And whereas he and others accused nonrevolutionary trade unionists of merely reinforcing a system of dependency, Fielden believed that violent strikers, such as coal miners in Ohio's Hocking Valley in 1884, constituted "the advance guard of a grand army of labor."[120] Activists used the Civil War as evidence that violence responded only to violence, balancing their tactics against those of hard war practitioners Sherman and Phil Sheridan. Like the conflict between blue and gray, this was a war that involved "armies," "battles," "mortal wounds," "scars," and "fortifications." Enemy apparatuses, which sought to "enslave the laborer," included judges, prisons, police forces, and "armies" both private (Pinkertons) and public (the National Guard) armed with Gatling guns and designed to protect the sovereignty of capital. "It is," according to one anarchist, "the slaveholder fighting his last battle for control of his slaves."[121] In the minds of such militants, only the alleged "red terror" could counter the "white terror" of plutocracy and its partners within the state.[122] Insisting that the very control of capital (and thus political power) *was* a form of violence and that forceful resistors were merely responding to existing victimization, revolutionaries presaged C. L. R. James's maxim with regard to Haiti's "Black Jacobins" that "the cruelties of property and privilege are always more ferocious than the revenges of poverty and oppression. . . .

For the one aims at perpetuating resented injustice, the other is merely a momentary passion soon appeased."[123]

Socialists deemed the Haymarket martyrs the ultimate emancipators. Executed by the state of Illinois in the fall of 1887 for their alleged role in the fatal bombing in Chicago's Haymarket Square on May 4, 1886, the five defendants were rebels against "slavery" and the "bravest apostles of liberty that ever lived."[124] Fielden, an English immigrant and lay preacher, described the aftermath of strikes and rioting at the McCormick Reaper Works as nonviolent as workers and labor leaders rallied in the city's West Side to advocate a reduced workday. "Socialists are not going to declare war; but I tell you war has been declared on us," the former teamster proclaimed.[125] In fact, the Haymarket meeting proved so subdued that Mayor Carter Harrison famously walked home before the rally had even adjourned. Although the demonstration had been nonbelligerent, someone in the crowd detonated a metal-based dynamite bomb that rocked the square just as Fielden, the last speaker to take the stage that evening, stepped down from the podium. Seven policemen and four workers soon lay dead, and Fielden and seven other agitators (only two of whom were present at the rally) were convicted of conspiracy. This judgment was returned despite a spirited defense that incorporated "antislavery heritage." The anarchists' "abolitionist" council was led by Union hero and Congressional Medal of Honor recipient William P. Black and his associates John Swinton, veteran and freethinker Robert Ingersoll, and Lyman Trumbull, formerly a Republican senator and coauthor of the Thirteenth Amendment.[126] While Knight leadership quickly distanced themselves from the prisoners, Chicago anarchists dedicated Memorial Day 1888 to the memory of the dead: August Spies, Adolph Fischer, George Engel, Louis Lingg, and Albert Parsons.[127]

Parsons in particular had self-defined as a "new abolitionist." Born in Montgomery, Alabama, Parsons was just thirteen when he volunteered with a group of Confederate irregulars in Texas, the Lone Star Grays. His older brother had risen to the rank of colonel in the 12th Texas Cavalry, and Albert eventually joined Parsons's Mounted Volunteers. With the Confederacy laid low, Parsons returned to Waco. There the teenager married Lucia "Lucy" Eldine Gonzalez, a former slave of African, Native American, and Mexican ancestry who would become a prominent revolutionary and founding member of the IWW. Parsons, a Republican scalawag and editor of *The Spectator*, which endorsed "the political rights of the colored people," was branded by Democratic opponents a "political heretic and traitor."[128] This ostracism led him to migrate to the Middle West in 1873 where, according to Jacqueline

Jones, "it was not a great leap from denunciations of chattel slavery and the planter class in the rural South to denunciations of 'wage slavery' and the capitalist class in the urban North."[129]

Parsons's Chicago was a mosaic of ethnic stratification, racialized boundaries, and labor division. By 1885, workers in Illinois were roughly 33 percent German, 19 percent Irish, 12 percent Scandinavian, 10 percent British, and 5 percent Polish, Czech, and Italian. Only 21 percent were English-speaking and native-born.[130] Viewing their own immediate material conditions as paramount, many workers surely agreed with the numerous labor leaders, radicals and reformers alike, who alleged that "wage slavery" was more exploitative than chattel slavery and made no consideration for the anti-Black legacy of bondage.[131] Such authorities utilized martial rhetoric to rouse solidarity and employed antislavery vernacular to provide a patriotic cultural framework through which foreign-born laborers, including those who were not "white on arrival," might assimilate into the movement. This meant that "conditionally white" workers from Europe quickly grasped the premium that US society placed on being "not Black." Management exploited this "not quite white" idea to impose hierarchy, separation, and competition, leading to the persistence of nationalism and racial segregation within the labor tradition.[132]

Parsons possessed an alternate social vision, despite his "race neutral" approach to organizing. In Chicago he adopted socialist and, later, anarchist politics, joining the Knights of Labor and representing the Workingmen's Party during the Great Railroad Strike.[133] As he gained national publicity, Parsons proved an important symbol: a "'typical' American in a movement filled with immigrants" who, according to Michael Kazin, was able to "spin a powerful narrative about his conversion from ignorant 'wage-slave' to apostle of freedom."[134] Soon a speaking circuit regular, Parsons deployed war memory to foment revolution. In Indianapolis on July 4, 1876, he used the nation's centennial to damn the "Aristocrats of Capital" who "brought the last civil war on our country to abolish black slavery, but left wage slavery as it was, while augmenting its ever-increasing cruelty."[135] Speaking to a crowd of 30,000 in Chicago's Market Square on July 23 the following year, the day before the Great Strike, Parsons bemoaned the supreme paradox that the capital consolidation that had been in some sense an outgrowth of Union victory now reduced proud old soldiers to a "Grand Army" of hunger and material deprivation.[136] Although the GAR had not yet reached the peak of its political influence, he acknowledged that many of its members were once again browbeaten, not by Confederate guns but by the private violence of industrialists. Declaring that Union veterans constituted a "Grand Army of

Starvation," Parsons urged worker-veterans to instead enroll their names in the "Grand Army of Labor."[137]

The Civil War profoundly shaped Parsons's worldview. Terming the condition of workingmen "enslavement by capital," he discovered "a great similarity between the abuse heaped upon poor people by the organs of the rich and the actions of the late Southern slave holders in Texas toward newly enfranchised slaves" and linked the failure of "40 acres and a mule" during Reconstruction to the capitalist system's propensity to protect and aggregate the resources of those in power. Portraying his radicalism as a "homegrown impulse," Parsons summoned the legacies of the American Revolution and the Slaveholders' Rebellion, avowing that whereas previous Americans had delivered themselves from political oppression, working people were now obliged to "liberate themselves from economic bondage." Having no doubt encountered this "third American revolution" narrative during his time with the Knights, Parsons now viewed anarchism as the vehicle for such change, as it was the "advance guard in the impending social revolution" against "industrial slavery," committed to the "up-lifting and emancipation of the wage-worker." "My enemies in the southern states consisted of those who oppressed the black slave," he explained. "My enemies in the north are among those who would perpetuate the slavery of the wage workers."[138]

Antislavery vernacular remained a valuable tool in Parsons's rhetorical arsenal while on the stump. In South Bend, Indiana, he censured the use of veterans to quell labor agitation and underscored the irony that capitalists now employed the men of a former army of freedom to impose a new form of "slavery." Parsons recalled how "the Grand Army of the Republic, which twenty-five years ago, drew its sword to liberate the black chattel slave from bondage, came to South Bend, and with gleaming bayonets and flashing swords riveted the chains of slavery upon wage-laborers and compelled them to submit to the dictation of the property beasts."[139] Meanwhile, the opposition press fearfully compared Lucy Parsons to anarcho-feminist Louise Michel, the "Red Virgin" of the Paris Commune. Parsons nevertheless used her forum as an investigative journalist for *The Socialist* to denounce the abuse of poverty-stricken Union veterans by Chicago's "slaveocracy."[140]

The prosecution's success in the Haymarket trial involved placating a friendly judge and convincing the jury—a jury from which union members were excluded—that Albert Parsons and the other so-called conspirators were not merely revolutionaries but raving, homicidal "dynamiters."[141] Alleging that intimations of violence were merely "expressions of ideas," Parsons explained that anarchists "do not make the revolution . . . they prophesize its coming."[142] He imagined himself on some level an inheritor of political tradition, quoting Thomas Jefferson and Patrick Henry (as well as John Brown) during the trial. Proposing leniency, Parsons's defenders highlighted what they adjudged as elements of fundamental Americanism within the anarchist cause, including freedom of speech and assembly and political resistance to perceived tyranny. Amid clemency pleas from as far away as Europe, federal amnesty toward former Confederates was also used as a precedent by which Parsons and the other convicts should be exonerated. Appealing directly to Terence Powderly in August 1886, Parsons claimed that the principles of socialism and anarchism were the same as those of the Knights: "the abolition of the wage-slave system" through "open rebellion against class rule."[143] Even AFL president Samuel Gompers asserted that if Jefferson Davis could be pardoned, so could a handful of men whose only crimes were their words and associations.[144]

Apologists painted Parsons and the other defendants as neo–John Browns. The antislavery martyr offered a salient point of comparison, even if the Haymarket litigants had not actually committed violence. One editor reminded readers that although Brown had been stamped as a criminal in 1859, popular memory had transformed him into an idol. Believing that while Parsons had "erred in detail," the editor pointed out that his broader aim of a "just and right condition of the workingman" was analogous to the righteousness of Brown's ambitions.[145] Another held that the Brown-Parsons resemblance was a false parallel, as Brown had gone to Harpers Ferry with the express purpose of breaking the law and the Chicago accused had not.[146] At a lecture delivered to New York's Ethical Society in Chickering Hall, Professor Felix Adler weighed the Chicago anarchists against Brown's legacy. "Today the revolutionists of extreme type quote John Brown's words and look to him as a patron saint," Adler explained. "They look to the means he used to inaugurate the emancipation of the slaves and claim that they are his disciples, following in his footsteps." Agreeing with the noble ends but not the violent means, he predicted that, unlike Brown, society would not come to endorse the aims of the anarchists. Yet Adler also concluded that the distinction between militant abolitionists and anarchists was "not obvious," as both had foregone the capacity for reform through peaceful, democratic means and sought instead to use targeted violence to improve society and "break the shackles of the slaves."[147]

It was for naught. Parsons was executed by hanging on November 11, 1887, and laid to rest in Chicago's Waldheim Cemetery with the red flag of revolution draped across his chest. In death, Parsons was further canonized as a "second John Brown."[148] In an essay titled "John Brown, Anarchist," written for the anarchist journal *Mother Earth* in 1907, Nicholas Kopeloff insinuated that abolitionists and all radical opponents of injustice were the original anarchists. He compared his subject to the martyred Parsons: "The difference between John Brown and the Chicago Anarchists is but this, the former lived, worked, and died for the liberation of the negro; the latter did the same for the modern white slave."[149] The *Mother Earth* founder, the famed anarchist-feminist Emma Goldman, made the same analogy in 1912, claiming Brown and Parsons as true "American revolutionists" willing to die for their ideals.[150] Paeans matched Parsons with militant antislavery figures from William Lloyd Garrison to David Walker; Benjamin F. Butler deemed him a victim of "judicial murder"; and Dyer Daniel Lum protested that he had been "strangled to death by the state."[151] Editors of London's *The Anarchist* considered Parsons's hanging more heinous than the crucifixion of Jesus Christ and "worse than the murder of John Brown . . . for it was supposed to be done by free men, and not slaveholders."[152] For his part, John Brown Jr., the son of the sainted abolitionist, claimed that both he and his father possessed a "Socialistic or Communistic faith" ingrained in Christ's teachings and as such had petitioned for a commutation of Parsons's sentence.[153] In a testament to the metaphorical power of Parsons as an abolitionist, as well as to the fundamental Americanness of the Haymarket martyrs, prairie poet Carl Sandburg later equated Parsons with freedom fighters of historical importance in his verse on his friend Eugene Debs: "Over in Valhalla, if Valhalla is not demolished, rebuilt, / renamed, he speaks at ease with Garrison, John Brown, / Albert Parsons, Spartacus."[154]

It was an appraisal that Parsons and other red republican progeny would have likely endorsed. Anarchists, Marxist industrial unionists, and revolutionary socialists alike conceived their causes as extensions of Gustave Paul Cluseret's radical democratic internationalism—pushing the radical boundaries of antislavery vernacular despite ideological, ethnic, and class divergences between and within their movements. This linking of slavery not merely to monopoly or corporate capitalism but to property itself held stark symbolic resonance. For one Socialist Laborite the choice was clear: "Either Socialism and Freedom, or Capitalism and Slavery."[155] Yet Parsons and others who conceptualized a left future never entirely discarded the vision, much less the stylings, of the Radical Republicans, as antislavery continued to influence the socialist imagination.[156] Meanwhile, Debs, who had fully radicalized by reading Laurence Gronlund, Karl Kautsky, and Karl Marx during his jail stint in Woodstock, Illinois, following the Pullman Strike, abandoned the conservatism of the Brotherhood of Locomotive Firemen and its emphases on sobriety and respectability politics.[157] With the fracturing of the SLP in 1899, Debs's organizations, the Socialist Party of America and the IWW, would further perpetuate ties between twentieth-century socialism and nineteenth-century abolitionism. By 1900, members drew on cultural politics following the Socialist Labor schism over whether to wage "political war" or "economic war" against capitalism. The goal of local socialist bodies became, according to former SLP member Julius Hammer, to "man the guns" while the national network helped "supply the ammunition" to be used against capital's "huge army of lackeys and labor fakirs." The aim was not to suppress militancy in favor of electoral legitimacy or political respectability but to foster "a Socialist army . . . a class-conscious army" as part of a "war for social emancipation."[158] Trade union halls, labor homes, third party stumps, and workshop floors became critical sites of the production of Civil War memory, where history and identity were created and regenerated. Even as a new farmer-labor party intent on blue-gray populism took shape in the early 1890s, the construction of a "red Civil War" would in time serve as a commemorative template for how future socialists connected the antislavery project and the Union cause to their designs for class-based transformation.

CHAPTER 5

# The Blue-Gray Campaign

## Populism and White Reunion

IGNATIUS L. DONNELLY saw the menace of corporate supremacy as something like a civil war. Once a fierce opponent of slavery, the self-proclaimed "father of the Populist Party" was concerned that the power of an undemocratic minority *still* endangered the existence of the republic.[1] A congressman during the Civil War era, Donnelly personified the arc from Radical Republican to Liberal Republican and from Greenbacker to Populist. A lawyer, novelist, and amateur scientist, he was perhaps best known as a science fiction author. Yet by the culminating decade of the nineteenth century, Donnelly feared the social reality of industrial capitalism far more than any imaginary world. His 1890 novel, *Caesar's Column: A Story of the Twentieth Century*, like the popular works of Edward Bellamy or Jack London, was of a popular trend of utopian and dystopian parables. A modernist and an eccentric, Donnelly, who would go on to write the famous preamble of the People's Party platform in 1892, linked the republican farmer with the Civil War veteran. He imagined 1988 as a future ruled by oligarchs, where farmers were no longer the "honest yeomanry" that had once made up the "armies . . . of Grant and Sherman."[2] One of the novel's property-leveling characters even threatens to abolish all corporations, comparing his strategy to that of Lincoln's Preliminary Emancipation Proclamation, in which the president gave Southern planters a window to adopt free labor ("break up their monopolies") or subject themselves to wholesale property confiscation. To Donnelly, the war demonstrated "how impossible it is, by any process of reasoning, to induce a privileged class to peacefully yield up a single tittle."[3]

Daring to "invoke the power of the nation, as was done in the great civil war of 1861," Donnelly and other Populists employed war memories to imagine a more cooperative variety of capitalism centered on greater democratic participation and economies of scale.[4] They drew from a shared past, to be sure, their ideas often grounded in tradition. Yet modernity and progress were essential to Populist reform, with the war and its aftermath spawning the backdrop for the profound changes in American life during the final quarter of the nineteenth century.[5] "Invocations of the past (as traditions) may occur as a means of resisting change or of achieving innovations," Michael Kammen contends, and Populists habitually called forth the sectional conflict to construct an "ethos of modernity."[6] Populism placed soldiers and veterans, as well as conceptions of bondage and liberation, in the service of sectional reconciliation along class or trade lines. This rapprochement often reinforced the existing racial hierarchy even as it created new prospects for Black political participation and challenged the Democratic Party cartel in the South.

Insisting that the political economy rested on power, not an "invisible hand," Populists crafted a philosophy of history rooted in both anti-elitism and the morality of labor. They co-opted a range of historical and ideological precedents: the Protestant work ethic, the protest of Thomas Paine, Jeffersonian agrarianism, Jacksonian democracy, transcendentalist self-reliance and virtue, and antislavery and free labor inheritances.[7] Both the utopian and conspiratorial intimations of early Republicans, who had offered small-scale capitalism as an alternative to both permanent wage labor and the slaveholding cabal, penetrated the Populist mind. All of these overlapping, reinforcing, and often disparate and contradictory identities were filtered through the violent upheaval of war and Reconstruction. The result was a form of democracy conceived, promoted, and communicated in the language of section, slavery, race, and social violence. Populism was ultimately defeated from without, by fraud, corruption, and coercion on the part of Bourbon Democrats, as well as from within, unable to resolve its ideological inconsistencies. The Populist movement's complicated collective remembrance highlights its failure to pacify, much less overcome, the deep racial and sectional contradictions that still radiated from the war years despite widening class divisions.

Civil War memory informed the currents and contradictions of Populist thought. Beginning with the Grange, Greenbacker, and Readjuster movements, veterans turned agrarian reformers—even many white Southerners—painted themselves as neo-abolitionists fighting economic enslavement. They often combined antislavery vernacular with conceptions of social and scientific progress. Courting (often understandably reluctant) African Americans and white Northerners and rejecting states' rights white supremacy, Populism's basic tenets and political strategies repudiated the Lost Cause.

Yet the People's Party's 1892 "blue-gray" presidential ticket of Union veteran James B. Weaver and former Confederate James Field was part of a cultural vehicle predicated on national reunion. In fact, the movement was profoundly shaped by the far-reaching trends of white reconciliation that swept through the American scene in the 1890s.[8] Imagining a country unified around the principles of producerism, democratization, and state activism, Populist representatives sought to transcend sectional issues and commonly rebuked leaders and publications that appealed to wartime division.[9] The hyper-patriotism of reunion also helped stave off possible attacks by opponents who, either in rhetoric or reality, saw Populists as American Communards.[10]

However, exploited by Democrats in the South and Republicans in the North, the upstart party's anti-sectional approach was poisoned by regional cleavages, party alignments, and loyalty litmus tests. While North-South issues might be circumvented by emphasizing class or vocational solidarity or old regional antagonisms of South and West against East, racial divisions could not be skirted or squelched. Although an effective and permanent coalition required the complete partnership of fully equal nonwhite laborers, Populist-style reconciliation often reinforced the color line even as it defied the Solid South and created new possibilities for Black political engagement. Once again, "whiteness" sabotaged solidarity. Attempting to nullify sectionalism through white-dominant reunion motifs while simultaneously promoting unity among farmers and workers created a commemorative incongruity that overlooked immigrant workers in the North and domineered African American farmers in the South. This political exclusion—demonstrated culturally—undermined the potential for broad, sustained class cohesion across racial and spatial boundaries.[11] Ultimately, the fraudulent and sometimes violent overthrow of Populism and fusionism restored two-party stability nationally and one-party rule in the South, facilitating both Jim Crow and an even whiter and more reactionary brand of sectional reunion.

## An Alliance of Old Soldiers

Sprung from the electoral drive of the Farmers' Alliance and its Ocala Platform of December 1890, the People's Party, commonly known as the Populists, emerged during the pivotal decade of white reconciliation. Although the Alliance furthered what James B. Weaver had called "the restoration of the South to fraternal feelings," sectionalism regularly burst forth as Agricultural Wheel and Alliance reformers wielded the Lost Cause and downtrodden veteran tropes. Using Confederate identity and concomitant whiteness as a binding agent risked fracturing class unity by conjoining struggling tenant and yeoman farmers with wealthy planters. It also potentially ostracized whole swaths of former Unionists in Southern states.[12] Combating sectionalism within agrarian movements, Alliance leaders urged a broader federation of workingmen, envisioning a party that might unite former Greenbackers, Knights of Labor, and Alliancemen, underpinned by the imagery of the old soldier.[13] Beginning with state party formation in Kansas and the Dakotas in 1889 and pressed by labor leaders including Terence V. Powderly, a faction of Alliancemen began seeking electoral substitutes. Having seen their numbers fall due in part to a lack of policy commitment from their Democratic Party representatives, Alliance members began to advocate for a national alternative to the Democrats.[14] The resulting People's Party proved more an association of reformers and industrial organizations than an archetypical political party.[15] Unanimously elected president of the Southern Alliance at Indianapolis in November 1891, Leonidas L. Polk commanded the loyalty of both Southern party leadership and Confederate veterans, such as Reuben Kolb of Alabama, and the rank and file of yeoman whites, many of whom had fought in the war.[16]

Opponents branded it "Jacobinism," "socialism," or "communism," using slurs once reserved for abolitionists and Yankee carpetbaggers, but Populism defied neat characterization.[17] Though appeals to a Black-white "harmony of interests" and professed "social equality" proved constant sources of tension, class and race power dynamics in fact varied by state, region, and community.[18] Populism is best categorized as an extension of the anti-monopolist left. However, its ranks included freethinkers, nonconformists, spiritualists, agnostics, utopians, prohibitionists, and assorted socialists and Christians.[19] With radicals having repudiated the laissez-faire chimera, which was by the 1890s a conservative and elitist aspiration, Populists sought freedom *from* fickle market forces. Reanimating preindustrial notions of independence, they proposed leveraging the democratic power of the state in pursuit of greater economic (and therefore political) autonomy for small farmers, shopkeepers, and workingmen. Such reform represented a "speedy return to the good old Democratic and Republican times which our martyred Lincoln established."[20] Richard Hofstadter believed Populism the climax of a long, "popular rebellion" that combined republican, democratic, and provincial elements in response to the rapid economic and demographic change wrought by industrial capitalism. But this resistance to certain facets of commercial change—the "soft" side of the farmers' "dual character"—derived from understandings of free labor.[21]

Indeed, although Populism contained both traditional and romantic notions of agrarianism that often obscured the hard commercial realities of changing technology, increased production, and land and capital concentration, most Populists in fact harnessed Civil War memory in the service of what they considered modernity and progress. Populists created new appeals to veterans, swiveling from both the bloody shirt and bourgeois reconciliation based primarily on the interests of the white middle and managerial classes. Like the Greenbackers, they defined their ideology as one transcending both corrupt partisan factions, outmoded party ideologies, and rancorous sectional divisions—one that united "producers" under a "true Republicanism" that combined Jeffersonian independence, Jacksonian democracy, and Lincolnian economic leveling.[22] As the first national political movement to insist explicitly that the federal government was an agent of positive freedom that had specific obligations to common people, Populism sponsored what Charles Postel describes as a "dramatic expansion of government regulation and control in the country's economic life."[23] Whereas John D. Hicks deemed Populism "the final defeat of the American farmer," others saw "success through failure" in the movement's eventual influence on Progressive Era reforms.[24]

Whiteness complicated this pursuit of modernity. Although Reconstruction had collapsed a decade and a half prior, perhaps a majority of legally eligible Southern Blacks still voted in the late 1880s and early 1890s, and they remained overwhelmingly loyal to the party of Lincoln, Grant, and Douglass.[25] Black people held considerable political power in eastern Virginia and North Carolina and in parts of the South Carolina Low Country, resulting in "low-key" yet subversive attempts by Populists to win Black votes, sometimes accompanied by radical interracial gestures.[26] Appealing to the materiality of farmers, white Populists often falsely believed that their interests and those of African Americans were identical. Some supported class-based cooperation only to impugn "unnatural" racial egalitarianism; many advocated political but not social equality between the races; and still others warned that interracial alliance would convert fundamentally conservative farmers into dangerous radicals.[27] When Blacks sat on Populist state councils and served as delegates to the national convention, a few white members viewed federal intervention as a way to protect their vulnerable comrades; others, as a repeat of the federal "intrusion" of Reconstruction. The party also divided largely along racial lines over the Lodge Force Bill, which would have permitted federal intervention to protect African American voters in the South.[28] As they had in the Colored National Labor Union and the Colored Farmers' Alliance, African American Populists ultimately carved out space within the white-dominated national framework, meeting in simultaneous or segregated conventions and rallies.

This tension between reactionary and radical impulses, and between the interracial rhetoric of the "democratic promise" and cynical political expediency and adherence to the color line, created deep organizational and ideological cleavages.[29] It was evident as early as the spring of 1892 that the movement was split between conservative and progressive forces, between leaders who wished to make silver a "single issue" and those who sought broader reforms through stronger alliances with socialists and interracial labor. As one union member explained in the American Railway Union's *Railway Times*, "I am a Populist from core to rind . . . [but] I do not believe that free coinage of silver and gold is all that the working millions want in this land of the poor and the home of the slave."[30] Despite the limitations and emerging contradictions within the Populist coalition, American Railway Union leader Eugene Debs, whose own Populist presidential candidacy failed to launch in 1896, defended the socialist position within the party and argued that, at the very least, the movement offered workers a greater opportunity than either the Republicans or Democrats to "vote their way from slavery to emancipation."[31]

Populism certainly proved an emancipatory force for countless rural women. Although they entered the Populist ranks for many of the same reasons men did, women built their movement on the intellectual and organizational edifice of abolitionism, women's rights, the Woman's Christian Temperance Union, and the Grange. The Farmers' Alliance in particular had afforded a Populist blueprint by providing women with equal membership, voting, and office-holding rights. Like men, Populist women sought greater economic freedom, but many were especially attuned to matters of political representation, financial dependency, and liberation from the double duty of both childcare and domestic labor in addition to grueling field work. For this reason, the novelist Hamlin Garland argued that no movement in US history, including antislavery, had appealed to women quite like Populism.[32] Led by celebrated orators, including Mary Elizabeth Lease, Populist women debated and broke apart over questions of suffrage, temperance, and their role within or outside gendered "spheres." They also participated in and benefited from the party's construction of cultural memory. Especially attuned to the power of history, exaggeration, and emotion, Populist author and lecturer Sarah E. Van De Vort Emery wrote of "new kinds of slavery" that had surfaced after the Civil War.[33] Texan and plantation mistress turned reformer Bettie Gay agreed, asserting that women's liberation entailed "acknowledging no master."[34] In addition to antislavery tropes, women added their own particulars to pervasive Civil War analogies. Churchwomen spoke of "wage slavery." Suffragists summoned Garrisonian abolitionism. Farm women in the Great Plains, pressured in the Populist newspaper columns not to stray from domestic matters, publicly hoped for a "second Abraham Lincoln" who might emancipate them from the "shackles" of toil.[35]

In nominally aspiring to liberate laborers of both sexes, Populists repurposed the regional language of antebellum Westerners and wartime Peace Democrats, pitting the more agrarian and extractive South, West, and Northwest against the financial East. This Yankee appraisal excoriated the East's wealth stratification, ethnic pluralism, and supposed dearth of republicanism. It was also part of a larger cultural critique between Eastern and Western and urban and rural America dating to the First Party System.[36] Proffering Westernness as an alternative to sectionalism, Populists viewed Southern and Western political alignment as a way to balance the economic advantages of the Northeast.[37] Others insisted simply that Western or Southern men best exemplified the agrarian, anti-monopoly, and producerist qualities of the nascent party.[38] As Edward L. Ayers maintains, "The farmers turned the language of town arrogance into a defiant language of agrarian pride and resistance."[39] Populist songs reinforced the political kinship of region, arguing that while Northern "gold bugs" and "Carnegie hires" dreamed of the South and West bending in submission, Populist "armies" were certain to sweep them from the field.[40] Former Republican and Greenbacker George S. Bowen, an Illinoisan who had built his reputation supplying clothes to the Union army, regarded Populism a continuation of Jeffersonian agrarianism and termed the party's electorate the "producers of the West and South."[41] Defending those his opponents termed "ignorant western voters," he maintained that the sections were misaligned and that Populists simply sought to "restore more equitable and just conditions throughout the country—east and west, north and south."[42]

This Populist reification of the imagined North-South binary culminated in the West in 1892, first at the party's organizing convention in St. Louis, then at its "Blue-Gray Reunion" in Omaha, Nebraska, on the Fourth of July. Promising to restore government to "the plain people," the party platform declared that the nation "cannot be pinned together by bayonets; that the Civil War is over, and that every passion and resentment which grew out of it must die with it."[43] The party's blue-gray presidential ticket of Kansas congressman and former Union general James B. Weaver with Virginian and Confederate veteran James G. Field challenged the New South's white Democratic power structure. So did African Americans who served as convention delegates. Highlighting the new politics of "wage slavery" (or any species of class politics) naturally demanded downplaying the old politics of sectional division.[44] Yet in attempting to eclipse the politics of section through a

FIGURE 5. "People's Party Candidates for President and Vice President, 1892." Linking farm and factory, North and South, Union veteran and Confederate veteran, Populist imagery tended to underscore "brother toilers" (farmer and labor organizations) and sectional amity. (Library of Congress)

white-dominant reconciliation that ignored the African American experience (emancipationism) or explicitly reinforced New South racial ideology, white Populists undercut the possibility of transcending the politics of whiteness. And when Black and white interracialists made either pragmatic or sincere efforts to overcome the color line in the name of class or trade mutuality, elite white institutions and racial reactionaries both outside and within the party responded with racial dog whistles and sectional rancor.

Alliance weeklies anticipated the Populist moment by the time the St. Louis convention met in February 1892.[45] Pronouncing the movement a "revolution," the once reluctant Leonidas L. Polk now endorsed the creation of a new party, with Knights of Labor leadership, including Powderly, looking on.[46] In doing so, Polk expunged the North-South cultural partition through an alliance of workers in the West, the South, and the Northwest.[47] From the gaze of Wall Street and anti-silver Grover Cleveland men in New York, this alignment against the East smacked of radical insurrection, and not without merit. People's Party newspaper titles—the *Comrade*, the *Revolution*, the *Agitator*, the *Tiller and Toiler*—combined American and English agrarianism and Fabianism with the ideology of Revolutionary America and France to form a new political vocabulary. The Populists' producerist vanguard of Alliance farmers, Knights, and the blue and the gray backed silver coinage, a graduated income tax, a postal savings bank, and the abolition of foreign and "excessive" corporate land ownership. Their platform proposed the nationalization of the telegraph, telephone, and railroad industries while leaving woman suffrage up to individual states. Party leaders were direct in their appeal to class, avowing that wealth belongs to those who toil and that interests and enemies of rural laborers were the same as those of urban workers.[48] The official Alliance history adopted in St. Louis was subtitled *The Impending Revolution*, and Thomas E. Watson of Georgia titled the party's campaign book *Not a Revolt; It Is a Revolution*. Indeed, Populists hyperbolized to defy assumptions about section and, oftentimes, race. Capsizing traditional understandings of white reconciliation and the Solid South—in effect challenging white power—meant that Populists often faced economic boycott, job or credit loss, personal and familial ostracism, and violent reprisal in the process.[49]

The St. Louis conference also spotlighted Civil War veterans. While some delegates, for whom the wounds of the 1860s were still raw, slung sectional mud, various overtures to old soldiers became part of the movement's culture.[50] Populists reasoned that the soldiers and victims of the late war were mostly farmers and farmers' sons, and too many were now "dead, pensioned, or on starvation wages."[51] Blunt sectionalism proved a calculated risk, as pro-Confederate Populists hazarded estranging expedient Black allies. Though

Polk rejected sectional politics, many members remained proud of their service in the Confederacy, adhering to basic Lost Cause tenets.[52] At the same time, Northerners who exploited the "Treasury of Virtue" against class enemies ran the risk of alienating national audiences. More commonly, white Populists framed emancipation as a gift bestowed by Union soldiers. At the People's Convention of Kansas's Second Congressional District in July 1890, A. F. Allen of Douglas County spoke of a "grand army of free Americans . . . forming to down the other slave power that is now seeking to enslave the toiling and laboring masses." Allen claimed that the war's primary legacy, Black liberation, had been achieved by workingmen: "The toilers and laborers of this country rescued this nation from the grip of the powers of American African slavery."[53]

Though engaged in a general shared struggle to transform the political economy, agrarians and socialists debated issues, jockeyed for leverage, and endeavored to find common ground. While socialists saw Populism as too agrarian and middle-class, that the two groups vied for the same members and votes is a testament to Populism's radicalism.[54] Polk's *Progressive Farmer*, for one, confronted monopoly and worker alienation through a materialism that Marxists would have recognized. Arguing that the interests of capital and labor were only accommodatable through worker gains, editors published soft socialist tracts, including Oscar Wilde's "The Soul of Man under Socialism," which deplored the "slavery of the machine." Once again, socialism was framed as "emancipation from Tyranny" and a means toward what Wilde described in London's *Fortnightly Review* as "true individualism": the security and leisure time of each person to cultivate their own interests and individuality.[55] The good of socialism, another author proposed, was the "restoration to man of his best use of the earth."[56] Although this notion of socialism as a restorative system resonated more with utopians than with Marxists in the Knights of Labor, it served as a bridge between Polk's disgruntled farmers and their intraclass brethren in the North's expanding megalopolises and between old soldiers. According to one Iowa journalist, the War for the Union had laid the foundation for the People's Party by "obliterating" sentimentality in favor of questions of economic power and interests. Such questions bled into nearly every corner of Populist thought.[57]

Despite its occasional red hue, Populism proved a rare example of late nineteenth-century radicalism that opponents struggled to pillory as imported, foreign, or "un-American." This was true in part because members so often linked their movement to the national bloodletting of 1861–65.[58] Former Greenbacker T. A. Bland viewed Populism in the vein of radical Antifederalists: anti-Hamiltonian, anti-English, and anti–"slave oligarchy."

But it was also innovative, using science and policy experts to apply logic and fairness to economic relations. To Bland, the Civil War had concentrated capital and political power among bankers and industrialists, as war debt was used to transfer wealth "out of the pockets of producing classes, into the pockets of non-producing classes." Yet the forward-thinking People's Party represented the Republican ideal reborn: political democracy and rough egalitarianism established on empiricism, modernity, and deeply American values. The party system that emerged was neither republican nor democratic, but "Monopolistic and Plutocratic." Nationalization of industries was more than smart policy; it was patriotic.[59]

Reconciliation played an even more pronounced role when party leaders met again four months later in Omaha. Volunteers displayed an ensign inscribed "The Blue and the Gray of the People's Party," while Paul Vandervoort, former GAR commander in chief, planned a national reunion of Union and Confederate veterans. Decrying the "money kings" of the "two Wall Street parties," protected by private armies of "Pinkerton bullets," labor-veterans mirrored Lincoln's oratory of the "government of the people, by the people, and for the people."[60] A brass band played familiar patriotic (and trans-sectional) tunes, including "Yankee Doodle," the "Star-Spangled Banner," and "Dixie," amid a packed Omaha Coliseum of roughly 10,000 participants. In addition to blue-gray comity, farmer and labor fused as Knights occupied various party committees and leadership roles.[61] Populists cited wartime emancipation as a precursor to the liberation of labor, comparing agrarian reformers and their attacks on the Money Power to how abolitionists had attacked the Slave Power prior to the Civil War.[62] In parts of the South, the People's Party was alternately known as the "Blue and Gray Party."[63]

The ticket frontrunner was Union veteran Walter Q. Gresham, a judge whom Middle Western Populists naturally paired with Lincoln. Born in Harrison County, Indiana, just upriver from Lincoln's boyhood home in Spencer County, Gresham practiced law in Corydon and New Albany, joined the newborn Republican Party, and won election to the Indiana House of Representatives in a majority Democratic district. During the war he served with distinction as an officer in Ulysses S. Grant's Army of the Tennessee and was wounded during the Atlanta campaign. His credentials and political connections cemented, he held various court and cabinet positions after the war. By the 1890s, Gresham's Populist admirers argued that his nomination would thankfully require him to abandon the party of emancipation, which was "banking on its old time record" of destroying slavery, even though "common people" now had no voice in "the Party of Lincoln and Grant."[64] Contending that "the Aristocracy of Wealth stands in the same position as the Aristocracy of Slaveholders in 1861," patrons trumpeted Gresham as a champion of "plain people," often presumably white. They hoped that a new emancipator of an upstart party might do for the producing classes what Republicans had done for chattel slaves.[65] One booster predicted simply that Gresham would "be to present political, financial, and industrial conditions what Abraham Lincoln was to human slavery."[66]

But to many Southern Populists, Gresham—a Republican, Union veteran, and "new Lincoln" from Indiana—had a sectional problem. On the other hand, despite being a Confederate veteran, Polk had leadership experience and ideological appeal both within and beyond the South, making him another party darling. Populism's anti-sectionalism and courting of Black voters forced Polk and other Confederate veterans to reject the Lost Cause credo even as they backed the racial order of Henry W. Grady's New South. One Boston editor believed that, unlike Gresham, who did leave the Republican Party later in 1892, Polk was popular in the West, the Northwest, and the South. Polk was therefore the only man who could break the "Solid South" from Bourbon control. Boyce foresaw a blue-gray ticket headed by "a Southern man and Confederate soldier" and supported by a Union veteran who "was a fighter while the war lasted but who had manliness enough to quit fighting since the war was over," a "Boy in Blue . . . who will follow us faithfully as they ever followed Grant and Logan." He saw that symbolic potential in Polk and Paul Vandervoort.[67] Even many pragmatic Black Alliancemen, whose expectations were far more tempered than those of their white counterparts, appeared willing to ignore Polk's white nationalism and forgive his opposition to the 1891 Colored Farmers' Alliance cotton picker strike and the Lodge Force Bill.[68] Although he had met the Western Alliance's call for a third party with some caution after the group's convention in Cincinnati in May 1891, by 1892, and with cotton prices still falling, Polk was fully prepared to move what remained of his Alliance toward a third party.[69] The *Progressive Farmer* backed the St. Louis conference platform and anticipated Omaha as an opportunity for sweeping finance and land reform, perhaps with its editor at the helm.

Yet Polk died suddenly of a bladder hemorrhage on June 11 while in Washington, DC, on his way to Omaha with an assembly of Confederate veterans. According to one editor, the Populists had lost "the one man in the country who could break the Solid South," and both major parties perhaps breathed a sigh of relief.[70] Predictably, obituaries of Polk recalled his singular ability to unify former Union and Confederate soldiers. "Who has done more to destroy sectionalism and join the hands of the Blue and the Gray?" one mourner pleaded.[71] Writing a widely circulated eulogy, Vandervoort described Polk as a bona fide comrade of every People's Party household. As a private from Illinois, Vandervoort had spent six months in Andersonville prison before rising through the ranks of the GAR, where as leader in the early 1880s he used pension reform to promote the organization.[72] He now praised his friend's "desire to unite the blue and the gray in bonds of federal union," and white Southern Populists agreed.[73] The old Confederate veteran had perished, according to Raleigh's *Special Informer*, so that the nation would become "a home of the people, not of plutocrats and slaves."[74]

## Uniting the Sections

James B. Weaver was a decorated combat veteran, but he was not nostalgic for war. A former Republican and Greenbacker, Weaver abhorred what he deemed the "extravagance" of military airs or social rank.[75] Seeking to illustrate his subject's modesty and lack of partisanship, one campaign biographer remarked that Weaver's home offered no indication that its inhabitant was a veteran. "No pictures adorn the walls of his parlor or his library depicting a war scene," he alleged. "There are no crossed swords over the mantel piece; no musket in the corner."[76] But what Weaver's domicile may have lacked in martial ephemera the Iowan made up for in political Weltanschauung, rife with veteran motifs. Like other Populists, Weaver spoke of his program in the same crusading terms that many partisans had used during the war, this time foreseeing an "impending revolution" between the Money Power and the so-called honest masses. A soldier's duty was central to this mission, and the party itself "a vast army leading the charge against the battlements of monopoly."[77]

Noting that "sectionalism seems to be absolutely banished," Populist newspapers published veterans' endorsements of a trans-sectional party ticket as the Omaha convention neared, arguing that the bloody shirt had been worn threadbare.[78] Airy hope of "sections united" also pervaded the popular response to the congressional run of William A. Harris of Kansas. Declaring the Civil War in Kansas finally over, Populists praised the nomination of Harris, a former cadet at the Virginia Military Institute and later a foot soldier in the Army of Northern Virginia. For bloody shirt–burying veterans, the poetry of a Confederate running for Congress from the state of Jayhawkers was unmistakable. Harris was even nominated by an ex-Union soldier who pointed to his own empty sleeve as evidence not of amity but of brotherhood and shared sacrifice. Harris had been put forth, in the words of a Kansas veteran, by "old men, whose eyes were dimmed by time, whose step was slow and tottered, whose hair was frosted as the driven snow, and who followed Grant, Sherman, Lee, and Johnson until the end."[79] Likening the episode to the magnanimity of Appomattox, one Ohioan deemed it a turning point in the story of North-South rapprochement. He expected the approaching Omaha convention to nominate a man who might "lead us out of the land of bondage, into a land of freedom."[80]

That deliverer turned out to be Weaver. In nominating a Union general at the head of the ticket, along with one-legged Confederate veteran James G. Field of Virginia as vice president, all on the Fourth of July, the People's Party sought to make reunion, reform, and republicanism mutually unexclusive. Although the selection of Field was opportunistic, alleviating disappointed Southerners who had anticipating one of their own (Polk), it was shrewdly depicted as a repudiation of loyalty politics.[81] Prefiguring the revisionist school of historians who blamed the war on a "blundering generation" of politicians, Weaver backers insisted that, in contrast to the weak-kneed lawmakers of the 1850s, the present crisis *must* produce courageous, principled leadership.[82] As one Populist reckoned, only a veteran could unify "the chaotic forces struggling for emancipation," and both Democratic and Republican Party leaders were as unfit to lead the current movement "as was the Whig Party under Henry Clay to lead in the struggle for the emancipation of the negro from chattel slavery."[83] "The People's Party Couples the Blue and Gray," headlines exclaimed, a union that at last offered "recognition that the South is in the Union."[84] Praising its legions of common soldiers, the Winnfield *Comrade*, Louisiana's first Populist newspaper, declared "the bloody shirt dashed with a force that has shaken the strongholds of the money power of Europe and America."[85] Others simply called the nominating convention a "Blue-Gray Reunion." Condemning "howlers of the bloody shirt" in both parties, the *People's Party Paper* celebrated that "veterans of the Union, led by one of their number, have shown that they will join the veterans of the Confederacy, led by a maimed and honored soldier of the lost cause, in a patriotic movement for the emancipation of the wealth producers from a thralldom galling as chattel slavery."[86]

The Omaha Platform itself was one of the most sweeping expressions of reform in US history. Building on the Alliance positions of St. Louis in 1889 and Ocala in 1890, the document held that the powers of government *were* the powers of the people. Its planks consisted of currency and land reform, including the nationalization of railroad, telegraphs, and telephone systems. Individual candidates and state parties also opposed lynching, child labor, lien laws, and the convict lease system and urged the establishment of state labor bureaus and greater protection for Black voters.[87] Spectators compared the reception on the convention floor to idealistic exuberance like that of the French General Assembly in the boisterous days of 1789.[88] Combining agrarianism with democratization, alongside Whig and Republican models of state activism, Populists embraced expanded government. As one member saw it, the party stood for "the principles of true Democracy, represented by Thomas Jefferson and Andrew Jackson, and the true principles of Republicanism, represented by Abraham Lincoln."[89] Rejecting the Southern racialized political tradition of small government and "states' rights," the platform was, according to one Populist, the same as that "advocated by Jefferson, Jackson, and Lincoln."[90] Moreover, the claim to both Jefferson *and* Lincoln—a Southerner and a Northerner—became a way for Populists to fuse political democracy with economic democratization *and* to bridge partisan and sectional divides.

The cult of the veteran proved as elemental to the farmer-labor insurgency as the GAR, and its conservative patriotism, was to the electoral base of Northern Republicans. The idea of producerist reconciliation among old soldiers was just as critical to the People's Party as the Lost Cause, with its romanticization of gray-bearded reactionaries, was to Southern Democrats. This Populist veteran creed was also part of a broader reimaging of bygone wars, battles, masters, bondmen, and revolutionists. As in other class-based movements, industrial barons, bankers, and corrupt politicos were, according to the *People's Party Paper*, the neo-"slavers." Plutocrats, meanwhile, were "traitors"; managers were "slave drivers"; defiant workers "runaways"; and "hireling" detective agencies "slave patrols." Industrial exploitation and financial monopoly had created "a slavery where white men are slaves."[91] Partisans draped their cause in war nostalgia because it was arithmetically true, as old soldiers predominated the party rank, file, and, most notably, leadership. They also did so because it was tactically effective. Populists saw their party branding as an outgrowth of the conflict over slavery because they viewed their material plight in part as resulting from the Civil War. Unchecked monopoly, unbridled wealth accumulation, and the growing political influence of capital illuminated unsettled war issues regarding the role of the state and the meaning of free labor. Yet in simultaneously portending a "second Appomattox" *and* courting African American voters—in promoting interracial politics between laboring classes with white men on top—movement architects created an implacable tension within their ranks.

Populists reinforced their image as a veterans' instrument in the vacuum created by Polk's death, employing blue-gray reunion, as one old soldier explained it, in order to blot out the Mason-Dixon Line and promote a "fraternal, unsectional brotherhood."[92] Merely a week after his nomination, at a memorial service for Polk, Weaver had recalled the story of a "Confederate boy" dying in his arms at Shiloh, in part to endear himself to the staunch backers of the former Alliance leader and ex-Confederate.[93] Now party leaders combined this Appomattox writ large—a conciliation of North, South, East, and West—with attempts, both tactical and sincere, to win over Black voters. As one Georgia Populist suggested, "radical change" was necessary to challenge Bourbon power and the historic "necessity of white supremacy in the South." Yet he also alleged that such transformation should upend the portent of "white slavery," a phrase frequently used by white party directors to facilitate Anglo-Saxon reconciliation.[94] Others, failing to account for race as a specific and insidious form of class oppression, judged that racial integration risked alienating white farmers or eliciting violence from Democratic reactionaries. The result was a Black Populism for those who had become disillusioned with the Republicans and concurred with white farmers on key economic questions. Yet, like its Colored Farmers' Alliance predecessor, this subgroup was separate from white Populism in expectation if not organization.[95]

Meanwhile, white Populists developed an alternate "bloody shirt." In a continuation of the damnation that Greenbackers had leveled at Samuel Tilden and James Blaine, agrarian radicals claimed that the Democratic presidential nominee, Grover Cleveland, was a Northeastern blue blood who had bought his way out of military service. They questioned his manhood, as this "Populist bloody shirt" became a tactical recounting of one's war record (or lack thereof) based on class rather than party or sectional critique. Aiming for his third consecutive popular vote victory, Cleveland had, in the words of one critic, "fought the South fiercely through a hired Hessian substitute."[96] This appraisal of the ruling class as gutless was part of a general party philosophy. For many Populists, experiences as soldiers in a momentous bloodletting reinforced their belief in common agency and the power of collective movements.[97] Time and again, Thomas E. Watson's *People's Party Paper* blamed party setbacks on the sectional or racial hatred stirred up by political and financial elites, or what one Kansan called "the men who never heard a bullet whiz."[98] The loyalty to the Civil War veteran was such that, to many farmer-laborers, affluence became antithetical to the experience of the war. Simply, being a "true" veteran disqualified one from being rich.

Populists frequently combined their class analysis with emancipationist memory while simultaneously attempting to countermand sectional division. One Kansas veteran explained, "The boys who wore blue did a grand and patriotic work when they preserved the Union and incidentally liberated four millions of black slaves." Yet he held no ill will toward the "old gray headed Johnnies," who had likewise experienced the hardships of march, bivouac, and battle. The real enemies, he avowed, were the faux patriot bondholders.

Now veterans blue *and* gray were engaged in what one Populist termed "the new and greater struggle for emancipation, emancipation of our producing classes from industrial slavery." But this "antislavery war"—one against the "moneyed oligarchy" and "centralized capital"—required more than the old partisan position of "marking the territory in which the institution of slavery should and should not spread."[99] A wider revolution was needed, wherein formerly rival armies were "united and marching in solid phalanx" in pursuit of a second and fully national liberation.[100] In part to downplay section, Weaver boosters north and south equated their man with Lincoln, insisting that both were Westerners, were third party outsiders, and originated from the working class.[101] The editor of the *People's Party Paper* explained that the great task of Populists in the South and West was to breach the "bloody chasm" created by the war and eradicate the "sin of sectionalism."[102] Editors elsewhere amplified the merit and manhood of "Fighting Jim," the honorific veteran who knew no section.[103]

A wave of campaign songs stressed the reconciliation au courant. Populist songbooks rendered allegorical armies, slaves, shackles, banners, cannon, and battle cries, marrying war-specific themes to People's Party positions including free silver, industry regulation, anti-monopoly, and anti-corruption. "Since We Were Fighting in Georgia" rued how common fighting men had been swindled by "cunning men of money" while off battling for a righteous cause, sent to their "half a million tombs."[104] "New Dixie Land" imagined a South without war, one of "no reeking sword or musket balls." It also beckoned non-elite Southerners, those in the field and the factory, to band with Westerners against rapacious tycoons.[105] Emma Ghent Curtis's "Them Jims," performed at New York's Cooper Union in September 1892, painted the candidates in a homespun earnestness—"no airs" or "aristocratic whims"—that pitted sectional reunion against elitism. Curtis's lyrics depicted two battle-tested warriors who, although impugning fratricidal war, were now prepared to fight plutocracy.[106] Similarly, Henri Fairweather's "Linked Ever More, the Gray and the Blue" accentuated reunion as the Populist linchpin, which stumpers foregrounded in the fall campaign.[107] The "People's Party Banner," sung to the tune of "Bonnie Blue Flag," conjured producers and old war enemies. An "army of the people . . . marching to victory," it warned, must unite or become "slaves" to "plutocratic laws":

> The soldiers of North and South
> Who wore the blue and gray,
> Discarded old animosities
> And let them die away.

Yes, we've joined our hands together,
Our old war wounds are healed,
We'll join with you in electing
Our Weaver and our Field.[108]

Other songs drew on sectional tropes and emancipation's unfinished legacy in both theme and form. "The Panic and Its Effects" likened farmers, miners, and mechanics to slaves and characterized Coxey's Army as a column of liberation. Echoing this theme of reform's legions, "We Are Coming" depicted Populism as a mighty battalion of "cringing slaves" now set to emancipate the masses through a Providential redemption.[109] "Voting for Justice and Freedom" was written to the music of "Battle Cry of Freedom" and, appropriating slave spirituals, Populists sang "Jubilee Song" to the tune of "John Brown's Body." Still others were reminiscent of wartime standards including "Bonnie Blue Flag," "Dixie," "Tramp, Tramp, Tramp," and "Marching through Georgia." Written by a white lyricist but narrated from the perspective of a "darkey" Populist, "The People Are Coming to Stay" avowed that Republicans and Democrats, who "have spat since fo' de war," now shared common ground in a people's movement and that bosses everywhere were likewise united in halting the insurgency. The fictional former slave praised Lincoln while also acknowledging the incompleteness of liberation:

I'm mighty proud of old Abe Lincoln,
And what he done for me,
But by the way I got to thinkin'
I still am far from free;
And I believe the once grand party,
That cared for slavery's tears,
Have joined right in for gold and barter,
With rebel brigadiers.[110]

Yet this overridingly white reunion did not fundamentally imperil the racial order despite providing a new mechanism for Black political participation by upsetting the South's Democratic hegemony. Nevertheless, conservatives winced at the party's subversive inflection and radical potential. Populist weeklies quoted socialist revolutionary theorists, including Marx; others tied the concept of revolution to distinctly native traditions and ideas.[111] While Weaver spoke to a political "revolution" through bottom-up electoral change, some of his allies pushed the analogy considerably further.[112] The Weaver-Field ratifying celebration in Los Angeles saw speeches, floats, and crowds holding signs that read "Tax the Incomes," "Public Ownership," "Equal Rights to All; Special Privileges to None," and "We Want the Earth, for It Is Ours." People's Party congressional candidate Marion Cannon of Ventura declared, "We are on the eve of the greatest revolution ever witnessed." If such transformational change did not occur at the ballot box, Cannon cautioned, it would come through bloodshed. "The storm," he warned, "is ready to burst."[113]

## Bloody Shirt Weaver

The Populist blue-gray campaign coincided with the publication of Weaver's *Call to Action: An Interpretation of the Great Uprising, Its Source and Causes.* A history of the centuries-long strife between owners and producers, Weaver's tome addressed how recent federal institutions, including the Senate and the Supreme Court, had colluded with private interests to subvert the public good.[114] The Iowan weighed US wealth inequality against that of ancient Rome and industrializing Britain, sketching the history of capitalism and its impact on common people. Weaver tackled issues including trusts, free silver, the national debt, corporate land ownership, private police forces, the banking system, and the monopolization of the transport and telegraph industries. He saw worker militancy and the response of state and corporate violence as part of a historical "uprising among the industrial people of the new world" and applied economic data, classical history, and Shakespearean literature to argue his case.

Although scholars have largely ignored *Call to Action* (Richard Hofstadter likens it to a "Jacksonian polemic"), the book reveals the Civil War as crucial to Populist conceptions of history, social philosophy, and political strategy.[115] Weaver explained that the second American revolution represented, above all, a transfer of supremacy from the Southern Slave Power to the Money Power in the urban North, or what leftist theoreticians after 1917 would term a "bourgeois revolution." "The slaveholder lost his human chattels and the Confederacy perished," he admitted, "but the tyranny of capital was not broken by the war." On the contrary, Weaver argued that it was augmented: "The money power gained all that the slaveholder lost." Anticipating the Progressive school interpretations of historians Charles A. and Mary Beard, this view saw the war as a shift in regional power in which two often complementary forms of "aristocracy" increasingly competed for cultural and political sway, from one of tremendous slaveholder influence to one of Northern dominion. Despite political restoration and slave liberation, Weaver insisted that "the battle for substantial and real emancipation has yet to be fought and it is but just ahead."[116]

To Weaver, the failure to secure the war's promises or address inequalities beyond the political began in Congress and on Wall Street and ended with the victimization of workers, farmers, and former slaves. Although he praised wartime governance, especially Charles Sumner and Benjamin Wade, Weaver maintained that the postwar intelligentsia (with the exception of Wendell Phillips) tragically "stopped with the overthrow of the outward form of slavery." The "inward" form of slavery, what his contemporaries called "wage slavery," was thus exacerbated by financial corruption that allowed corporations to supersede the influence that the "slave oligarchy" had enjoyed at its zenith. Through the exploits of common people, the Radical Republicans had "succeeded in breaking the chains of chattel slavery and prepared the way for the complete triumph of man over those who lived by the enslavement of labor." Yet in privileging capitalist "slave drivers" over workers' interests, wartime leaders precipitated a new conflict that in fact persecuted the true victors of the late war—enlisted men who had "strengthened the public credit by their valor and blood."[117]

The tensions within the Reconstruction program—liberalism versus radicalism—highlighted the urgency of Weaver's producerist vision. Some Populists theorized the postwar South as a site of extended conflict, not only in a literal sense but in terms of policy and power relations. The most obvious lay not in Black political and civic rights (a topic to which Weaver dedicated little energy so as not to alienate white Southerners) but in land reform. Like some of his Radical Republican forebears, Weaver insisted that the inability of every man to possess a small, self-sustaining landholding was the root of political and economic tyranny. Tracing the history of land consolidation from England's enclosure movement to corporate land grabs by extractive resource enterprises in the American West, Weaver, who fretted the United States might devolve into an Old World despotism, explained how "land monopoly" fed wealth inequality and class stratification.[118] He maintained that the outgrowths of 1861–65, including currency deflation, public debt, and the demonetization of silver, had facilitated these unprecedented concentrations of wealth—"colossal fortunes [with] no parallel in the annals of the modern world."[119] A primary reason for this inertness of land reform lay in congressional legislation and judicial review.[120] State and federal courts had repeatedly sided with corporate over labor interests on property rights pretexts.[121] Furthermore, Congress had allocated public lands to favor speculators and railroad conglomerates over subsistence farmers. Soldiers returning home from war were especially entitled to free or affordable access to arable public lands, or what Weaver termed the "liberty to occupy the soil."[122] Although grounded in settler-colonial assumptions about "empty" space and racialized notions of land improvement, Weaver's "veteran-settler" idea argued that to be "emancipated" as a worker meant "more than mere relief"—it entailed greater control of one's own mechanisms of production.[123]

Despite his martial hyperbole, Weaver's vision was not a violent one. He viewed electoral politics—a "call to action" at the ballot box and a "revolution" of the people against "class laws" and "special privileges"—as preferable to the alternative of a "tragic revolution" in the factories and on the farms.[124] Like many later sociologists, Weaver appeared to have viewed wealth inequality and hyper-accumulation (rather than poverty) as the primary impetuses of the type of political violence and social foment that characterized revolutionary France—a scenario he sought desperately to avoid.[125] Weaver's ideal was a political economy in which private interests were subordinate to public welfare.[126] He acknowledged that industrial production had indeed ushered in new material possibility and the capacity for a permanently advanced standard of living.[127] However, corporate capitalism, like property, was not "natural" but a social construction.[128] To that end, capitalism and democracy were frequently antagonistic forces. Yet, like most Populists, Weaver's anticapitalism was less dogmatic than situational, denouncing mostly concentrated capital and inequitable markets. The Iowan possessed, like William Jennings Bryan after him, "Lincolnian refrains" regarding the popular accountability of political and private institutions.[129] The blue-gray ticket offered proof that citizens understood the profound economic questions that were "hidden from the contending forces in that gigantic struggle."[130]

Political opponents fired back. Countering Populist cooperationism, Republicans co-opted the labor-veteran label under the banner of unfettered markets. Rather than advocating a "revolution" of victimized farmers and industrial workers, Republican liberalism propagated the "self-made man" mythos that legal equality alone ensured equity. As one conservative editor professed, just as the "sword and shoulder straps worn by workingmen in the late war" were identical to those of the wealthy, workers had every opportunity to leverage their identical civic rights into social mobility. This "Horatio Alger myth" of meritocracy maintained that the wealthy of tomorrow were the laborers of today and that those who failed to rise were simply lacking in effort or character. Equal laws led to just outcomes, Republicans argued, and by delineating themselves as casualties of an economic war, Populists, veterans and all, were guilty of dishonorable, even effeminate comportment.[131]

Bourbon Democrats, meanwhile, used sectionalism to direct scorn and violence against Populist "race traitors" who challenged Democratic class status and the region's white unity. They accused Populists of betraying Anglo-Saxon supremacy, defaming the memory of the Confederacy, and threatening the Solid South.[132] To Democratic editors in the South, "Bloody Shirt Weaver" was the "most radical of radicals," his third party posture merely a front to disseminate redistributive policies that would jeopardize white ruling-class authority.[133] Antagonists cried that Weaver's tacit support for the Lodge Force Bill was part of an extensive personal history of enmity toward Dixie. "He hates the South," one editor maintained. Rousing the specter of a return to Reconstruction, he warned that Weaver sought to "shackle [white Southerners] with bayonets" and instate a monstrous "negro rule."[134] Opponents in St. Tammany Parish, Louisiana, branded Weaver "the most ultra of Southern hating Republicans," evoking lynching imagery to make their point. The Democratic Party, they argued, was the only thing protecting white men from having "ropes around their necks."[135] Rebuking Weaver due to his former Republican affiliation, one Virginia congressman complained that the Iowan had "exhausted the vocabulary in his denunciation of the Southern people."[136] Grover Cleveland supporters derided Weaver as a "bummer," the nickname for Sherman's troops who had purportedly laid waste the Georgia and Carolina countryside, and accused him of stealing hogs, abusing his military authority, and capriciously placing local civilians under arrest.[137] One party newspaper in Greensboro, North Carolina, complained that every time Southern Democrats encounter a whiff of Populism, "the air becomes filled with blue devils, Union soldiers."[138]

The weightiest charges came from Pulaski, Tennessee, where Weaver had served as provost marshal in 1863. In mid-July the *Pulaski Citizen* published sworn affidavits from local residents claiming that Weaver had engaged in criminal behavior, including arbitrary taxation and arrest of citizens. The story was syndicated throughout the nation. Both Bourbon and Alliance Democrats grew convinced that Weaver had been, as one editor phrased it, "the most vindictive and bitter hater of the South in all the Union army."[139] Populist publications, including the *National Economist* and the *People's Party Paper*, retorted that although they were now "arm-in-arm, laying flowers upon graves of the blue and gray" in order to bond the West and South, both Weaver and Field had been "blood-waders" during the war, preferable to deserters and "court proof" gentlemen. Although Populist newspapers published counterclaims from Pulaski locals, the damage of the Pulaski incident was considerable, a testament to the influence of Democratic media and sectionalism's persistence.[140]

Weaver's campaign tour of Georgia that September proved especially chaotic. His first speech at Waycross's Opera House drew a crowd of around 500 spectators, nearly half of whom were African Americans. Alongside Union Labor Party veteran Mary Elizabeth Lease, daughter of an exiled Irish revolutionary, promoter of Black suffrage, and by 1892 a famed Populist orator, Weaver spoke for an hour.[141] When the old soldier accused state Democrats of encouraging small farmers to "vote your families into bondage," he was deliberately tapping into the most primal fears of the region's dependent agrarians and small-scale yeomanry, white and Black.[142] His public reception devolved after that. The *Atlanta Journal* ran a full-page story on Pulaski, copies of which were distributed to townspeople prior to his campaign stops. Although Weaver pleaded to "bury the issues of the past" and focus on the Money Power, hostile congregants egged him and his wife in Macon, where Democratic adversaries drowned out his speech by playing "Dixie." They met similar resistance in Columbus, Madison, Augusta, and Elberton. Shouted down from the balcony of Albany's Mayo Hotel by what Weaver described as a "howling mob," he castigated typical "southern intolerance."[143] Fearing worse awaited him and his troupe in Atlanta, Weaver abandoned his Georgia swing altogether.[144]

The *People's Party Paper* compared the hostility to the tumult that had preceded secession. Given the state's deep political divisions and episodes of violence, particularly within Thomas E. Watson's own congressional race, this allusion transcended mere hyperbole. The publication blamed the madness on the bloody shirt, insisting that Weaver was assaulted due to his Union service. But Watson also avowed that this unmanly partisanship was socially and economically skewed. "Remember this is not done by the ignorant and lower classes," one editor explained, but by "high class public manipulators," including Bourbon politicians and the media.[145] Weaver himself was careful to exonerate veterans, blaming the attacks on "organized rowdyism" orchestrated by Democratic elites. He maintained that "disorderly behavior does not proceed from the ex-Confederate soldiers, who are, almost without exception, manly in their conduct and generally in sympathy with out movement."[146]

While the Democratic press either ignored Weaver or condemned him as a Yankee interloper, Republicans used the bedlam in Georgia to characterize blue-gray reunion as a delusion and to reinforce preexisting assumptions about Southern intransigence.[147] Allies of Republican nominee and Union veteran Benjamin Harrison painted white Southern Democrats as a "lawless and ungovernable race of people" and, in this case, a riotous mob of "drunken hoodlums and foul-mouthed Clevelandites," equating them to the so-called anarchists of 1789 Paris. Even to Populism's bloody shirt–waving Republican opponents, Weaver's mistreatment constituted the heinous "persecution of a Union soldier," revealing once again the "insurrectionary spirit of the Democratic party."[148] One Kansas editor offered the Georgia circuit as proof that Alliancemen "shoot in one direction in the North and in another in the South."[149] While in Georgia that entailed former "traitors" shooting northward, in North Dakota, for instance, "loyal Union men" slandered the Populist gubernatorial candidate as a "southern sympathizer" for having been a "Missouri guerrilla" during the war.[150] In one Kansas congressional district, a faction of Populists protested Democratic influence in the state party by forming the Abraham Lincoln Republican Party, a political "halfway house" that employed Unionist memory to help restore GOP influence.[151] While most dyed-in-the-wool Republicans deemed Weaver an honorable Union soldier at the helm of a misguided cause and portrayed Cleveland as an anti-veteran draft dodger, others drew a harder line by castigating Field and insisting that it was treasonous for any Union veteran to vote a ticket that included an ex-rebel.[152] Although Democratic leaders cynically and self-servingly exploited wartime hatreds to protect their material interests, much white Southern derision toward Weaver was rooted in genuine sectional animus, and it is unlikely that a Confederate veteran such as Polk would have received similar treatment (though he may have faced ostracism outside the South). Even to some white Southern Populists who defied sectional politics in other ways, being represented by a Union veteran seemed somehow unconscionable.[153]

The campaign stayed on theme, underscoring reconciliation yet often isolating the Northeast and courting Black supporters yet ignoring racial justice issues and race-specific matters. Weaver intentionally cold-shouldered the Lodge Force Bill; Field called it a distraction. Another consequence of this emphasis on rural issues in the West and South was a relative neglect of industrial workers in the East and Great Lakes region. Populists won the endorsement of Powderly and the (rapidly declining) Knights of Labor, but the burgeoning American Federation of Labor and its leader, Samuel Gompers, formally eschewed party politics. Informally, AFL members were highly active in local races and, though they largely sidestepped socialist and populist mass movements, frequently lobbied for specific reforms at the national level.[154] Moreover, Weaver's agrarian-heavy message and erratic campaign route bypassed industrial hotbeds from Boston to Pittsburgh to Chicago, and the party failed to make inroads with urban workingmen who would have otherwise been a snug ideological fit.[155] Nevertheless, on Labor Day in Dallas, accompanied by a brass band, surrounded by both American and Confederate flags, and beneath a banner that read "The War Is Over," Weaver spoke to an enthralled crowd of 2,000. One rapt editor claimed that "Dixie appeared to be waltzing with Yankee Doodle."[156]

It was not to be. The People's Party ultimately yielded significant returns in the Southwest and the Great Plains, winning a host of state-level seats, electoral votes from six states, and 8.5 percent of the national vote for president, garnering over 1 million votes. Yet the Weaver-Field ticket failed to gain traction in the Upper South and Midwest. Although Weaver received 15.7 percent of all votes cast in the former Confederacy, including 37 percent in Alabama, where state Republicans endorsed the Populist ticket, Populism all but collapsed in South Carolina and Florida, remained highly localized in Louisiana, and imploded in North Carolina after Polk's death.[157] In the Populist hotbeds of Alabama and Georgia, where Reuben Kolb with his "Negro plank" was narrowly defeated for governor and Tom Watson was ousted from his congressional seat, the election was marked by fraud on the part of state Democrats, with party elites relating Populist insurgents to alien, extortionist carpetbaggers.[158] This setback also marked the effective end of both the Farmers' Alliance and the Knights of Labor.[159] Although the 1894 and 1896 campaigns would highlight the relative success of fusionist strategy, with Democrats outside the South and Republicans within, the Populist cultural appeal to the Civil War veteran peaked in the fall of 1892.

## The Campaign Over

Countless white supporters nevertheless viewed the Weaver-Field campaign as a critical reconciliatory moment. Sanguine editors saw the degree of blue-gray ticket support as "evidence that the hatchet is buried, the war is over and the bloody shirt has lost its power," and Weaver himself took heart that state-level gains had "awakened fraternal feelings in all sections."[160] At the AFL's annual convention in Philadelphia one month after Weaver's defeat, an infirm John Swinton declared it "time for the struggling work people of the eastern cities to link arms with the advancing farmers of the resurgent West."[161] Boston's *Labor Leader* agreed, hoping the silver issue might at last "weld together the farmers of the West and the mechanics of the East."[162] Yet to many Populists, the terms of asectionalism were predicated as much on whiteness as on class. As one North Carolinian rejoiced, farmers and workers in the Middle West and Great Plains were at long last "tired of the everlasting nagging at the South" and of Republicans "harping on the nigger."[163] Martial imagery remained vital to this détente. With the "campaign over," the "brush of battle ceased," and the "results of the late war" tallied, Populists assessed their mark on the cultural and political landscape.[164]

Even as the People's Party feted a toiler's reconciliation at the national level, sectional divisions and party alignments continued to determine local and state strategies. In North Carolina, for instance, where the party courted African American votes and fused with Republicans in 1896 and 1898, Populists who feared losing Black votes argued that no alliances be made with pro-silver

Democrats, many of whom complained of "negro domination" within the movement.[165] As such, white Populists in Dixie used "emancipation" pragmatically. North Carolina's Marion Butler was a Knight and Allianceman who became a "middle of the road" Populist senator (which had a specific anti-fusionist meaning). He detested Democratic corruption and viewed sectionalism as something to be overcome by political realignment stemming from commercial bonds between the South and the Middle West, the Great Plains, and the Far West.[166] Butler had formerly edited the Clinton *Caucasian*, whose masthead affirmed the editor's commitment to "Pure Democracy & White Supremacy," and was far less eager than Tom Watson to engage Black voters.[167] Yet "fusion"—vote trading, ticket splitting, and ticket sharing—with state Republicans made Lincolnian memory especially expedient in the Tar Heel State. Despite his white supremacist bona fides, Butler, like other white Southern Populists, perceived the Great Emancipator's legacy as a return to a more egalitarian—if nostalgic—agrarianism.[168]

While Democrats countered swelling Populist ranks with fraud and violence, as the economic depression that began in 1893 expanded, old soldiers continued to use the People's Party as a vehicle of both financial reform and neo-emancipationist memory.[169] In Illinois, where the People's Party State Committee operated in Lincoln's shadow, members claimed their crisis was the greatest since 1861. Equating workers to chattel slaves, they lamented "Abraham Lincoln's Awful Prophesy" of a political system controlled by moneyed interests, a "Goldocracy" replacing the old slaveocracy.[170] The association of Lincoln with agrarian dissent proved poetic when Populists met in Springfield in July 1894 on the heels of a new statewide labor-Populist alliance backed by Clarence Darrow, Lyman Trumbull, and Henry Demarest Lloyd. In an act of solidarity with socialists and industrial workers, the conference endorsed the nationalization of mines, the public ownership of municipal services (railways, gas, electric), and an eight-hour workday.[171] These themes pervaded across and beyond the prairie. With sincere conviction, the editors of the *Kansas Agitator* lambasted anti-Populists who emphasized the preservation of the Union as the war's principal aim, insisting that "the crowning glory of the war was the extinction of slavery." "There is not an intelligent soldier today but would hang his head in shame if the slaves had not been liberated by that war," the editor argued. Yet this racial liberalism also fit within a more orthodox story of social change. Emancipation, they alleged, was a continuation of the revolution initiated by George Washington and Jeffersonian disinterestedness. Melding Jacksonian democracy with Radical Republican egalitarianism, the editors conjured the symbolic power of

Lincoln. The martyred president, they explained, "spelled labor, liberty, and love with a big 'L,' equality with a big 'E,' fraternity with a big 'F,' humanity with a big 'H,' and justice with a big 'J.'"[172]

Pro-silver Republicans adopted similar rhetoric. Echoing Frederick Douglass's 1894 claim that their former party had been converted "into a party of money rather than a party of morals," the Independent Republicans of Ohio maintained that the GOP had devolved from Lincoln and Grant's party of human rights to the party of property rights, asserting that the remonetization of silver fit within the early party's free labor tradition.[173] Anti-Republican Populists, on the other hand, sometimes refused to appropriate the sixteenth president, linking Republican policy to monopoly and widening inequality or viewing him instead as a contemporary symbol of Radical Republican "misrule." One editor maintained that Republicans were weaponizing Lincoln as "the only friend and benefactor" of the Black race in order to obscure a party program that facilitated "the stupendous increase of millionaires and paupers" and the growing "unequal distribution of wealth."[174]

The Populists' use and abuse of Lincoln's likeness, depicting him as either a proto-Populist or predecessor of Wall Street cronyism, obscured the Rail-splitter's unformed views on the relationship between labor and capital, which People's Party representatives cited with great alacrity and interpretive certainty. Living prior to the ascendance of industrial capitalism, Lincoln possessed quotable but amorphous ideas about the working class, which he did not conceive of as a permanent or separate group with particular sets of interests.[175] Even so, Populists appropriated Lincoln's maxims regarding labor (rather than capital) and workers' right to strike as the "true standard of value."[176] Revered passages included Lincoln's March 1864 reply to the New York Workingmen's Association, in which he alleged that "the strongest bond of human sympathy, outside the family relation, should be one uniting all working people of all nations and tongues and kindreds," and Lincoln's first annual message to Congress on December 3, 1861. Stated in a previous form to the Wisconsin Agricultural Society in September 1859, the speech reiterated the interdependence of labor and capital but alleged "labor is prior to, and independent of, capital . . . and deserves much the higher consideration."[177] Populists viewed this speech as antithetical to the Gilded Age reality of perpetually subordinate labor offset with a dash of private charity. "It is quite a step from the doctrine of Lincoln to the doctrine of Carnegie [elite paternalism]," the *Kansas Agitator* protested, "but the Hanna doctrine is still worse, for it puts capital first and labor nowhere."[178] When the national antitrust movement held its inaugural meeting in 1900, participants opted to meet on February 12, Lincoln's birthday, in Chicago. Members, including Weaver, established the American Anti-Trust League in the "Land of Lincoln," cognizant of the symbolic spirit of the "Great Emancipator."[179]

The most exalted incorporation of Lincoln's labor dialogue came from Democratic-Populist presidential candidate William Jennings Bryan. By 1896, most Eastern and Midwestern Populists reckoned that the party's best means of attaining national power lay in fusion with Democratic candidates, a strategy pushed at the St. Louis convention that year. The "Popocrat" nomination of Bryan, a youthful Illinois-raised pro-silver Nebraskan, challenged once again the sectional binary by replacing the North-South blood feud with East-West imaginings.[180] Although Bryan distanced himself from the People's Party, opponents tagged him a dangerous leveler and courier of a "second civil war." "The election of Abraham Lincoln resulted in our first civil war—the interests of the South were at stake," one critic noted. "The election of William Jennings Bryan will result in our second civil war—the interests of the whole nation will be at stake." Whereas the Old South's slave property had been "worth millions," he maintained, the personal property of the industrial North that Bryan now supposedly jeopardized was "priceless," and any threat thereto was certain to initiate another "rebellion."[181]

The critic was right about one thing: Bryan's conscious emulation of Lincoln. Although the populist (though never Populist) Democrat would come to be known as the "Commoner," it was Bryan who touted Lincoln as a "man of the people."[182] Grandstanding in Chicago on Labor Day 1896, Bryan quoted the Great Emancipator at length, pairing himself with his fellow Illinoisan in that they both believed that capital was but the fruit of labor.[183] While incensed Republicans charged Bryan with demagoguery and attempting to foment class war through the co-optation of their party icon, Bryan maintained that the Lincoln tradition was essentially reconciliationist.[184] Speaking in Arlington National Cemetery on Decoration Day 1894, he indulged old soldiers, as well as the widows and children of the fallen, both Union and Confederate, between passages of Lincoln's Gettysburg Address. And while Bryan reminded the audience that the preservation of the Union was the "greatest triumph in all history," he likewise maintained that "no greater victory can be won by citizens or soldiers than to transform temporary enemies into permanent friends."[185]

Silver Populists used the Lincoln metaphor to endorse Bryan and attack his opponent, Republican and Civil War veteran William McKinley. Paralleling the silver movement with the antislavery cause, Marion Butler cursed McKinley's insistence that the pro-silver faction back a gold standard consensus for the sake of economic stability: "How ridiculous it would have been for Abraham Lincoln in 1860 to have said he was in favor of freeing the slaves, but that until the consent of the Southern slave owners could be gotten, that he and all of the abolitionists should stand up boldly and support the institution of slavery."[186] Bryan men also painted their candidate's anti-imperialism as within Lincoln's free-labor vision of a small-producing (and often white) republic. To many reformers, imperial expansion was the logical capstone of "wage slavery" and the drive for cheap labor. To radicals, its voracious demand for new commodities and markets exemplified the obvious conclusion of capitalism itself.[187]

The contentious 1896 People's Party convention in St. Louis saw the farmer-labor enterprise fuse with Bryan's Democracy, with Georgian Tom Watson as the vice presidential nominee on a separate Populist ticket. Though Bryan-Watson patrons argued that the duo would have a reconciliatory effect on both sectional relations and disgruntled anti-Bryan Populists, the marriage created substantial rifts inside the party.[188] Some Southern Populists insisted that backing Watson was simply a matter of regional honor.[189] Anti-Bryan Watson proponents, meanwhile, argued that the "North and South would come together, as one people," with an independent Watson ticket along with a Northern running mate.[190] This intraparty divide was made worse when Bryan refused to adopt Watson and chose a different vice presidential candidate, the "Yankee banker" Arthur Sewall of Maine.[191] Although the Democratic meeting in Chicago's Coliseum revealed "GAR copper buttons" alongside "those who wore gray," invitations to reunion could not heal partisan fracture. Much of the party's program, centered increasingly on the single issue of silver, grew depthless, further reducing the Populists' early interracialism. Party members spoke ever more of internal "fire-eaters," "traitors," and "Copperheads," as well as "reconciliation" not among sections but among party factions, especially in North Carolina, where the formal alliance with the Democrats proved a blow to the Populist-Republican fusion.[192] Ultimately, Bryan lost because McKinley's promise of a "full dinner pail" sufficiently appealed to urban workers. The Republican swept the industrial Northeast and crucial Midwest, where groups of Union veterans called "Patriotic Heroes" had campaigned for him on a cannon-mounted train car, proclaiming "1896 is as vitally important as 1861."[193] Even Terence Powderly returned to his Republican roots.[194]

The national People's Party splintered following Bryan's defeat, destroying what Matthew Hild contends was "the last best chance for a biracial coalition of the farm, mine, and factory."[195] The Populist use of "reunion" revealed and perpetuated hallmarks of whiteness that were antithetical to interracial alliance. Yet if white reunion did not extinguish most pretenses of racial liberalism, much less radicalism, fusion with national Democrats in 1896 did. By 1898, with Populism waning and the AFL moving sharply toward exclusive craft unionism, old soldiers' reunions also publicized partisan blending, Republicans and Populists, blue and gray. "Better a decade of love and peace than a cycle of the mutilations and of the memories of civil war," one editor explained, having attended an educational conference in Richmond. "It would be impossible for this assemblage of Northern and Southern men, met here in the old capital of the Confederacy, the storm-center of the great Civil War, to forget that eventful struggle, but its memories have knit the men closer together, not pulled them apart."[196] United by the Spanish-American War, the Blue and Gray Association of the Knights of Labor now encamped with Republican and Populist representatives.[197] Remarking on American empire-building in the Caribbean and the South Pacific, one Ohio editor marveled at "Republicans, Democrats, Populists, the blue and the gray, all advancing on the common enemy."[198]

The People's Party theme of sectional reconciliation along class lines remained white-dominant, resulting in modes of commemoration rooted in nostalgia and wartime service that undercut interracial potential in both political culture and association. Although the *Progressive Farmer* continued to champion agrarian reform and international bimetallism, backing Bryan in 1896, by the century's turn the newspaper rejected Black-white cooperation. Most white Southern Populists followed suit. The People's Party's collapse and the racial segregation federally sanctioned by *Plessy v. Ferguson* converged in the years before a new editor, Clarence Hamilton Poe, took the reins in 1899, his columns running thick with savage race-baiting and white reconciliatory themes amid war with Spain. Deeming Reconstruction the "saddest picture in the annals of the English-speaking race," Poe applauded the "total withdrawal" of African Americans from the political process and warned that, as during Yankee occupation, social and political rights for Blacks had brought about "negro crime" against white womanhood.[199] Connecting racial advancement to government expenditure, the editors simultaneously excoriated "old soldiers" in the North whose pensions allegedly devoured the federal budget while romanticizing the ways and whiteness of the pre-industrial Old South. This Lost Cause interpretation cohered with the racial retrogression of Tom Watson and others. Although some dissenters resisted the intensifying reconciliatory tide, Populists in the South, and old soldiers among them, mostly viewed this political and economic restoration among whites—"rancor renounced," "dissolved differences," and "forgetting the things which are behind"—as a testament to the splendor of racial nationhood.[200]

Nevertheless, African Americans continued to vote in large numbers throughout the 1890s in Polk's North Carolina, and in 1896 a Republican-Populist fusion upended Democratic Party preeminence. In what amounted to a "virtual revolution," Republicans won control of the state legislature for the first time since Reconstruction, this time in coalition with Populists and aided by Knight mobilization of Black voters.[201] Portraying themselves as the party of law, order, and justice in contrast to Democratic "political slavery," fusionists denounced Black disenfranchisement, the politics of "race prejudice," and white Democratic violence, warning that Bourbons might resurrect the Red Shirts and other forms of Reconstruction era political bloodshed.[202] Running strongest in the eastern and western portions of the state and weakest in the more commercial Piedmont, fusionists alleged that Democrats were beholden to Northern capitalists and accused them of strategically employing white supremacy—with well-placed cries of "negro domination"—in order to divide white and Black voters.[203] One Populist identified this Democratic practice of "nigger yelling," maintaining that "this same man who is screeching his throat sore about the 'nigger,' is a banker or bondsman." The Democrats, he insisted, were "running a campaign on the assumption that the people of the state are fools, and can be eternally haggled and frightened [by race fears]."[204]

Fusionists were headed by Daniel Lindsay Russell, the state's first Republican governor since Reconstruction and its last until the party's "Southern Strategy" seven decades later. A Confederate veteran turned scalawag, Russell had won a seat in Congress through a federation with Greenbackers in 1878, and by the late 1890s he endeavored to broaden the Republican Party in the former slave states. Russell saw Southern Republicanism as "commemorative of Abraham Lincoln," tying Lincolnian activism to New South modernity. "Mr. Lincoln was born in the South," Russell explained, and had "saved the government and freed the slave" even as Southern "opposition and reaction" curbed those gains. To be sure, although Reconstruction—civil and political equality—was "startling in its radicalism," it failed in attempting to "execute the element of force," and its decline was disastrous for freedpeople. Russell asserted that the "paper decrees" of the Thirteenth, Fourteenth, and Fifteenth Amendments meant little if the federal government was willing to withdraw from the South, leaving policy to be enforced by an antagonistic "master class" that was "unalterably hostile to that policy." Now interracial possibility again imperiled this "united white sentiment."[205]

Yet contemporaneous events challenged Russell's suggestion that the South's newfound urbanity and industry threatened white supremacy, rather than altered or reinforced it. To a large degree, unfree and uncompensated

Black labor built the New South's infrastructure, as the "slavery by another name" of convict leasing underwrote emergent steel, timber, brick, turpentine, and mining industries. In North Carolina, Russell's policies—and the prospect of successful Black-white politics—drew the ire of white planters and incorrigible white supremacists. When he supported reducing property requirements on voting, Democratic opposition charged him with being a "nigger lover," degrading Confederate veterans, and undermining the "natural" racial order.[206] Even so, Russell was elected governor in 1896 in large part by the votes of former slaves in the state's "Black Second" Congressional District, home to George H. White, the last Black congressman from the South until the 1970s. To whites, Russell's victory constituted "negro rule," and 1898 saw a coordinated attempt by state Democrats to oust all Black politicians and white allies through threats, economic coercion, extortion, and outright violence, led by a reanimated Red Shirt faction composed of Wilmington's white elite.[207] One Populist deemed this neo-Redemption worse than the Ku Klux Klan owing to its expanded targets, including white men who wore gray: "The Klan never made an arsenal of one hundred villages, nor plotted against free speech, nor attended public meetings and polling places armed with rifles and shot guns. . . . They did not refuse Confederate veterans the right to vote."[208]

In many ways, the fall 1898 Wilmington Insurrection signaled both the conclusion of the national Populist upsurge and the end of an era in which radical class-based coalitions employed war symbols to appeal to coalitions of Civil War veterans. In what proved to be the largest coup d'état in US history, white Democrats led by Russell nemesis and Confederate veteran Alfred Waddell attacked and overthrew the local Republican regime and destroyed the city's Black-owned newspaper. The violent Thermidor returned the state to one-party rule and, as Michael K. Honey notes, shored up the "undisputed power of an oligarchy of landlords, commercial leaders, and industrialists."[209] Contemporary newspapers—those that both supported and opposed the massacre—likened it to the War of the Rebellion, terming it the "revolution of 1898," a "race war," and a "second civil war."[210] Ignatius Donnelly's lofty dreams had rested upon the assumption that racial reconciliation was an integral part of healing sectional wounds. He and others like him put forth noble ideas that were cut down on the blood-soaked streets of Wilmington.

The fraudulent and often violent overthrow of Populism and the gradual changeover of white Populists back into the Democratic Party signaled a watershed in Black disenfranchisement and the hastening of Jim Crow. But what C. Vann Woodward termed the "forgotten alternative" of interracial farmer-labor politics also collapsed in part under the weight of its own fluid contradictions.[211] As Gerald H. Gaither concedes, "There now seems to be a general recognition that the walls between the two races were too high for Populism to have ever succeeded." However, contributing factors to the Populist decline—fusion with national Democrats, state-level anti-Populist chicanery and violence, and the Populists' appeal to sectional reconciliation without or above racial reconciliation—were highly contingent as possibilities turned abruptly and in real time.[212] In terms of collective memory, Populism represented a forceful blow to the Lost Cause tradition of states' rights white supremacy, as any direct and public challenge to white unity in the New South was itself a remarkable act.[213] The people's movement also confronted entrenched class interests, bringing African Americans into the political arena in great numbers and recalling the interracial democracy of Reconstruction.[214] Yet in promoting white reunion at the expense of an emancipationist legacy that highlighted interlocking oppressions, Populism too often precluded or subordinated a vast and materially predisposed bloc of Southern workers: African Americans. Instead, Populism's hierarchy of remembrance mirrored the party's personnel and policy. Because whiteness undermined genuine class solidarity, sectionalism proved mystifying and the dominant parties insurmountable. Culture did not cause, but certainly illuminated, systematic failings. The Populist collapse was the result of commemorative as well as political missteps.

CHAPTER 6

# Citadel of Labor

## The American Federation of Labor and Reformist Memory

DYER DANIEL LUM reckoned Decoration Day less a day of collective mourning than of collective action. Taking a "wider view of the field" on the holiday in 1885, Lum, a bookbinder who had been an officer in the 14th New York Cavalry, maintained that while US soldiers had fought for "Liberty and Union," the war's disastrous results included "the enrichment of army contractors; financial speculators in national necessities; the centralization of authority; the creation of monied aristocracy; and the tendency of industrial enterprises to concentrate into monopolies." Although the second American revolution had saved the republic and expanded the bounds of human freedom, the farther-reaching objectives for which some Radical Republicans had struggled remained incomplete. Impatient with the pace of labor reform, Lum became an anarcho-syndicalist, a Labor Reform Party candidate, a Knight in the Knights of Labor, and, for a time, publisher of *The Alarm*. His libertarian socialist and anti-statist writings, including *The Economics of Anarchy*, advocated the breakup of the state as to dissolve land titles, abolish of rent and interest, overthrow the wage system, and enable genuine worker cooperation.[1] Accordingly, Lum's war memory was that of an unfinished revolution against inequality. "In preserving the union we created a new union—of capital," he railed. A "new war cry" was necessary to achieve economic freedom.[2]

In late April 1886, mere days before a turn of events in Chicago's Haymarket Square altered forever the destiny of the US labor movement, Lum published a piece titled "American Workingmen Are Called Upon to Arm Themselves."[3] Insisting that electoral politics were necessary but insufficient, he submitted that workers could choose to be either "slaves" or "free men" but that the latter would require confronting the extortive Money Power and the "arbitrary states of the markets." In an about-face from the Civil War, the legions of federal bayonets were now the instruments of capital, and workingmen were left to stake their own "emancipation." Positing that militant agitation was within the American republican and individualist traditions, Lum's left-wing liberty called on workers to "be your own man . . . seek your own self" in order to undermine their "economic masters." "Personal independence," he asserted, was not subjugation by the fickleness of an "invisible hand" but the right to labor and organize. Lum described in Marxian terms that workers had evolved from slavery to serfdom and from serfdom to wage labor. The end goal, however, was working-class emancipation through economic democracy and control of production. Contrasting capital aggregation and the "fixed" status of the working classes with the utopian capitalism of free labor, he probed, "Do you not realize . . . times have changed since our civil war, if your memory goes back beyond that event?" Indeed, Lum claimed that while the republic had achieved political and "mental" freedom, "free thought" and the "free ballot" were insufficient for worker liberation, which required economic freedom. The veteran wondered how social immobility, the dearth of unemployment relief, the perils of the industrial workplace, the squalor of urban living conditions, and the insecurity of old age could possibly be "the outcomes of our republican institutions." Political liberty and religion, which emphasized "contentment and submission," engendered a false sense of security. Instead, Lum urged international solidarity, the systematic study of revolutionary socialism, and the unfurling of the red flag of the International.[4]

This indictment of liberalism—civic rights combined with faith in the fairness of markets—underscored the degree to which the grievances of urban workers still mirrored those of Reconstruction era land reformers. It also betrayed the rifts between craft and industrial unionism, anticipating debates within the American Federation of Labor. To be sure, the Federation's early years were shaped in part by the syndicalism of socialists and anarchists such as Lum, who attempted to shape the upstart organization as they had the Knights of Labor.[5] They brought with them cultural understandings of "free labor," particularly as it pertained to "slavery" and "emancipation." The AFL also provided masses of workingmen a model of battle, resistance, and abolition—a framework by which old soldiers north and south might reconcile their former differences in opposition to a "new slavery." As a promoter of an anti-political "mutualist" strategy, Lum insisted that the war had been a conflict between two "rival industrial systems" that had "opened new paths to fortune, incited new passions, and found means to gratify them." He saw in the New South the same wave of contractors, speculators, and monopolists who commanded the industrial North. Disappointed with the war's results, Lum exposed the "free-labor" chimera and avowed that real sectional reconciliation was being achieved by the capitalist class: "To-day, South and North alike admit the fundamental principle of our industrial system, the corner stone of our economic structure: *Free labor is cheaper than slave labor!* The South are converted; the poverty of a factory population is no longer an Eastern peculiarity. The gray meets blue in hearty union to draw dividends and cut coupons. They have found free labor the *cheapest*."[6]

Lum's interpretation of the Civil War as a partial revolution—an event that had emancipated some workers but enslaved others—was common during the Long Gilded Age, including to the ideologies and identities of countless Federationists.[7] However, as the Federation veered from being complementary to competing with industrial unions, its use of war imagery abandoned anti-capitalism. Mirroring the anti-revolutionary leadership of Samuel Gompers, the AFL moved increasingly away from labor militancy and electoral strategy, meandering toward conciliation and nationalism as leaders and "respectable" workers sought compliance in the throes of World War I and government repression of the labor left.[8] The AFL's labor patriotism was more than an attitude; it was a "set of cultural practices" that included collective memory. The rise of national blue-gray reconciliation paralleled the Federation's maturation. Whereas worker collectivism and fraternity appealed to the sensibilities of veterans' organizations, reform and labor agitation also possessed the capacity to undermine the preservationist identities of Union veterans as protectors of law and social order. Just as strikes served as proxies for military battles, Labor Day, Decoration Day, and Fourth of July marches became stand-ins for military parades, often with militia and veterans' auxiliaries, notably the GAR, in attendance. These incubators of nationalist pageantry in which white (and "becoming white") workingmen venerated the veteran alongside the industrial soldier, and the union label alongside the American flag, proved critical to AFL legitimacy.[9]

At the same time, "Jim Crow unionism" saw owners manipulate workers through racism even as those workers forged their own identities, created cultural practices, and comprehended their interests as "white." Those securely within the fortress of whiteness—and those pursuing admittance—not only accepted "white" as normative but also were inclined to view themselves primarily as members of a ruling race rather than, or in addition to, members of an oppressed class.[10] Labor conservatism and worker exclusion exacerbated racial separation and imbalance, widening the crisis of trust between working-class Blacks and white-led labor organizations. The sectional "healing" espoused by AFL bureaucrats came at the cost of not only African American inclusion but also labor radicalism, as racial segregation undermined any possibility of genuinely transformational politics. Indeed, AFL "emancipation" became synonymous with a balance between capital and labor and the incremental improvement of conditions for workingmen *within* capitalism. The Federation's antislavery symbolism and its representations of Lincoln in particular became rallying cries for piecemeal reform and against party politics and labor militancy. Labor's overall shift toward economic nationalism at the expense of revolutionary internationalism was gradual, but it occurred most evidently within Federation leadership and institutions and was affirmed through the Civil War memory they constructed.

## The Abolitionist Party of 1894

As the century mark approached, industrial unionists, anarchists, and revolutionary socialists were folding within or fighting a losing battle against the newly formed American Federation of Labor. Evolved out of the Federation of Organized Trades and Labor Unions and established in Columbus, Ohio, in December 1886, the Federation sought to revive the National Labor Union's eight-hour movement through an assembly of craft unions, some of the largest and most influential being the carpenters and joiners, cigar makers, ironworkers and steelworkers, iron molders, and typographers.[11] Organizing by trade rather than by city or region, the AFL coordinated beyond temporary movements, farmer-labor insurgencies, or divisive party politics—in some sense surviving by trying to do less.[12] Although national Republicans regularly charged AFL leadership with delivering votes to Democrats, Federationists formally eschewed partisanship, courted only those they categorized as "skilled" workers, and took a conservative approach toward strikes and direct action. Focusing on bread-and-butter issues, Federation leaders paired their organizational identity with notions of respectability, sobriety, antiradicalism, xenophobia, and masculinity. They countenanced the permanence of capitalism, and accepted wage labor, class divisions, and the dependent condition of workers as fixtures of the capitalist system.[13] By its 1894 convention the organization remained split between a rank and file who were often sympathetic to socialism (through either Marxist or non-Marxist avenues) and a more conservative management who viewed the AFL as a bulwark against industrial unionism and revolution.[14] Moreover, unlike the Knights of Labor, AFL members opposed the introduction of "greenhorn" workers who might dilute "skilled" trades, and administrators regularly exploited divisions of race, ethnicity, and region in order to suppress radicalism and refuse so-called unskilled workers.[15]

AFL members often understood this racial blackballing as necessary to protect their organizations. As Alexander Saxton finds, the rapid collapse of both the Knights and Eugene Debs's American Railway Union verified for many workers the structural deficiencies of catchall membership, when in fact more-inclusive industrial unions bore the brunt of employer attacks *because* they were more threatening to owner interests. Meanwhile, racial exclusion reciprocated economic exclusion, conditioning craft unionists, and their leaders in particular, to think in restrictive and self-preservationist terms. AFL bosses often characterized as "not white" any worker who might enter the labor market and compete with skilled "white" workers. They targeted laborers of African, Chinese, and eastern and southern European ancestry, widening the chasm between their craft unions and the remainder of the labor force, which was largely "unskilled" and disproportionately nonwhite and non-male. The result was that the self-defense of organized tradesmen was often predicated on gendered notions of "manhood," as well as on the adoption and extension of white racism, including white nationalism.[16]

The championing of so-called exceptional American rights and democratic institutions gradually became part of AFL culture, fostered by its longtime leader, Samuel Gompers. Although Gompers had talked openly in AFL's early years of inevitable class struggle and even identified as an anti-capitalist, he grew to reject industrial unionism and independent working-class politics. At the same time, a mushrooming labor bureaucracy became wedded to phased negotiation and détente with big business, lagging behind its constituents on such issues.[17] Even as many low-ranking Federationists rebuked capital-labor mutualism, Gompers defended his anti-socialist and anti-party stances through national tradition.[18] "In America we are trade unionists; in Russia we would be revolutionists," Gompers explained. "We don't need revolution."[19] Gompers's caution paralleled the gradualist wing of antislavery agitation, drawing through lines to antislavery politics. The AFL's depiction of Lincoln was that of a benevolent liberator and author of the most important democratic instrument ever penned by an American, the Emancipation Proclamation.[20] Projecting this Great Emancipator image, Gompers initially equated workingmen with slaves and capitalists with slave masters, highlighting their power to abuse and safeguard exploitation.[21] He called the War for the Union a "war of slave emancipation," and his adherents saw themselves as metaphorical soldiers, "effective as that of any regular military force," in an army of human freedom.[22]

Gompers's union model was that of the citadel, protecting those inside and excluding those beyond the walls. The citadel gates periodically opened, as when Gompers called for the organization of African American workers. After appointing George L. Norton, a Black man and secretary of St. Louis's Marine Firemen's Union No. 5464, general organizer in 1891, Gompers championed interracial strike actions and sent their details to AFL organizers across the South. Black-white unity was evidence that "the spirit of freedom, independence, and emancipation is dawning," he predicted. "The final emancipation of the wage worker will be contested by the white and black laborer shoulder to shoulder."[23] However, the AFL fortress became increasingly exclusionary after 1901. While corporate firms, business associations, and local chambers of commerce sought total employer control of the workplace and the nonrecognition of unions through "open shops" (a forerunner of "right-to-work" laws), Gompers in 1903 called for a "solid phalanx of the grand army of labor" to protest against "capitalist invasion of our rights." Once again expressing politics through martial traditionalism, he insisted that any hope for "the perpetuation of liberty and our republican institutions, lies in organized labor."[24]

AFL members also approximated themselves to "an army of labor" that would deliver workingmen by throwing off slavery's chains and achieve "industrial freedom."[25] Reviving and repurposing the language of the sectional crisis, Federationists consistently compared laborers to bondmen and unions to military organizations, emphasizing liberation as the ultimate aim. Labor's struggle was one against "autocratic interests" akin to the slaveocracy and its deliverance the same as the "emancipation fought for by our forefathers."[26] "We are all soldiers in one army advancing to the conquest of one sole aim," resolved one worker, advocating that the "different divisions of the grand army of labor" unify for "the struggle for the emancipation of the working class."[27] Fitting emancipation into a longer history of working-class struggle dating to classical antiquity, one member termed "the emancipation proclamation of Spartacus . . . the last great and unsuccessful struggle for the emancipation of labor."[28] "The brunt of battle . . . the real battle," another professed, was one of "economic, social and political emancipation."[29] This reform model was part and parcel of a general resurgence in trade unionism, in which the AFL's membership swelled from 297,000 in 1897 to over 1.6 million in 1904, comprising roughly 20 percent of all industrial workers.[30] As the AFL expanded, countless workingmen viewed its mission as a continuation of the Civil War and as one phase of a historical "emancipation." As proclaimed by socialist Herbert Newton Casson, himself a friend of both Gompers and Scottish trade unionist and Labour Party founder Keir Hardie, as well as a relative of the legendary Confederate Stonewall Jackson, "Great was the revolution of 1776! Great was the emancipation of 1863! But greater than both will be the uprising that will soon make another date!"[31]

Frank Keyes Foster, the AFL's first national secretary and head of the Massachusetts state chapter, as well as editor of the *Boston Labor Leader*, saw the civil strife as the greatest threat to the republic since the sectional crisis and viewed his growing assembly of workers as occupying the role of antislavery radicals on the eve of the Civil War. "The Abolitionist party of 1856 has its prototype in the labor organization of 1894," he explained, comparing "the onslaught against wage slavery" to "the movement championed by Garrison, Phillips, and Pillsbury." Although workingmen were numerically superior to organized abolitionists, he considered them at a greater disadvantage because the influence of the Money Power dwarfed even that of the Slave Power. What was needed was not only a war—the "citadel of labor" against the "battering rams of monopoly"—but confederation among labor reformers. Seeking to push workers out of various radical labor camps and into the Democratic Party, Foster nevertheless explained that "political action" and "party action" were not necessarily the same thing and, in the vein of antislavery immediatism, advocated an "awakening" of the public consciousness in addition to office holding.[32]

Irish-born veteran John O'Brien concurred. A soldier in the 4th Connecticut Infantry and 1st Connecticut Heavy Artillery, and later president of the Oregon state AFL, O'Brien argued that while workers were not engaged in an *actual* war with capitalists, unionization depended on replicating the martial composition of the War of the Rebellion. Having seen combat at Petersburg, O'Brien viewed the US Army—its "collection of men armed for war . . . companies, battalions, regiments, brigades and divisions under proper officers"—as a model for working-class organization. Trade unions, he maintained, "must be an army in some sense," as coordinated coercion required a "militant character" response. The better workers comprehended "the art of war," the better they might transform from "mob" to "phalanx" to "legion." Like his predecessors in the Knights of Labor and the Socialist Labor Party, O'Brien understood the conflict between labor and capital as an allegorical if not literal battle, insisting that labor tactics of the strike, the boycott, and the picket all required soldierly discipline. Federationist David Kiely was direct: "Our present industrial system is industrial warfare. . . . Our enemies have 90 percent of the munitions."[33] Just as the battles to save the Union and free the slaves "showed the world the military power of the United States," trade unionization could disclose the strength of the American laborer. Through this prototype, workingmen might rightly "cross lances with capital, then one campaign should, like the war of the Rebellion, which did away with slavery, show that labor is equal if not superior in strength to capital."[34]

The "perpetual civil war" in question was an alternative to physical war. Workers framed the conflict against "shop slavery" as patriotic, with loyalists and traitors, flags and professions of nationalism. In the antislavery vernacular of AFL journals, Federationists were "common soldiers in the grand army of labor"; strikebreakers were not only "scabs" and "mercenaries" but apostates, often slandered as "deserters," "shirkers," or "copperheads," equated to wartime turncoats.[35] Notions of loyalty mirrored their sectional predecessors. One Federationist defined "traitor" as a worker who feigns sympathy with the union cause or buys the nonunion label. "He is like the soldier who enlists in time of peace and deserts when the war begins," he contended.[36] "Treason," another averred, "is the only word to describe the acts of a workingman who strives to keep alive divisions in his own ranks on the day of battle."[37] Pinkertons and Baldwin-Felts agents, meanwhile, were emissaries of privatized violence and—as hirelings rather than citizen-soldiers—antithetical to American principles. Claiming that the United States had entered a new and continuous form of fratricide, one editor likened company guards and private police forces to the hired swords of medieval warlords.[38] Unlike the levy en masse or the people's army of 1861–65, these mercenaries for the aristocracy constituted agents of a new feudalism.

Labor opponents employed the same symbolic license, equating unions to rebels and slaveholders. However, the real crime of union men as viewed by corporate bosses was not their national disloyalty but their militancy in the service of so-called time theft and interference with private property. Some owners argued that tradesmen were more despotic than slavers. Supporting "open shops" (a workplace habitat that workingmen deemed equivalent to being "shackled"), breakfast food magnate C. W. Post, who was born and raised in Lincoln's Springfield, Illinois, wailed that "more tyranny, assaults, destruction of property, general violence and murder have been committed by members of labor unions in trying to force and enslave white men than were ever perpetuated by the owners of the black slave before the Civil War."[39] Anti-union propagandists and open shop advocates such as David M. Parry's National Association of Manufacturers compared Gompersism, with its relatively modest eight-hour advocacy and boycott tactics, to the French Revolution's Reign of Terror. Supposing labor organization "un-American," they connected the AFL to the foreign-born anarchism of Leon F. Czolgosz, who assassinated President William McKinley in September 1901. To Federationists, meanwhile, open shoppers were, in the vein of slaveholding Confederates, nothing less than "traitors to America" and working people.[40]

AFL songbooks reinforced these sectional imaginings. Composers drafted labor songs to the tune of popular wartime works. "Buddy, Won't You Roll Down the Line," well-known during the 1890s, described an instance in which "free labor rebelled" against the convict lease system.[41] Opponents deemed Coxey's Army, which marched on Washington, DC, to protest mass unemployment following the Panic of 1893, both a "second civil war" and a form of "insurrection and rebellion . . . likely to create a spirit such as that which John Brown brought to life at Harpers Ferry." Coxey's jobless dissidents stepped to "Marching with Coxey," which was composed to "Marching through Georgia" and written by an AFL member.[42] A song to the tune of "John Brown's Body" accompanied the 1901 AFL convention in Scranton, Pennsylvania. The lyrics envisioned an "army" of skilled workers—coopers, bakers, hatters, carpenters, bottle blowers, brickmakers, engravers, musicians, bicycle makers, jewelry repairmen, barbers, waiters, and horseshoers—all engaged in a "march of triumph," paralleling that of the Union armies four decades prior.[43] So-called unskilled workers were conspicuously absent from this producerist cavalcade.

The AFL's left wing provided a militant shank to the antislavery vernacular. Writing a series of essays for the *American Federationist*, member of the German labor left Gottlieb A. Hoehn advanced the radicalism of an earlier generation of socialists. Possessing a Marxian commitment to international worker self-liberation above the "sentimental songs" and "false freedom" of nationalism, Hoehn maintained that such class struggle was a battle—a "howling . . . fighting . . . scrambling" conflict that required the use of real or rhetorical weapons on the part of workers. According to Hoehn, formerly of Chicago's *Arbeiter Zeitung* and now editor of the *St. Louis Labor World*, which was committed to the socialist wing of the AFL, unorganized workers were used criminally as a "machine of warfare" and as "industrial soldiers . . . in capitalist profit mills." He avowed that the key to overthrowing capitalism lay in Marx's dictum that the liberation of the proletariat must be achieved by the working class itself. "The emancipation of labor," Hoehn explained, means "the emancipation of humanity, the abolition of class interests . . . of wage slavery."[44]

The violent character of large-scale strikes, or "rebellions," in Tennessee, Pennsylvania, Colorado, and Idaho further legitimized the language of slavery and emancipation. East Tennessee's Coal Creek Rebellion in the summer of 1891 began when owners replaced white and Black payroll miners with convict laborers. Witnessing columns of armed union men support striking miners, Chattanooga Federation of Trades representative H. H. Schwartz cheered Black and white cooperation among the miners and invoked the interracialism of the War of the Rebellion. "The captains of the different companies are all

Grand Army men," he observed. "Whites and negroes are standing shoulder to shoulder."[45] Anarchist Alexander Berkman maintained that revolutionary influence might "complete ultimate emancipation" among employees at Homestead, Pennsylvania, where steelworkers fought pitched battles against the state militia and Pinkerton agents loyal to owner Andrew Carnegie and manager Henry Clay Frick in the summer of 1892.[46] In Colorado, where the radical Western Federation of Miners sought "the emancipation of labor from the thralldom of monopoly," toilers demanded liberation from capitalist "masters."[47] To conservatives—capitalists, jurists, and the police—these were illegal insubordinations committed by traitorous "rebels."[48]

Formed in 1890, the United Mine Workers of America also exercised the language of "slave pens," "white slavery," and "a new bondage" to defend its numerous striking actions throughout the Middle West and Pennsylvania. An ethnically polyglot and interracial industrial union of workers in bituminous and anthracite mines, United Miners often viewed the Civil War not as consummation but as one step on the road to worker liberation, as well as an unfortunate watershed in favor of wealth imbalance and corporate control. As one miner saw it, the Confederacy, "whose cornerstone was slavery," had been replaced by "another confederacy whose cornerstone is slavery . . . a confederacy of millionaires."[49] Emphasizing worker conditions over market trends and credit networks, miners found owners tantamount to feudal barons and slave despots. They used "serfdom," "bondage," and "wage slavery" interchangeably to describe their oppressors.

Again, class unity was an alternative to literal war. According to the wife of one southern Indiana miner, whereas the emancipation of Black slaves had been achieved by "an agonized nation and baptized with blood and tears," a new emancipation for "wage slaves of the whole country" might be "a peaceful victory . . . enforced by the will of millions of united men."[50] Despite conventional interpersonal racism on the ground, which often devolved into outright white-unionist-on-Black-"scab" violence in places like Virden, Pana, and Carterville, Illinois, in 1898 and 1899, many white miners understood that more equal alliances with Black workers, who faced all of their hardships and then some, were the only way to effectively confront capital. White editorialists called forth Emancipation Day and racial justice revolutionaries, from Toussaint L'Ouverture to John Brown. Strategically, and perhaps cynically, white striking miners attempted to persuade nonunionized Black workers that "scabbing" was a betrayal of the work of the Emancipation Proclamation.[51] Meanwhile, Black unionists used emancipationist apologues and venerated the memory of Reconstruction (which remained very rare among white labor) to defend their labor work and recruit African

American workers. The names of the exalted included Frederick Douglass, Hiram Revels, Blanche Bruce, and John R. Lynch.[52]

The Pullman Strike of May 1894, a wildcat work stoppage that spread from Chicago to Sacramento, and one in which dozens of strikers were killed by state authorities and company police, was quickly dubbed the "Debs Rebellion" after the trainmen leader.[53] By July 4, 1894, Debs, speaking in Chicago, predicted a "civil war," this one along class lines, in which 90 percent of the United States would be arrayed against the other 10 percent.[54] He tied this specter of renewed domestic conflict to his idol and frequent reference point, Lincoln, by insisting that the slain president had predicted a "contest between producing classes and the money power" near the end of the war and that this reflection "gave the great emancipator his gloomiest forebodings." This time, however, Debs warned of a new enslavement in which "employees will be reduced to a condition scarcely removed above chattel slavery."[55] This notion of armed defiance, and armies of millions, outfitted not in woolen blue and gray but in workers' threads, pervaded even as aging veterans faded from visibility within the labor resistance.

Ultimately, President Grover Cleveland used two long-dormant Civil War statutes concerning domestic insurrection as justification to send troops into Chicago and quell the uprising, against the wishes of Illinois governor John Peter Altgeld.[56] Although Gompers had sided with the efforts of federal authorities to end the strike and other AFL leaders felt that the American Railway Union's defeat validated a more conservative, negotiation-based scheme, the Federation's masses remained committed to strike tactics as a new labor-Populist alliance arose in Illinois. "Pullman" became a rallying cry for later worker struggles, with unionists pairing their involvement with the old abolitionist cause through collective memory. A tremendous canvas banner displayed in the Cooper Union that July in support of striking railroad men made that connection explicit:

> They hanged John Brown, but Chattel
> Slavery passed away.
> They arrested Gene Debs, and may kill him,
> But White Slavery will pass away.
> Such souls go marching on.[57]

Influenced by the outbreak of war in Cuba, one worker compared mine owners during the Lattimer Massacre in the fall of 1897, in which nineteen unarmed anthracite coal miners of German and Slavic descent were killed by a police posse in Luzerne County, Pennsylvania, to bloodthirsty Spanish soldiers. The European American miners, meanwhile, with a reputation as underpaid strikebreakers and beholden to deeply exploitative company housing and retail, were "slaves." "Miners were bondsmen," one Federationist maintained, "bound to their employers as rigidly as though they were lawful slaves of their masters." Resistance demanded a military-like alliance in which workers must "organize and stand united . . . shoulder to shoulder in the grand army of labor."[58] The strike led to an upsurge in United Mine Workers membership, and rhetorical pugnacity grew in relation to strike actions.

## Labor Aristocracy

Conceptions of "labor emancipated"—the abolition of workingmen through industrial consolidation—varied, becoming more and more predicated on conciliation and reform. Summoning John Brown and Wendell Phillips, both craft and industrial unionists grasped the importance of radicalism outside the party system; many also called for independent workers' parties.[59] AFL leaders, however, were more likely than the common run to eschew revolutionary politics even as they divided over questions of decommodification and an independent labor party. Although AFL delegates in 1894 officially adopted parts of socialist Thomas J. Morgan's eleven-point measure endorsing the nationalization of railroads, telegraphs, telephones, and mines (a measure heavily influenced by both socialists and Populists), they vetoed the preamble of the "political programme" advocating third party action, a strategy Gompers vehemently attacked. In a final repudiation of the AFL's socialist minority, the delegates likewise rebuffed the plank calling for "collective ownership by the people of all means of production and distribution."[60]

In rhetoric as well as policy, conservatism tended to flow from the top down. AFL treasurer and longtime conservative John Brown Lennon, who had come out of the Journeymen Tailors Union, considered himself engaged in "a warfare for industrial emancipation" through which evolutionary (rather than revolutionary) trade union agitation might result in "the emancipation of labor."[61] Although Frank Duffy termed the AFL "a mighty army," it was "an army of peace." "Their 'arms' are not those of warfare or bloodshed," he reminded readers, but the "tools of industry."[62] Such sentiments mirrored Gompers's own conservative drift. "There are two ways by which great material and social improvements in the condition of the people come about," Gompers explained before the House Labor Committee just after the turn of the century. Contrasting the "rational" Anglo temperament with Bourbon volatility and explaining that judiciousness was a particular characteristic of the "great Anglo-Saxon race," he cautioned against "the method of the

French Revolution" in favor of an evolutionary style more in line with what he deemed quintessentially American traditions.[63]

This rightist use of the antislavery vernacular supplemented the AFL's larger pivot in the late 1890s against both industrial unionism and farmer-labor alliance and toward racialization. Gompers's half-hearted professions of organization regardless of race, sex, or nationality were undercut by the chauvinistic practice and policy of local chapters, as well as by the reality that Blacks, women, and the foreign-born were inordinately employed in "unskilled" labor, effectively locking them out of the AFL's "labor aristocracy."[64] Industrialization profoundly impacted sex relations and gender roles, often creating or exacerbating forms of domination within both the workplace and the home. Women critiqued the system accordingly, using the same antislavery vernacular as men to insist that freedom from "wage slavery" should apply equally to them. Addressing the ubiquity of women's oppression and attacking the paradoxical choice many women faced between wage slavery and an abusive marriage in pursuit of the "emancipation of women," feminist-socialist Meta Stern Lilienthal held that nearly all women are "either dependent on wage slaves or they are wage slaves themselves."[65] Although women, three-quarters of them single, constituted at least 20 percent of the industrial labor force by century's turn, the vast majority were judged as "unskilled."[66] As such, the Federation spurned this massive and especially oppressed bloc in favor of white male preference.

This restrictive approach also ostracized "unorganizable" and "racially in-between" workers of Italian, Polish, Russian, Greek, Czech, Romanian, and Lithuanian descent in favor of craft unions dominated by white, native-born workers. These racially unassimilable workers were often labeled "anarchistic" and "communistic" or, in the case of Hungarians, un-Americanized "Hunkies" who were "content to be driven like slaves."[67] White workingmen deployed racial theories against the growing numbers of "unskilled" and semiskilled foreign-born: Italian menial laborers, meat-packing Bohemians, Slavic miners and steelworkers, Jews in light industry occupations, and, most of all, East Asians, against whom Knights of Labor in the Far West had established a pattern of expulsion and violence.[68] In the context of *Plessy v. Ferguson*, the Spanish-American War, and the bureaucratization of race science, native-born unionists accepted and internalized stereotypes about "new" immigrants as not only violent radicals but also not fully white. On the road to Taylorism and the scientific management of labor, owners masterminded new forms of "efficiency" and "least cost" practices based on segregation and concepts of racial in-betweenness. Facilitating this process, and taking their cues from a national political and cultural system that normalized and prioritized whiteness, "white on arrival" workers designated ethnics-in-the-making "off-white," "conditionally white," or "temporary Negroes."[69] Gompers himself called for "racial purity" as a source of strength within both the trades and the nation-state.[70]

White workers across the AFL hierarchy continued to direct white supremacy against Black workingmen. "Jim Crow unionism" and "Jim Crow locals" combined explicit provisions for "white-born" applicants with de facto methods of apprenticeship discrimination, rigged technical examinations, and licensing and initiation fees to block African American and foreign-born membership. Through the myth of "Negro strikebreaking," owners and laborers alike exaggerated the extent to which "hordes of ignorant blacks" consciously crossed the picket lines of striking whites, thus rationalizing a sharp color line in both industrial hiring and union halls. Craft and trade segregation buttressed or rendered superfluous state-level legal segregation laws as, even in the event of legal integration, Black workers would not be permitted entry into decent-paying union jobs.[71] Meanwhile, whereas conservative race leaders including Booker T. Washington urged capitalists to employ African American laborers precisely *because* they were disinclined to radicalism and not tempted by the "red flag of anarchy," W. E. B. Du Bois advised Black workers to organize along class lines and fight discrimination within labor's ranks. Such integration always risked reviving sectional passions, such as it did in early 1898 with the "Southern Confederacy of Labor," created in Atlanta to resist the Northern pattern of racial inclusion within AFL unions.[72]

At the same time, rank-and-file white workers also used antislavery vernacular to push back against top-down conservatism. One AFL newspaper called for the organization of workers of all colors, avowing that the "master class" relied on the color line to keep workers divided. "The colored races are members of the wage slave class," the editor reminded readers, and must be so organized that "in order that the working class of the world may achieve its emancipation."[73] Although Frank Duffy insisted that Labor Day was to wage workers what Emancipation Day was to African Americans, Puerto Rican unionist Angel Becerra lamented the AFL's abandonment of May Day celebrations, which he thought an optimal tool to form "one grand army all over the world in a concerted effort to resist capitalistic greed and oppression."[74] Craft unions, including the National Union of United Brewery Workmen, fitted emancipationism within their foreign-born subcultural frameworks. The Marxist-heavy brewers became part of a "grand army of skilled craftsmen" that promoted "solidarity, man for man from roof to cellar, all for each and each for all," espousing both economic (strike and boycott) and political (worker party) action.[75] Untold numbers of AFL socialists, including conservative "slowcialists" such as Milwaukee's Victor Berger, who backed municipal "sewer socialism" and assured capitalists that well-treated workers provided the best bulwark against strikes and economic disruptions, nevertheless damned Federationist leadership for placating capital, echoing charges of plutocracy that were once leveled against Southern slaveholders.[76] The old abolitionist John Swinton favored industrial unionism and renounced the AFL's craft union approach as insular and divisive.[77] Other workers predicted that Federation membership would soon include a majority of all wage earners, leading to a "second civil war" (presumably bloodless) in which trade unions not only reformed but overtook capital. "The second Civil War is now going on," one worker conceded; "every newspaper contains accounts of battles, skirmishes, victories and defeats" of "armies of wage-workers" in danger of becoming "the human chattels of the great trusts." The stakes were just as high as the first war, he swore, and the principles of strikers and union organizers were "as true as was any military general who wore the blue or the gray."[78]

Yet emancipationist language contrasted with the AFL's de facto exclusion, as male supremacy and white supremacy mutually reinforced to the detriment of an authentic working-class program. By 1900 thirty-nine of the eighty-two AFL affiliates were entirely white, another twenty-seven contained only a few nonwhite members, and many explicitly barred nonwhite workers in their charters. AFL leaders, many of whom believed that they must accept corporate and Jim Crow prerogatives or perish, deemed even organized Black tradesmen second-class workers, compliant and voiceless. Gompers backed the organization of Black workers largely to protect the gains of whites by preventing African Americans from being used as scabs.[79] Other Federationists saw the uplift of white workers as historically dependent on some form of solidarity (though typically not equality) with Black people. In his brief history of US trade unionism, which he deemed necessary to combat all forms of "slavery," Hugh McGregor groaned that the South's white underclass had never been emancipated, and their relative elevation by Black chattel slavery resulted only in the creation of a class of "white trash," detested by both masters and Black slaves.[80] The notion that "white slavery" was worse than chattel slavery remained ubiquitous, with some Federationists pointing to the absence of so-called paternalism as evidence that factory work was in fact more exploitative than the Old South's peculiar institution. They avowed that no slaveholder could have secured services so cheap as industrial workers.[81] Some veterans insisted that nonunionized African American laborers owed it to white workingmen not to cross the picket line because, in the words of one battle-scarred Union man and striking miner, they had fought to free enslaved Black people and were now under threat of being "enslaved" by chattel-slaves-turned-scabs.[82]

Despite the sanctioning of "white slavery," which further divided the workforce by racializing legitimate or "skilled" labor toward whiteness and privileging the experiences of white workers, AFL leaders viewed party politics and the endorsement of political candidates as a likely source of member division and organizational disintegration. Federationist captains rejected a parliamentary politics-based approach and growled that political division among veterans—the "damnable selfishness of party affiliation in the breasts of the grand army"—had hindered class consciousness for decades.[83] In 1895 labor leader William Curtis Pomeroy, former Knight and founder of the Waiters' League of Chicago, underscored this connection between white veteranhood and trade unity on the one hand and party loyalty on the other:

> I want to get a carpenter to join the trades union movement. . . . This carpenter is a Grand Army man, and nearly all carpenters who are old enough are Grand Army men, and he is a Republican. He says, "I am perfectly willing to join the trades union as such, but I will not join a political party in opposition to my ideas." He is wrong perhaps; we may all agree that he is wrong, but we want him in the trades union, and you cannot get him if he has to desert his party and adopt the policy of a new political party . . . advocating against everything for which he fought during the war. The Democrat is the same.[84]

In their rejection of party politics and labor militancy, AFL leaders sought to integrate ideological variety—and thus sheer numbers—into their movement. To Gompers, partisan inclusivity (more than racial or gender inclusivity) was a means of coalition building; tradition was necessary to offset revolution and establish political equilibrium. As he explained in February 1896, both radical and conservative "blend our cause into the great factor of an aggressive, moving body of the grand army of labor, determined to secure present amelioration in the conditions of the toilers, and finally to secure their entire emancipation. . . . We want the work of all."[85] Yet pro-electoral and Lassallean-oriented unionists employed wartime vernacular to reinforce their positions as well. As one Colorado carpenter declared, "The infantry forces of labor organizations are in absolute need of the cavalry and batteries of political action in the great conflict for industrial freedom and the emancipation of wage slavery."[86] Gompers played the role of Lincoln. Speaking in Cardiff, Wales, to a group of British and Irish trade unionists in the fall of 1895, he connected British workingmen to the antislavery cause: "Although during the great American War the moneyed classes of England stood on the side of slavery," he thanked "the weavers and spinners of Lancashire" who "refused to recognize the belligerent South and stood up for the freedom and rights of man."[87] Gompers echoed similar themes to a crowd at Burkes' Hall in Lowell, Massachusetts, in February 1898, likening labor's cause to that of antislavery. "The same blackguardly accusations that are argued against the men who discuss the labor question," he maintained, "were hurled at the head of Wendell Phillips, Abraham Lincoln and all those who were opposed to slavery."[88] They were—like the land reformers, currency populists, revolutionary socialists, and organized workingmen before them—the neo-abolitionists, working toward what workingmen termed a "greater emancipation" that would transcend mere civic and political rights.

The Federationist press turned Civil War symbolism, and Lincoln in particular, into a rallying point for reform. AFL leadership regularly demanded that Honest Abe's birthday be made a national labor holiday, and members consistently recycled Lincoln's adage about the "strongest bond of human sympathy" being that which "unites all working people," as well as his assessment of labor and capital from his second inaugural address.[89] As Daniel T. Rodgers notes, perhaps the most enduring theme in the history of US labor has been its "appeal to the dignity of labor and the worth of those who did the world's 'real' work."[90] In this sense, the rail-splitting Illinoisan was the embodiment of a "real" worker—an autodidact who understood, according to one carpenter, that the cornerstone of the republic was a "healthy, happy, contented, prosperous and self-satisfied working class."[91] AFL man J. E. Potts speculated that, after signing the Emancipation Proclamation, Lincoln would have eventually warned that "the time would come when whites would have to be emancipated."[92] Just as the sixteenth president conjectured that the country could not remain half slave and half free, union men maintained that shops could not remain half unionized and half nonunionized.[93]

As always, the Lincoln image satisfied a range of practical and ideological needs. Some Federationists saw in him a paragon of the white labor tradition, reflecting their own forms of reactionary economic and racial nationalism; others highlighted Lincoln's supposed radicalism and ultimate willingness to challenge property relations through uncompensated emancipation. Some trade union leaders used the Lincoln metaphor to attack Daniel De Leon and the Socialist Labor Party, or insist on the fruitlessness of debating with industrial unionists. To them, Lincoln represented a certain homespun, if Anglo-Saxon, steadiness and practicality. Even the Emancipation Proclamation was less a revolutionary symbol than a carefully assessed policy solution to an inescapable problem. This so-called grounded utilitarianism precluded anarchism, socialism, or radical interracial or cross-gender organization.[94]

Though greatly diminished, the Knights continued to play a token role in local Lincoln remembrance, often alongside the AFL. When W. W. Stone, a rabidly anti-Chinese Knights leader and president of San Francisco's Lincoln Monument League, found himself at the helm of an effort to both procure a statue of Abraham Lincoln for Golden Gate Park and establish "Lincoln Day" as a statewide observance, the enfeebled Knights of Labor, now led by former Greenbacker and Populist James Richard Sovereign, joined with local GAR chapters and members of the Women's Relief Corps to heartily endorse the measures.[95]

Most workers on the shop floor, however, deemed Lincoln a great commoner sprung from the producing classes. Merrill Peterson terms this version of Lincoln as identifiable with ordinary Americans, which peaked during the Great Depression, as the "Man of the People."[96] Like muckraking Progressive Era reformer Ida Tarbell, turn-of-the-century workers marveled at Lincoln's rise from "that class known in the South as 'poor whites.'"[97] In a 1904 essay titled "The Conflict of the Classes," labor journalist Margaret Scott Hall recalled that "when the blight of slavery cursed the nation, the mighty man of the people, Abraham Lincoln, stepped in from the obscure ranks of labor to be the champion of the weak." Now, Hall insisted, working people must summon his spirit to forward "the cause of liberty."[98] According to United Brotherhood of Carpenters and Joiners of America chairman Alexander Law, corporate employers were, like slaveholders of old, "exploiters of the people," engaged with the masses in an "irrepressible conflict." He warned that such oligarchs should be dealt with as Lincoln did the "oppressors" of 1861.[99] When Lincoln's son Robert Todd Lincoln, who sat on the Pullman Sleeping Car Company's board of directors, acknowledged in 1915 that African American porters did not make a living wage and therefore relied on tips to supplement their meager income, labor editors pounced. The symbolism of the headline, "Lincoln's Son Admits Railroad Slavery," was lost on no one. That the progeny of the Great Emancipator was now implicated in a network of "wage slavery," and one specifically against the Black working class, was a testament to the descent of free-labor ideals.[100]

Both the AFL and its opponents drew from the same well of commemoration. Labor enemies and xenophobic editors, asking whether the American people shall be "Lincoln Americans" or "Samgomperites," contrasted the wholesome sixteenth president with the AFL's supposed radicalism.[101] Asking "Shall it be Samuel Gompers, or Abraham Lincoln?," one editor claimed that unions were neither patriotic nor law-abiding.[102] Mocking the "Grand Army" of workingmen, reactionary tabloids objected to Gompers's unremitting allusions to Lincoln. Complaining that the labor leader had "referred for the seventeenth time to what Abraham Lincoln had said on this or that occasion" during a speech, one critic chided both the predictability of Gompers's innuendo (that no matter the issue, he was certain that Lincoln would have sided with workers) and the alleged insincerity, since Gompers himself was not a member of the working class.[103]

The AFL's appropriation of the Civil War had an inordinate impact on the trajectory of reconciliation among white veterans. Following patterns established by the Central Labor Union and the Knights, the AFL combined industrial and veterans' organizations—army and labor—at parades, speeches, picnics, and encampments dating back to the early "Labor Days" of the 1880s. Although GAR membership peaked in 1890, reunion culture grew alongside the Federation for the next two decades as old soldiers, veterans' bands, and Grand Army posts became fixtures of the Labor Day arena. Made a federal holiday in 1894, Labor Day quickly became, behind Memorial Day, the second most popular calendar date for old soldier reunions and an occasion to celebrate "labor's emancipation." Although created as a safe and government-sanctioned alternative to the more revolutionary May Day, Labor Day also evolved during the early and mid-1880s from militant socialist, Knights of Labor, and Central Labor Union demands that cities and states recognize an official labor holiday. Despite the holiday's contested (some would argue sanitized) origins, it came to represent to workers, according to one observer, what Emancipation Day was to African Americans.[104] As the century turned, the AFL became a fixture at Union and Confederate gatherings, GAR bivouacs, and blue-gray reunions. Grand Army men used Labor Day for monument unveilings and soldiers' and sailors' association reunions; labor leaders congressed at old soldiers' homes; and both war veterans and Federationists banded their gatherings with the nostalgia of old settlers' gatherings.

Throughout the 1890s, celebrations of "Labor's Great Army" became amalgamations of old soldiers and Republican, Democratic, and Populist partisans, as well as sites of overlap between workers and a shrinking base of Civil War veterans where the bloody shirt and sectional wounds were cast opened, mended, exposed, or suppressed.[105] Labor Day 1896 in Topeka, Kansas, for example, combined a massive labor parade with a state GAR reunion; a reported 10,000 soldiers attended.[106] In Canton, Ohio, in 1908, Grand Army members, headed by their brass band, led the Labor Day procession, followed in rank by a union of steam engineers.[107] The Thirty-Second Annual Encampment of the GAR, held in Cincinnati over Labor Day 1898, featured a "peace parade" of veterans and dozens of civic and industrial organizations that marched before an estimated crowd of half a million spectators.[108] The national encampment in Denver seven years later divided the festivities into three days: Labor Day, composed of workers and manufacturers of various persuasions; Military Day, which honored Spanish-American War veterans, the Sons of Union Veterans, and the Women's Relief Corps; and GAR Day, which featured a parade of veterans.[109]

Labor fetes became enmeshed with the Columbian quadricentennial celebrations of 1892. In Indianapolis, where one prominent display spotlighted blue and gray veterans shaking hands, cadets, martial societies, Zouaves, Turnverein members, socialist and fraternal groups, and members of the German-American Veteran Association marched alongside typographers, bookbinders, painters, plumbers, iron molders, carpenters, cigar makers, railroad men, stonemasons, and carriage and wagon workers. Because white reconciliationist and Union-liberationist motifs often coexisted, especially in the Middle West, a grand display representing "Emancipation" featured a Lincoln impersonator holding a copy of the proclamation in one hand and a broken chain in the other, "emblematic of bondage broken."[110] A Congress on Labor convened in August 1893 in Chicago's "White City," site of the nation's illustrious Columbian Exposition. The medley of reformers included Gompers, Terence Powderly, Frederick Douglass, Jane Addams, Henry George, and Booker T. Washington. Eugene Debs addressed a crowd of 25,000 just days after police clashed with unemployed packinghouse workers who were picketing on the lakefront nearby.[111] In the preceding months, exposition promoters had championed the classical colonnades, grand avenues, and coursing Venetian waterways as testaments to labor—"that great army of skilled artisans and workmen, all citizens of this republic." Grand Army members and officials, meanwhile, were instrumental in long-term vision and day-to-day organization. These included Black veterans such as Dr. George Wellington Bryant. Born a slave near Winchester, Kentucky, Bryant had been a drummer in the 54th Massachusetts Infantry before becoming a member of GAR Colonel Shaw Post 343, commissioner general of the National Emancipation Monument Association, and a regular on the veteran lecture circuit.[112] The World's Columbian Exposition also enlarged the scale of dignitaries and labor-veteran fusion. There, Union general and future Republican president William McKinley presided over militias, cavalry, and army regulars, alongside throngs of workingmen.[113]

Gompers himself became active in veterans' politics, advocating for an old soldiers' insurance bill to replace the federal pension system.[114] Part of an ideologically diverse lot that included William Howard Taft, Henry Watterson, Ida Tarbell, William Jennings Bryan, and Mark Twain, Gompers served on the board of trustees of the Lincoln Farm Association to preserve and promote Lincoln's boyhood home near Hodgenville, Kentucky.[115] Exploiting the era's proliferation of reconciliation scripts, he was likewise active in Grant Day celebrations and, with industrialists and imperial architects such as John D. Rockefeller and Alfred Thayer Mahan, as well as a smattering of famed Civil War generals, he administered the Ulysses S. Grant Monument Municipal Inaugural Committee and was instrumental in its unveiling.[116] Moreover, Gompers consistently referenced the war for the Union in popular discourse and gave public speeches specifically on Lincoln, including one to the Jackson Heights Press Club of Elmhurst, New York, in which he insisted that the Great Emancipator's spirit and ideals endured in the "work and lives of the toiling masses of America."[117]

The AFL chieftain buttressed his economic nationalism with Lincolnian memory, wielding it in the service of specific Federation campaigns. This eventually included using the first Republican president to stump for Democratic candidates. The AFL's initial foray into national electoral politics came in 1908 in support of Democrat William Jennings Bryan, whom Republicans and National Association of Manufacturers propagandists smeared as a "socialist." Gompers insisted that it was the duty of workingmen to back Bryan—the very same "duty . . . to preserve that form of government, for the preservation of which, Lincoln said '*Men died at Gettysburg*.'"[118] Bryan lost, but Gompers never relinquished the theme. Speaking in Washington, DC, on Labor Day 1916, he claimed that the "work of human freedom was not ended by Lincoln," praising the recent Seamen's Act and Clayton Antitrust Act.[119] Addressing striking shoemakers in Worcester, Massachusetts, in the summer of 1920—an action he deemed a protest against "slavery"—Gompers explained that Lincoln's freeing of the slaves was never intended to leave "loop holes" to "make it a crime for workers, white and black, to leave their jobs."[120] One pro-labor editor echoed Gompers's point: "If men were forced to work against their will the Emancipation Proclamation of Abraham Lincoln and 13th Amendment would be annulled."[121] United Mine Workers leader John L. Lewis and others linked the right to strike with Lincoln's professed consideration for labor and his opposition to all forms of "tyranny" over workers. "With Abraham Lincoln, I thank God that we have a country where men may strike," Lewis avowed.[122] For Gompers and Lewis, this point was political as well as ideological. While transforming a complicated president into a labor idol was indeed opportunistic, AFL leaders sincerely believed that worker organization—and labor action in the pursuit of workplace justice—converged with Lincolnian principles.

Gompers and other AFL captains also often formally—and expediently—recognized Lincoln's birthday, even using the anniversary to make symbolic interracial overtures, such as inviting Black delegates to discuss the conditions of African American wage earners.[123] As the keynote speaker at a "Lincoln Dollar Dinner" fundraising banquet celebrating the 101st anniversary of Lincoln's birth in February 1910, Gompers, along with directors of the Central Labor Union, painted the secular saint as a "man of the people," a "friend of the common people," and the "President for the working classes." The program featured a reading of the Gettysburg Address, the singing of "The Battle Hymn of the Republic," and a GAR color guard led by assistant adjutant general of the Department of the Potomac. Summoning the *Dred Scott* decision, Gompers pronounced that, rather than his famous espousal of emancipation, Lincoln's "great declaration" was in fact his 1859 address before the Wisconsin State Agricultural Society in Milwaukee that "labor should be considered above capital." He urged contemporary political leaders to echo that sentiment.[124] Eulogizing the "Savior of the Union" to an audience of 1,200 on Long Island the following year, Gompers added to the mythos of "Lincoln the laborer," christening the Illinoisan the "champion of the downtrodden."[125] Meanwhile, AFL membership, such as in the case of a "Lincoln Dinner" held by New York's Workingmen's Committee of One Hundred in the spring of 1900, denounced the co-opting of Lincoln's memory by politicians pretending to be speak for the laboring classes.[126]

The notion of Lincoln as a crypto–trade unionist permeated the AFL ranks. In 1913, as the United Brotherhood of Carpenters and Joiners of America, like much of the nation, celebrated the massive blue-gray reunion that marked the Battle of Gettysburg's fiftieth anniversary, Alexander Law asked a central question regarding the bloodshed of 1861–65: "What was it all about?" The answer was slavery, but not merely slavery of the Old South variety. Inquiring whether people or corporations should rule, Law stressed that Lincoln's "government of the people, by the people, for the people" applied to labor's fight for better hours, wages, and conditions. He compared the antebellum slaveocracy to mill owners in his own time, paralleling chattel slaves with industrial ones. Connecting union men with Union men, Law was certain of Lincoln that "were he alive today he would undoubtedly be with the union men as he was in the days of '61." The Gettysburg commemoration, he suggested, should be an occasion to once again fight against the anti-democracy of corporate power. It was labor's occasion.[127]

Upon his death in December 1924, eulogies for Gompers, like those for Debs two years later, paired the fallen commander with his beau ideal. Maintaining that the martyred president from the prairies of Indiana and Illinois had inspired the future AFL boss as far back as his childhood in England, one Associated Press report insisted that young Gompers wept upon Lincoln's death. And when Lincoln's body lay in rest at New York's city hall during the funerary train procession from Washington, DC, to Springfield, Gompers allegedly waited all day in a congregation of mourners in order to glimpse his slain hero. From his own working-class roots as a cigar maker, the boy Gompers supposedly vowed to emulate the "friend of the common laboring people."[128] But as the AFL's representation of the sixteenth president as a benevolent white liberator grew, leaders used Civil War vernacular to fuse reform with workplace accommodation and industrial nationalism.[129] Indeed, when Federation lieutenants yoked Lincoln and the antislavery cause to their conservative bureaucracy, they did so in the service of a growing loyalty consensus among trade union leadership. The AFL's Abraham Lincoln was fully draped in the American rather than the red flag.

## Labor Loyalty

The industrial patriotism driven by the AFL's Lincoln mythos had imperial implications that culminated in the top-down consensus push during World War I. Stimulated by economic crises of overproduction, underconsumption, and the desire for new commercial markets, the Spanish-American War proved a turning point in both the AFL's conservative migration and the story of white reunion. Veterans north and south had allied against a foreign enemy, and the federal government, with McKinley at the helm, formally committed itself to sectional rapprochement.[130] The essence of labor nationalism also shifted. Some anti-imperialists, including Carl Schurz and Thomas Wentworth Higginson, linked abolitionism to opposition to empire. While Gompers would serve as vice president of the Washington, DC, Anti-Imperialist League, channeling Ulysses S. Grant's famous campaign motto "Let Us Have Peace," his isolationist credentials were dubious.[131] Gompers denounced the potential for "slave labor" anywhere within the US imperial project, but he supported war with Spain and the Philippine annexation, raised no objection to Theodore Roosevelt's Panama Canal or the dollar diplomacy of William Howard Taft, and backed US intervention in Mexico.[132] According to Bernard Mandel, Gompers "accepted imperialism as part of the American fabric, working only to improve the conditions of labor within the framework."[133] Gompers's own references to "wage slavery" and the "emancipation of labor," so common in his speeches of the 1890s, slowly disappeared as he became more bound to the National Civic Federation, a politically moderate institution designed to ameliorate disputes between capital and labor that grew into a patriotic organization during the "preparedness" lead-up to World War I.[134] Meanwhile, most of the Federation's multitudes possessed anti-imperialist sensibilities, and, associating militarism abroad with reaction at home, many came to oppose both the annexation of Hawaii and the US military invasions in Cuba and the Philippines. Yet common worker voices were muted in comparison to the national outcry for war, and much leadership welcomed the benefits of overseas expansion in the Caribbean and the Pacific, as empire successfully reinforced the AFL's model of business unionism.[135]

This amalgamation of the union man with patriotism and the veteran as a defender of both industry and nation was on full display in Los Angeles in the fall of 1911. Two brothers, John J. and James B. McNamara, both members of the International Association of Bridge and Structural Iron Workers, were convicted of a late-night bombing that set an inadvertent fire, ultimately killing twenty-one people. Their target was the newspaper of anti-labor editor Harrison Gray Otis, lately embroiled in an open shop dispute.[136] The *Los Angeles Times* bombing, which the press termed the "crime of the century," was a cause célèbre that involved some of the most notable personas of the Progressive Era: muckraking journalist Lincoln Steffens, publisher E. W. Scripps, IWW director William "Big Bill" Haywood, and President Taft. Debs noted the irony that the bombs had killed only the paper's "wage slaves" rather than their "masters," and Gompers, fearing a public backlash against the labor movement, quickly denounced the attack while also seeking defense for the McNamaras.[137] The AFL Executive Council retained celebrity litigator Clarence Darrow and raised additional funds through Labor Day parades and the production of a feature film, *A Martyr to His Cause*, which premiered in Cincinnati to a crowd of 50,000 people. Although the McNamaras were found guilty, the court case led to the creation of a Commission on Industrial Relations at the urging of Louis Brandeis, Jane Addams, and others.[138] Radicals compared the defendants to militant abolitionists, including John Brown.[139]

One of the lesser known defendants that November was seventy-two-year-old George W. Morton. A socialist and Union veteran, Morton had ditched the Republican Party after witnessing its devolution into a "party of capitalists."[140] Now he was on the stand and charged by the prosecution with reading subversive periodicals, including the *Social-Democrat* and the *Appeal to Reason*, which by 1910 was the most widely circulated socialist newspaper in the country. Slandered as disloyal, Morton protested, "You! You ask me that! Me who fought to save this government! No, I am not against the government!" The inconsistency of the prosecution was self-evident, and the labor press decried the harassment of a venerable old soldier, waxing lyrical about Morton's testimony of loyalty to the US government. In this sense, Morton represented not only the virtuous worker but also the belief that the war had been fought by workingmen, its memory tied to the aims of the AFL.[141]

At the same time, the Socialist Labor Party excoriated the AFL as unsatisfactorily militant. Far from being "ready to fight" against the traitorous capitalist class, craft unions had been, in the words of one socialist, "reduced to a mere benevolent organization . . . an ambulance service on the industrial battlefield, taking care of the wounded, burying the dead, and stripping itself of all other functions." This emasculation of the trades movement and indictment of its leadership as equivalent to a nurse in the midst of carnage was a rebuke of Federationist conservatism, presented in martial and honor-bound terms. Rather than engaging in reformist union organization, socialists claimed that US workers should be "forming their phalanxes . . . drilling their battalions . . . and getting ready for [capital's] overthrow" in conjunction with comrades in France, England, Italy, Germany, Scandinavia, Argentina, and elsewhere. "The whole of this labor movement," one De Leon man explained, "must become saturated with Socialism, must be placed under Socialist control, if we mean to bring together the whole working class into that army of emancipation."[142]

AFL leadership's acceptance of militarism and foreign intervention metastasized into outright trade union nationalism during the Great War. Gompers's former pacifism waned as he skirted the role that capitalist imperialism had played in instigating the conflict. Instead, he sensed the cataclysm as an opportunity for new international standards concerning labor law and arbitration.[143] Even as workers circulated anti-war petitions featuring his likeness alongside that of Lincoln, Gompers countenanced preparedness after the *Lusitania* affair that became a public endorsement by January 1916, increasingly denouncing leftist anti-militarism out of ideology and self-preservation.[144] Such a position proved divisive as prominent Federationists, including socialist Adolph Germer of the Illinois United Mine Workers, called on workers to "desist from affiliating with any branch of the military."[145] Appointed to President Woodrow Wilson's Council of National Defense in 1916, Gompers hoped to use his influence to place labor leaders in key policy-making positions, maintaining that "American organized labor is loyal to America, loyal to the core." He soon reversed the AFL's previous stance of noninterference in anti-war activities, pledging "labor loyalty" to the Wilson administration. Gompers believed the war was one of British democracy versus German autocracy and arraigned German American socialist leaders as "agents of the Kaiser."[146] This position squared with both his affinity for England (where he had grown up) and his rising conservatism. Gompers likewise attacked labor partisanship, lambasted socialists (whose anti-war views he linked to Prussianism and outright treason), assailed the Russian Revolution, and resisted the nationalization of industries, often in opposition to his own disciples, such as with the 1920 AFL convention's Plumb Plan. Overwhelming shop floor hostility to preparedness and the "Plattsburgh idea"—which one editor deemed the "cloak and mantle for militarism"—was exacerbated by anti-Anglo sentiment among the Irish, Jewish anti-czarism, and large numbers of ethnic German, Hungarian, and Czech workers.[147] Many AFL members, especially those aligned with the Socialist Party of America, backed the national war referendum proposed by the trades-organized "Keep Out of War Committee."[148] Yet Preparedness Day parades grew to include more and more trade unionists. Although the anti-preparedness *International Socialist Review* deplored that Chicago's June 1916 parade, the nation's largest, had been "engineered and dominated by economic masters," the editor marveled at the event's marshalling of labor: "Never before has working class power been massed anywhere in the United States since the Civil War as on this day."[149] The trade union majority pivoted sharply after Congress's declaration of war, with most AFL workers following the "super-patriotic course" of their leadership. Meanwhile, the AFL Executive Council presented President Wilson a "blank check," guaranteeing the organization's full support for war so long as its leadership was afforded some control over wartime labor policies.[150]

The European war and its uses of nationalism drove a wider wedge between radical workers and old soldiers, as veterans' organizations were expected to protest "seditious" socialism.[151] Amid demands for political consensus and movements such as Labor Loyalty Week and the American Alliance for Labor and Democracy within the AFL, Gompers and others increasingly linked conceptions of the Civil War to labor flag-waving.[152] Gompers used the anniversary of Lincoln's birth in 1918 to avow that the bloodletting in France was not a "war for capital." He compared Wilson to the Great Emancipator, predicting that criticism would soften and that the former would, in due time, also be universally praised as a champion of democracy.[153] As he became further alienated from the more radical and redistributive European labor movement, Gompers aped the Wilsonian rhetoric of popular democracy, American destiny, and anti-Prussianism. In 1917 Gompers was appointed president of the American Alliance for Labor and Democracy, a coalition of pro-war unions that looked to snuff out anti-war sentiment among fellow workers. Vindicated by Allied victory, he spoke to enlisted men aboard the SS *Rotterdam* in the spring of 1919 and described a great and glorious war for freedom and humanity unequaled in world history. In telling of a "great crusade" of civilization versus barbarism, Gompers reinforced the labor jingoism that De Leon and Debs viewed as corollary to the bourgeoisie's division and conquest.[154]

Mounting fears of Bolshevism and "anti-Americanism" led workingmen to redouble their emphasis on tradition and patriotism. Union festivities saw AFL locals embrace loyalty leagues and zealous anti-Bolshevik politicians.[155] New government propaganda bureaus, spearheaded by George Creel's Committee on Public Information, painted a portrait of US labor as being divided between "alien workers" and "true Americans." Using the AFL as a foil against the IWW, the antiradical propaganda sheets of the America First Publicity Association declared that "Abraham Lincoln was wiser than any Bolshevik" and that Gompers and his Federationists had proven that Leninism was nothing more than a "false doctrine."[156] Meanwhile, Gompers used class-based language to entwine Civil War memory to a newfound "super-patriotism," defending Wilson's foreign war and domestic repressions.[157] A conduit between national political leadership and US workers, Gompers broadcast that German militarism and "kaiserism" were antithetical to the traditions and symbolic lineages of US labor.[158] As one carpenter avowed, the Great War had fostered a "great impetus to our Americanism," and he dedicated that new nationalism to "the memory of . . . Abraham Lincoln, the great emancipator."[159]

By the third decade of the twentieth century, the memory of the Civil War had given animating force to reinvigorated racial and loyalty politics within and beyond the AFL. The symbolic assimilation of organized labor into the patriotic body politic through the Federation's culture of unshakable political allegiance worked hand-in-glove with wider trends of white nationalism during the apex of anti-Black racism. Constitutive of enduring bourgeois anxieties about change from below that saw socialism as racial integration and "race mixing" as communism, white fears of Black advancement and agitation merged with ruling-class dread of anarchism and Bolshevism, culminating in widespread white-on-Black violence and anti-socialist mania during the Red Summer of 1919. Meanwhile, the blue-gray reunion that began in earnest in the 1880s crested at Gettysburg in 1913, hastening North-South accommodation of Jim Crow. The white reconciliation movement also facilitated the imaginative integration of the South back into the nation-state, including through electoral politics, culminating with the election of Southerner Woodrow Wilson in 1912. Labor fraternity often paralleled blue-gray fraternity, and the memory of 1861–65 proved a device to both foster labor nationalism and sow accord among old soldiers. When former AFL treasurer and Confederate veteran Gabriel Edmonston died in 1918, comrades linked his memory to a broader strain of patriotic nostalgia. Gompers himself honored the war record of the man who had served under James Longstreet, and Secretary General Frank Duffy thought it fitting that a tribute to Edmonston in 1920 should coincide with the Fifty-Fourth National Encampment of the GAR—a testament to a conflict transcended and a nation healed.[160] But "healing" came at the cost not only of African American cultural memory but also of labor radicalism and a transformational working-class project. Dyer Lum's "war cry"—his revolution against the *very existence* of the wage system—was silenced by what was largely a top-down compromise with owners and triangulation against both nonwhite and radical workers. Seeking mutual arrangement with big business, AFL bureaucrats utilized the residue of the Middle Period to shape a more conservative organizational language, political outlook, and institutional philosophy. Gompers and others envisaged the Civil War not as an inclusive stage of impending proletariat revolution but as a nostalgic event of national trial, rejuvenation, and harmony—a harmony now mirrored by newly balanced relations between labor and capital as well as between white workingmen.

CHAPTER 7

# The Blue and the Gray and the Red

## The Rise and Repression of Proletarian Memory

CONFEDERATE VETERAN John Taylor Chappell was living in Richmond's Church Hill neighborhood in 1886 when he became secretary of the city's Knights of Labor. Meeting in the *Labor Herald* offices, founding members coordinated with various worker societies, accepted no one who had betrayed other labor organizations, and rejected the use of violence except as a means of self-defense.[1] Haymarket and its aftermath had radicalized several Richmond Knights, turning them toward independent socialist politics. Chappell proposed growing the Knights of Labor through the promotion of socialism and damned the capitalist system for pauperizing the true producers of wealth and creating a planetary gap between rich and poor.[2] In contrast to many of the city's white Knights, Chappell proved an unflinching advocate of interracial labor organization and a staunch ally of Black movement politics. Combating the city's oppressive industrial conditions, he forwarded a socialism rooted in the "natural law" of equity, premised on the idea that all people required—and could claim a right to—food, clothing, and shelter.[3] When Chappell hosted the first meeting of the Socialist Educational Club of Richmond in February 1898, questions from members proved diverse: "Would not socialism destroy one's individuality?" "What would be done with surplus production?" "Would machines replace physical laborers?" The group read and analyzed socialist literature, including works by Daniel De Leon, Henry George, and Edward Bellamy, author of the best-selling utopian fiction *Looking Backward*.[4]

At the same time, Chappell had long struggled with the "flood of memories" from the late war.[5] In 1890, partly as a coping mechanism, he decided to write his memoirs, insisting from the outset that his chronicle would be unique. While other autobiographies were given to aggrandizement or political motive, his would underscore the unheroic nature of warfare.[6] Chappell impugned "idealistic, imaginative, and exaggerated" war writing in favor of a "matter-of-fact, free and easy, every day style" that would appeal to working people. Above all, he emphasized the hardships faced by common soldiers. The war's savagery remained haunting, and those nightmares led him to consider the conflict's randomness and futility, even fostering pacifist inclinations.[7] The "ghosts" of Chappell's short stories were not supernatural; they existed within his living memory.[8] Alternative politics and the possibility of a freer future offered Chappell hope. He was not alone. In addition to Civil War veterans, turn-of-the-century socialism drew mass converts from across the political, literary, artistic, theological, and academic spectrum: John Dewey, Jack London, Helen Keller, Eugene O'Neill, Carl Sandburg, Florence Kelley, Isadora Duncan, Reinhold Niebuhr, and Upton Sinclair. For adherents, Civil War memory was an overture to worker collectivism, a binding agent amid internal schism, an expression of patriotism, and a harbinger of either political reform or social revolution.

Members of what became the Socialist Party of America invoked an especially motley remembrance of the second American revolution. While some drew on such disparate wartime leaders as James Garfield and George B. McClellan to advocate a softer nationalism, incremental reform, and Christian socialism, others quoted Lincoln and John Brown alongside Marx to validate calls for international industrial emancipation.[9] Pairings of class rebels with abolitionists tied socialism to domestic tradition and rendered the Civil War part of a revolutionary struggle. Previous generations of white workers had largely ignored the memory of Reconstruction owing to the success of Reconstruction's opponents, and later the influential Dunning School, in framing the era as one of "negro misrule," statist tyranny, and military occupation (which, to many workers, connoted brutal worker suppression, especially after the 1877 strikes). There were obvious political risks in venerating the ideas and figures of what Claude Bowers would defame as the "Tragic Era." However, the new socialist movements of the early twentieth century guardedly began to defend Reconstruction both as a juncture of critical rights (the Reconstruction Amendments) and as a cross-racial, working-class project. Though an unapologetically interracial advocacy of Reconstruction would not take flight until the Third International, socialists often moved in revolutionary commemorative directions. Party conventions featured antislavery themes as well as portraits of Marx and Engels draped with the American flag.[10] The most prominent socialist newspaper, the *Appeal to Reason*, consistently presented the Civil War as a momentous—albeit incomplete—occasion of human freedom. Socialist leader Eugene Debs, like Lincoln, became a messiah figure. Although Debs often prudently conjured national tradition and appealed to a patchwork of so-called American ideals, his supporters also commemorated the sectional conflict as subversive and transformational. Debs's left nationalism called on workers to renew wartime militancy in the name of workplace democracy and a new emancipation of labor.

For many, this liberation meant anti-capitalist industrial unionism. Touting a self-management shop model, the provocative and factious Industrial Workers of the World claimed and modified one of the most contentious legacies of the abolitionists: the defiance of absolute property rights.[11] Born out of the socialist left wing, IWW "Wobblies" acknowledged that chattel slavery was a property regime in which workers both produced *and* functioned as commodities, exposing the essential constructedness of property relations and questioning their legitimacy. Socialists argued that the Emancipation Proclamation, as well as Radical Republican economic activism and bids for land redistribution, had provided an analogue for the seizure and decommodification of private property. Former calls to "confiscate the slaves!" and "confiscate the plantations!" were replaced by those to "confiscate the industries!" Both the Socialist Party and the IWW demonstrated how organized workers gave voice to the idea of "liberation" as part of a historical class-based insurgency. Although the socialists' analysis, including their emphasis on economics, harmonized with certain elements of the prevailing Progressive school of Civil War historiography, their avowals for a continuation of the war's most revolutionary elements were unique within white American society. However, the federal government's subduing of radicalism and industrial unionism throughout the ultranationalism and mandated patriotism of World War I and the Red Scare undermined the socialists' long-standing narrative of the war for the Union as a working-class war. Memory and power went hand in hand as anti-red hysteria reinforced the decline of revolutionary Civil War memories, which in turn yielded before a rising industrial patriotism.

## The Emancipated Shall Be the Emancipators

The two decades between the Socialist Labor Party fracture and the First Red Scare were a "golden age of American socialism" in which the rising Socialist Party of America encompassed a kaleidoscope of Marxist, Christian, utopian, reformist, and internationalist ideas. Devotees believed that collective ownership would make good on the Founders' rhetoric concerning democracy and equality.[12] Socialists split into left, right, and center camps; into revolutionary and evolutionary advocates; and into a ballot-conscious majority and a bomb-conscious minority. Whereas the socialist center and left saw class struggle as their lifeblood, the right presented socialism as also benefiting nonworkers. The surging movement remained divided between middle-class reform against corporatism and working-class revolution against capitalism—between revolutionary socialism and "parlor socialism."[13] While socialists emphasized different degrees of union and party work, the Socialist Party pledged itself to assisting trade unions.[14] Less ethnic and insular than the Socialist Labor Party and less traditionalist than Gilded Age cooperationist socialists, who feared above all that industrial capitalism was displacing autonomous small-craft production, Progressive Era Marxians were often modernists who believed that science and technology could be harnessed to egalitarian ends. Both the ethnic and modernist left coexisted with larger outgrowths of Greenbackism and Populism. Indeed, a "plain-folk socialist movement" swept through the workplaces and small farms of the Midwest and the Great Plains, with Kansas's *Appeal to Reason* as its mouthpiece and Indiana's Debs as its political standard-bearer. Often explicitly Protestant, this socialism was rooted in economic radicalism, as well as in the labor theory of value, biblical justice, and distrust of Eastern capital consolidation. In this sense it echoed time-honored Middle American antipathy toward coastal elites, the slaveocracy, and, to some extent, racial pluralism. Noting that the racial hue of these "prairie Reds" was overwhelmingly white, Michael Kazin alleges that "Thaddeus Stevens still had no successor on the grassroots left."[15]

As the Socialist Party splintered from the Socialist Labor Party, socialists drew on Civil War tropes to bolster viewpoints and censure opponents. Members linked conceptualizations of "slavery," "emancipation," "slavers," "treason," "grand armies," and "Reconstruction" to specific bloc tactics and general party developments. For instance, whereas proponents of direct action or (in very rare cases) even tactical violence self-identified as neo–John Browns, opponents saw them as latter-day "guerrillas."[16] Socialists of all stripes used antislavery vernacular to win support by tapping into a familiar American language *and* by creating a new left nationalism. Americanizing Socialist Labor Party symbols, Debs, who often channeled the "spirit of '76," linked the red flag to the patriots of Bunker Hill, insisting that the emblem of democratic revolt from Giuseppe Garibaldi to Bloody Sunday carried the same "revolutionary spirit that gave us the republic."[17] As a century of national expansion, disintegration, and reunification gave way to one of unprecedented productive capacity and widening internationalism, Debsians looked back to the previous generation's great drama and its indubitable leader, Lincoln.[18]

Socialists had long used sectional phrases such as "irrepressible conflict" and "impending crisis" to refer to the class struggle, and that antislavery discourse took on new meaning with the rise of another prairie liberator.[19]

The aim of the Socialist Party was, according to Debs, to "organize the slaves of capital to vote their own emancipation," and the party rose rapidly as Socialist Labor Party rolls diminished.[20] In a development the *Social Democratic Herald* headlined as "Enthusiasm Paralleling Abolitionist Days," the newly consolidated party nominated Debs for president in 1900.[21] But that year proved merely a dress rehearsal, and the upstart Socialist Party soon outpaced its older, more ethnic antecedents. Socialist membership was relatively young, and perhaps 80 percent of members were native-born.[22] While Civil War veteran socialists were limited, the native origins of the party's base, as well as opponents' contention that socialist principles were antithetical to "American ideals," led to an insistence among Debsians that their politics were indeed patriotic. Promoting the overthrow of the capitalist system and "the emancipation of the working class from wage slavery" during his opening campaign speech in Indianapolis, Debs garnered over 400,000 votes for president in 1904—nearly five times his 1900 tally. The Socialist Labor Party nominee, New York printer Charles Hunter Corregan, netted just 31,000.[23] In 1908, 800,000 Americans went to see Debs's "Red Special" train car. The barnstorming whistle-stop tour embodied a newfangled and dynamic era of political campaigning. The Hoosier gave up to ten speeches a day at massive rallies, replete with red flag displays, trunks of socialist literature, and a sixteen-piece brass band.[24] Accepting the party nomination with a declaration that workers "are and always have been the world's slaves," Debs's popular vote count—and the overall popularity of the Socialist Party—peaked in 1912 with over 900,000 votes.[25]

The Socialist Party remained bifurcated on matters of race, as the regularity of abolitionist imagery did not produce the effect of racial leveling. Far from it. Writing in the *New Review* in 1912, W. E. B. Du Bois would refer to the "Negro problem"—ignoring the race-class nexus in favor of a "color-blind" class struggle—as the "great test of the American socialist."[26] From the outset, race was one of the most widely debated issues within the Socialist Party, which included segregationists and white supremacists. The party's founding convention in 1901 saw delegates deliberate and ultimately adopt a resolution of "equal rights for all human beings without distinction of color, race or sex." But others pinpointed African Americans as a uniquely oppressed and exploited subset of workers. Led by Debs, Isaac Max Rubinow, and John Spargo, some white Socialist Party leaders mostly passed Du Bois's "test" by vigorously attacking the color line. Their attention to racism helped cultivate

FIGURE 6. Undated photo of Eugene Debs making a speech. Debs was for a generation perhaps the most tactical and spirited ambassador of Civil War imagery and the antislavery vernacular on the American left. (Library of Congress)

an influential cadre of Black socialists, including A. Philip Randolph, John H. Adams, Edward D. McKay, and William Costley, who predated the Black Marxism of Chandler Owen and Cyril Briggs, as well as the better-known antiracist work of the Communist Party.[27]

Wielding their own radical traditions, many Black socialists understood the connection between antiracist cultural politics and antiracist movement building. Wilfred Adolphus Domingo, who was active in the Socialist Party's Twenty-First Assembly District in New York, laid out a blueprint for how radicals might employ left nationalism. The Jamaican-born Domingo, onetime editor of the *Negro World*, navigated the terrain of Harlem's Black socialists, Marcus Garvey's Universal Negro Improvement Association, and the broader New Negro movement. He published a socialist journal, the *Emancipator*, and eventually joined the African Blood Brotherhood alongside other anti-Garvey Black Marxists. In a Socialist Party pamphlet on race—one that nevertheless assumed numerous Black stereotypes—Domingo listed the means by which socialists might better energize class consciousness among African Americans. He explained that the party should first separate itself from the racially discriminatory practices of the AFL, as well as broadcast how owners exploit race so as to divide workers and subvert labor dissent. At the same time, socialists could draw on the war's legacy to win Black workers. This adoption of antislavery memory included better communicating long-standing left-wing positions in defense of the Reconstruction Amendments and summoning nineteenth-century abolitionism by pointing out that "Christ, William Lloyd Garrison, Horace Greeley, John Brown and Abraham Lincoln were abused as radicals in their day."[28]

Often accommodating themselves to racism or paternalism, socialist women found common cause with white and Black men as "slaves" on a new industrial "plantation." In her deliberately provocative 1912 pamphlet titled *Nigger Equality*, socialist lecturer Kate Richards O'Hare professed that while white socialists "don't love the 'nigger' . . . don't admire the shape of his nose or the color of his skin," his ankle was nevertheless "riveted on the wrists of white workers," their fates intertwined. O'Hare recited to African American men in the South that "while Abe Lincoln and the boys in blue were smashing your shackles of chattel slavery the capitalist class of the North was forging the shackles of economic slavery on both you and the men who fought to free you. . . . Now you are both slaves of the same master."[29] Other women, such as Caroline Hollingsworth Pemberton, used their blood ties to the war to address myriad problems socialists faced in confronting the "Negro question." The niece of Confederate general John C. Pemberton, whose army had ignominiously surrendered to Ulysses S. Grant at Vicksburg, she was an avid socialist writer and in 1901 published a series of essays in New York's *Worker* that explained slavery as a racialized labor system, extolled the history of slave resistance, and contested a host of Lost Cause myths. Discerning the interconnected issues of racism, classism, and sectionalism, Pemberton argued that the true task facing African Americans was "the labor problem plus the inherited prejudices of employer and fellow workmen in the North, plus the bitter jealousy in the South of a proud people who were conquered by the sword while defending their beloved dogmas that 'the negro is not a man.'"[30]

For many socialists, white and male consciousness stunted alliance potential by disregarding the extent to which the fight for material inequality concerned race and gender. The national Socialist Party eschewed Jim Crow, rejecting Louisiana's notorious segregationist "negro clause" in 1903 despite fears among Southern socialists that Democrats would label them racial "miscegenators." However, the party remained most popular in the Middle West, where allusions to free labor and independent producerism often invoked an earlier—and whiter—brand of trade unionism or republicanism. The extent to which Debs, who boycotted segregated gatherings, ignored the dialectic between race and class in favor of a "color-blind" class struggle has likely been overstated, and the party's antiracist contingent consistently denounced anti-Black bigotry as both morally wrong and strategically counterproductive.[31] Even so, right-wing socialists "Jim Crowed" potential Black comrades and defended segregation as "natural." They maintained that, to its detriment, capitalism had driven various races and ethnicities to live among one another.[32] Other white attitudes were simply paternalistic. The *Chicago Socialist*, which disavowed all racial particularism, warned African American readers that any emancipatory attempt outside of socialism was futile.[33] Despite the words and speeches of white antiracists and occasional meetings dedicated to racial equality, such as the Lincoln Emancipation Conference of 1909, the Socialist Party ultimately lacked a sustained or unified system of warming white workers to the idea that their own liberation was contingent upon Black liberation.[34]

The notion that the Civil War had been but one step in a historical process of worldwide emancipation had grown in stature among Gilded Age industrial workers. However, the "scientific" analysis of the war as a means toward global working-class liberation largely failed to address anti-Black racism as a force derived from but often seemingly independent of economics. Holding court in New York City's Union Square on May Day 1910 and led by an aging veteran of the Paris Commune, Lucien Sanial, socialist speeches aroused a revolutionary spirit. Yet those who held banners proclaiming "Capitalism is Slavery" emphasized "white slavery," ignoring the fact that the masters of chattel slavery could legally own another's body and constitutionally sell an enslaved woman's children. Rather than speaking to various forms of domination and their connection to capitalism while also locating sites of overlap for potential interracial unity, white socialists too often framed labor exploitation as a story of "white" victimhood.[35] This failure, even by revolutionaries, to identify specific forms of oppression within class oppression opened the door for more direct forms of racism within the movement. Hypermasculinity and xenophobia proved similar hindrances to solidarity. Socialists contested East Asian workers, with many echoing the anti-Chinese sentiments of earlier generations despite appeals from the Japanese Socialist Party that the Socialist Party "be true to the exhortation of Marx."[36]

Leadership likewise fractured over the role of women, as socialist-feminists linked economic power to political rights and sexual freedom in order to counter a social position that May Walden labeled "women's slavery."[37] Although the party officially supported suffrage and recognized capitalism's role in fostering poverty, hunger, sex work, and broken families, socialist men nonetheless tended to ignore gender-unique issues or fully subsume them beneath the labor question. Socialist men tended to especially reject the suggestion that the patriarchal household was a site of domination. In fact, many happily foresaw women existing in mostly domestic roles after socialism mitigated the need to supplement their husbands' income.[38] At the same time, socialism built on decades of women's activism in labor through networks of political rights, abolitionism, and agrarian reform. In particular, women's socialism thrived in the small towns of the Upper Midwest, with their long-standing reform institutions, and in the West, where, rather than adhering to Victorian domesticity, rural labor provided a greater degree of male-female equality despite the lack of physical separation between work and home.[39]

By and large, women employed the same antislavery vernacular as men, often in the service of gender-specific causes. For example, white male workers frequently used the term "white slavery" to distinguish industrial oppression (and the so-called unnaturalness of persecuting white men) from antebellum race-based slavery. However, for women the phrase came to denote not merely exploitative wage work but also the gendered injustice of sex slavery. As socialist and cofounder of the National Birth Control League Jessie Ashley maintained, the fight against "slavery" was one against all its forms: Black, white, sex, and wage, or any hindrance to "economic freedom."[40] Though many socialists cold-shouldered destitute immigrants and people of color, socialist women worked especially in these communities, tying questions of inequality and social cooperation to marriage, sex, and bodily autonomy. Birth control pioneer Margaret Sanger, too, was active in the Socialist Party and the IWW and wrote columns for the *New York Call*, a socialist daily.[41] Overall, working-class women as well as middle-class teachers, missionary types, and suffragettes used the Civil War era's metaphors and cultural memory to craft a distinct and convincing message about why the emancipation of women could be achieved only by curtailing the ills of for-profit and least-cost production.[42]

Conservative socialists, on the other hand, expected the party to facilitate a masculinized (and ostensibly white) blue-gray reconciliation, even at the expense of sexual equality and interracialism. Reminding *Appeal* readers that "they fought against each other on the question of chattel slavery, but now they fight together for the overthrow of wage slavery," one member noted in 1903 that the party was having a conciliatory effect upon former sectional enemies.[43] Reconcilers hoped that Debs's speeches might prove a commonality for "the old soldiers of blue who wore the red banner of Socialism . . . and the old soldiers of gray who wore the same red banner." One editor marveled that previous belligerents were "today fighting side by side under the red banner of universal brotherhood."[44] But this camaraderie was frequently predicated on indifference or hostility toward Black voters, issues, and alliances. Though Socialist Party partisans had declared as early as 1901 at the party's founding convention in Indianapolis that there were discrete differences in the statuses of Black and white workers owing to added discrimination, political disenfranchisement, and the threat of lynching against the former, many white socialists continued to challenge what Morris Hillquit bemoaned as the "singling out of the negro race," especially in the South and Middle West.[45]

For his part, Debs scrupulously exploited the free/slave binary. When a malcontent from the peanut gallery barked that socialism was a wasted vote, Debs shot back, "That's right. Don't vote for freedom—you might not get it. Vote for slavery—you have a cinch on that."[46] He equated the Goulds and the Vanderbilts to a slaveholding cabal.[47] Pronouncing "Arouse, Ye Slaves!" in the pages of the *Appeal to Reason* during the 1906 IWW miner strikes in Idaho and Colorado, Debs painted capitalists as enslavers and labor leader cooperationists as traitors to the working class.[48] In a "declaration of revolt" against the undue imprisonment of *Appeal* editor Fred D. Warren and what he viewed as the Supreme Court's pandering to big business, Debs made overtures to antislavery nationalism. Comparing the US courts to czarist Russia, he quoted Lincoln, who he never ceased to point out was "cordially hated by the slave owners and their supreme court." Now, Debs maintained, the crisis was not slavery in the South but the "slavery of the whole working class," and he avowed it patriotic to celebrate Lincoln's birthday by making war upon the "capitalist courts."[49] Though Debs observed that Lincoln was "not an oracle who spoke for all coming ages," he persistently called forth the consecrated president.[50]

Hoosier friends and neighbors echoed the Great Emancipator parallels. In testimony collected after Debs's imprisonment, Terre Haute natives described "Our Gene" as civic-minded, Christianly, bighearted, and, most of all, a loyal and patriotic American. Charles Gerstmeyer, a local physician, dubbed Debs "a political Wendell Phillips . . . who has roused the old parties from their sodden sleep."[51] Labor organizer and Socialist Party national executive secretary Adolph Germer agreed, predicting that "historians of the future will record his place beside other immortals who championed the cause of human freedom."[52] Admirers imagined Debs a "Lincoln-like figure" who was enchanted by antislavery luminaries.[53] Another recalled his moral composition as "the stuff of which Abe Lincolns and John Browns are made," with his stature, gaunt face, and Midwestern affect bearing close resemblance to the former.[54] Debs biographer Walter Hurt weighed his subject against Lincoln:

> Lincoln was epochal; Debs is epochal. Like Lincoln, Debs is elemental. Debs will loom larger in history than does Lincoln, in the same degree that the proportions of a limited chattel slavery are exceeded by those of a universal wage-slavery. Lincoln lacked the cosmic perspective of Debs. In his great heart he doubted the expediency of the Emancipation Proclamation, and signed it only under irresistible political pressure. Lincoln was great; Debs is greater. Lincoln proclaimed that the black man should be free. Debs proclaims that *all* men shall be free.[55]

Debs cultivated his own image as a latter-day abolitionist, invoking antiracist renegades to imagine a redemptive future. At his 1920 trial in Cleveland, Debs likened his persecution to that of slain Illinois abolitionist newspaperman Elijah P. Lovejoy. Avowing that Lovejoy was "opposed to chattel slavery just as I am opposed to wage slavery," Debs reminded the gallery that Lovejoy, Wendell Phillips, William Lloyd Garrison, Thaddeus Stevens, and Gerrit Smith were all "regarded as monsters of depravity" in their own time yet had rightfully become heroes in popular memory. He postulated that the same pattern of the future recognition of radicalism would also hold true for socialists.[56] Debs also fervently expressed his admiration in both public and private for John Brown, whom he termed "an immortal old rebel," often recommending readings and passages to his admirers.[57]

Antislavery memory, particularly that of sanctified abolitionists, helped sustain Debs while incarcerated. Convicted of violating the Sedition Act for a speech made against the war in Canton, Ohio, in June 1918, Debs was imprisoned the following year. He served time first in West Virginia's Moundsville State Penitentiary before being transferred to Atlanta Federal Penitentiary, from where, as an inmate, he would run for president in 1920. As Ernest Freeberg maintains, Debs continued to see in Brown "a kindred spirit in the long fight for human liberation." The Hoosier who had once made a pilgrimage to Harpers Ferry, the site of John Brown's attempted slave insurrection, now also sat in a West Virginia jail. This parallel was lost on neither Debs nor his visitors, whom he regaled with stories about the militant prophet. Sympathetic journalists and adoring supporters drafted commentaries and dispatched letters affixing the suffering Debs to an antislavery past. One admirer even sent a "dream picture" in which Debs received the title of "Emancipator" from Lincoln's ghost. Despite the bare existence of prison life, the socialist carried with him two sacred artifacts related to the radical abolitionist cause: a candle and a button that had been owned by Brown.[58]

Debs's emancipationist commemoration helped earn him the esteem of Black leftists, including A. Philip Randolph, founder of the Brotherhood of Sleeping Car Porters, and Du Bois, who voted for Debs in 1904 and whose *Souls of Black Folk* likely inspired Debs's "The Negro in the Class Struggle," both published in 1903. But Debs's adoration for abolitionists was not limited to men. In a tract honoring Elizabeth Cady Stanton, Debs defined the antislavery suffragette as "one of the heroic figures of her age." Upon visiting Stanton's birthplace, he proclaimed her one of the "greatest leaders and crusaders that ever consecrated [herself] to the cause of freedom," a forerunner of the neo-abolitionist socialist crusade that spanned race and gender.[59] As one Debs partisan declared in 1918, "The Socialists today occupy the same position as did the Abolitionists. The Socialists are engaged in a new Abolition movement to liberate all workingmen from the bondage of concentrated wealth."[60] "Abraham Lincoln had every belief of a Socialist," another alleged. "If he were alive today, he would be the first man to uphold Socialism."[61]

Debs fastened abolitionism to his assumptions about political revolution, despite their partial contradictions. May Day was an extension of Emancipation Day, in which the "slaves of all the world" might raise the red flag. "The great discovery the modern slaves have made," he asserted, "is that they themselves their freedom must achieve."[62] As Debs saw it, the organization of the American Antislavery Society was a symbolic framework for the Socialist Party; the militancy of John Brown sanctioned industrial unionism; and Garrison, Douglass, and Phillips provided radical precedents for socialist leadership. Describing his thoughts on the coming of the Civil War and African American emancipation in a 1904 pamphlet titled *The American Movement*, Debs insisted that Turnverein and utopian socialists, most of whom were abolitionists, instinctively moved "toward collective society, industrial freedom, and social justice" prior to Marx's scientific foundation. In particular, he lauded Horace Greeley, pioneer of early American socialism, for his labor positions. Meanwhile, Debs maintained that the War for the Union and the Paris Commune reenergized US labor and socialist movements, setting the pace for their struggle against Gilded Age capital.[63]

Debs expanded his emancipationist sensibilities with age. Diagnosing slavery as the war's cause, he noted that antislavery activists had seen through the "American contradiction." Chattel slavery "developed to its highest power" and controlled all branches of government, Debs pointed out. And the majority of white people "in their ignorance . . . supported the institution." Those who dissented were deemed "agitators, demagogues, and disturbers of the peace" and persecuted accordingly.[64] He reiterated such themes in a speech to Black workers in New York City in 1923. Introduced by comrades A. Philip Randolph and James O'Neal, author of *The Next Emancipation*, Debs provided a laundry list of those he deemed American heroes and forerunners of his own cause. "I have read some history," he pronounced. "I have read of such stalwart figures as John Brown, Frederick Douglass, Wendell Phillips, Elijah Lovejoy, Denmark Vesey, Sojourner Truth, and others; I have followed with pride the record of their contribution to human progress." He singled out for recognition female abolitionists who had "espoused the cause of their sex" while also condemning Black slavery: Elizabeth Cady Stanton, Susan B. Anthony, and Maria Childs. As with abolitionism, Debs theorized that posterity would validate socialism. "These historic characters," he posited, "came into their own only after they were dead and then garlands were woven for their graves."[65]

Debs then turned his message from vindication to white supremacy and racial justice. He maintained that he had always believed in racial equality and felt ashamed of the crimes of the white race. Laying blame on powerful institutions, including the church, Debs recounted the horrors of the transatlantic slave trade and reminded his audience of the central role that Black volunteers had played in the American Revolution. He insisted that, in terms of racial disparities, inequality of outcome was only a result of unequal histories. Recounting his own experiences with segregation in the South and anti-Black discrimination within labor as head of the American Railway Union during the Pullman Strike, Debs's message to African Americans was one of solidarity: "If you are excluded, so will I be excluded; if you cannot be admitted, I will not speak." He proclaimed to be always "on the black man's side" and against "those who are attempting to keep him in servitude." The Jim Crow of Southern Democrats was manifest enough, but Debs also blamed Republicans for calling themselves the "party of Lincoln" despite trafficking in xenophobia and Black exploitation.[66]

Most strikingly, Debs emphasized that American slavery was unique in its racial character, scale, and barbarism. "If there is any institution in the history of the world," he admitted, "the reconciliation of which should turn the cheek of humanity crimson with shame, it is the infamous institution of chattel slavery in the United States. . . . There is no parallel to it in sheer, stark brutality in all the history of the world." Debs grieved that a majority of white Americans still supported a "slave system" driven by politicians, statesmen, businessmen, preachers, and editors who, through policy and rhetoric, made it appear as though bondage was "ordained by God himself." Debs alleged that the ideology of masterhood kept non-elite whites deferential, leading to "the race question as we understand it resolving itself into a class question." As such, the slaves' story—the history of every underclass, in fact—would not be front and center until history was written about, by, and for not the ruling class but those whom Debs called "common people." This history, however, might be patronized by bourgeois allies such as Wendell Phillips, a supporter of the nascent labor and socialist movements whom Debs surmised "the great towering, commanding intellectual and moral figure . . . the real champion [African Americans] had from first to last." Or Abraham Lincoln, whom Debs held was "vilified as no other American statesman ever was by that cruel and relentless power that organized the Ku Klux Klan after the war, and which is now seeking to revive that fanatical institution for the persecution of the Negro." Or John Brown, whom Debs trademarked "the greatest hero of them all" for his singular militancy and willingness to sacrifice, agreeing with Victor Hugo's assessment that he was a far greater liberator than George Washington. Censuring William Lloyd Garrison's views to the contrary, Debs avowed that the end of slavery was just the beginning of struggle for the Black race, who, like other white workers, now awaited "the liberating hour" of revolution that might create "a land without a master, a land without slaves." Like the abolitionists of old, Debs's socialists were simply waiting for the world to catch up.[67]

## Prairie Reds

A journalistic firebrand on the Great Plains soon became the nation's foremost socialist mouthpiece. Founded in Kansas City in 1895 by Indiana-born Julius Augustus Wayland, who had been affected by the popular Gilded Age socialism of Bellamy and Laurence Gronlund, the *Appeal to Reason* broadened its circulation following the Populist collapse. In 1897 Wayland moved production to Girard, Kansas, where readership increased along with Socialist Party membership. The tabloid soon boasted three-quarters of a million readers—an "Appeal Army" that was nine-tenths native-born and white. Although printing slowly faded with Wayland's death in 1912 and, later, amid government suppression following the Bolshevik Revolution, at its peak the *Appeal* was the most significant socialist newspaper in US history. Its members styled themselves a new-wave GAR—the "Grand Army of Revolution" embroiled in a "War for Human Emancipation."[68] Muckraking and sometimes sensational in style, bold two-inch letters dominated the nameplate, urging workers to "THROW OFF THE BONDS OF SLAVERY . . . YOU HAVE BUT YOUR CHAINS TO LOSE."[69] Left-wing dignitaries brightened its pages. Debs, Jack London, Ben Hanford, and Mother Jones all editorialized; Upton Sinclair's classic on workplace injustice, *The Jungle*, appeared in serialized form.[70] Part of Wayland's stated mission was to "Yankeefy," or Americanize, the socialist movement, and his columns situated the ostensibly radical West against the effete and aristocratic East, insisting on the former's revolutionary potential.[71] As such, the *Appeal* brimmed with antislavery vernacular, setting the template for the type of Middle American Civil War imagery employed by Debs and his prairie socialists.

Like its agrarian and labor predecessors, the *Appeal* beckoned Civil War veterans and trumpeted old soldiers in its membership rolls. Editors referred to these "recruits" as its "GAR Brigade" or the "Grand Army of the Appeal," and the gazette featured their testimonies as both socialists *and* Union veterans, declaring the former a natural continuation of the latter.[72] "One of the remarkable things about the Appeal Army is the number of Abraham Lincoln veterans of the civil war it contains," one editor stated. "They enlisted in the battle for human freedom in 1860, and they are still fighting."[73] Espousing reform socialism directed toward public ownership, the *Appeal*'s editors urged old soldiers to "vote as they shot." "You shot to free men from slavery," one reminded readers; "socialism will also free men from slavery—wage slavery."[74] Debs's 1904 and 1908 vice presidential candidate Ben Hanford agreed that a new battle between capital and labor required the mass mobilization of disenfranchised Black workers in order to forge a "Grand Army of Socialists."[75] Viewing this hypothetical interracial brotherhood as a postscript to the Union army furthered the *Appeal*'s frequent expression of a distinctly American socialism.

Socialists melded radical politics with left nationalism to entice aging Union veterans by upholding the highly popular pension system. Conjoining military veteranhood with industrial veteranhood in the name of workers' compensation and an old-age annuity, socialists argued that soldiers were workers and workers soldiers—both were producers of wealth rather than owners of production.[76] Accordingly, the Civil War pension system should be expanded to include not only men who had donned blue but "soldiers of industry" as well. It was not hyperbolic for socialists to equate industrial and battlefield deaths. As the century turned, as many as 35,000 workers died each year in workplace accidents and roughly 1 million were injured.[77] One socialist charged that "the number of wage earners killed and maimed every year on the railroads, in the mines, factories and other industries in our country is approximately equal to the number of soldiers killed and wounded in any one year of our great civil war, with all its terrible battles."[78] In fact, with Union veterans having defended themselves against detractors' claims that they were "socialists" and "communists" for lobbying for federal pensions, socialists appropriated that message by painting the pension system as proto-socialist.[79] The editor of the *Kansas Agitator* explained that socialism *was* mutualism—the kind of mutualism that old soldiers had promoted during 1861–65 and now boosted through veterans' grants.[80] Socialism, however, not only would expand the pension system, he reminded readers, but would abolish war altogether.[81]

Like earlier leftists, the *Appeal* characterized the Civil War as simultaneously liberating *and* a vehicle for plutocratic ascent. The "war for emancipation" was also, according to socialist C. L. Phifer, a sectional competition centered on bourgeois property relations in which the pendulum of institutional power or national "mastery" shifted from slaveholders to Northern industrialists.[82] South Dakota socialist and Catholic priest Robert W. Haire explained that although the war for the Union had ended the historical era of "barbarism," the world had currently entered the age of "despotism," which could be eradicated only by the overthrow of capitalism.[83] Marxists also viewed the conflict over chattel slavery as constitutive of a historical process. In a survey of "the ideas that have influenced civilization," an editor of the *Chicago Socialist* attested that the war had led modern workers to challenge ownership in production *in addition to* ownership in person.[84] In testimony before a federal court in September 1909, Fred D. Warren explained the role of emancipation within the socialist theory of history, arguing that while courts had once shored up the power and privilege of slave owners, they now defended "industrial masters."[85] The war had given rise to a class of the "reckless rich," one that rivaled the opulence and licentiousness of France's Old Regime.[86] Within this Marxian interpretation (one that Marx himself might well have taken issue with), the war was a bourgeois revolution, to be sure. But many socialists held that it had primarily empowered not workers but owners.[87]

Nevertheless, socialists stressed that while wartime power rearrangements had benefited capitalists, the conflict was "not fought out by capitalists, but by armies and navies almost entirely recruited from among the working people."[88] Debs voters argued that for these soldiers, now veterans, 1861 began a new consideration of class consciousness. One advocate recalled the deprivations of the Union soldier to make this point: "The memory of how soldiers in the Civil War were furnished with rotten shoes, shoddy blankets, spoiled food, poor powder, and ancient muskets . . . still lingers in the minds of some of those who did the fighting in that war."[89] Even so, like Marx, countless socialists believed that emancipation had advanced the cause of *all* workers; that freedpeople represented the first wave of an international emancipation of labor; that Union soldiers were both liberators and workingmen; and that the destruction of the planter class at least created the possibility of a worker-led socialist revolution.

Socialism's heyday hastened a stream of academic thought that broadened how the proletariat was conceived of, presaging the "common man" themes of the Great Depression. This slant on the emerging Progressive school of Civil War historiography, embodied by Charles A. and Mary Beard and Howard K. Beale, presented soldiers as workers, Black slaves as a bonded proletariat, and white planters and Northern industrialists and financiers as usurpers of emancipatory forces. As such, socialists used left nationalism to color the industrial struggle as a continuation of the Civil War and Reconstruction.[90] Factories were "slave pens"; workers were "wage slaves" driven by the lash; strikes were "slave revolts"; and capitalists represented the plantation master reincarnate.[91] Punctuating the class component of the master-slave relationship, one socialist warned, "There is no limit to the outrages which a master class will inflict upon a slave class, nor to the fury and slaughter with which a slave revolt will be put down."[92] While editors praised the abolitionists and soldiers who eradicated chattel slavery, they maintained that socialists "have a cause that will abolish all kinds of slavery."[93] Veterans, the logic went, should have a special place within this class struggle owing to their wartime experience as liberators of labor. Massachusetts veteran Henry L. Ferry, by 1911 residing at the Mountain Branch National Military Home in Johnson City, Tennessee, noted the growing popularity of socialism among his comrades. He explained that "the men who fought to free the chattel slave are fast awakening to the fact that although they freed one kind of slave they did not abolish human slavery."[94]

*Appeal* contributors tied this industrial freedom to the legacy of abolition. They analogized slaveholders to postwar industrialists in that the power of both rested on surplus value (theft of time and labor) and both usurped democracy through economic clout.[95] Conversely, labor leaders were "a new Wendell Phillips for our times"; militants were "John Brown reborn"; and anti-labor court rulings were "another Dred Scott decision." As Wayland resolved, "We stand with reference to the abolition of wage-slavery exactly where William Lloyd Garrison, Wendell Phillips, and Theodore Parker stood with reference to the abolition of chattel slavery."[96] Black socialist and fellow Kansan George Washington Woodbey also connected labor with antislavery struggle, comparing owners to masters and police and strikebreakers to slave patrols, as both were "the watchdogs of capitalism." Like Debs, Woodbey believed that socialism would complete the work of the abolitionists and the Emancipation Proclamation.[97] Emphasizing their comparable victimhood and political marginalization, one white socialist affirmed that "the advocate of a labor state is as unpopular in a capitalist society as the abolitionist was in the Carolinas before the Civil War."[98] Socialism versus capitalism was, according to Wayland, as primal a political issue as free labor versus slavery.[99] Lionizing the "battles for freedom won in the past," editors insisted that "just as the hated abolitionist labored to free the negro from chattel slavery so are the hated Socialists striving to free all workingmen, white and Black, red and yellow, brown and mixed, from wage slavery."[100]

Socialists debated the degree of worker agency in the forthcoming "emancipation." Equating Progressive reform leadership to sectional conciliators (Cotton Whigs and Northern Democrats), philosopher and *Appeal* contributor James MacKaye asserted that the "great compromisers of the antebellum period, Clay, Webster, Douglas and their ilk, sought to deal with the institution of slavery as our advocates of regulation seek to deal with that of capitalism."[101] Rather than top-down policy subject to the whims of elections, socialists insisted that the emancipation of the working class must come through worker ownership via industrial unionism, led by workers themselves. This converged with standard Marxist theory. "The Socialist party is the twentieth century emancipation party," one member explained, "and for once the emancipated shall be the emancipators."[102] The implication that the emancipation of 1863 had relied on a contingent of non-enslaved emancipators squared with the prevailing view of the War of the Rebellion as one in which white men were the primary drivers of historical transformation. Although he acknowledged the unique oppression of Black laborers in the United States and recognized the revolutionary potential of chattel slaves, according to Robin Blackburn even Marx himself "tended to believe that slaves needed external deliverance."[103]

The memory of John Brown marched on above all others within the ranks of the Socialist Party and the pages of the *Appeal*. In a radicalized version of the Great Emancipator myth, a militant white abolitionist rather than a white politician or reformer was for many socialists the decisive agent of Black emancipation. Their Brown was a sane, heroic egalitarian, and if not a socialist then at least a forerunner to the movement. He was an outlaw, to be sure, but only in the sense that all revolutionaries are outlaws. This protosocialist Brown fit within a positively American vein, along with Jefferson, Paine, and Washington, all of whom had usurped unjust law. Furthermore, socialists contended that the Republican appropriation of Brown was sheer hypocrisy because he had broken the law by inciting domestic insurrection and attacking property rights.[104] Insisting they were Brown's true successors because socialism was the next step in human emancipation, radicals transformed their icon into a communitarian saint: "He freed the negro slaves.

. . . All the powder-burning and years of war that followed were merely incidental. He was that figure that made human freedom a vital issue."[105] Asking, "Who shall be the John Brown of wage-slavery?," Debs labeled the grizzled agitator "history's greatest hero . . . the bravest man and most self-sacrificing soul in American history."[106]

Socialists grafted Brown onto party themes and specific labor campaigns. During the Colorado labor wars of 1903–4, Debs compared striking Western Federation of Miners workers to martyred abolitionists, avowing that to hang innocent men was the surest way to animate their cause. In 1859 the slaveholding elite had hanged Brown, Debs recalled. Yet by 1861 Lincoln had been elected president and legions of Union soldiers marched into battle to the anthem of "John Brown's Body." In 1865, Debs continued, "less than six years after John Brown was murdered, as the mine owners of Colorado now threaten to murder union leaders, the slave owners were annihilated and chattel slavery was wiped from the earth in a storm of iron and a deluge of blood." The metaphor was simplistic but rhetorically effective: while extractive capitalists were akin to the slaveholders of old, and they benefited from the scales of power, wage workers were the new chattel slaves, and their emancipatory efforts would surely be redeemed by history. Dramatizing the continuation—or at least the transferability—of the antislavery struggle, Debs concluded, "Then it was chattel slavery. Now it is wage slavery. Then it concerned a few Negroes. Now it embraces all the workers of the world."[107]

The socialist veneration of Civil War–era antislavery included the movement's subversive fringe and the progressive wing of the Republican Party. If John Brown was the heartbeat and starry-eyed visionary in the *Appeal*'s pantheon of abolitionist forebears, then Wendell Phillips was the organization's most direct intellectual antecedent. The *Appeal* insisted that Phillips was a full-blown apparatchik, owing to his platform as a Massachusetts gubernatorial candidate that included a professed end to poverty, the "overthrow of the profit-making system," and the "abolition of privileged classes." Socialists praised Phillips as a "comrade in the great war of emancipation" for his expansive understanding of "abolition" and for transitioning the struggle from chattel slavery to "industrial slavery."[108] Occasioning the anniversary of his death, one editor championed him an inspiration to all revolutionists: "If he were alive today he would be at the head and front of the Socialist movement."[109] Socialists believed that, in addition to abolitionists, many Reconstruction era Radical Republicans had been anti-capitalist progenitors. Such descendants included Charles Sumner and Thaddeus Stevens, whose interest in Confederate property confiscation and land redistribution earned him singular esteem. Chicago organizer Theodore Vind even maintained that, were he alive in the early twentieth-century, Lincoln would have been a Bolshevik.[110] The *Appeal* lamented the "dead, putrid carcass" of the formerly great Republicans: "Once it was the receptacle of such living fire as Thaddeus Stevens and Abraham Lincoln, but now only maggots of the McKinley order fatten on its putrescence!" Socialists viewed this Republican embrace of big business as a fundamental betrayal of both Lincoln's small producerism and Stevens's economic leveling, as the party changed orientation toward "a government of the corporations, by the corporations, and for the corporations."[111]

The *Appeal*'s reverence for abolitionism included a blueprint for economic democracy. Socialists insisted that, through emancipation, activist economic planks, and calls for land redistribution, Radical Republicans had provided a correlate for the seizure and conversion of private property.[112] In addition to the American seizure of British goods during the Revolution, the uncompensated destruction of chattel slavery had supplied "a parallel by which to judge the possible trend of the change from wage slavery to co-operation and real democracy." Positing that property rights were often inimical to republicanism and that expropriation of production was, in theory, no more confiscatory than levying a tax, socialists sometimes concluded that violence could prove a prerequisite for such change. "If the class struggle becomes violent, the possibility is that the property of the capitalists will go the same way the property of the slave owners went."[113] Capitalism, they argued, with its course toward trusts and monopolies, was a sort of reverse welfare state in which, through the owner's seizure of the worker's surplus value, wealth was redistributed upward. Socialism sought to prevent this form of "confiscation."[114]

To many, Lincoln had been a pioneering confiscator. The socialist representation of the prairie president was largely that of a radical ascended from and whose memory belonged to the working class. The *Appeal* ran features of Lincoln's most labor-friendly pronouncements and voiced that his antislavery—the ownership of one's own body and labor—was a forerunner to labor's self-emancipation.[115] Henry M. Tichenor, socialist and editor of the freethinking publication the *Melting Pot*, listed Lincoln as one of the handful of greatest men in world history, along with Paine, Marx, and, to "future history," Vladimir I. Lenin.[116] Kansas socialists agreed, alleging that Lincoln Republicanism was precisely the same as their own reform model. Citing the Rail-splitter's regard for labor, one editor argued, "If you were an Abraham Lincoln Republican then, you believe exactly what the socialists teach now."[117] Another asked simply, "Will another Abraham Lincoln rise to strike from the limbs of the workers the galling chains of a slavery more damnable, cruel and relentless than chattel slavery—the chains of wage slavery?"[118]

At the same time, socialist workers contested the co-opting of Lincoln's memory by owners. Arguing that there was no way to reconcile Lincoln's memory with "our present system of wage slavery," the *Black Hills Daily Register*, an organ of the Western Federation of Miners, decried that Lincoln was celebrated by the "pro-slavery press of today." The publication maintained that those same power brokers were the real victors of the war, as "the soldiers who saved the country, and their children, have been reduced to a slavery infinitely worse than that of the chattel slaves of the south." Meanwhile, writing in celebration of Lincoln's birthday, the editor proclaimed that capitalists now "exploited in the name of Lincoln." "They grind up the souls and bodies of millions in the factories and sweatshops," he bemoaned, "invoking the name of Lincoln to justify the infernal crime."[119] Believing that farmers and Civil War veterans inherently understood socialism's cooperative tenets, James MacKaye deemed capitalist oligarchy "un-Lincoln-like." Genuine socialism, MacKaye explained, "rationally follows from universally accepted American traditions," including equality and republicanism. In this sense socialism not only was rooted in discrete domestic heritages but was in fact synonymous with them. Indeed, socialism "could be called democracy or even nationalism, Americanism, collectivism, or anything suggestive of its real character, and expounded in the common sense American fashion of Lincoln."[120]

Historians Hermann Schlüter and Bernard Mandel have challenged this view of Lincoln as primarily the "friend of the working man." They insist that although the early Republicans were a coalition of classes, Lincoln himself mostly represented the interests of capital and possessed little coherent understanding of particular workingmen's issues. Lincoln saw himself as a member of the petite bourgeoisie and, as a free labor advocate, denied the very existence of a permanent wage-earning class with its own set of interests.[121] This position is predictable, given that Lincoln lived prior to the zenith of industrial capitalism. While Lincoln's reputation as an ally of working people was well earned due to his common origins and paramount role in emancipation, the free-labor system, which viewed wage work as a temporary condition and held that prosperity required only hard work and thrift, was predicated on a belief in merit and unlimited mobility that rendered class extraneous. Barry Schwartz terms this socialist appropriation of Lincoln a "peculiar affinity" rooted in the sixteenth president's supposed views on economic equality. Schwartz, like Schlüter, argues that Lincoln did not view himself as part of the working class, nor did he perceive the Civil War as a class conflict.[122] Nevertheless, the Great Emancipator remained essential to the construction of left nationalism and the collective memory of radical labor.

FIGURE 7. *The Liberator*, February 1919. The editorial offspring of *The Masses*, Max Eastman's *The Liberator* was a miscellany of socialist and left-wing news, literature, and art whose name summoned the famed and controversial abolitionist publication of William Lloyd Garrison. The magazine frequently referenced Abraham Lincoln, helping solidify the Great Emancipator's position as the historical figure most frequently appropriated by the Socialist Party, the Industrial Workers of the World, and the Communist Party. (Collection of the author)

Lincoln conceptualized a quixotic small-scale capitalism that was especially concerned with so-called equality of opportunity (though by no means equality of outcome). However, Lincoln's capitalism is less important than the fact that, to turn-of-the-century leftists, the romanticization of his producer ideal embodied just how oppressive corporate capitalism had become.

Socialists promulgated this class-conscious Lincoln. On the centennial of Lincoln's birth, the *Appeal* explained that the martyred president was fundamentally a "revolutionist" who "sprang from the 'lower class' and never forgot it" and whose antislavery impulses derived from his innate understanding of poverty and exploitation. The first state ruler to arise from and represent the proletariat, Lincoln "never pandered to power; never catered to the rich, and never sought to 'shine' in society." In fact, he "hated those who exploited. . . . He hated the power that crushed the masses." The *Appeal* rationalized Lincoln's perceived political conservatism—his alleged slowness to emancipate—by highlighting the necessity of electability and retention of the border states during the war's early months. "Wendell Phillips was needed in his place, stern, fiery, uncompromising; John Brown, brave, reckless, determined; so Charles Sumner, Thaddeus Stevens, Gerrit Smith, and William Lloyd Garrison. Each had his part. . . . Lincoln had the most difficult task." This interpretation of Lincoln as less an antislavery conventionalist and a reluctant emancipator than a social leveler hamstrung by political realities demanded that his legacy be wrested from the moneyed classes.[123] For Christian socialists, Debs, Lincoln, and Jesus Christ, who one minister claimed also belonged to a "Grand Army of Self-Respecting Workingmen," became interchangeable, mutually reinforcing embodiments of the American worker.[124] On the other end of the theological spectrum, atheists such as Charles Chilton Moore also praised Lincoln. Moore, whose free-thought newspaper, the *Blue-grass Blade*, endorsed temperance, vegetarianism, and the separation of church and state, insisted that "those in control of the government . . . hate and despise a socialist today as they did an abolitionist 50 years ago."[125]

Other socialists mapped sophisticated historical analyses underscoring the centrality of the Civil War to contemporary socialism. Radical economist Scott Nearing requisitioned the antislavery legacy in his examination of the "new slavery" of unemployment, poverty, and the "mental slavery" of capitalist culture. Writing during the height of the Dunning School of Southern historiography—a highly influential white supremacist perspective of Reconstruction that highlighted the alleged horrors of the era (Black "misrule," Radical Republican despotism) in order to justify the Jim Crow system—Nearing downplayed the singular inhumanity of chattel slavery. He alleged that even modern plutocrats who, like antebellum slaveholders, advocated reforms, gave to charity, or were "kind" to their "slaves" could not escape the fact that they were still "slaveholders."[126] Likewise, in his unpublished "Development of the Communist Movement in the United States of America," Socialist Party left-winger William F. Kruse explained that the problem of the American Revolution, which had been immediately undercut by an antidemocratic Federalist "counterrevolution," was not fully solved until the establishment of US industrial development. In the Marxist posture, Kruse, a two-time Socialist Party congressional candidate from Illinois and the Workers Party of America gubernatorial candidate in 1928, maintained that the Civil War was a bourgeois revolution that pitted an oligarchical and backward South against a more modern, diverse, and industrializing North. He largely eschewed the knotty issues of ideology and insisted that the Republicans'—and Union—victory resulted from an alliance between workers and agrarians, among homesteading farmers and foreign-born radicals and the small-town petite bourgeoisie. The outcome was not only industrialization, financialization, and the emergence of US workers as part of a global wage-earning class but also the government's expanded colonial ambitions. Kruse surveyed the tension between "wage slavery" and chattel slavery reform, the role of racism in the labor movement, the indifference of workers toward third party agrarian radicalism, and state intervention on behalf of capitalists during labor stoppages. His conclusions ultimately tied Beardian interpretations to his own moment of early twentieth-century US imperialism, which, like Lenin, Kruse understood as peak capitalism.[127]

That apex burst wide open in Belgium and France in 1914. Announcing a "War against War!," most American socialists initially emphasized the commonalities of working people in defiance of national alliances.[128] On April 7, 1917, the day after the US declaration of war against Germany, socialists held a rally in St. Louis, where, despite the departure of a pro-war minority, the majority followed the examples of Jean Jaurés in France, James Connolly in Ireland, and Rosa Luxemburg in Germany by committing to international working-class solidarity. Surmising it an imperial competition instigated by "predatory capitalists" who exploited "race hatred" and "false patriotism," anti-war legions measured themselves against the abolitionists who had opposed the Mexican War on moral grounds.[129] Their ranks included such prominent women as Jane Addams, Emma Goldman, and Helen Keller, who encouraged the "Appeal Army" to "strike against preparedness" rather than remain "obedient slaves" to a government bent on hostility.[130] Socialists soon organized mass anti-war and anti-draft resistance, opposing Woodrow Wilson's Espionage Act, which made it illegal to interfere with military recruitment, and the Sedition Act, which criminalized so-called disloyalty toward the US government (defined as public opposition to the war). For his political repression, the editors of Chicago's *American Socialist* labeled Wilson a "puppet of the master class" who enforced "political slavery" onto workers bound by "capitalist chains."[131] Ultimately, hundreds of thousands of workers avoided conscription; Wilson's State Department deported thousands of enemy "aliens," including Goldman; and Debs was imprisoned for his Canton anti-war speech.

Anti-war dissidents embraced left nationalism associated with the Civil War era. Asserting that intervention was the most monumental question faced by the nation since 1861, war opponent George P. West held steel, oil, motor, and newspaper industries responsible for moving the situation forward. A journalist who frequently reported on labor violence, including to the US Commission on Industrial Relations, West predicted that the US forces might end up invading Mexico to "protect investments." Unlike a conflict of national salvation such as the war for the Union, this new conflict—waging war on foreign soil—was one of "commercial and industrial imperialism," backed by J. P. Morgan and John D. Rockefeller in order to "protect Wall Street dollars already bloody with exploitation at home." Moreover, one could not fight a war for the rights and liberties of foreign nations when those rights and liberties were not protected in Youngstown, Ohio; Bayonne, New Jersey; or Ludlow, Colorado.[132] There existed a long-standing feeling among socialists that the United States was becoming "Europeanized," not only in its foreign policy—its zeal for military intervention and expansion—but also in its state oppression and entrenched social stratification.[133] Such fears spoke less to the reality of 1917 as a watershed, given that the United States had always been a settler colony and racial empire, than they did to how even most socialists at least acknowledged the use-value of nationalism. They demonstrated as much by continuing to tie conceptions of working-class liberation to domestic leaders, myths, and republican and democratic traditions.

## Smashing the Chains of Slavery

Left nationalism morphed yet again in 1905 when Debs, De Leon, Lucy Parsons, James Connolly, William "Big Bill" Haywood, and others founded the Industrial Workers of the World. Emerged from the radical faction of the Socialist Party, the IWW—whose members were called "Wobblies"—included revolutionaries committed to supplanting capitalism through international confederation. Composed largely of "unskilled" labor (tenant farmers, textile workers, miners, and lumberjacks), Wobblies recruited across skill, ethnic, and racial lines. The IWW practiced the industrial unionism popularized in *Industrial Socialism* and the *International Socialist Review* and avowed that the primary battle against capital would be waged less at the ballot box than in the workshops.[134] Accordingly, Wobblies sought not the reformer's aim of fewer hours or a fairer wage within an oppressive system but "complete emancipation from wage slavery," critiquing the essence of production and the nature of labor itself.[135] The IWW crested in influence and activity with the Lawrence, Massachusetts, "Bread and Roses" textile strike of 1912, where a competing anarchist faction from Boston paraded banners urging unity between the "SLAVES OF THE WORLD . . . NO GOD! NO MASTER!" and the Paterson, New Jersey, silk strike the following year.[136] It caught on internationally, too, primarily in English-speaking countries: Britain, Canada, Australia, New Zealand, and South Africa. Membership required but one qualification: "Are you a wage worker, exploited by a capitalist master?"[137] With its motto of "One Big Union" and its publication, *Solidarity*, whose masthead spotlighted the word "emancipation," the IWW soon became a radical if sectarian alternative to the AFL, whose designers were convinced that the Federation could never become an anti-capitalist vehicle. As if to prove their point, Samuel Gompers and other labor bureaucrats aggressively red-baited the movement, calling it a "socialist plot" and later tacitly supported IWW repression.[138]

The Wobblies also represented a new pinnacle in labor's celebration of proletarian culture, constituting an "overalls brigade," or what Haywood called "socialism with its working clothes on."[139] Members rebuked the respectability politics of the AFL through song, symbol, and scathing satire. Insisting that the nationalist symbols, including the US flag, had always accompanied institutions of oppression against workers, they adopted the red flag of revolution and consciously rejected nationalist and top-down history. "Let us celebrate not the battle of Bunker Hill, but the battle of Homestead, the first great labor war in the modern industrial era," *Solidarity* recommended.[140] As such, the so-called revolutionary patriotism of abolitionist iconography became commonplace within IWW halls, as allies and opponents alike branded Wobblies with the same monikers that had been given to slavery's opponents, as well as with the wartime epithets directed at the Union armies of the West: "bummers," "tramps," and "ragged warriors." And this workingmen's culture was multihued. Unlike the Jim Crow unionism of the AFL, the IWW openly defied the color line, uniting Irish longshoremen and white mill workers with African American laborers in Philadelphia and piney woods Louisiana, respectively.[141]

Like its socialist antecedents, the IWW cultivated a fluid institutional memory rooted in the militancy of the Civil War era, envisioning a new—and revolutionary—deliverance through the international organization of workers. Aping William H. Seward's famed 1858 speech, the IWW manifesto, drafted prior to the body's first meeting at Chicago's Brand's Hall in June 1905, was premised on an "irrepressible conflict," this one "between the capitalist class and the working class."[142] Wobblies were the self-defined successors of radical antislavery. Carl Sandburg himself later concluded that he "knew the Abolitionists better for having known the IWW."[143] With Debs resigning due to the organization's lack of electoral emphasis and De Leon and his Marxist faction of "politicals" expelled in 1908, Wobblies construed direct action as tantamount to combat. Industrial unionism was more than mere labor formation; it was, according to IWW president Richard O. Sherman, an order to "prepare for war before war is declared" by way of regimen, drill, and hardened discipline.[144] Speaking on issues ranging from tactics to dues, Sherman drew time and again on the martial metaphor. Hoping to stave off "desertion" among the rank and file, he explained that "an army without a commissary train is worth nothing in the field. . . . You got to feed the soldier if you expect him to go to the firing line and fight."[145] As in combat, industrial unionism meant militant solidarity. To Wobbly J. S. Schatzke, this included a vow that "the working man shall not take orders in the shape of a soldier to shoot down his fellow workingmen."[146]

Wobblies often considered worker liberation an outgrowth of the Civil War while simultaneously contemplating a "color-blind" emancipatory movement far broader than that of 1863.[147] Although IWW leaders had pragmatic reasons for arguing that the slavery of wages was the most historically exploitative form of labor, worse even than chattel slavery, such postulation sometimes promoted "white slavery" tropes. Claiming that the wage system was "worse than chattel slavery," Haywood explained that he would "rather be a big buck nigger on a plantation in the south before the days when chattel slavery was wiped out," because whereas wage earners were worth only $1.50 a day, productive slaves represented an investment of thousands of dollars and were guaranteed shelter, clothing, food, and medical care.[148] In a treatise titled "Slave, Serf and Laborer," Abner Woodruff maintained that both feudal serfs and chattel slaves were more secure than wage earners, who were merely free to "change from a bad master to a worse one."[149] Woodruff's *Evolution of Industrial Democracy* further theorized on the history of slavery from the ancient world through feudalism and development of a new "wage slave" class. He exposed capitalism's abominable "fiction" that "all men are free and equal" and that wages alone—and the falsehood of market choice—relieved owners of all obligation to those who did not control production. When a disposable worker possesses nothing but his labor power, Woodruff reasoned, and his "master" (employer) is under no obligation to protect him, he is in some ways less free and as much a "slave" as anyone.[150]

Wobblies also employed abolitionist imagery to underscore their belief that "race hatred" benefited only the ruling class. In a pamphlet titled *Colored Workers of America: Why You Should Join the IWW*, leaders used the words of Lincoln to avow that race prejudice served merely to divide and conquer, as racial disunity segmented the labor force.[151] For others, this "strongly felt continuity with the Old Abolitionist movement" led to an outright rejection of whiteness. Often denouncing America's "white mystique," IWW members identified the concept and codification of race as a mechanism of worker control. Despite residual Sinophobia among Wobblies in the West, they tended to interpret abolitionist agitation as labor agitation and violence against abolitionists, such as the 1837 murder of Elijah P. Lovejoy and the destruction his printing press in Alton, Illinois, as anti-labor violence. One of the most widely circulated Wobbly tracts, Justus Ebert's *IWW in Theory and Practice*, lauded nineteenth-century abolitionists as the movement's revolutionary predecessors: "Lovejoy's press was thrown into the river and he himself was afterward murdered. William Lloyd Garrison was dragged through Boston streets with a rope around his neck. John Brown was hanged. Yet his soul marches on, not only to the abolition of chattel slavery, but of wage-slavery, too; John Brown still lives, reincarnated in the abolitionists of modern times. Dreamers! Yes! . . . So were the abolitionists of chattel slavery."[152]

The pages of the *Industrial Pioneer*, the IWW's monthly publication housed in Chicago, were rife with antislavery vernacular, featuring images and cartoons that advanced the servitude metaphor. Industrial workingmen were "slaves," and concepts such as "master," "shackles," and "bondage" presented a portrait of class struggle across time by authors including Illinois socialist Mary Marcy, who, in remembering the "freedom to slaves" in early medieval France, saw workers as bondmen within an enduring and evolving spirit of self-manumission.[153] This march-of-progress interpretation of the past used abolitionist symbols as explicitly revolutionary devices. In a piece titled "Smashing the Chains of Slavery," Vern Smith, a Wobbly and later the Moscow correspondent of the Community Party's *Daily Worker*, predicted a "great strike of all industries" against concentrated capital in which Pinkerton men and Baldwin-Felts agents—the "expeditionary forces of slavery"—would attempt to subdue the working classes.[154] Yet, like many white Wobblies, Smith also acknowledged race-specific disadvantages among working-class African Americans. Writing a searing exposé on "present-day negro slavery" during his travels throughout the South, Smith cited the unique threats that lynching, whippings, threats, and intimidation posed to Black agricultural workers.[155] As in other labor organizations, white IWW members debated the extent to which African Americans were either *within* or *distinct from* other wage workers of the "new slavery."

IWW anthems conjured the revolution of 1861–77. The most renowned song in the IWW's *Little Red Song Book* was Ralph Chaplin's "Solidarity Forever," written in 1915 to the tune of "John Brown's Body."[156] Pleading "Arise, ye slaves!" and "no more tradition's chains," Eugene Pottier's "The Internationale" was sung at the IWW's first convention, and Wobbly tunes including Richard Brazier's "When You Wear that Button," Covington Hall's "Us the Hobos and Dreamers," and Pat Brennen's "Down in the Mines" contrasted slavery with liberty, imagining the IWW as an instrument of emancipation that might overturn the "slavepen."[157] E. S. Nelson's "Workingmen Unite" featured themes of slavery, masterhood, and liberation; so did the popular works of Joe Hill.[158] IWW symbols and songs commonly featured John Brown, comparing him to persecuted anarchists Nicola Sacco and Bartolomeo Vanzetti as deliverers murdered by a callous legal system.[159] "When the Cock Crows: To the Memory of Frank Little Hanged at Midnight," written by Arturo Giovannitti, one of the architects of the Lawrence strike, situated a martyred Wobbly within a legacy that began with Brown and included the Haymarket conspirators.[160] The title of the popular tune "Hold the Fort" had its origins in William T. Sherman's Atlanta campaign, and Frank Brechler's "Workers, Shall the Masters Rule Us?" was sung to the melody of the ubiquitous Civil War song "Just before the Battle, Mother."[161] IWW poetry reiterated these emancipatory themes, as works by Giovannitti, Hall, and other Wobbly poets paid tribute to abolitionists.[162] Printed anonymously in *Industrial Solidarity*, the poem "Hold Fast: The Cry of the Striking Miners" compared mine workers to Union soldiers: "We, too, had our Fredericksburg and our Appomattox, in the war to preserve the Union."[163] For their part, rank-and-file Wobblies recognized the antislavery motifs as rooted in the recent past, as did their successors. When the Congress of Industrial Organizations was created in 1935, it too adopted "Solidarity Forever."[164]

Despite their pledged internationalism, the Wobblies' connection of the union cause with the Union cause resembled the left nationalism of the Socialist Party. As Franklin Rosemont explains, the Civil War and Reconstruction were vivid within IWW historical memory, and the "new master class . . . recognized the winged words of the Wobblies as dangerous tocsins of revolt and revolution."[165] This left nationalism in the service of international revolution stood in sharp contrast to what Wobblies deemed the false consciousness of "industrial patriotism." Gustave Hervé's *Patriotism and the Worker* explained that, in order to justify its existence, capitalism required mythology, and thus fraudulent history, pertaining to progress and Social Darwinist notions of merit. Hervé's work claimed that "the child's brain is stuffed with stories of alleged 'heroes' of U.S. history from George Washington to Theodore Roosevelt as a preparatory schooling for the future slave to acquire the necessary respect for and obedience to his master." The tonic to such rancid nationalism, Hervé reckoned, was "ONE BIG UNION of all slaves against all masters . . . emancipation from 'patriotism' and masters of whatever nationality."[166]

The IWW represented "the slave side of the class struggle," and its driving force of history was, in the words of Richard O. Sherman, a figurative battle, "the class struggle between master and slave." Class warfare was, in fact, the linchpin of revolution.[167] IWW organizer Joseph Ettor alluded to this tension while speaking on the 1912 Lawrence textile stoppage. Drawing a line between abolitionists and striking garment workers, as well as between antebellum slaveholders and Lawrence's mill owners, Ettor pleaded for clemency in his trial testimony: "Massachusetts refused to give the apostles of abolition to the rule and to the lust of the cotton kings of the South. It refused to allow their blood to act as so much balm to the cuts and to the wounds of the cotton planters of the South." Summoning Phillips and Garrison, Ettor predicted the ramifications of his so-called criminality: "John Brown was hanged and the cry went up, 'A social criminal,'" Ettor recalled. Yet "within two years the noblest that this nation could offer, were marching through the fields of this country singing: 'John Brown's body lies mouldering in the grave, But his soul goes marching on.'"[168]

What French radicals termed *la guerre sociale* included an element of industrial vandalism, which both Wobblies and their enemies interpreted as something akin to guerrilla warfare. Modes of resistance proved a dilemma for the IWW as, according to Melvyn Dubofsky, "references to John Brown, the terrible swift sword and sabotage made Wobblies appear violent and even criminal."[169] While largely metaphorical, the concept of an irregular conflict against the capitalist class—a tactic of the under-resourced—pervaded Wobbly thought. Writing on the "horrors of respectability," worker Edward C. Hayes explained, "Those who have no hope of ordinary, conventional, 'respectable' [political] success, and upon whom the existing status presses cruelly," were far more likely to accept direct action—action that was always "opposed by prestige and by the well-situated classes." "It was thus that the abolition of slavery . . . was once passionately resisted," he reminded readers.[170] The tactical and intellective roots of this "collective bargaining by force" dated to the Luddites and militant antislavery and increased as corporate-backed vigilante groups, such as the Knights of Liberty in Oklahoma, waged low-intensity war against the IWW.[171] Wobbly Ben H. Williams explained that sabotage, whether passive or destructive, whether being idle on the job or blowing up a machine, was first and foremost a "WAR MEASURE, made necessary by the nature of the class struggle."[172] Many Wobblies viewed dispossessed workers on skid row and in hobo camps not as *lumpenproletariat* but as a class with revolutionary potential, capable of waging a bushwhacking-style war against owners through "jungle crimes" such as robbery, transportation impairment, the disruption of communications, or arson. As one IWW editor made clear, migrant workers were "admirably fitted to serve as the scouts and advance guards of the labor army. . . . They may become the guerrillas of the revolution—the *francs-tireurs* of the class struggle."[173]

As with nationalism and militarism, Wobblies repudiated sectionalism, which they considered a useful diversion for power brokers and antithetical to movement building.[174] The IWW saw class solidarity as an antidote to regional, as well as national, animosities. More than their Greenbacker, Knight, and Populist predecessors, these industrial unionists endorsed North-South "reunion" not as an embrace of white supremacy but through a new mode of class consciousness. That consciousness recognized that workers Black and white had far more commonalities than differences and understood racism—designed to circumscribe those commonalities—as a principal tool of the ruling class. This involved portraying white Southerners as singularly American *and* as part of an international struggle. For example, *Seattle Union Record* editor Anna Louise Strong's free verse poem "Centralia Pictures" implied that having ancestry from both the South and Lincoln's prairies made one quintessentially American and also a more cosmopolitan worker.[175] On speaking to the Brotherhood of Timber Workers in Alexandria, Louisiana, in 1912, part of a tour of Southern lumber camps that summer, Haywood wrote in the *International Socialist Review*, "The lumber barons will not loosen the stranglehold on their ill-gotten profits until they have exhausted every weapon that Capitalism has armed them with. But now that the workers of the Southland have joined hands with their fellow workers of the North, there can be but one result . . . VICTORY!"[176] This class-based sectional rapprochement did not preclude emancipationist memory or allusions to the Union cause. Expanding the movement's political "forefathers" to include abolitionists, Haywood, writing in 1918 in the socialist monthly *The Liberator* (the title of which invoked Garrison's famous abolitionist periodical), reminded readers that such men and women had "waged war . . . against chattel-slavery—these were the titanic battles that were fought, bringing us to the threshold of the greatest of all wars—the class war. Abolish the wage system, is our battle cry."[177]

Acolytes found in Haywood their abolitionist. Though not engaged in Debs's level of Lincolnian mythmaking, Haywood regularly cited the Great Emancipator, and workingmen yoked their living liberator to the martyred president, viewing Haywood as the militant counterpoint to Debs's political redeemer.[178] One Louisiana laborer predicted that the tide of popular opinions, so polarized in 1921, would turn in favor of Haywood as it had the radical abolitionists. Americans would someday monumentalize the Wobbly leader as they had John Brown, providing him his own Osawatomie lore. Like Haywood, this laborer maintained that Brown had been "the direct actionist of his day," both warriors who sought to "eradicate human suffering."[179] IWW journalist Jack Phillips agreed. Asking, "Will there be marching songs written to Bill Haywood someday as the same kind of a 'traitor' as John Brown?," he equated Haywood's industrial democracy—resisting the "shackles of wage slavery"—with Brown's aim of slave salvation. Although Wobbly tactics were similar to Brown's in their zealotry, Phillips held that they were not punitive, lethal, or necessarily violent. Yet just as the pietistic abolitionist had been largely dismissed as a "traitor" in his own time only to find redemption in public memory, so too would Haywood and the IWW.[180]

The IWW used Lincoln's memory in various contexts within specific strikes, demonstrations, and campaigns. Recognizing that one's station resulted not from a lack of work or thrift but from impersonal social and market forces, Wobblies spurned the "self-made" Lincoln while organizing the unemployed to not scab on their "fellow slaves."[181] Using Lincoln's birthday to call attention to this "unemployment problem," Detroit IWW locals staged a mass demonstration in frigid temperatures on February 12, 1914. They demanded municipal lodging and a job guarantee, and local leader Arthur Christ explained that Lincoln's words "with charity for all" offered a self-evident counterpoint to the avariciousness of Henry Ford and other capitalists.[182] "We are the modern abolitionists fighting against wage slavery," Wobbly James P. Thompson avowed in 1918. Like the philosophies of Garrison, Douglass, and Phillips concerning demonstration and public protest, Thompson and others firmly believed that industrial unionism was merely an extension of Lincoln's doctrine of "government of the people, by the people, for the people."[183] This symbolic inheritance of radical abolitionists and runaway slaves buttressed the organization's support for the Russian Revolution.[184] But when the US Justice Department began raiding IWW halls in the fall of 1917, eventually indicting 165 members with conspiracy, Jack Phillips hoped for honorable treatment, reiterating that the values of the Wobblies were aligned with "the traditions of fair play associated with Abraham Lincoln."[185] As an attempt to Americanize radicalism and craft a radical reading of US history in order to jump-start a workers' democracy, the leftist attachment to Lincoln would continue through and beyond the Progressive and New Deal eras.

Meanwhile, the socialist divergence over revolutionary versus evolutionary strategy continued to spotlight Civil War tropes, crescendoing in January 1912 at Cooper Union. Occupying the same stage where Lincoln had, in effect, launched his presidential bid half a century earlier, the socialist right-winger Morris Hillquit disputed Haywood. The ostensible issue was the ballot box and the picket line, and tactics related to both. But the subtext centered on Socialist Party respectability and IWW encroachment into the party inner circle.[186] Radical spectators equated the event to Lincoln's famous oration, and some imagined the rousing parley as a Lincoln-Douglas debate redux, with Haywood occupying the former role. An atypically cautious Haywood, who had championed the occasional use of violence on the part of workers in defiance of capitalist "law and order," arraigned the corrupt and reactionary AFL and espoused industrial unionism. The theoretician Hillquit, who wanted Haywood to choose between his two organizational loyalties, felt the IWW "anarchistic" and advocated an electoral and educational approach for the Socialist Party in coordination with the AFL, predicting that Federationists would soon be won over to socialism.[187] Following the verbal spar, Afro-Caribbean socialist organizer Hubert Harrison, who would later turn toward Pan-African politics owing to the indifference of white socialist leaders toward race, assured Haywood that "while Douglas had won the debate, Lincoln had carried the country."[188] In other words, Harrison, the "father of Harlem radicalism," believed that although Hillquit had triumphed in the contest with party leadership, most US workers stood with Haywood and would hereafter adopt his position.

They would not. Pushed toward the American flag—in part by the "red hue" of Leninism—the Socialist Party proved susceptible to factionalism from within and to reaction from without, undermining the red Lincoln vision. One might contend that the refusal of the party's left-wingers to work tactically with the AFL and their neglect of political activity impaired a potential socialist coalition. Yet the expulsion and defection of the Socialist Party's left camp, who had fought for industrial unionism and civil rights and overseen the party's greatest gains between 1909 and 1912, greatly reduced the organization's dynamism. The movement of left-wingers into the IWW also diminished the force and coherency of party commemoration. This ideological dilution—reforming capitalism rather than rejecting it—rendered the Socialist Party at times indistinguishable from the middle-class progressivism into which much of its energy was subsumed. Led by John Spargo, a cluster of socialists broke from the Socialist Party in early 1918 for the newly formed (and short-lived) Social Democratic League of America, which emphasized electoral strategy, rebranded the *Appeal to Reason* the *New Appeal*, and, most critically, supported US intervention in World War I. Rightward political thrust moderated collective memory. Social Democratic League member Allan L. Benson, who had been the Socialist Party presidential candidate in 1916,

FIGURE 8. "Lincoln—Why Not Form a New Party? We Did Once," *Reconstruction*, June 1920. Seeking a conservative balance of labor against capital, disaffected socialist and war proponent Allan L. Benson's aptly titled magazine used Abraham Lincoln to propose the formation of a third party comprising farmers and laborers that might also alleviate owner grievances about strikes and halts in production. (New York Public Library)

would soon begin publication of the non-socialist magazine *Reconstruction*, which used Lincoln and the early Republican model to advocate the creation of a new third party.[189] Overall, the radical Lincoln of the workingman was undone by the reformist, middle-class Lincoln of the party's legal, ministerial, business, and craft union leadership bloc. This disjuncture within the Socialist

Party and isolation from the IWW and the AFL weakened all three to the point that conservative wartime pressures and government frontal assaults validated conservative craft union leadership, facilitating the "normalcy" and "business unionism" of the 1920s.[190]

The Russian Revolution nevertheless represented a break in the clouds before a storm of hypernationalism and federal repression, momentarily altering the meaning and possibilities of radicalism in the United States. In some sense, Bolshevik triumph had the same effect on US Marxists that John Brown's raid had on pacifist abolitionists in 1859. The potential for the direct seizure of property and power was now on the table, and, as Michael Kazin reminds, the emergence of the Communist Party and its influence on labor had some American workers "imagining that they could capture their own equivalent of the Winter Palace."[191] Longshoremen in San Francisco demanded seats on the board of directors and partial ownership of their shipping firms; workers in the Pacific Northwest declared a "Seattle Soviet" in what became a five-day general work stoppage involving 65,000 workers in February 1919. As radicals disseminated thousands of pro-Soviet pamphlets that decried "wage slavery" and urged workers to seize the means of production, anti-labor voices used the anniversary of Lincoln's birth to support "alien" deportation and malign the "Seattle Revolution" as "un-American."[192] Although many of the AFL members who participated in the work stoppage disavowed "Red conspiracy," differentiating between trade unionism and the "Red revolutionists" of the IWW, to antiradicals the Seattle General Strike smacked of pure Bolshevism.[193] Minnesota governor Joseph A. A. Burnquist warned that Lincoln's most dire prophecies of the potential of lawlessness and domestic revolt were coming true, fed by the specter of Lenin.[194]

The Bolshevik Revolution, the suppression of antiwar dissent, and the anti-ethnic and ultrapatriotic consensus of World War I led to a torrent of reaction against the American left. This often came from within labor itself, as many viewed Leninism as thoroughly outside the domestic tradition of the Lincolnian producer, the toiling veteran, and the "brothers' war." Though labor secretary William Bauchop Wilson, former secretary-treasurer of the United Mine Workers, declared that "the struggle of the masses to get away from slavery" had been the central theme of class relations "from the time that Moses led the Israelites out of bondage in Egypt until Lincoln issued the Emancipation Proclamation," he excoriated "Bolshevist agitation" and its alleged connection to the IWW.[195] This antiradicalism expedited the persecutions of leftist leaders including Emma Goldman, Alexander Berkman, and Debs (convict #9653) as well as thousands of arrests, many warrantless, and the deportation of over 500 foreign-born citizens under the Palmer Raids.

Although the perception of Wobblies as violent opponents of American entry into World War I was more rhetorical than real, the IWW's syndicalism and anti-electoralism made them especially vulnerable to mounting anti-left restriction. As industrial unionists endeavored to connect the plight of soldiers and sailors to those of workers, federal agencies and lawmakers, some of whom backed IWW-control bills, increasingly deemed anti-war sentiment tantamount to "treason," an idea legislated into being through the Espionage Act.[196] Exploiting wartime notions of disloyalty and "un-Americanness," militantly anti-union and "pro-business" coalitions rebranded the open shop movement the "American Plan" in 1919. Union membership would decline from 5 million to 3.5 million over the course of the next decade.[197]

Facing a more united anti-labor front following the war, defensive-minded labor officials responded with conciliation and triangulation. To reformist politicians and trade union bureaucrats who had endorsed both World War I and Red Scare suppression, "emancipation" became fully synonymous with the improvement of conditions for workingmen *within* capitalism. The collapse of the Second International and the expulsion of the left wing of the Socialist Party facilitated this rightward trajectory. Openly renouncing socialism, business unionists such as Gompers abandoned even token gestures toward some possible future of worker control.[198] The defection of the small but vocal core of revolutionists to the IWW had served only to mitigate the AFL's militancy, augmenting what Debs termed its "labor-dividing and corruption-breeding" racism, xenophobia, and bureaucracy.[199] While Gompers had long eschewed the "impossible dreams" of worker-commanded industries, by 1918 his nationalism and increased hatred of socialism was part of a "timid lobbying strategy" and overall worldview that perceived capitalist governance as both inevitable and irreversible.[200] Even to right-wing socialists, this acquiescence to owners amounted to "treason" committed by class "traitors."[201] Encouraging storefront closing on Decoration Day, carpenters' unionist and Minnesota Civil War veteran J. H. Baker had insisted that union labor should honor the "progressive and patriotic spirit" of the soldier, the veteran, and the nation-state.[202] That was the labor patriot's credo.

Revolutionary memory of the Civil War did not vanish. Black workers, for one, continued to connect emancipation with the general strike. Debsians likewise adhered to their left nationalism, remembering the War for the Union as part of a lineage of world historical change. Despite accusations by opponents that they represented the most subversive elements of sectional extremism, Wobblies maintained that even the revolutionary industrial organization of workers—strikes, sabotage, direct action, and even allegations of violence and criminality—fit within an abolitionist canon. Yet even antiracist annals were ultimately only as potent as the exiguous memory-makers who constructed and sustained them. Indeed, large numbers of white leftists continued to use Civil War memory to paint Black working-class oppression as coincident to or markedly less important than (rather than intersecting or on a spectrum with) white working-class oppression. They had not, in effect, abolished white preference or white normalcy, much less white identity. As such, they too often neglected to accept—and certainly to articulate—capitalism as not merely a system of exploitation but an apparatus that, by equipping its beneficiaries with the power to create and reproduce racial and gender difference for their own advantage, scrupulously organizes and gives added force to racism and misogyny, thus pitting certain groups of workers against others. The legal suppression of socialism and the marginalization of industrial militancy through censorship, deportations, mass arrests, beatings, brandings, murders, and lynching depleted of its social power the interpretation of the Civil War as one stage of an international working-class revolution. The motors that curbed interracial industrial unionism were fueled in part by the cultural transformation of radical antislavery from proletarian heroism to reformist flag-waving. The concomitant repression of the revolutionary left heightened nativism and stymied the idea of the War for the Union as a part of a global class struggle. As radical working-class memory receded, white reconciliation and Lost Cause tropes, the handmaidens of Jim Crow, filled the commemorative void. Quickened by the war's Golden Jubilee years of 1911–15, popular history emphasized national restoration and maintained that both secession and Reconstruction, and specifically the latter's interracial politics, had been profound mistakes. The dedication of the Lincoln Memorial in 1922, shortly after Debs was released from the Atlanta penitentiary, began a new mainstreaming of the Lincoln symbol, including throughout the white South.[203] In the aftermath of the Great War, AFL commander Hanford MacNider had explained how to win and retain political influence in the coming decades. His model: the Grand Army of the Republic. MacNider reminded audiences of the social impact once engendered by Union veterans and boasted that the AFL's numbers were far larger than that of the GAR. The trick to wielding effective influence, he avowed, was for this new grand army of labor to remain "fair, tolerant, clean, straight," and, most importantly, "American."[204]

# Epilogue

## Resurrecting John Brown's Body

THE YEAR 1936 found the United States in the midst of its greatest domestic upheaval since the Civil War. With the capitalist system waning, union militancy was on the rise. As during Reconstruction, factions of beleaguered laborers—"slaves" of the Great Depression—came to see public works and federal intervention as midwives of liberation.[1] With nineteenth-century farmer-labor movements still a part of living memory, countless workers viewed either social democracy or socialism as a viable alternative to a fickle and often brutal—and still politically vulnerable—"free market" ideal.[2] The economic reforms and relief programs of Franklin D. Roosevelt's administration had eased collective hardship. However, unemployment still stood at nearly 17 percent. In the political arena, conservatives and business owners took direct aim at the Second New Deal. Meanwhile, what Eric Hobsbawm terms "the patriotism of the Left" was critical to political fights against right-wing anti-liberalism, anti-communism, and blood-and-soil nationalism, undergirded by an aggrieved and revanchist petite bourgeoisie.[3] The surging Communist Party, first prodded by Lenin toward the "Negro Question" at the Second Congress of the Comintern in 1920, imagined itself as a bulwark against fascism. Popular Front Communists became the only US working-class organization outside the Black community to confront white supremacy head-on.[4] Having formerly criticized FDR's agenda as hopelessly capitalistic and even as a form of "industrial slavery," Communists now devised alliances with Democrats, the NAACP, and the CIO, seeking to grow their status as an independent left-wing political bloc *and* prevent the ascendency of the New Deal's right-wing opponents.[5]

Resurgent revolutionary politics aroused revolutionary Civil War memory. The Popular Front era, midway between the right-wing offensives of the First Red Scare and Cold War, proved a fleeting window of radical cultural possibilities. For Communists, "Americanization" was critical both as a political strategy and as a commemorative theme. Yet the process of "Americanizing" Marxism also revealed how the very tools required to expand leftist projects can also facilitate their absorption, co-optation, and demise. A reimagined *Daily Worker* blended mass culture with popular history and "American revolutionary traditions."[6] Social realist artists, from *New Masses* illustrator Hugo Gellert to Japanese American Communist Eitaro Ishigaki to Mitchell Siporin, who drew inspiration from radical Mexican muralists, translated Civil War images onto modern labor causes. At their 1936 party convention, Communists displayed placards of John Brown and Frederick Douglass, as well as massive banners that read "Communism Is Twentieth Century Americanism." In addition to commemorating the sixteenth president's birthday with Lincoln-Lenin rallies each February, the Communist Party named community clubs after antislavery luminaries: John Brown, Harriet Tubman, Frederick Douglass, Sojourner Truth, and Elizabeth Cady Stanton. The party, which leader Earl Browder called "the most consistent fighter . . . for the defense of our flag," used cultural production to "carry on the work" of Lincoln and the antislavery generation.[7] Overall, Browder's Communists were, according to Nina Silber, the inheritors of "an intellectual legacy that saw in the Civil War period the roots of an indigenously American radical tradition."[8] Appeals to the American past grew alongside the party. Bolstered by an influx of young people and women, it soon claimed 80,000 members, with its female membership increasing fivefold over the course of a little more than a decade.[9]

The Communists' reading of US history did not build consensus within the ranks. Tension persisted between those, influenced by Black Marxists including W. E. B. Du Bois and C. L. R. James, who looked to situate Marxism within the lived experiences of nonwhite workers and others who merely accessorized Marxism with nonwhiteness. Nevertheless, white Communists, regardless of whether their antiracism was more tactical or driven by inner belief, understood the expediency of a usable past and largely embraced Black history; vocal segments of African Americans responded in kind.[10] When Black Communists Hosea Hudson and Angelo Herndon likened their organizing efforts to a restored abolitionism that might "finish the job of freeing the Negroes," white comrades agreed. James S. Allen, whose defense of the "Scottsboro Boys" represented to many Southern whites a reconstituted carpetbagger threat, saw the Communist Party as a means by which to "complete the unfinished tasks of revolutionary Reconstruction."[11]

FIGURE 9. Eitaro Ishigaki's *Emancipation of the Negro Slaves* (1937, removed 1938), formerly in the Harlem courthouse in New York City. A John Reed Club and Federal Art Project member, Ishigaki's work compared fascism to slavery. (Smithsonian)

Abolitionist imagery saturated the culture of the movement and was used to highlight interracial democracy. Composed and performed by Communists Earl Robinson and Paul Robeson and adopted by the Popular Front and featured at Communist Party conventions, the cantata *Ballad for Americans* recalled chattel bondage, Abe Lincoln, and the Gettysburg Address, even sampling the slave spiritual "Go Down Moses."[12] One verse borrowed equally from slave rebels and Marxist theory by explaining that "a man in white skin can never be free while his black brother is in slavery."[13] While Communism indeed offered African Americans a coherent framework through which to understand poverty and racism, Black Communists in the South eschewed European models, instead interpreting Communism through Black cultures of opposition and traditions of resistance, including abolitionism and Black nationalism.[14] Some Black Communists combined bondage hymns and sorrow songs with Communist Party tunes; others drew a straight line between the "Party of Lincoln" and the "Party of Lenin."[15] To them, Communists were the "new Yankees," Stalin the "new Lincoln," and the Soviet Union a "new Ethiopia." "The first Civil War didn't free [Black tenant farmers]," one comrade maintained. "But this one will."[16]

A Communist tract printed in 1935, and accommodating the party policy of "self-determination for the Black Belt," *The Struggle for Negro Emancipation* considered the practical and historical dynamics of interracial class struggle. Tying antiracism to anti-capitalism and affirming that labor's liberation depended on the capacity of white workers to overcome race prejudice, the manifesto warned that, just as "the Fascist South" rested on slavery and Jim Crow, creeping global fascism would disproportionately impact people of color.[17] At the same time, reform alone could not combat a ladder of capitalist exploitation with working-class African Americans positioned on the lowest rung. This was especially true of New Deal policies that denied relief to tenant farmers, sharecroppers, and domestic workers, who were disproportionately Black. Rather, the lessons concerning racial (and therefore class) emancipation lay in radical history—in Nat Turner, Frederick Douglass, and John Brown. Echoing contemporary Black scholars such as Du Bois and Eric Williams and anticipating the "New History of Capitalism" of the twenty-first century, the pamphlet identified the transatlantic slave trade and race-based chattel slavery as instrumental to the construction of commercial (and later industrial) capitalism and understood slave resistance as part of an expanded battle against owners. White supremacy worked as a wedge, precluding cross-racial, working-class consciousness and alliance. Yet the triumph of wage labor over the slave labor system—the triumph of wage capitalism over the alternative capitalism of chattel slavery—*did* lead to unparalleled liberation. Though the Emancipation Proclamation and the Thirteenth Amendment "did not free the Negroes in any human sense of the word," they nevertheless brought Black people one step closer to the (albeit often limited) opportunities of white workers regarding individual movement, basic education, and the possibility of organizing.

In other words, through the efforts of abolitionists and slaves, the Civil War had "laid the basis for a real struggle for freedom, whereas under slavery there was no prospect except submission or futile revolt." Moreover, despite the valid criticism of Richard Wright (himself a Communist) and others that Northern radicals had oversimplified the experiences of Southern Blacks, *The Struggle for Negro Emancipation* underscored what many Communists saw as the singular revolutionary potential of African Americans.[18] That potential entailed rural Blacks in the Deep South, whom Lenin had characterized as an "oppressed nation," ostensibly primed for "self-determination." Such readiness was due to their numbers as workers, their historic hostility to the white ruling class, and how the solidarity forged during slavery, including the coordination of the Underground Railroad, had supposedly conditioned Black people to protect fellow victims of oppression.[19] "The uprisings of Cato, Gabriel, Denmark Vesey, and Nat Turner are remembered by all revolutionary workers who are trying to overthrow capitalist wage-slavery today," the authors explained. The universalist demands of Reconstruction had further demonstrated the so-called revolutionary character of working-class African Americans. As such, "emancipation" was not so much a legal event in 1863 but an ongoing struggle that bound the fate of Black people to that of all other workers.[20]

The use of Civil War memory in the service of militant interracialism was embodied by Augusta Jackson's poem "The People to Lincoln, Douglass." A Black Communist feminist, Jackson was a member of the Southern Negro Youth Congress and the editor of its newspaper, *Cavalcade*.[21] She and other Black female Southern Negro Youth Congress leaders undertook the "Woman Question," which attacked both the patriarchal nature of the nuclear family and the problem of "male chauvinism" within party ranks. Jackson's poetry spoke to these interactions of class, race, and gender. As Robin D. G. Kelley explains, her works also betrayed the extent to which Black Communists wielded the second American revolution to advocate "a politics of inclusion and self-determination—a vision of interracial democracy combined with black militancy, economic fairness without explicit references to socialism, and an uncompromising antisegregationist discourse inextricably linked to a celebration of African American heritage." This radical solidarity meant effectively highlighting both the "similarities between poor whites and blacks as well as forms of oppression unique to the black experience":

> Up from the people,
> Poor white and black, slave alike,
> Horny-handed from the frontier
> and farm . . .
>
> Fred Douglass, in Maryland, you
> endured the cut of the slavers'
> lash 'till blood flowed
> But Abe, you felt it, too, up there
> in Illinois . . .
>
> We are free now—all the people
> of America—black and white
> and Indians
> Free from slavery—yes,
> Free from land, too,

> And bread, and power to rule ourselves,
> Free from happiness and leisure.
>
> Abe Lincoln clench your fists once
> more, straighten your back,
> and take the hand of Fred
> Douglass, the ex-slave,
> And turn to the people—
> We are ready, again, Abe Lincoln.
> We, the people will drive out the
> slavemaster . . . [22]

While opponents vilified the Communist Party in the same way white supremacists had demonized early Republicans—condemning it as a "nigger party"—its three-time African American vice presidential nominee, James W. Ford, equated Earl Browder to Douglass and Lincoln. Others claimed the Communists were the inheritors of runaway slaves and the "climax of the American revolutionary tradition."[23] "It was not Marx, Lenin, and Stalin whom Communists cited in their addresses," one editor observed; "rather it was Douglass, Lincoln, and the heroes of the American Revolution from whom they drew their inspiration."[24] The official introducing Secretary General Browder as the party's presidential nominee even called him the "*new John Brown of Osawatomie*."[25] Staunch anti-communists drew a similar conclusion. In his final novel, the white supremacist screed *The Flaming Sword*, author Thomas Dixon rebuked the Communist Party's "miscegenation" and derided the Kansan Browder as "The John Brown of 1936!"[26]

Speaking that year in Springfield on Lincoln's birthday, Browder insisted that workers should draw on the Great Emancipator in order to guide the nation through this next "conflict between the forces of entrenched privilege and political reaction." Fearing rising fascism abroad and the New Deal's shortcomings at home, Browder claimed that Americans were "repeating the experience of Civil War days" and argued that it was "left to the Communist Party to revive the words of Lincoln." In comparing 1860 and 1936, he maintained that both periods represented a constitutional crisis with progress and justice hamstrung by a reactionary Supreme Court, likening the court's invalidation of FDR's National Recovery Act to the *Dred Scott* decision. Browder likewise praised John Brown and the abolitionist militants, noting the irony with which the Republicans had become a purely counterrevolutionary party, "exploiting" Lincoln's name.[27]

Browder's Lincoln was cloaked in the red flag. Unlike Roosevelt, Lincoln had grasped the utility of third party formation and the necessity of property confiscation, Browder contended, as well as the relationship between the emancipation of Black slaves and the liberation of workers everywhere. Browder cited Marx's affinity for Lincoln, as well as his popularity among the First International, as evidence of the Rail-splitter's leftist inclinations. Although he acknowledged that Lincoln, "having played his role before the rise of monopoly capital," would not have understood the major issues of 1936, Browder constructed a usable if mythic version of the great man as one who represented "all the best traditions" of US democracy. He then took aim at the Roosevelt administration's record on racial justice: "Under Lincoln the Negroes were freed from slavery; under Roosevelt they are suffering a thousand Scottsboro and Herndon cases." Only a revolutionary workingmen's party—one uniting socialists, Communists, tenant farmers, trade unionists, and Black workers—could effectively replicate the Radical Republican coalition of Reconstruction. "Revolution is the essence of American tradition," Browder concluded; "revolution is the essence of the teachings of Lincoln."[28]

Browder's red-hued Lincoln both differed from and comported with the prevailing view by 1936 of the Civil War as a nationalist achievement and of the Great Emancipator as a "common man." This interpretation provided a salve for Americans witnessing the swell of fascism yet feeling crushed by the weight of the Great Depression and a world at war. On the left, meanwhile, *The Masses* damned the "new slavery," called for a second Reconstruction, excoriated the "war" on labor, and compared industrial bosses to whip-toting masters, including the nefarious Simon "Marse" Legree.[29] The National Negro Congress, the most radical interracial labor–civil rights coalition since Reconstruction, constructed an anti-capitalist folk culture through the memory of slave rebels including Gabriel Prosser, Denmark Vesey, and Harriet Tubman.[30] Depicting Black workers as bondservants in need of a "second emancipation" from the "shackles of company union slavery," members tied the Marxist interpretations of Du Bois and Herbert Aptheker to the Black past. Speaking before the National Negro Congress in April 1940, Congress of Industrial Organizations head John L. Lewis—whose shared birthday with Abraham Lincoln led CIO leaders to theorize a profound symbolism between the two men—shrewdly quoted Frederick Douglass to endorse labor solidarity as a means toward civil rights. For both Douglass and Lewis, certain forms of wage labor were "only a little less galling and crushing in [their] effect than chattel slavery."[31]

Workers internationalized anti-fascist Lincoln. Comparing fascism to chattel bondage and the Great Emancipator to an anti-fascist, white and Black American workers formed the Abraham Lincoln Brigade and sent over 3,000 volunteers to fight Francisco Franco's Nationalists during the

FIGURE 10. Meeting of the Second National Negro Congress in Philadelphia, October 15, 1937. Like the Communist Party, the National Negro Congress embodied the Popular Front practice of featuring African American and antislavery figures in its political culture. (Pennsylvania State Archives)

Spanish Civil War, helping elevate the US Civil War's great martyr and political emancipator to the status of "red hero" for European and Third World revolutionaries.[32] The now-undersized Socialist Labor Party also tied Lincoln to worldwide revolution. National secretary Arnold Petersen, for one, drew a direct line running backward that linked the SLP cause to that of Lincolnian small producerism, racial leveling, democratization, and rough egalitarianism.[33] "America was proclaimed the land of the free even while millions were in abject slavery, cowering under the lash of the slave-driver," he reminded. Quoting Lincoln, Petersen argued that capitalists who opposed global "proletariat emancipation" were the "lineal descendants" of the political moderates who "objected to the 'rude,' 'name-calling,' and 'impatient' Abolitionists"; socialists were, naturally, the inheritors of William Lloyd Garrison and Wendell Phillips. Emancipation, he avowed, was, like socialism, an approximation—an unfinished project. It was now up to socialists to "carry forward the Emancipation Movement."[34]

Although radicals continued to couple the war's legacy to the labor and budding civil rights movements, the emergent notion of Lincoln as a "common man"—albeit one with cooperative tendencies—who rose through pluck and hard work derived from proprietarian and capitalist ideologies. This merit-spawned Lincoln also facilitated the popular belief that the Civil War era was part of a distinctly American drama capped not with a looming emancipation of the world's workers but with an already-consummated national renewal. Highlighted by the Communist Party's catchphrase of "Communism as Americanism," leftists also moved away from international and foreign-born symbols, including Marx, in favor of safer, nationalist themes. This delicate cultural process of using the iconography of patriotic statehood in the service of international solidarity and revolution was both necessitated by and catalyzed the Popular Front and the patriotism of World War II.[35] New Dealers constructed Lincoln as a "friend of the working man," even if the "workingman's Lincoln" was, like industrial unionism, ever more stripped of its revolutionary implications.[36] This sentiment was propagated in popular literature through Carl Sandburg's representations of the Illinoisan as a homespun folk hero. Even "revisionist" academics including James G. Randall praised the prairie poet and Lincoln biographer as a "beloved interpreter of the American spirit."[37] As part of the "Lincolnizing of America," the image of the Great Emancipator as an epic and godlike savior grew to coexist with that of the rustic and humble plainness of his log cabin background.[38]

The vast majority of the war generation having died, political and social circumstances homogenized Civil War memory around both antebellum wistfulness and the splendor of restored nationhood. The nationalization of Lincoln mythology during the New Deal era—the expansion of the Lincoln civic religion to promote political belonging across sections and the adoption of Lincoln in the white South—coincided with, and perhaps rendered permissible, the striking reemergence of Old South nostalgia during the 1930s.[39] Elements of the Lost Cause also transcended section. David O. Selznick's *Gone with the Wind* (1939) and the military histories of Douglas Southall Freeman, both sympathetic to the Confederacy, proved nationally fashionable due to, not in spite of, the contours of Union victory. War anniversaries boomed, despite economic depression. Colonel U. S. Grant III and J. C. Pemberton clasped hands at Vicksburg's "Surrender Monument"; President Roosevelt, who in 1935 approved the creation of a national park at Appomattox, cited the "sectional hatreds" caused by Reconstruction on the Antietam battlefield; and, despite some initial signs of irreconciliation, a proposed blue-gray reunion commemorated the seventy-fifth anniversary of Gettysburg. Even the vast majority of reformers and organized workingmen recalled the war not as a precursor to wider class upheaval but as an intensely patriotic preservation and sanctification of the nation-state.

The Cold War further decimated the left. Permanent mass anti-communism made it infeasible for workers—even militant ones—to resurrect the revolutionary, international, and anti-capitalist Civil War memory of 1886, or even of 1936. Midcentury dreams of radicalizing and globalizing the New Deal through an international Popular Front gave way to Henry Luce's "American Century" of nuclear hegemony, consumer culture, patriarchal conformity, and economic-imperial foreign policy. The "Good War" against fascism provided new nationalist mythologies surrounding "Victory Culture" that were less bound by class and minority status as more Americans shared in a society of widespread affluence owing to social democratic programs, historically progressive taxation, and high union membership.[40] Meanwhile, a succession of federal anti-labor and anti–civil liberties actions, from the Smith Act through the McCarran Act, spearheaded a mass culture of domestic anti-communism. The nationalizing experience of total war alongside automobilization, suburbanization, urban renewal, and community atomization hastened this "official" (state-imposed) repression of the left, facilitating the forced loyalty and union bureaucratization that helped scuttle Henry A. Wallace's 1948 social democratic presidential campaign. Confronted by McCarthyism, in addition to the Red Scare inside the Democratic Party, trade union leadership, and middle-class reform organizations such as the NAACP, the Communist Party languished. By the mid- and late 1940s, increasing sectarianism—directives from Soviet leadership that immobilized partnerships with social democrats and nonsocialist reformers—left the party vulnerable to right-wing onslaught. Assaulted and exposed on various fronts, the Communist Party's working-class independence was ultimately derailed by the Democratic corporate base and conservatives in its Southern wing, its members purged from the CIO, and what remained of its influence sheepdogged into a capitalist party.[41] This establishment absorption of the Communist Party and draining of its political energy also stripped Browder-style nationalism of its leftist connotations within a new type of consensus politics reliant on fealty to "American civilization."[42] The red memory of the Civil War as a precursor to class revolution waned. Indeed, just as white reunion erased the Black emancipation narrative, relegating it to subaltern status, the gradual political concessions of labor to capital and radicalism to reform, crowned by the "ideological freeze" of the Cold War, undercut the Civil War's proletarian overtones.[43]

The ascendant American Federation of Labor, meanwhile, promoted a different type of "war." Industrial work was now and again "slavery," but it was slavery without an anti-capitalist alternative. The disagreements between capital and labor perhaps constituted a "civil war," but it was a civil war of armistice and incremental victories. Capitalists might even be "traitors," but they were obstacles to be attended to and negotiated rather than destroyed. The coupling of "slavery" with Nazi (and later Soviet) totalitarianism, designed to unify American public opinion against foreign enemies, not only unmoored the concept from the historical specificities of Black enslavement and worker exploitation but implied that slavery's antithesis was in fact liberal capitalism.[44] By midcentury, business elites had fully mutated "free labor," once a celebration of small producers, into "free enterprise," a fetishization of the managerial class, repudiation of state-sponsored social programs, and guiding component of capitalist ideology.[45] Though leftists still underscored emancipation from "wage slavery" and attempted to connect Lincoln's legacy to other "common men," conservatives twisted and contorted Lincolnian memory into a crypto-libertarianism or proto-neoconservatism in order to oppose New Deal programs, champion unregulated markets, and escalate Cold War imperialism. While business unionists continued to espouse a type of labor liberation, these notions became more symbolic in character as the labor movement's anti-revolutionary bureaucracy committed itself to the piecemeal negotiation of workingmen's conditions *within* the capitalist system. Whether of a reactionary or liberal pluralist slant, uncritical interpretations of US history as a unified story—a march of progress free of class conflict—empowered the rising consensus culture. In fact, the approach to the conflict's centennial saw state-sanctioned Civil War memory reinforce Cold War themes, including militarism, anti-communism, the trampling of civil liberties, racial and gender subordination, middle-class pro-business disposition, and labor antiradicalism.[46] A supposedly shared history had become synonymous with so-called shared values.

This conservative drift spoke to the ebbs and flows—but overall decline—of labor radicalism between World War I and the Second Red Scare. The mid-century rise of middle-class consumerism amid the Cold War's amplified moral nationalism largely sheared the collective remembrance of 1861–65 of its subversive class implications. The breakdown of anti-capitalist organizations and the defeats of broader liberal-redistributive and social democratic political coalitions, which ultimately laid the groundwork for the neoliberal turn of the 1970s, undermined the popular memory of homegrown working-class militancy. The notion of Eugene Debs's "antislavery war" as but one stage in a progression of social transformation from below—long sustained by radical worker and industrial democratic institutions—was further marginalized in favor of an interpretation of the war as a lodestone of labor patriotism and economic nationalism, as well as a watershed in US nation-building. With the red flag loosened, subdued, and vilified, the foreseeable memory of the Civil War would be draped safely and triumphantly in the Stars and Stripes.

# Notes

## INTRODUCTION

1. Swinton, *1860—Lincoln.*
2. Debs, *Letters*, lxxvii.
3. *Marshalltown (IA) Evening Times-Republican*, February 26, 1906.
4. *New York City Sun*, November 27, 1895; *Topeka Advocate*, December 11, 1895.
5. Socialist Labor Party, *They Stand for Emancipation.*
6. *North Platte Semi-Weekly Tribune*, May 28, 1915.
7. Le Prade, *Debs and the Poets*; Cannon, *Debs Centennial*, 17, Eugene V. Debs Pamphlet Collection, Cunningham Library, Indiana State University, Terre Haute.
8. *New Leader*, October 30, 1926.
9. *New York Times*, October 26, 1906.
10. *Young Socialists' Magazine* 12, no. 9 (September 1918).
11. Salvatore, *Eugene V. Debs*, 311.
12. Currarino, *Labor Question*, 14.
13. *Appeal to Reason*, October 16, 1909.
14. Salvatore, *Eugene V. Debs*, 295.
15. *Salt Lake City Broad Ax*, November 2, 1918.
16. *Washington Times*, February 17, 1912.
17. Salvatore, *Eugene V. Debs*, 275.
18. Freeberg, *Democracy's Prisoner*, 99–100; McCarthy and McMillian, *Radical Reader*, 3.
19. Rehmann, *Theories of Ideology*, 22.
20. Hobsbawm and Ranger, *Invention of Tradition*, 9.
21. E. Thompson, *Making of the English Working Class*, 9–11.
22. Robinson, *Black Marxism*, 208–40.
23. T. Allen, *Invention of the White Race*, 1.

24. Fields and Fields, *Racecraft*.

25. Marx, *On America*, 247; Blackburn, *Unfinished Revolution*, 54.

26. Marx and Engels, *Civil War*, 1, 191.

27. DeVault, *United Apart*, 182.

28. Green, *World of the Worker*, 33.

29. Mandel, *Labor*, 182.

30. Green, *World of the Worker*, 52.

31. de Man, *Psychology of Marxian Socialism*, 144.

32. Buhle, *Marxism*, 56–63.

33. E. Foner, *Reconstruction*, 228–29.

34. Roediger, *Wages*, 175.

35. Dawley, *Class and Community*, 238.

36. Andrew Zimmerman, "Second American Revolution," in Downs and Masur, *World the Civil War Made*, 308.

37. Greene, *Pure and Simple Politics*, 68.

38. Fink, *Workingmen's Democracy*, 3–13.

39. Lause, *Free Labor*, 175.

40. John L. Brooke, "Consent," in Pasley, Robertson, and Waldstreicher, *Beyond the Founders*, 209.

41. E. Thompson, *Making of the English Working Class*, 9–11.

42. Trotsky, *Literature and Revolution*, 115.

43. Engle, "Yankee Dutchmen"; Montgomery, *Citizen Worker*, 98.

44. Hobsbawm, *Age of Capital*, 145.

45. Fink, *Workingmen's Democracy*, 22.

46. Roediger and Foner, *Our Own Time*, 85.

47. Gourevitch, *From Slavery to the Cooperative Commonwealth*, 7.

48. Fink, *Long Gilded Age*, 7.

49. Gerteis, *Class and the Color Line*, 24–25.

50. Dean, *Agrarian Republic*, 2.

51. Gourevitch, *From Slavery to the Cooperative Commonwealth*, 7–17.

52. E. Foner, *Reconstruction*, 29.

53. Lause, *Civil War's Last Campaign*, 134.

54. Fink, *Long Gilded Age*, 14–17; Hobsbawm, *Age of Empire*, 54.

55. Montgomery, *Citizen Worker*, 90–93.

56. Ava Baron, "Gender and Labor History," in Baron, *Work Engendered*, 1–46; Savage, *Standing Soldiers*, 178, 186.

57. Silber, *This War Ain't Over*, 177; Meier and Rudwick, *Along the Color Line*, 18; Jackson, *Soledad Brother*, 251.

58. Traverso, *Left-Wing Melancholia*, xiv, 55–56.

59. McConnell, *Glorious Contentment*, 58, 81–82, 116.

60. McConnell, 210; Harris, *Across the Bloody Chasm*, 18.

61. Blight, *Race and Reunion*, 276.

62. Horton, *Race and the Making of American Liberalism*, 74.

## CHAPTER 1. King Labor

1. *Wheeling (WV) Daily Register*, July 6, 1868.
2. Stuckey, *Slave Culture*, 289.
3. Lause, *Free Labor*, xiii.
4. Saxton, *Rise and Fall*, 298.
5. Mandel, *Labor*, 67, 166.
6. Saxton, *Rise and Fall*, 7–8.
7. Mandel, *Labor*, 139.
8. Schlüter, *Lincoln, Labor, and Slavery*, 39.
9. Mandel, *Labor*, 89, 94; Buhle, *Marxism*, 76.
10. *Anti-slavery Bugle* (New Lisbon, OH), September 7, 1850.
11. Wilentz, *Chants Democratic*, 95, 102, 198, 317; *New York Daily Tribune*, August 6, 1850; *Anti-slavery Bugle*, April 14, 1848.
12. Mandel, *Labor*, 77.
13. Roediger, *Wages*, 87.
14. *Ottawa Free Trader*, February 18, 1848.
15. E. Foner, *Free Soil*, xxv.
16. Mandel, *Labor*, 68.
17. *Anti-slavery Bugle*, April 14, 1848; Marx, *Capital*, 414; Marx, *On America*, 274–75.
18. Tuchinsky, *Horace Greeley's "New York Tribune,"* x–xiii; Sotheran, *Horace Greeley*, 1.
19. *Anti-slavery Bugle*, July 20, 1850; *American Whig Review* 11 (New York: 1850), 673; Wilson, *Rise and Fall of the Slave Power*, 165.
20. Mandel, *Labor*, 194.
21. Foner and Shapiro, Northern Labor and Antislavery, x.
22. Buhle, *Marxism*, 71, 91.
23. Rodriguez, *Slavery in the United States*, 500.
24. Cunliffe, *Chattel Slavery*, 110n24.
25. Quoted in Roediger, *Colored White*, 103.
26. Stanley, *From Bondage to Contract*, 33.
27. Dray, *There Is Power in a Union*, 57–58.
28. Blackburn, *Unfinished Revolution*, 18, 47.
29. E. Foner, *Free Soil*, 120.
30. E. Foner, 63, 269.
31. E. Foner, 91.
32. Lause, *Free Labor*, 10; Basler, *Collected Works of Abraham Lincoln*, 5:537.
33. *Cincinnati Republikaner*, October 22, 1859, reprinted in *The Liberator*, December 9, 1859.
34. Efford, *German Immigrants*, 1–15; Blackburn, *Unfinished Revolution*, 1–2, 24; Mandel, *Labor*, 167.
35. J. Miller, *Abandoned*, 178.
36. Montgomery, *Beyond Equality*, 90.

37. Du Bois, *Black Reconstruction*, 57; Blackburn, *Unfinished Revolution*, 39; Du Bois, *Souls of Black Folk*, 17–18.

38. *Spirit of Democracy* (Woodsfield, OH), June 18, 1862.

39. *Cleveland Leader*, October 10, 1862.

40. D. Davis, *Inhuman Bondage*, 10.

41. E. Foner, Reconstruction, 24.

42. Marx and Engels, *Civil War*, 200.

43. Blackburn, *Unfinished Revolution*, 54.

44. Andrew Zimmerman, "Second American Revolution," in Downs and Masur, *World the Civil War Made*, 315.

45. Marx and Engels, *Civil War*, 281.

46. Rachleff, *Black Labor in Richmond*, 101, 144, 28, 44.

47. E. Foner, *Reconstruction*, 102–5.

48. Gourevitch, *From Slavery to the Cooperative Commonwealth*, 4; Hahn, *Nation without Borders*, 289.

49. Du Bois, *Black Reconstruction*, 598–99, 604; McPherson, *Struggle for Equality*, 247.

50. Oubre, *Forty Acres and a Mule*, 31–45; Du Bois, *Souls of Black Folk*, 26–31; E. Foner, *Reconstruction*, 58–59.

51. Quoted in *True Southerner* (Norfolk), February 1, 1866.

52. Quoted in Messer-Kruse, *Yankee International*, 29.

53. *New Orleans Tribune*, November 10 and 14, 1865.

54. *True Southerner*, December 14 and November 24, 1865.

55. *True Southerner*, March 22, 1866.

56. Hahn, *Nation without Borders*, 289–91, 304; Montgomery, *Beyond Equality*, 80.

57. Stampp, *Era of Reconstruction*, 122–27; Zornow, "'Bluff Ben' Wade"; Nimtz, *Marx, Tocqueville and Race*, 144.

58. E. Foner, *Reconstruction*, 377.

59. Hahn, *Nation without Borders*, 350.

60. Oakes, "Real Problem with White Abolitionists."

61. Shaffer, *After the Glory*, 76; Du Bois, *Black Reconstruction*, 601; Oubre, *Forty Acres and a Mule*, vii.

62. Quoted in Montgomery, *Citizen Worker*, 15.

63. White, *Republic for Which It Stands*, 44.

64. E. Foner, *Reconstruction*, 106–10; Du Bois, *Black Reconstruction*, 632.

65. Hahn, *Nation without Borders*, 351; Richardson, *Death of Reconstruction*, 66.

66. Lause, *Free Labor*, xiv.

67. Steven Hahn, "What Sort of World?," in Downs and Masur, *World the Civil War Made*, 346–47.

68. Du Bois, *Black Reconstruction*, 216, 680, 346.

69. Feagin, *Racist America*, 30.

70. Sylvis, *Life, Speeches, Labors, and Essays*, 286, 81.

71. Dray, *Power in a Union*, 79.

72. Edwards, *Angels in the Machinery*, 40.

73. Montgomery, *Beyond Equality*, 196, 227–33.

74. *Workingman's Advocate*, April 16, 1866.

75. Sylvis, *Life, Speeches, Labors, and Essays*, 82.

76. Litwicki, *America's Public Holidays*, 70; Green, *Death in the Haymarket*, 21.

77. Sylvis, *Life, Speeches, Labors, and Essays*, 233, 128.

78. Gourevtich, *From Slavery to the Cooperative Commonwealth*, 98–101.

79. *Workingman's Advocate*, June 2, 1866; Glickman, *Living Wage*, 33–34.

80. Sylvis, *Life, Speeches, Labors, and Essays*, 233.

81. *Workingman's Advocate*, July 7, 1866.

82. Sylvis, *Life, Speeches, Labors, and Essays*, 232–35.

83. *Chicago Tribune*, June 5, 1865; Merritt, *Masterless Men*, 40–41, 56.

84. *Cleveland Leader*, June 6, 1865.

85. *Workingman's Advocate*, April 16, 1866.

86. *The Working-Man's Banner* (New York: Currier and Ives, 1872), http://www.loc.gov/pictures/item/2003656593/ (accessed November 30, 2017); White, *Republic for Which It Stands*, 214.

87. *New National Era*, September 15, 1870.

88. Salvatore, *Eugene V. Debs*, 17.

89. *Rock Island (IL) Evening Argus*, September 19, 1868.

90. Dray, *Power in a Union*, 83–85.

91. Rachleff, *Black Labor in Richmond*, 61–62, 65.

92. Rachleff, 41, 61–62.

93. P. Foner, *Organized Labor and the Black Worker*, 35–46.

94. Merritt, *Masterless Men*, 326–27.

95. P. Foner, *Organized Labor and the Black Worker*, 39–40.

96. "Appeal to the Workingmen of America," May 1872, folder 10, box 1, International Workingmen's Association Records, 1871–1877, Wisconsin Historical Society, Madison.

97. David Armitage Boyd, "The Labor Movement of Detroit," unpublished manuscript, Labor Papers, 1878–1939, Joseph A. Labadie Collection, Harlan Hatcher Graduate Library, University of Michigan.

98. Renshaw, *Wobblies*, 40; M. Davis, *Prisoners of the American Dream*, 30–31.

99. *Iron Molders' International Journal*, November 1873, 163, 178, and December 1873, 195, Iron Molders-Sylvis Society Collection, Gelman Library Special Collections, George Washington University, Washington, DC.

100. *Workingman's Advocate*, August 11, 1866.

101. Blackburn, *Unfinished Revolution*, 69.

102. Blackburn, 78.

103. Johnson, *Broken Heart of America*, 155.

104. E. Foner, *Reconstruction*, 586.

105. E. Foner, 582–84.

106. Du Bois, *Black Reconstruction*, 16, 55.

107. Du Bois, 670.

108. Du Bois, 584.

109. Rachleff, *Black Labor in Richmond*, 34.

110. McConnell, *Glorious Contentment*, 212.

111. Greene, *Pure and Simple Politics*, 26.

112. Efford, *German Immigrants*, 9; Du Bois, *Black Reconstruction*, 580.

113. Dailey, *Before Jim Crow*, 43.

114. Cook, *Civil War Memories*, 54.

115. Blair, *Cities*, 128–30.

116. *Richmond Daily Dispatch*, June 3, 1881.

117. *Tribune*, May 31, 1881, Scrapbook, 1881, vol. 21, box 213, William Mahone Papers, 1853–1895, Rubenstein Library, Duke University (hereafter WMP).

118. *Richmond Whig*, June 8, 1881, WMP.

119. *Richmond Whig*, June 8, 1881, WMP.

120. *John Brown and William Mahone: An Historical Parallel Foreshadowing Civil Trouble* (Richmond: C. F. Johnston, 1880), Clippings, 1887–1889, box 205, WMP.

121. Dailey, *Before Jim Crow*, 81.

122. Dailey, 82.

123. Dailey, 79, 67.

124. Blair, *Cities*, 140–41.

125. P. Foner, *From the Founding*, 21–22.

126. Blair, *Cities*, 136–37.

127. Rachleff, *Black Labor in Richmond*, 90–91, 101.

128. "Address to Colored Virginians," Scrapbook, 1881, vol. 21, box 213, WMP.

129. Rachleff, *Black Labor in Richmond*, 103; Dailey, *Before Jim Crow*, 47.

130. *Daily Evening Traveler*, February 2, 1882, folder 31, box 216, WMP.

131. Unknown newspaper, April 24, 1888, Clippings, 1887–1889, box 205, WMP. Wilson's attitude shifted after Mahone joined the Republican Party.

132. Blair, *Cities*, 130–31.

133. Rachleff, *Black Labor in Richmond*, 101.

134. Dailey, *Before Jim Crow*, 79, 90.

135. Quoted in Dailey, 90.

136. *Emporia (KS) Weekly News*, October 27, 1881.

137. Dailey, *Before Jim Crow*, 46, 138–41.

138. Blair, *Cities*, 130.

139. *Shenandoah Herald* (Woodstock, VA), March 29, 1882.

140. *Staunton (VA) Spectator*, June 21, 1881.

141. *National Republican* (Washington, DC), November 14, 1883, Danville Massacre Scrapbook, box 216, WMP.

142. *Virginia Star*, November 15, 1883, Danville Massacre Scrapbook.

143. Quoted in Rachleff, *Black Labor in Richmomd*, 108.

144. *Staunton Spectator*, April 25, 1882.

145. *Cambria Freeman* (Edensburg, PA), November 18, 1881.

146. *Alexandria Gazette*, November 14, 1883.

147. *Shenandoah Herald*, March 29, 1882.

148. Dailey, *Before Jim Crow*, 167.

149. Janney, *Remembering the Civil War*, 351n87; Blight, *Race and Reunion*, 306.

150. *Indianapolis Journal*, April 28, 1888; Kammen, *Mystic Chords of Memory*, 108.

151. *Butler (PA) Citizen*, June 10, 1892.

152. *School and Tariff Advocate*, September 24, 1889, Clippings, 1887–1889, box 205, WMP.

153. Quoted in Blight, *Race and Reunion*, 293.

154. Blair, *Cities*, 8–9.

155. *Wilmington (DE) Daily Gazette*, July 31, 1874.

156. Messer-Kruse, *Yankee International*, 28–31.

## CHAPTER 2. Southern Palm, Northern Pine

1. Quoted in Lause, *Civil War's Last Campaign*, 113–14.

2. Mitchell, *Skirmisher*, 104–5.

3. *Weekly Chillicothe (MO) Crisis*, June 24, 1880.

4. "Labor and Its Tribulations," box 1, Mary E. Ryder folder 3, Labor Collection, 1830–1935, Missouri Historical Society, St. Louis.

5. Degler, *Other South*, 288–91; Lause, *Civil War's Last Campaign*, 164.

6. Lause, *Civil War's Last Campaign*, 18.

7. Hahn, *Nation without Borders*, 350.

8. Hild, *Greenbackers*, 3–4.

9. P. Foner, *From the Founding*, 482–84.

10. Salvatore, *Eugene V. Debs*, 38.

11. O'Malley, *Face Value*, 96, 114.

12. "Document No. 1, National Greenback Labor Party," box 11, Luman Hamlin Weller Papers, Wisconsin Historical Society, Madison.

13. "Address of the National Committee of the National Greenback-Labor Party," John Francis Bray Papers, Joseph A. Labadie Collection, Harlan Hatcher Graduate Library, University of Michigan, Ann Arbor (hereafter JALC).

14. Hild, *Greenbackers*, 32–33.

15. *Workingman's Advocate*, May 19, 1866; E. P. Allen to Charles F. Bates, January 21, 1888, Charles F. Bates Papers, JALC; "Document No. 1, National Greenback Labor Party," box 11, Luman Hamlin Weller Papers.

16. Rogers, *One-Gallused Rebellion*, 263–65; Adam and Gaither, *Black Populism*, 152.

17. Independent Greenback Party Notebook, 1876 (kept by Thomas J. Durant, secretary), New York Historical Society.

18. *Weekly Chillicothe Crisis*, February 12, 1880.

19. Sklar, *Corporate Restructuring*.

20. Campbell, *True Greenback*, 6, 31–32.

21. Hild, *Greenbackers*, 23.

22. "The Money Question. Speech of S. F. Norton of Chicago, Illinois, Delivered at Newton, Iowa, September 20, 1877," Correspondence Greenback Party, March 1878–January 1888, Charles F. Bates Papers, JALC; *Boston Weekly Globe*, September 1, 1880.

23. *St. Paul Daily Globe*, September 6, 1878.

24. *True Northerner*, March 7, 1879, David Woodman Scrapbook, Bentley Library, University of Michigan, Ann Arbor.

25. Steven Hahn, "What Sort of World?," in Downs and Masur, *World the Civil War Made*, 345.

26. Ricker, *Greenback-Labor Movement*, 110.

27. P. Foner, *From the Founding*, 486.

28. Mitchell, *Skirmisher*, 94–96.

29. Gustafson, *Women and the Republican Party*, 59.

30. Norgren, *Belva Lockwood*, 127.

31. Edwards, *Angels in the Machinery*, 40–41.

32. *Frankfort (KS) Bee*, July 9, 1880.

33. Mitchell, *Skirmisher*, 71.

34. Lause, *Civil War's Last Campaign*, 54.

35. *Weekly Chillicothe Crisis*, January 29, 1880.

36. William P. Innes letter, October 12, 1880, Correspondence Greenback Party, March 1878-January 1888, Charles F. Bates Papers, JALC.

37. *People's Party Paper* (Atlanta), September 9, 1892; Mitchell, *Skirmisher*, 77–79.

38. Lause, *Civil War's Last Campaign*, 50.

39. *Frankfort Bee*, July 8, 1880.

40. Avrich, *Haymarket Tragedy*, 47–48.

41. Ricker, *Greenback-Labor Movement*, 139.

42. Mitchell, *Skirmisher*, 102.

43. Lause, *Civil War's Last Campaign*, 93, 96.

44. Reprinted in *Weekly Chillicothe Crisis*, July 29, 1880.

45. *Wheeling (WV) Daily Intelligencer*, September 25, 1880.

46. *Frankfort Bee*, September 24, 1880.

47. Lawrence, *National Greenback Labor Songster*, 6, 11.

48. Lawrence, 22–24.

49. Lawrence, 4.

50. Lawrence, 5, 18.

51. Schindler, *Labor Greenback Song Book*.

52. Lawrence, *National Greenback Labor Songster*, 47.

53. Randall, *Political Catechism*, 4–17.

54. Dacunha, *Irrepressible Conflict Resumed!*, n.p.

55. *Weekly Chillicothe Crisis*, September 16, 1880.

56. *Weekly Chillicothe Crisis*, October 7, 1880.

57. Randall, *Political Catechism*, 18–20.

58. Randall, 18–30.

59. *Weekly Chillicothe Crisis*, October 25, 1883.

60. *Weekly Chillicothe Crisis*, February 12, 1880.

61. "Yaple's Speech Accepting the Fusion Nomination," George L. Yaple Scrapbook, Bentley Library, University of Michigan, Ann Arbor.

62. "Copperheadism Refuted," George L. Yaple Scrapbook.

63. "The What Is It?," "Yaple Rally Song," and "Yaple Will Speak To-Night," George L. Yaple Scrapbook.

64. George L. Yaple Scrapbook, pp. 39–39.

65. Lause, *Civil War's Last Campaign*, 86, 64–65; Mitchell, *Skirmisher*, 98–99; Gustafson, *Women and the Republican Party*, 46–49, 212; *Chicago Alarm*, May 30, 1885; Katz, *From Appomattox to Montmartre*, 185.

66. *Frankfort Bee*, July 8, 1880.

67. *Frankfort Bee*, October 22, 1880.

68. Mitchell, *Skirmisher*, 103.

69. Anderson, *All-American Anarchist*, 74.

70. Lause, *Civil War's Last Campaign*, 172; Messer-Kruse, *Haymarket Conspiracy*, 63.

71. *Weekly Chillicothe Crisis*, June 24, 1880.

72. P. Foner, *From the Founding*, 486.

73. Rodgers, *Work Ethic*, 222; Puette, *Through Jaundiced Eyes*, 75.

74. Dulles, *Labor in America*, 121.

75. *Mexico (MO) Daily Ledger*, August 5, 1880.

76. *Lexington (MO) Daily Intelligencer*, August 14, 1880.

77. *Meridional* (Abbeville, LA), August 28, 1880.

78. *St. Paul Daily Globe*, September 23, 1880.

79. *Nebraska Advertiser* (Brownville), August 5, 1880.

80. *Staunton Spectator*, August 3, 1880; *Spirit of Democracy*, August 24, 1880.

81. Lause, *Civil War's Last Campaign*, 90.

82. *Helena Weekly Herald*, November 4, 1880.

83. Ritter, *Goldbugs and Greenbacks*, 52.

84. Lause, *Civil War's Last Campaign*, 162, 105, 211.

85. Ricker, *Greenback-Labor Movement*, 111.

86. *Weekly Chillicothe Crisis*, September 25, 1884.

87. *Weekly Chillicothe Crisis*, January 31, 1884.

88. "Speech of Butler, September 21, 1878," Correspondence Greenback Party, March 1878-January 1888, Charles F. Bates Papers.

89. *Democratic Northwest* (Napoleon, OH), May 15, 1884; Clark, Craig, and Wilson, *History of Public Sector Pensions*, 126.

90. *Columbus (NE) Journal*, October 15, 1884.

91. *New York Times*, August 20, 1884.

92. Clark, *People's Party Document*, 1–15.

93. Rodgers, *Work Ethic*, 161.

94. Lauck, *Prairie Republic*, 35.

95. Pollack, *Populist Response*, 5.

96. Postel, *Populist Vision*, 181–83.

97. Lester, *Up From the Mudsills of Hell*, 50, 73–76.

98. Postel, *Equality*, 73, 89, 96.

99. Ayers, *Promise of the New South*, 223; Kindell and Demers, *Encyclopedia of Populism*, 533–34.

100. *Progressive Farmer* (Winston, NC), February 10, 1886 (hereafter *PF*).

101. *PF*, March 3, 1886.

102. *PF*, March 10, 1886.

103. "Great Day at Atlanta," newspaper clipping, folder 133, Leonidas L. Polk Papers, Southern Historical Collection, Wilson Library, University of North Carolina, Chapel Hill (hereafter LLPP).

104. "To the Supreme Council of the National Farmers Alliance and Industrial Union," 1891, folder 99, LLPP.

105. Ayers, *Promise of the New South*, 265.

106. *PF*, April 14, 1886.

107. *PF*, March 31, 1886.

108. "Great Day at Atlanta," newspaper clipping; see also *The Special Informer*, June 22, 1892, newspaper clipping, folder 231, LLPP.

109. *PF*, February 10, 1886.

110. *PF*, April 21, 1886.

111. *PF*, September 29, 1887.

112. "New Revolution," newspaper clipping, folder 133, LLPP.

113. Gaither, *Blacks and the Populist Movement*, 76, 102, 27–30; Ayers, *Promise of the New South*, 258.

114. *PF*, March 17, 1886.

115. *PF*, March 3 and February 17, 1886.

116. *PF*, February 10 and 17, 1886.

117. *PF*, March 24, 1886.

118. McGreevy, "Farmers, Nationalists, and the Origins of California Populism," 471–95.

119. Wilfrida and Henry Fairweather, "Linked Evermore the Gray and the Blue," series 1, folder 99, LLPP; Polk to J. W. Denmark, March 12, 1892, folder 226, LLPP.

120. *Los Angeles Herald*, October 20, 1891.

121. Hild, *Greenbackers*, 116–17.

122. "To the Supreme Council of the National Farmers Alliance and Industrial Union."

## CHAPTER 3. Against Masters and Money Power

1. Rabinbach, *Human Motor*, 228–34.

2. *Journal of United Labor* 4, no. 3 (July 1883): 530–31 (hereafter *JUL*).

3. Brecher, *Strike!*, 9.
4. *Richmond Daily Dispatch*, July 28, 1877; Dray, *Power in a Union*, 116–19.
5. Hahn, *Nation without Borders*, 431.
6. Stowell, *Streets, Railroads, and the Great Strike of 1877*, 2.
7. P. Foner, *Great Labor Uprising*, 12–13.
8. Saxton, *Rise and Fall*, 303–4.
9. Gourevitch, *From Slavery to the Cooperative Commonwealth*, 69.
10. Phelan, *Grand Master Workman*, 2.
11. Salvatore, *Eugene V. Debs*, 74–80.
12. Fink, *Long Gilded Age*, 25.
13. P. Foner, *From the Founding*, 16, 57.
14. Rodgers, *Work Ethic*, 32.
15. Dulles, *Labor in America*, 65.
16. Loughran, *Republic in Print*, 427.
17. Green, *Death in the Haymarket*, 23.
18. Andrew Zimmerman, "Second American Revolution," in Downs and Masur, *World the Civil War Made*, 317.
19. *Chicago Alarm*, December 8, 1888.
20. Peck, "White Slavery and Whiteness."
21. Loughran, *Republic in Print*, 427–32.
22. E. Foner, *Free Soil*, xvii.
23. Roediger, *Colored White*, 113.
24. Ignatiev, *How the Irish Became White*, 94.
25. Lause, *Free Labor*, 11; Wilentz, *Rise of American Democracy*, 721.
26. Roediger, *Wages*, 68, 145; Kelley, *Race Rebels*, 30–31.
27. Roediger, *Working toward Whiteness*, 115.
28. E. Foner, *Free Soil*, xix.
29. Lause, *Free Labor*, xiii–xiv.
30. Merritt, *Masterless Men*, 262; Carsel, "Slaveholders' Indictment."
31. *Portage Sentinel* (Ravenna, OH), February 21, 1849; *Idaho Semi-Weekly World*, December 28, 1867.
32. Ignatiev, *How the Irish Became White*, 102, 81, 49.
33. Mandel, *Labor*, 122.
34. Roediger, *Colored White*, 113.
35. Mandel, *Labor*, 24.
36. Merritt, *Masterless Men*, 220, 1; Mandel, *Labor*, 24.
37. Douglass, *Autobiographies*, 330.
38. Horton, *American Liberalism*, 74.
39. Dray, *Power in a Union*, 66.
40. *Workingman's Advocate*, August 25, 1866.
41. Horton, *American Liberalism*, 74.
42. Donovan, *White Slave Crusades*, 32–36.
43. Postel, *Equality*, 138–47.
44. Fink, *Long Gilded Age*, 17.

45. *Workingman's Advocate*, August 11, 1866.
46. Horton, *American Liberalism*, 75.
47. Glickman, *Living Wage*, 31–32.
48. Glickman, 33–34.
49. *JUL* 4, no. 5 (September 1883): 556.
50. *Chicago Alarm*, May 30, 1885.
51. Roediger, *Wages*, 35.
52. Horton, *American Liberalism*, 76–77.
53. Glickman, *Living Wage*, 33.
54. *JUL* 5, no. 10 (September 1884): 795–96.
55. Warren, *Legacy of the Civil War*, 58–59.
56. Stanley, *From Bondage to Contract*, 85–86.
57. Fink, *Workingmen's Democracy*, 122; Andreas, *History of Chicago*, 289.
58. Rodgers, *Work Ethic*, 167–68.
59. *Albany Express*, April 1, 1886, Thomas B. Berry Scrapbooks, Bentley Library, University of Michigan, Ann Arbor.
60. Jama Lazerow, "Power and Respectability," in Boris and Lichtenstein, *Major Problems*, 245–47.
61. "The Secessionist Movement: Powderly's Enemies Growing Stronger," Thomas B. Berry Scrapbooks.
62. Rodgers, *Work Ethic*, 176–77.
63. Mandel, *Labor*, 77.
64. Green, *World of the Worker*, 32.
65. Kazin, *American Dreamers*, 91.
66. Friedrich Engels to Florence Kelley Wischnewetsky, December 28, 1886, https://www.marxists.org/archive/marx/works/1886/letters/86_12_28.htm; Lapides, *Marx and Engels*, 141.
67. Gourevitch, *From Slavery to the Cooperative Commonwealth*, 175–76; Dray, *Power in a Union*, 122–25.
68. Rodgers, *Work Ethic*, 155, 174.
69. P. Foner, *Organized Labor and the Black Worker*, 47; P. Foner, *From the Founding*, 54.
70. *Journal of the Knights of Labor*, March 16, 1889.
71. Hahn, *Nation without Borders*, 425.
72. Buhle, *Marxism*, 56–63.
73. Hild, *Greenbackers*, 95.
74. Weir, *Beyond Labor's Veil*, 186–90.
75. Gourevitch, *From Slavery to the Cooperative Commonwealth*, 69.
76. Kaufman, *For the Common Good?*, 238n28.
77. Leikin, *Practical Utopians*, 55.
78. Postel, *Equality*, 179.
79. Knights of Labor, *Proceedings of the General Assembly*, 1690–91.
80. P. Foner, *From the Founding*, 122.

81. O'Donnell, *Henry George*, 9–10.

82. George, *Henry George*, 8–10, 149.

83. Richard White, "Utopian Capitalism," in Beckert and Desan, *American Capitalism*, 119–39.

84. *Chicago Tribune*, August 22, 1887; *Wilkes-Barre (PA) Times Leader*, August 18, 1887.

85. Postel, *Equality*, 206–12.

86. *Scranton Daily Times*, June 18, 1878; Scrapbook I and II, box 264, Terence V. Powderly Papers, Catholic University of America Research Center and University Archives, Washington, DC (hereafter TVPP).

87. Quoted in Horton, *American Liberalism*, 76.

88. *JUL* 3, no. 5 (September 1882): 308, box 116, TVPP.

89. *JUL* 4, no. 1 (May 1883): 477, box 116, TVPP.

90. Edward J. Blum, "'To Doubt This Would Be to Doubt God,'" in Wright and Dresser, *Apocalypse and the Millennium*, 232.

91. *Journal of the Knights of Labor*, July 17 1890; "Address of the General Master Workman," [1891?], 3, box 217, TVPP.

92. "Address of the General Master Workman," September 4, 1883, 3–4, box 217, TVPP.

93. "Address of the General Master Workman," [1886?], 4, box 217, TVPP.

94. "Address of the General Master Workman," September 1, 1884, 11–12, box 217, TVPP.

95. *Appeal to Reason*, September 20, 1902; Weir, *Knights Unhorsed*, 23–46.

96. *Journal of the Knights of Labor*, January 16 1890, box 118, TVPP.

97. District No. 84 Knights of Labor broadside, George Ainsley Barksdale Scrapbook, 1861–1889, Virginia Historical Society, Richmond; Greg D. Kimball and the *Dictionary of Virginia Biography*, "John Taylor Chappell (1845–1915)," *Encyclopedia Virginia*, http://www.encyclopediavirginia.org/Chappell_John_Taylor_1845-1915.

98. Rachleff, *Black Labor in Richmond*, 28–31, 107.

99. Gerteis, *Class and the Color Line*, 94.

100. Rachleff, *Black Labor in Richmond*, 137–39.

101. *JUL* 11, no. 13 (October 1885); Rachleff, *Black Labor in Richmond*, 139.

102. *JUL*, May 8, 1886.

103. *JUL*, May 17, 1886.

104. *Labor Herald* (Richmond), April 24 and March 13, 1886 (hereafter *LH*).

105. *LH*, April 24, 1886.

106. Montgomery, *Beyond Equality*, 26.

107. *LH*, July 3, 1886.

108. Glickman, *Living Wage*, 34; Montgomery, *Citizen Worker*, 98.

109. *LH*, May 22 and April 17, 1886.

110. Monroe, *Democratic Wish*, 79.

111. Slotkin, *Fatal Environment*, 157.

112. *LH*, June 19, 1886.

113. *LH*, April 17, 1886.

114. *LH*, June 26, 1886.

115. Gabor Boritt, "The Right to Rise," in Davis et al., *Public and Private Lincoln*, 57–70.

116. *LH*, March 27, 1886.

117. *LH*, July 3, 1886.

118. *LH*, June 26, 1886.

119. *LH*, June 19, 1886.

120. *LH*, March 13, 1886.

121. *LH*, March 13 and March 20, 1886.

122. *LH*, May 17, 1886.

123. *LH*, May 8, 1886.

124. *LH*, June 19, 1886.

125. Horton, *American Liberalism*, 77; Postel, *Equality*, 247.

126. *LH*, June 19, 1886.

127. P. Foner, *From the Founding*, 67.

128. P. Foner, 70.

129. Foner, *Organized Labor and the Black Worker*, 47–49; Nell Irvin Painter, "Black Workers," in Birnbaum and Taylor, *Civil Rights*, 217.

130. Rachleff, *Black Labor in Richmond*, 127.

131. *LH*, May 1, 1886.

132. Dray, *Power in a Union*, 115.

133. *LH*, April 17, 1886.

134. *LH*, March 20, 1886.

135. *LH*, March 13, 1886.

136. Weir, *Beyond Labor's Veil*, 46.

137. Beckel, *Radical Reform*, 125.

138. Painter, "Black Workers," 217.

139. Horton, *American Liberalism*, 75.

140. *JUL* 1, no. 1 (May 1880): 15, 142.

141. *JUL* 3, no. 2 (June 1882): 243.

142. *St. Paul Daily Globe*, November 1, 1885; *Bismarck Weekly Tribune*, October 16, 1885; *Great Falls (MT) Tribune*, October 24, 1885.

143. *Wichita Daily Eagle*, June 1, 1886.

144. *St. Paul Daily Globe*, May 31, 1886.

145. *Wheeling Daily Intelligencer*, May 31, 1886.

146. *Journal of the Knights of Labor*, January 30, 1890.

147. *St. Paul Daily Globe*, November 1, 1885.

148. Weir, *Beyond Labor's Veil*, 58.

149. *Indianapolis Journal*, May 26, 1890.

150. *Washington Evening Star*, March 18, 1906; *Farmer and Mechanic* (Raleigh), March 16, 1909.

151. *Indiana State Sentinel*, July 6, 1887; Ozanne, *Labor Movement*, 11; Bureau of Labor and Industrial Statistics, *Second Biennial Report*, 378–82.

152. *Wheeling Daily Intelligencer*, August 23, 1886.

153. *Springfield (OH) Daily Republic*, April 1, 1887.

154. *St. Paul Daily Globe*, September 13, 1887.

155. *Emporia Weekly News*, March 14, 1889.

156. *Maysville (KY) Daily Evening Bulletin*, October 6, 1887.

157. Knights of Labor, *Proceedings of the General Assembly*, 1525–26.

158. *Omaha Daily Bee*, May 13, 1894.

159. *Washington Morning Times*, September 3, 1895.

160. *Topeka State Journal*, September 8, 1898; *Kansas City Journal*, September 5, 1898.

161. *Labor World* (Duluth), November 10, 1900.

162. *Anaconda (MT) Standard*, October 21, 1895.

163. *State Journal* (Jefferson City, MO), May 17, 1878.

164. P. Foner, *From the Founding*, 157–58.

165. Montgomery, *Citizen Worker*, 89, 95–97.

166. *St. Paul Daily Globe*, August 14, 1890.

167. *Journal of the Knights of Labor*, February 12, 1891.

168. *Journal of the Knights of Labor*, October 12, 1893.

## CHAPTER 4. The Red Flag of Emancipation

1. *Belmont Chronicle* (St. Clairsville, OH), May 11, 1871.

2. Katz, *From Appomattox to Montmartre*, 4–8, 211n23.

3. Cluseret, *Solidarity of Nations*.

4. Steven Hahn, "What Sort of World?," in Downs and Masur, *World the Civil War Made*, 340.

5. Philbeam, *French Socialists*, 176; Long, *France and Its Revolutions*, 315.

6. *New York Times*, February 24, 1870.

7. Pierce, *Memoir and Letters of Charles Sumner*, 128.

8. Fink, *Workingmen's Democracy*, 22.

9. *Washington Sentinel*, March 14, 1855.

10. *Sumter Banner*, April 3, 1850.

11. *New York Herald*, October 28, 1853, and February 28, 1860.

12. P. Foner, *From the Founding*, 29.

13. Hass, *Socialist Labor Party*, 24.

14. Kazin, *American Dreamers*, 85–86.

15. T. Draper, *Roots of American Communism*, 31.

16. *Platform and Constitution of the Socialist Labor Party*, 224–26, reel 35, Socialist Labor Party Papers, Wisconsin Historical Society, Madison (hereafter SLPP).

17. Marx and Engels, *Civil War*, 191.

18. Dray, *Power in a Union*, 128; P. Foner, *From the Founding*, 448–49; Renshaw, *Wobblies*, 41.

19. Forgacs, *Gramsci Reader*, 246–74.

20. Hass, *Socialist Labor Party*, 10; P. Foner, *From the Founding*, 279–80.

21. Seretan, *Daniel DeLeon*, 202.

22. *Common Cause* 2 (July 1912): 333.

23. *Weekly People* (New York), April 6, 1901.

24. "Let Us Argue," reel 35, SLPP.

25. "Liberté, Egalité, Fraternité!," reel 36, SLPP; meeting of November 2, 1879, Socialist Labor Party Records, Tamiment Library and Robert F. Wagner Labor Archives, New York University.

26. *Weekly People*, April 13, 1901.

27. London, *When God Laughs*, 260.

28. *Northwest Enterprise* (Anacortes, WA), July 19, 1884.

29. *Washington Evening Star*, July 21, 1896; US Bureau of Labor, *Report on Strike of Textile Workers in Lawrence*, 503; IWW, *Proceedings of the Second Annual Convention*, 519–20, 415.

30. *Petroleum Centre (PA) Daily Record*, September 17, 1872.

31. *Weekly People*, April 3, 1901.

32. *Labor Argus* (Charleston, WV), February 9, 1911.

33. Congressional Commission on Industrial Relations, *Industrial Relations*, 10,641.

34. *Commercial Telegraphers Journal* 15 (October 1917): 348.

35. Johnson, *Soul by Soul*, 72.

36. *Weekly People*, April 6, 1901.

37. *Weekly People*, May 4, 1901.

38. "Downfall of the Small Producer," 48, reel 36, SLPP.

39. "Confiscation," 148, reel 36, SLPP; "Confiscation," 442, reel 11, Victor L. Berger Papers, Wisconsin Historical Society, Madison.

40. Bax, *Short History of the Paris Commune*.

41. Shawki, *Socialism*, 114–15; Weir, *Knights Unhorsed*, 26.

42. Robinson, *Black Marxism*, 218.

43. "Capitalism in the South," 54, reel 36, SLPP.

44. P. Foner, *From the Founding*, 43.

45. Workingmen's Party of the United States, *Proceedings*, 13–23.

46. *Workmen's Advocate* (New York), October 26, 1889.

47. Workingmen's Party of the United States, *Proceedings*, 14.

48. *Workmen's Advocate*, October 26, 1889.

49. Seretan, *Daniel DeLeon*, 83; Johnpoll and Johnpoll, *Impossible Dream*, 250.

50. *St. Paul Daily Globe*, March 8, 1881.

51. *Indianapolis Journal*, November 26, 1888.

52. McLellan, *Karl Marx*, 159.

53. Socialist Labor Party, *Proceedings of the Tenth National Convention*, 145.

54. P. Foner, *From the Founding*, 493–95.

55. Seretan, *Daniel DeLeon*, 72.

56. *National Republican* (Washington, DC), October 22, 1880.

57. Schnierov, "Chicago's Great Upheaval," 5.

58. Stan Nadel, "German Immigrant Left," in Buhle and Georgakas, *Immigrant Left*, 73.

59. Montgomery, *Citizen Worker*, 100; Green, *Death in the Haymarket*, 91.

60. Blackmar, *Kansas*, 845.

61. Kipnis, *American Socialist Movement*, 53; Secrist, "Economic Analysis," 369.

62. Sotheran, *Horace Greeley*, xxxv.

63. Hinton, "American Labor Organizations," 49.

64. Hinton, *John Brown and His Men*, v–vi.

65. Andrew Zimmerman, "Second American Revolution," in Downs and Masur, *World the Civil War Made*, 318.

66. Hinton, *John Brown and His Men*, 219.

67. Hinton, 449.

68. Hinton, 462.

69. Hinton, 600.

70. Gilpin, *John Brown Still Lives!*, 73.

71. Malin, *John Brown and the Legend of Fifty-Six*, 445.

72. Hinton, *John Brown and His Men*, 437–38.

73. Hinton, 326.

74. Hinton, 162.

75. *Carpenter* 28, no. 7 (July 1908): 22.

76. *Carpenter* 11, no. 1 (January 1891): 2.

77. P. Foner, *From the Founding*, 96; *Carpenter* 10, no. 9 (September 1890): 1.

78. *Carpenter* 1, no. 4 (August 1881): 2, 5; *Carpenter* 1, no. 3 (July 1881): 3.

79. *Carpenter* 5, no. 12 (December 1885): 2; *Carpenter* 5, no. 9 (September 1885): 1.

80. *Carpenter* 3, no. 9 (September 1883): 4.

81. *Carpenter* 20, no. 3 (March 1900): 13.

82. *Carpenter* 5, no. 12 (December 1885): 3.

83. *Davenport (IA) Daily Times*, May 19, 1904.

84. *Carpenter* 14, no. 1 (February 1894): 9.

85. *Carpenter* 16, no. 4 (April 1896): 3.

86. *Carpenter* 2, no. 11 (November 1882): 2

87. *Carpenter* 4, no. 4 (April 1884): 4

88. *Carpenter* 2, no. 8 (August 1882): 6.

89. *Carpenter* 15, no. 7 (July 1895): 6.

90. *Carpenter* 13, no. 5 (May 1893): 3.

91. Koenig, "American Anarchism," 130.

92. Dray, *Power in a Union*, 133–34.

93. J. Jones, *Goddess of Anarchy*, 92.

94. Roediger and Rosemont, *Haymarket Scrapbook*, 97, 177.

95. J. Jones, *Goddess of Anarchy*, 78–79; Green, *Death in the Haymarket*, 89.

96. Messer-Kruse, *Haymarket Conspiracy*, 137–49.

97. Fink, *Long Gilded Age*, 124.

98. Dray, *Power in a Union*, 137.

99. Green, *Death in the Haymarket*, 131.

100. Roediger and Rosemont, *Haymarket Scrapbook*, 94.

101. *Alarm* (Chicago), December 3, 1887.
102. *Alarm*, June 13, 1885.
103. *Alarm*, June 13 and August 22, 1885.
104. P. Foner, *From the Founding*, 40.
105. *Alarm*, August 25, 1888, and November 19, 1887.
106. *Alarm*, June 27, 1885.
107. *Alarm*, July 14, 1888.
108. *Alarm*, June 16, 1888.
109. *Alarm*, May 30[?], 1885.
110. *JUL* 5, no. 10 (September 1884): 802.
111. *Alarm*, January 5, 1889.
112. *Alarm*, November 19, 1887.
113. *Alarm*, February 11, 1888, and April 18, 1885.
114. J. Jones, *Goddess of Anarchy*, 170; *Alarm*, November 5, 1887.
115. *Alarm*, August 22, 1885.
116. *Alarm*, January 5, 1889.
117. J. Jones, *Goddess of Anarchy*, 349–50; *Alarm*, September 8, 1888.
118. *Alarm*, August 4, 1888.
119. Messer-Kruse, *Haymarket Conspiracy*, 156.
120. Messer-Kruse, 148.
121. *Alarm*, July 27, 1885, October 3, 1885, and October 17, 1883.
122. *Alarm*, July 7, 1888.
123. James, *Black Jacobins*, 89; Genovese, *From Rebellion to Revolution*, 110.
124. *Anarchist* 1, no. 9 (December 1887): 1, 9.
125. Quoted in Dray, *Power in a Union*, 144.
126. Roediger and Rosemont, *Haymarket Scrapbook*, 93.
127. *Alarm*, June 16, 1888.
128. Albert Parsons, "Autobiography," in P. Foner, *Autobiographies of the Haymarket Martyrs*, 49.
129. J. Jones, *Goddess of Anarchy*, 46.
130. Renshaw, *Wobblies*, 30.
131. Roediger and Rosemont, *Haymarket Scrapbook*, 94.
132. Roediger, *Working toward Whiteness*, 13, 72.
133. Green, *Death in the Haymarket*, 56–57; Dray, *Power in a Union*, 129.
134. Kazin, *American Dreamers*, 88.
135. J. Jones, *Goddess of Anarchy*, 58.
136. Schneirov, *Labor and Urban Politics*, 72; Dray, *Power in a Union*, 115; Arneson, *Encyclopedia of U.S. Labor*, 1,061.
137. Green, *Death in the Haymarket*, 76.
138. Parsons, "Autobiography," 50–90; J. Jones, *Goddess of Anarchy*, 121.
139. Parsons, *Life of Albert R. Parsons*, 41.
140. J. Jones, *Goddess of Anarchy*, 76, 109.
141. Avrich, *Haymarket Tragedy*, 262–67.

142. Green, *Death in the Haymarket*, 131; Parsons, "Autobiography," 68–69; Dray, *Power in a Union*, 153.

143. *World*, August 26, 1886, box 118, TVPP.

144. Dray, *Power in a Union*, 156.

145. *Lucifer, the Light-Bearer* (Valley Falls, KS), July 5, 1895.

146. *Detroit Free Press*, November 7, 1887.

147. *Philadelphia Times*, November 14, 1887.

148. *Alarm*, November 19, 1887.

149. *Mother Earth* 1, no. 12 (February 1907): 34–37.

150. *Mother Earth* 7, no. 1 (March 1912): 209.

151. *Alarm*, March 24, 1888, November 19, 1887, and June 16, 1888.

152. *Anarchist* 1, no. 9 (December 1887): 9.

153. Roediger and Rosemont, *Haymarket Scrapbook*, 143; P. Foner, *From the Founding*, 113.

154. Sandberg, *Selected Poems*, 142–43.

155. "Our Surplus Labor," 53, reel 36, SLPP.

156. Green, *Death in the Haymarket*, 131.

157. Salvatore, *Eugene V. Debs*, 150.

158. Socialist Labor Party, *Proceedings of the Tenth National Convention*, 280, 136, 274, 319, 198.

## CHAPTER 5. The Blue-Gray Campaign

1. Brock, *American Crisis*, 64; Hicks, *Populist Revolt*, 162–163, 400.

2. Hofstadter, *Age of Reform*, 68, 75.

3. Donnelly, *Caesar's Column*, 82–83, 54.

4. Donnelly, 84.

5. Postel, *Populist Vision*, 11–12.

6. Kammen, *Mystic Chords of Memory*, 10; Postel, *Populist Vision*, 4.

7. Gaither, *Blacks and the Populist Movement*, 200; Pollack, *Populist Response*, 5–12.

8. Janney, "'I Yield to No Man,'" 397.

9. R. Miller, "Farmers and Third-Party Politics," 294; R. Miller, *Populist Cartoons*, 69; Janney, "'I Yield to No Man,'" 397–98.

10. O'Conner, *Iron Wheels*, 305.

11. Patrick J. Kelly, "The Election of 1896," in Fahs and Waugh, *Memory of the Civil War*, 189.

12. Mitchell, *Skirmisher*, 107; Lester, *Up from the Mudsills of Hell*, 73–74.

13. Matthew Hild, "Workingmen's Democracy," in Beeby, *Populism in the South Revisited*, 47.

14. Ayers, *Promise of the New South*, 266.

15. Postel, *Populist Vision*, 12.

16. Woodward, *Origins of the New South*, 235–47.

17. Woodward, 240–41.

18. Gaither, *Blacks and the Populist Movement*, x–xi, 198.

19. Kazin, *American Dreamers*, 103; Kipnis, *American Socialist Movement*, 48.

20. "Populist Platform. Principles of the Fourth Party in Vermont Politics," circa 1896, series 1:2, folder 12, Marion Butler Papers, Southern Historical Collection, Wilson Library, University of North Carolina, Chapel Hill (hereafter MBP).

21. Hofstadter, *Age of Reform*, 19, 95.

22. Gaither, *Blacks and the Populist Movement*, 82.

23. Hofstadter, *Age of Reform*, 4–5, 61, 94–95; Postel, *Populist Vision*, 17.

24. Hofstadter, *Age of Reform*, 121.

25. Gaither, *Blacks and the Populist Movement*, 51.

26. Ayers, *Promise of the New South*, 269–70, 272–73.

27. David Lubin letter, May 31, 1897, series 2.4, folder 763, MBP.

28. Gaither, *Blacks and the Populist Movement*, 47; Ayers, *Promise of the New South*, 251, 256–57.

29. Gaither, *Blacks and the Populist Movement*, 113, 80.

30. Quoted in P. Foner, *From the Founding*, 327–32.

31. Salvatore, *Eugene V. Debs*, 159; Kipnis, *American Socialist Movement*, 48–50. Debs changed his mind about conservative electoral alliances and middle-class panaceas after the defeat of William Jennings Bryan's free silver presidential campaign in 1896.

32. Postel, *Populist Vision*, 70.

33. Adams and Thornton, *Populist Assault*, 75–75.

34. Postel, *Populist Vision*, 85.

35. Ostler, *Prairie Populism*, 226.

36. "Whereas" statement, 1892, series 2.3.2, folder 713, MBP.

37. J. Devine to Marion Butler, July 16, 1895, series 1:2, folder 10, MBP.

38. B. O. Flower to Marion Butler, December 14, 1894, series 1:1, folder 8, MBP; and Jo A. Parker to N. A. Dunning, October 11, 1895, series 1:2, folder 11, MBP.

39. Ayers, *Promise of the New South*, 255, 264–66, 281.

40. *People's Voice* (Wellington, KS), August 12, 1892.

41. George S. Bowen to Henry Clews, June 4, 1896, folder 8, Box 53, George S. Bowen Papers, Chicago Historical Society.

42. Bowen to Clews.

43. "National People's Party Platform, Adopted at Omaha, Nebraska, July 4, 1892," series 2.3.2, folder 713, MBP.

44. Woodward, *Origins of the New South*, 255.

45. P. Foner, *From the Founding*, 301.

46. Polk to J. W. Denmark, February 17, 1892, folder 100, Leonidas L. Polk Papers; Gaither, *Blacks and the Populist Movement*, 43.

47. Ayers, *Promise of the New South*, 259.

48. *Jamestown (ND) Weekly Alert*, March 3, 1892.

49. Woodward, *Origins of the New South*, 251–59.

50. McMath, *American Populism*, 109.

51. *PF*, October 24, 1893.

52. Ayers, *Promise of the New South*, 249–51.

53. *Kansas Agitator* (Garnett), July 21, 1890.

54. Pollack, *Populist Response*, 68–72, 85.

55. *PF*, January 5, 1892, and May 26, 1891.

56. *PF*, September 17, 1895.

57. Postel, *Populist Vision*, 10.

58. Woodward, *Origins of the New South*, 247.

59. Bland, *People's Party Shot and Shell*, 5–17, Tamiment Library and Robert F. Wagner Labor Archives, New York University; see also series 3, box 1, folder 21, Charles H. Kerr Company Papers, Newberry Library, Chicago.

60. *Seattle Post-Intelligencer*, July 3, 1892.

61. *Rock Island Daily Argus*, July 5, 1892.

62. *PF*, March 6, 1894.

63. *Salt Lake Herald*, July 3, 1892.

64. D. W. Clark to Walter Q. Gresham, June 29, 1892, Walter Q. Gresham Papers, Indiana Historical Society, Indianapolis.

65. C. A. Power to Walter Q. Gresham, June 26, 1892, Walter Q. Gresham Papers.

66. S. M. Owen to D. M. Fralwiler, June 24, 1892, Walter Q. Gresham Papers.

67. Boyce to Polk, April 13, 1892, folder 103, Leonidas L. Polk Papers.

68. Postel, *Populist Vision*, 174; Gaither, *Blacks and the Populist Movement*, 75.

69. Ayers, *Promise of the New South*, 251–52, 260.

70. Ayers, 260.

71. *People' Party Paper* (hereafter *PPP*), June 17, 1892; *Kansas Times* (Atwood), July 8, 1892.

72. Pratt, *Gray Agendas*, 28.

73. *PF*, June 28, 1892.

74. *Special Informer*, June 22, 1892, Folder 231, Leonidas L. Polk Papers.

75. Weaver, *Call to Action*, 363.

76. Allen, *James Baird Weaver*, 27.

77. *PPP*, July 1, 1892.

78. *PPP*, September 14, 1894; *Los Angeles Herald*, July 2, 1892.

79. *PPP*, October 28, 1892.

80. *PPP*, June 24 and July 1, 1892.

81. Gaither, *Blacks and the Populist Movement*, 77.

82. "Populism, Democracy, and Political Chaos," ca. 1896, series 2.3.2, folder 716, MBP.

83. Newspaper clipping, ca. 1896, series 2.3.2, folder 716, MBP.

84. *Rock Island Daily Argus*, July 5, 1892; *Democratic Advocate* (Westminster, MD), July 9, 1892.

85. Quoted in *Colfax (LA) Chronicle*, September 10, 1892.

86. *PPP*, July 8, 1892.

87. Woodward, *Origins of the New South*, 244–55.

88. Mitchell, *Skirmisher*, 153.
89. "To Members of the People's Party," January 1896, series 2.1, folder 640, MBP.
90. "Whereas" statement, 1892, series 2.3.2, folder 713, MBP.
91. *PPP*, October 28 and June 24, 1892.
92. *PPP*, July 1, 1892.
93. *PPP*, July 15, 1892.
94. *PPP*, June 10, 1892.
95. Postel, *Populist Vision*, 173–93.
96. *PPP*, September 30, 1892.
97. *PPP*, July 1, 1892.
98. *PPP*, October 28, 1892.
99. Newspaper clipping, ca. 1896, series 2.3.2, folder 716, MBP.
100. *PPP*, June 24, 1892.
101. *PPP*, October 21, 1892; Andrew Neather, "Labor Republicanism," in Bodnar, *Bonds of Affection*, 82–101.
102. *PPP*, June 24, 1892.
103. *Dakota Farmers' Leader* (Canton, SD), July 22, 1892; *Richmond Dispatch*, March 6, 1892.
104. Stelle, *People's Party Song Book*, 29–30.
105. Stelle, 2–3.
106. *Kansas Agitator*, October 6, 1892.
107. *PF*, December 6, 1892.
108. *Dakota Farmers' Leader*, November 4, 1892.
109. Stelle, *People's Party Song Book*, 9, 18–19.
110. Stelle, 15–30.
111. *People's Voice*, August 12, 1892.
112. *Wichita Daily Eagle*, September 21, 1892.
113. *Los Angeles Herald*, July 17, 1892.
114. Weaver, *Call to Action*, 5.
115. Hofstadter, *Age of Reform*, 63.
116. Weaver, *Call to Action*, 20.
117. Weaver, 18–36, 86.
118. Weaver, 285–90.
119. Weaver, 292.
120. W. Ross, *Muted Fury*, 51.
121. Engel, *American Politicians*, 231.
122. Weaver, *Call to Action*, 166, 283.
123. Weaver, 203.
124. Weaver, 20, 362.
125. Weaver, 294.
126. Weaver, 220, 266.
127. Weaver, 333.
128. Weaver, 242–43.

129. Engel, *American Politicians*, 232.

130. Weaver, *Call to Action*, 424.

131. *Dodge City (KS) Globe-Republican*, June 3, 1891. For data on the "self-made man," see Frances W. Gregory and Irene D. Neu, "The American Industrial Elite," in W. Miller, *Men in Business*, 202; and Montgomery, *Beyond Equality*, 14–15, 31.

132. Ayers, *Promise of the New South*, 255.

133. *Hickman (KY) Courier*, August 19, 1892.

134. *State Chronicle* (Raleigh), August 9, 1892.

135. *St. Tammany Farmer* (Covington, LA), September 10, 1892.

136. Mitchell, *Skirmisher*, 167.

137. *PF*, September 27, 1892.

138. Ayers, *Promise of the New South*, 262.

139. *St. Tammany Farmer*, September 10, 1892.

140. *People's Voice*, August 12, 1892.

141. Fischer, *Liberty and Freedom*, 402.

142. *Wichita Daily Eagle*, September 21, 1892; Mitchell, *Skirmisher*, 170.

143. *Wichita Daily Eagle*, September 21, 1892; *Abilene (KS) Weekly Reflector*, September 29, 1892; *Los Angeles Herald*, September 22, 1892.

144. Arnett, *Populist Movement*, 151–52; Woodward, *Origins of the New South*, 259–60.

145. *PPP*, September 30, 1892.

146. *PPP*, September 30, 1892.

147. *Omaha Daily Bee*, November 4, 1892.

148. *Omaha Daily Bee*, October 22, 1892.

149. *Abilene Weekly Reflector*, September 29, 1892.

150. Goodwyn, *Populist Moment*, 210.

151. Argersinger, *Populism and Politics*, 143; Argersinger, *Limits of Agrarian Radicalism*, 118.

152. *Worthington (MN) Advance*, October 27, 1892; *Saline County Journal* (Salina, KS), July 21, 1892.

153. Ayers, *Promise of the New South*, 261.

154. Saxton, *Rise and Fall*, 308.

155. Mitchell, *Skirmisher*, 160.

156. *People's Voice*, September 16, 1892; Mitchell, *Skirmisher*, 168.

157. Hild, *Greenbackers*, 174–75; Ayers, *Promise of the New South*, 275.

158. Rogers, *One-Gallused Rebellion*, 213–14; Woodward, *Origins of the New South*, 262–63; Ayers, *Promise of the New South*, 276–79.

159. Hild, *Greenbackers*, 175.

160. *PPP*, November 4 and 25, 1892.

161. P. Foner, *From the Founding*, 310.

162. Quoted in P. Foner, 313.

163. George Wilson to Marion Butler, May 30, 1896, series 1:2, folder 19, MBP.

164. *PPP*, November 25, 1892.

165. James Shepard to Marion Butler, April 30, 1896, series 1:2, folder 17, MBP.
166. Mitchell, *Skirmisher*, 163; Postel, *Populist Vision*, 269–70.
167. Postel, *Populist Vision*, 197.
168. Speech, January 1896, series 2:1, folder 640, MBP.
169. Ayers, *Promise of the New South*, 283–85.
170. People's Party State Committee of Illinois, folder 2, box 54, George S. Bowen Papers.
171. P. Foner, *From the Founding*, 317–19.
172. *Kansas Agitator*, October 26, 1893.
173. Stauffer and Gates, *Portable Frederick Douglass*, 398; "Independent Republicans of Ohio," folder 2, box 55, George S. Bowen Papers.
174. *Salt Lake City Broad Ax*, September 7, 1895.
175. Schlüter, *Lincoln, Labor, and Slavery*, 173, 179; Mandel, *Labor*, 156–57; Schwartz, *Abraham Lincoln and the Forge of National Memory*, 205.
176. Basler, *Collected Works of Abraham Lincoln*, 4:7, 212.
177. Lincoln, *Abraham Lincoln Speeches and Writings*, 97, 296.
178. *Kansas Agitator*, March 29, 1901.
179. P. Foner, *From the Founding*, 382–83.
180. Ayers, *Promise of the New South*, 293–96.
181. *Advocate* (Topeka), February 3, 1897.
182. Schwartz, *Abraham Lincoln and the Forge of National Memory*, 143.
183. *Breckinridge News* (Cloverport, KY), September 30, 1896.
184. *Indianapolis Journal*, September 9, 1896.
185. *National Democrat* (Washington, DC), June 2, 1900,
186. Butler to Zebulon Vance Walser, September 1, 1896, series 1.2, folder 27, MBP.
187. Kipnis, *American Socialist Movement*, 95.
188. John S. Dore to Butler, August 3, 1896, series 1.2, folder 24, MBP.
189. Grigsby E. Thomas Jr. to Butler, August 26, 1896, series 1.2, folder 26, MBP.
190. "Tom Watson," newspaper clipping, series 1.2, folder 26, MBP.
191. J. W. Dollison to Butler, August 21, 1896, and J. F. Rhoads to Butler, August 27, 1896, series 1.2, folders 25–26, MBP.
192. Ayers, *Promise of the New South*, 296–97.
193. Goodwyn, *Populist Moment*, 281.
194. Hild, *Greenbackers*, 191–92.
195. Hild, 201.
196. *PF*, April 28, 1903.
197. *Kansas City Journal*, November 2, 1898.
198. *Hot Springs (SD) Weekly Star*, May 6, 1898.
199. *PF*, June 30, 1903.
200. *PF*, April 23, 1901, and March 24, December 8, and July 1, 1903.
201. Crow and Durden, *Maverick Republican*, 50; Hild, *Greenbackers*, 181, 199.
202. "To the People of North Carolina," October 25, 1898, box 1, folder 8, Cyrus Thompson Papers, Southern Historical Collection, Wilson Library, University of North Carolina, Chapel Hill.

203. Crow and Durden, *Maverick Republican*, 50; "Why Was This Done," ca. 1900, aeries 2:1, folder 640, MBP.

204. Letter to Butler, July 19, 1900, series 2:1, folder 640, MBP.

205. "Republicanism in the South," ca. 1899 (presumably written by Russell), folder 19, Daniel L. Russell Papers, Southern Historical Collection, Wilson Library, University of North Carolina, Chapel Hill.

206. Edmonds, *Negro and Fusion Politics*, 59, 108, 55; "Col. Waddell" letter, 1896, series 2:1, folder 640, MBP.

207. Ayers, *Promise of the New South*, 299–304; Edmonds, *Negro and Fusion Politics*, 56; Hild, *Greenbackers*, 202.

208. Letter to Butler, July 19, 1900, series 2:1, folder 640, MBP.

209. Michael K. Honey, "Racial Violence," in Cecelski and Tyson, *Democracy Betrayed*, 178.

210. *Semi-weekly Messenger* (Wilmington, NC), November 4 and December 9, 1898; *PF*, October 18, 1904.

211. Woodward, *Strange Career of Jim Crow*, 45.

212. Gaither, *Blacks and the Populist Movement*, ix.

213. Woodward, *Origins of the New South*, 244.

214. Blight, *Race and Reunion*, 294.

## CHAPTER 6. Citadel of Labor

1. Lum, *Economics of Anarchy*.
2. *Alarm*, May 30, 1885; Lause, *Civil War's Last Campaign*, 192.
3. Avrich, *Haymarket Tragedy*, 317–20.
4. *Labor Herald*, May 1, 1886.
5. Ashbaugh, *Lucy Parsons*, 181.
6. Lum, *Social Problems*, 87–88.
7. Greene, *Pure and Simple Politics*, 68.
8. Hobsbawm, *Age of Capital*, 99.
9. Schneirov, *Labor and Urban Politics*, 319.
10. Roediger, *Wages*, 12.
11. P. Foner, *From the Founding*, 141–43, 171.
12. Kazin, *American Dreamers*, 94.
13. P. Foner, *Policies and Practices*, 352; J. Jones, *Goddess of Anarchy*, 121.
14. P. Foner, *From the Founding*, 290–91; P. Foner, *Policies and Practices*, 73–74.
15. Green, *World of the Worker*, 32.
16. Saxton, *Rise and Fall*, 301-16.
17. P. Foner, *From the Founding*, 176–77.
18. Greene, *Pure and Simple Politics*, 68.
19. Samuel Gompers, "The American Labor Movement," Denver, Colorado, August 25, 1906, Samuel Gompers Scrapbook, reel 1, George Meany Memorial AFL-CIO Archive, Hornbake Library and Special Collections, University of Maryland, College Park (hereafter SGS).

20. *Carpenter* 30, no. 10 (October 1910): 6.

21. *American Federationist* 11, no. 7 (July 1904): 596 (hereafter *AF*).

22. *Carpenter* 8, no. 11 (November 1888): 2; *AF* 1, no. 3 (May 1894): 52.

23. P. Foner, *From the Founding*, 197–98.

24. *Commoner* (Lincoln, NE), October 16, 1903.

25. *AF* 3, no. 8 (October 1898): 162.

26. *Carpenter* 27, no. 5 (May 1907): 19.

27. *AF* 1, no. 8 (October 1894): 173.

28. *AF* 2, no. 7 (September 1895): 122.

29. *AF* 3, no. 9 (November 1896): 187.

30. Olsen and Mendoza, *American Economic History*, 30–31; Dunlop and Galenson, *Labor in the Twentieth Century*, 29–33; W. H. Foster letter, November 20, 1881, Early Federation Records, 1881–1889, George Meany Memorial AFL-CIO Archive, Hornbake Library and Special Collections, University of Maryland, College Park; P. Foner, *Policies and Practices*, 27, 174.

31. *Carpenter* 29, no. 5 (May 1909): 53; Brundage, *Socialist Utopia*, 56.

32. *AF* 1, no. 1 (March 1894): 5.

33. *Carpenter* 25, no. 7 (July 1905): 6.

34. *AF* 1, no. 9 (November 1894): 189–90.

35. *Carpenter* 22, no. 10 (October 1902): 9; *Labor World*, November 25, 1905.

36. *Carpenter* 22, no. 7 (July 1902): 13.

37. *Carpenter* 22, no. 7 (July 1902): 8.

38. *Day Book* (Chicago), May 15, 1914.

39. *Carpenter* 25, no. 4 (April 1905): 4.

40. P. Foner, *Policies and Practices*, 36–37, 42–49.

41. P. Foner, *From the Founding*, 219.

42. *Evening Bulletin*, April 24, 1894; P. Foner, *From the Founding*, 242.

43. *Scranton Republican*, January 6, 1901.

44. *AF* 5, no. 9 (November 1898): 175; S. Miller, *From Prairie to Prison*, 85, 134.

45. R. Lewis, *Black Coal Miners*, 24; P. Foner, *From the Founding*, 221–22.

46. Dray, *Power in a Union*, 176.

47. P. Foner, *Policies and Practices*, 404.

48. P. Foner, 397.

49. *United Mine Workers' Journal*, June 14, 1894.

50. Ibid., October 22, 1891.

51. *United Mine Workers' Journal*, December 28, 1893, and June 4, 1891.

52. *United Mine Workers' Journal*, May 12, 1892, and June 8, 1893.

53. P. Foner, *From the Founding*, 261.

54. *Roanoke Times*, July 5, 1894.

55. *Progressive Farmer*, July 17, 1894.

56. P. Foner, *From the Founding*, 268.

57. P. Foner, 276.

58. *AF* 5, no.1 (March 1898): 12.

59. *United Mine Workers' Journal*, February 13, 1896; *National Labor Tribune*, February 7, 1891.

60. Hild, *Greenbackers*, 190; Greene, *Pure and Simple Politics*, 63; Archer, *Why Is There No Labor Party in the United States?*, 220.

61. *AF* 1, no. 7 (September 1894): 142.

62. *Carpenter* 26, no. 8 (August 1906): 6.

63. *AF* 11, no. 7 (July 1904): 597.

64. P. Foner, *Policies and Practices*, 220–22.

65. Lilienthal, *Women of the Future*, 22.

66. Claudia D. Goldin, "Work and Wages," in Cott, *History of Women*, 256.

67. Laurie, *Artisans into Workers*, 197; P. Foner, *Industrial Workers of the World*, 282.

68. Saxton, *Rise and Fall*, 310–13.

69. Roediger, *Working toward Whiteness*, 13–15, 72–73.

70. P. Foner, *Policies and Practices*, 256–62.

71. Woodward, *Strange Career of Jim Crow*, 98; P. Foner, *Policies and Practices*, 233–45.

72. P. Foner, *From the Founding*, 348–57.

73. Quoted in P. Foner, *Policies and Practices*, 278–79.

74. *Carpenter* 29, no. 9 (September 1909): 2; *Carpenter* 27, no. 6 (June 1907): 29–30.

75. Proceedings of the Thirteenth Convention, 159, United Brewery Workers Records, Gelman Library Special Collections, George Washington University, Washington, DC; P. Foner, *Policies and Practices*, 197.

76. P. Foner, *Policies and Practices*, 109.

77. P. Foner, 195.

78. *Labor Argus*, October 18, 1906.

79. Saxton, *Rise and Fall*, 312; Green, *World of the Worker*, 46.

80. *Carpenter* 20, no. 6 (June 1900): 3.

81. *Carpenter* 23, no. 2 (February 1903): 4.

82. *Carpenter* 21, no. 10 (October 1901): 7.

83. *Labor Argus*, April 23, 1908.

84. Quoted in Archer, *Why Is There No Labor Party in the United States?*, 198.

85. Gompers, *Samuel Gompers Papers*, 4:129.

86. *Carpenter* 33, no. 1 (January 1913): 36.

87. Gompers, *Samuel Gompers Papers*, 4:59.

88. Gompers, 435.

89. *Lincoln (NE) Commoner*, December 4, 1908.

90. Rodgers, *Work Ethic*, 174.

91. *Carpenter* 25, no. 6 (June 1905): 10.

92. *Carpenter* 28, no. 3 (March 1908): 15.

93. *Carpenter* 27, no. 5 (May 1907): 25.

94. *Labor World*, June 30, 1906.

95. *San Francisco Call*, April 21, 1897; Stone, "The Knights of Labor," 225–26.

96. Schwartz and Schulman, "History, Commemoration, and Belief"; Schwartz, "Collective Memory," 482–86; Peterson, *Abraham Lincoln*, 30.

97. *Arizona Republican* (Phoenix), March 4, 1907.

98. *Carpenter* 24, no. 12 (December 1904): 9.

99. *Carpenter* 26, no. 2 (February 1906): 2.

100. *Day Book*, May 5, 1915.

101. *New Iberia (LA) Enterprise and Independent Observer*, November 8, 1919.

102. *New York City Sun*, October 26, 1919.

103. *Salt Lake Herald*, April 28, 1895; *Topeka State Journal*, June 5, 1920.

104. *Pittsburgh Daily Post*, September 2, 1890.

105. *Inter Ocean* (Chicago), September 5, 1893; *Topeka State Journal*, September 29, 1896.

106. *Kansas City Journal*, September 29, 1896.

107. *Stark County Democrat* (Canton, OH), September 10, 1908.

108. *Wichita Daily Eagle*, September 9, 1898.

109. *Clayton (NM) Enterprise*, March 31, 1905.

110. *Indianapolis Journal*, October 22, 1892.

111. J. Jones, *Goddess of Anarchy*, 242.

112. World's Columbian Exposition, *Columbian Exposition*, 2, 394–395; Pietila, *Not in My Neighborhood*, 27.

113. *Indianapolis Journal*, October 22, 1892.

114. *Washington Times*, August 17, 1917.

115. *Rock Island (IL) Argus*, November 8, 1911.

116. "Leaflet: Souvenir of Grant Day, New York City, April 27, 1897" and "Grant Monument Inaugural," reel 5, SGS.

117. "Statement for the Jackson Heights Club Regarding Abraham Lincoln, February 1, 1923," reel 4, SGS.

118. Quoted in P. Foner, *Policies and Practices*, 354.

119. *Salt Lake Herald-Republican*, September 3, 1916.

120. *Producers News* (Plentywood, MT), June 18, 1920.

121. *Brattleboro Daily Reformer*, July 17, 1922; *Washington Evening Star*, July 15, 1922.

122. *Washington Times*, October 28, 1919.

123. *New York Age*, February 16, 1918.

124. *Washington Evening Star*, February 13, 1910.

125. *Washington Herald*, February 13, 1911.

126. *New York Times*, March 11, 1900.

127. *Carpenter* 33, no. 7 (July 1913): 31.

128. *Indianapolis News*, December 16, 1924.

129. *Carpenter* 30, no. 10 (October 1910): 6.

130. Cook, *Civil War Memories*, 110.

131. P. Foner, *From the Founding*, 404–31.

132. "Samuel Gompers on War," *Chicago Times-Herald*, April 17, 1898," and "Wants

No Slave Labor," *World*, August 1, 1898, reel 5, SGS; Scott C. Bone, "Gompers, American" and "Sam Gompers: Patriot," reel 1, SGS; Scipes, *AFL-CIO's Secret War*, 9–10.

133. Mandel, *Samuel Gompers*, 206.

134. P. Foner, *Policies and Practices*, 385.

135. Scipes, *AFL-CIO's Secret War*, 1–2.

136. Renshaw, *Wobblies*, 21.

137. Kipnis, *Movement*, 351, 357.

138. Weir, *Workers in America*, 437–439.

139. Kipnis, *American Socialist Movement*, 357.

140. *Marion (OH) Daily Mirror*, November 7, 1911.

141. *Labor Journal* (Everett, WA), November 17, 1911; *Day Book*, November 7, 1911.

142. Socialist Labor Party, *Proceedings of the Ninth Annual Convention*, 8–10, 27.

143. P. Foner, *Labor and World War One*, 43–44.

144. *Roseburg (OR) Review*, February 14, 1917; McKillen, *Making the World Safe*, 94.

145. Kazin, *War against War*, 89.

146. McKillen, *Making the World Safe*, 116–17; P. Foner, *Labor and World War One*, 304.

147. P. Foner, *Labor and World War One*, 41, 65–67.

148. P. Foner, 97.

149. P. Foner, 72.

150. P. Foner, 102–8.

151. Eugene B. Stinde to Robert Burkham, December 26, 1919, Julius J. Goldberg Papers, Missouri Historical Society, St. Louis.

152. AFL Labor Files, 1899–1924, SGS.

153. *Washington Evening Star*, February 13, 1918.

154. "Speech by Mr. Samuel Gompers, April 7, 1919," reel 3, SGS.

155. Building Trades Council and Central Trades and Labor Union of St. Louis to David R. Francis, September 24, 1919, David R. Francis Papers, Missouri Historical Society, St. Louis.

156. *Harrisburg Telegraph*, April 26, 1919.

157. Howell Harris, "Shaping of Federal Labor-Relations Policy," in Boris and Lichtenstein, *Major Problems*, 431.

158. *Washington Evening Star*, August 31, 1918.

159. *Carpenter* 38, no. 2 (February 1918): 16.

160. *Carpenter* 38, no. 7 (July 1918): 50–51; *Carpenter* 40, no. 11 (November 1920): 17; Gompers, *Gompers Papers*, 2:122–23.

## CHAPTER 7. The Blue and the Gray and the Red

1. Richmond Knights of Labor Association Ledger, April 5, 1895, Notebook of John Taylor Chappell and Samuel Michael Chappell, Albert and Shirley Small Special Collections Library, University of Virginia, Charlottesville (hereafter NJTC).

2. Alex B. McCulloch letter, January 31, 1898, and Richmond Knights of Labor ledger, February 1, 1897, NJTC.

3. Undated letter, "What is Socialism?," NJTC.

4. Richmond Knights of Labor ledger, February 8, February 14, and March 21, 1898, NJTC.

5. "Ghosts" and "Steward's Luck," NJTC.

6. "The Evacuation of Yorktown, as Seen by a Private Soldier," ca. 1890, John Taylor Chappell Papers, Virginia Historical Society, Richmond.

7. "The Battle of Rich Mountain," ca. 1890, John Taylor Chappell Papers.

8. "Ghosts," NJTC.

9. *Washington Socialist*, November 12, 1914; *Morning Examiner* (Ogden, UT), February 21, 1909; *World's Cresset* (Fowler, MO), November 16, 1911.

10. Kipnis, *American Socialist Movement*, 215.

11. Oakes, "Slavery Is Theft."

12. Fink, *Long Gilded Age*, 121.

13. Kipnis, *American Socialist Movement*, 177, 234–35.

14. P. Foner, *Policies and Practices*, 368.

15. Kazin, *American Dreamers*, 110–17.

16. Kipnis, *American Socialist Movement*, 392–420; P. Foner, *Industrial Workers of the World*, 165.

17. Kazin, *American Dreamers*, 103; *Appeal to Reason*, October 16, 1909 (hereafter *Appeal*).

18. Schwartz, *Lincoln and the Forge of National Memory*, 205.

19. *Detroit News*, June 27, 1885, John Francis Bray Papers, 1822–1896, JALC.

20. Kipnis, *American Socialist Movement*, 114.

21. Kipnis, 99.

22. Kipnis, 104; Fink, *Long Gilded Age*, 126.

23. Debs, *Opening Campaign Speech*; Renshaw, *Wobblies*, 83.

24. Kipnis, *American Socialist Movement*, 212; Young, *Age of Charisma*, 74; *New York Times*, October 5, 1908.

25. "Acceptance Address and Letter Socialist Candidates Debs and Seidel, 1912," box 8, folder 143, Bernard J. Brommel–Eugene V. Debs Papers, Newberry Library, Chicago.

26. D. Lewis, *W. E. B. Du Bois*, 275.

27. Heideman, *Class Struggle*, 1–20.

28. Heideman, 199–232.

29. Kate Richards O'Hare, *Nigger Equality*, Eugene V. Debs Pamphlet Collection, Cunningham Library, Indiana State University, Terre Haute.

30. Quoted in Heideman, *Class Struggle*, 20.

31. W. Jones, "'Nothing Special to Offer the Negro.'"

32. Kipnis, *American Socialist Movement*, 131–32.

33. P. Foner, *Policies and Practices*, 382.

34. Heideman, *Class Struggle*, 23–25.

35. *New York Tribune*, May 1, 1910.
36. Kipnis, *American Socialist Movement*, 277.
37. Fink, *Long Gilded Age*, 143.
38. Kipnis, *American Socialist Movement*, 260–61.
39. J. Ross, *Socialist Party of America*, 61.
40. *Progressive Woman*, April 1913.
41. Brown, *Birth Strike*, 65.
42. Buhle, *Marxism*, 71, 91.
43. *Appeal*, October 10, 1903.
44. *Appeal*, February 11, 1911.
45. P. Foner, *From the Founding*, 402.
46. Kazin, *American Dreamers*, 122.
47. Debs, *You Railroad Men*, box 7, folder 119, Bernard J. Brommel–Eugene V. Debs Papers, Newberry Library.
48. *Appeal*, March 10, 1906; *American Socialist* (Chicago), October 31 and December 12, 1914; Kipnis, *American Socialist Movement*, 324.
49. *Appeal*, January 7, 1911.
50. Debs, "Negro and His Nemesis," 396.
51. J. H. Hollingsworth, "Eugene V. Debs: What His Neighbors Say of Him," box 7, folder 91, BDP.
52. Germer, "Eugene V. Debs," box 7, folder 121, BDP.
53. Claessens, *Eugene Victor Debs*, 4–7.
54. *Eugene Victor Debs: The Centennial Year*, 49, box 8, folder 155, BDP.
55. Hurt, *Eugene V. Debs*, 15, EVDPC.
56. "Debs: The Voice of Labor: Extracts from His Address to the Jury at His Trial in Cleveland, Ohio, 1920," box 7, folder 103, BDP; Salvatore, *Eugene V. Debs*, 295.
57. Debs to Ralph Chaplin, January 5 and January 27, 1925, Ralph Chaplin Papers, JALC.
58. Freeberg, *Democracy's Prisoner*, 152–53.
59. Debs, "The Life Story of a Great Woman," July 28, 1922, folder 4, Eugene V. Debs Collection, Indiana State Library, Indianapolis.
60. *Salt Lake City Broad Ax*, November 2, 1918.
61. *Washington Times*, February 17, 1912.
62. Debs, "Revolution: May Day Address in *New York Worker*, April 27, 1907," box 9, Socialist Party of the United States of America Records, 1909–1965, WHS.
63. Debs, *American Movement*, 8–17, box 7, folder 94, BDP.
64. "Address of Eugene V. Debs," n.d., folder 6, Eugene V. Debs Collection, Indiana State Library.
65. Debs, "Appeal to Negro Workers, October 30, 1923," 1, 17, box 7, folder 95, BDP.
66. Debs, 2–6, 18.
67. Debs, 8, 15–18, 29.
68. England, *Wonderful Appeal Army*.
69. Kipnis, *American Socialist Movement*, 248–49.

70. Martinek, *Socialism and Print Culture*, 48; Kazin, *American Dreamers*, 118.

71. Kipnis, *American Socialist Movement*, 44–45, 147–48.

72. *Appeal*, December 15, 1917, and March 21, 1908.

73. *Appeal*, August 19, 1905.

74. *Appeal*, April 18, 1914.

75. *Appeal*, November 28, 1908, and June 29, 1907.

76. *Appeal*, July 29, 1911.

77. Wrobel, *America's West*, 56.

78. *Appeal*, January 27, 1912, and January 8, 1916.

79. Sloane, "Pensions and Socialism"; Marten, *Sing Not War*, 214; *Wheeling Daily Intelligencer*, September 12, 1887.

80. *Kansas Agitator*, May 12, 1905.

81. *Kansas Agitator*, September 30, 1904.

82. *Appeal*, October 25, 1913, and October 12, 1912.

83. Peterson and Vaughn-Roberson, *Women with Vision*, 56; *Madison (SD) Daily Leader*, November 30, 1900.

84. Quoted in *Montana News* (Lewiston), November 19, 1908.

85. *Wenatchee (WA) Daily World*, September 11, 1909.

86. *Wenatchee Daily World*, March 3, 1906.

87. Marx and Engels, *Collected Works*, 254–55, 281; Blackburn, *Unfinished Revolution*, 212; Kulikoff, *Abraham Lincoln*, 105.

88. *Appeal*, May 2, 1908.

89. *Appeal*, December 25, 1915.

90. *Indiana Socialist*, June 21, 1913.

91. *Indiana Socialist*, April 5, 1913; *Appeal*, March 16, 1912.

92. *Appeal*, September 24, 1921.

93. *Indiana Socialist*, June 28, 1913.

94. *Labor Argus*, December 14, 1911.

95. *Labor Argus*, August 3, 1907.

96. *Appeal*, March 21, 1908.

97. Heideman, *Class Struggle*, 13–14.

98. *Appeal*, June 10, 1922.

99. *Appeal*, August 31, 1912.

100. *Appeal* November 7, 1908.

101. *Appeal*, December 21, 1918.

102. *Appeal*, August 28, 1909.

103. H. Draper, *Karl Marx's Theory*, 68; Blackburn, *Unfinished Revolution*, 57; Heideman, *Class Struggle*, 3–9.

104. *Appeal*, December 1, 1906.

105. *Appeal*, November 7, 1908.

106. Debs and Reynolds, *Debs*, 371–75.

107. Appeal, November 24, 1917; see also Eugene V. Debs, "The Anniversary of Class War in Colorado (June 25, 1904)," https://www.marxists.org/archive/debs/works/1904/040625b-debs-anniversaryclasswarcolorado.pdf.

108. *Appeal*, November 24, 1917.
109. *Appeal*, February 3, 1912.
110. *Lake County Times* (Hammond, IN), December 8, 1919.
111. *Appeal*, June 2, 1906.
112. *Appeal*, April 19, 1913.
113. *Appeal* March 23, 1907.
114. *Appeal*, January 15, 1898.
115. *Appeal*, October 8, 1904, April 5, 1913, and May 10, 1913.
116. *Appeal*, July 8, 1922.
117. *Goodland (KS) Republic*, August 31, 1906.
118. *Black Hills Daily Register* (Lead, SD), February 11, 1911.
119. *Black Hills Daily Register*, February 17, 1910.
120. *Appeal*, December 21, 1918.
121. Schlüter, *Lincoln, Labor, and Slavery*, 168–85; Mandel, *Labor*, 156–57; Mandel, "Communications."
122. Schwartz, *Lincoln and the Forge of National Memory*, 204–8.
123. *Appeal*, February 13, 1909.
124. *Fulton County News* (McConnellsburg, PA), March 2, 1904.
125. *Blue-grass Blade* (Lexington, KY), June 28, 1908.
126. Nearing, *New Slavery*, 41.
127. William F. Kruse, "Development of the Communist Movement in the United States of America," William F. Kruse Papers, Abraham Lincoln Presidential Library, Springfield, IL.
128. *American Socialist*, March 13, 1915.
129. Berger, *Victor L. Berger*, 722; P. Foner, *Labor and World War One*, 35–39; Wentworth, *Patriotism*, EVDPC.
130. P. Foner, *Labor and World War One*, 15.
131. *American Socialist*, October 24, 1914.
132. *American Socialist*, February 26, 1916.
133. "A Picture of European Life," p. 26, George A. Schilling Scrapbook, Abraham Lincoln Presidential Library, Springfield, IL.
134. Kipnis, *American Socialist Movement*, 312–13.
135. P. Foner, *Industrial Workers of the World*, 13, 111; Rosemont, *Joe Hill*, 28.
136. Renshaw, *Wobblies*, 133–56.
137. P. Foner, *Labor and World War One*, 123.
138. P. Foner, *Industrial Workers of the World*, 26, 33; P. Foner, *Labor and World War One*, 304.
139. Green, *World of the Worker*, 60–61; Kazin, *American Dreamers*, 126.
140. P. Foner, *Industrial Workers of the World*, 131–32.
141. Kazin, *American Dreamers*, 127.
142. IWW, *Proceedings of the First Annual Convention*, 6.
143. Rosemont, *Joe Hill*, 255.
144. IWW, *Proceedings of the Second Annual Convention*, 46.
145. IWW, *Proceedings of the First Annual Convention*, 473.

146. IWW, 186.

147. Debs, *Craft Unionism*, folder 16, box 1, Franklin Rosemont Papers, Newberry Library, Chicago (hereafter FRP).

148. IWW, *Proceedings of the First Annual Convention*, 578–79.

149. Woodruff, *Advancing Proletariat*, 10.

150. Woodruff, *Evolution of Industrial Democracy*, 7–21.

151. Heideman, *Class Struggle*, 154.

152. Quoted in Rosemont, *Joe Hill*, 253–55.

153. *Industrial Pioneer* (Chicago), July 1923, 10; Marcy, "Run-Away Slaves," 23–24, box 6, series 2, FRP.

154. *Industrial Pioneer*, December 1924.

155. *Industrial Pioneer*, July 1921, 3–4.

156. IWW, *IWW Songs*, EVDPC; P. Foner, *Industrial Workers of the World*, 155.

157. Kornbluh, *Rebel Voices*, 240, 260, 299.

158. Kornbluh, 11.

159. Neville, *Twentieth-Century Cause Célèbre*, 146.

160. Kornbluh, *Rebel Voices*, 306–7.

161. Kornbluh, 105–6, 179.

162. Rosemont, *Joe Hill*, 255.

163. Kornbluh, *Rebel Voices*, 364–65.

164. Billington, *Fire in the Minds of Men*, 633n131.

165. Rosemont, *Joe Hill*, 255–56.

166. Hervé, *Patriotism and the Worker*, 1.

167. IWW, *Second Annual Convention*, 352, 42, 333.

168. Kornbluh, *Rebel Voices*, 190–93.

169. Dubofsky, *"Big Bill" Haywood*, 64.

170. Hayes, "Horrors of Respectability," 202.

171. P. Foner, *Labor and World War One*, 295.

172. Kornbluh, *Rebel Voices*, 52.

173. Kornbluh, 65.

174. P. Foner, *Industrial Workers of the World*, 555–56.

175. Kornbluh, *Rebel Voices*, 271–73.

176. Kornbluh, 265.

177. Kornbluh, 334–35.

178. Dubofsky, *"Big Bill" Haywood*, 65; Conlin, *Big Bill Haywood*, 86.

179. *Iron County (MO) Register*, October 27, 1921.

180. Phillips, "Haywood."

181. P. Foner, *Industrial Workers of the World*, 436.

182. P. Foner, 441–42.

183. J. Thompson, "Industrial Unionism," 370.

184. P. Foner, *Industrial Workers of the World*, 68.

185. Phillips, "Department of Justice," 407; Christensen, *Political Trials in History*, 214.

186. Wallace, *Greater Gotham*, 733.

187. Dubofsky, *"Big Bill" Haywood*, 59; Kipnis, *American Socialist Movement*, 388–89.

188. Perry, *Hubert Harrison*, 175; P. Foner, *Industrial Workers of the World*, 397; Fink, *Long Gilded Age*, 136.

189. *Reconstruction* 2, no. 6 (June 1920): 1.

190. Kipnis, *American Socialist Movement*, 421–29.

191. Kazin, *American Dreamers*, 150–51.

192. Brecher, *Strike!*, 105.

193. Howard Abramowitz, "The Press and the Red Scare," in Edsforth and Bennett, *Popular Culture*, 72; *Carson City Daily Appeal*, June 4, 1919.

194. *Topeka State Journal*, February 13, 1919.

195. *Carpenter* 39, no. 11 (November 1919): 17.

196. "Proclamation for Workers' Independence," May 1, 1919, David R. Francis Papers, Missouri Historical Society, St. Louis; P. Foner, *Industrial Workers of the World*, 554–57.

197. Fink, *Long Gilded Age*, 16.

198. Mandel, *Samuel Gompers*, 250; P. Foner, *Policies and Practices*, 385.

199. Kipnis, *American Socialist Movement*, 336, 371.

200. Green, *World of the Worker*, 48–49.

201. *Social-Democratic Herald* (Chicago), February 25, 1905.

202. *Labor World*, May 30, 1903.

203. Kammen, *Mystic Chords of Memory*, 416; Janney, *Remembering the Civil War*, 292.

204. American Federation of Labor, *Proceedings of the Forty-first Annual Convention*, 286.

## EPILOGUE

1. Silber, *This War Ain't Over*, 114.

2. Kelley, *Hammer and Hoe*, xix.

3. Hobsbawm, *Age of Extremes*, 136.

4. Robinson, *Black Marxism*, 219; Smith, *Subterranean Fire*, 124–25.

5. Amter, *Industrial Slavery*.

6. Storch, *Red Chicago*, 218.

7. Smith, *Subterranean Fire*, 134; Donald, "Getting Right with Lincoln"; Central Intelligence Agency, *Communist Party*, 54–57.

8. Silber, *This War Ain't Over*, 1.

9. Storch, *Red Chicago*, 219.

10. Buhle, *Marxism*, 170–71.

11. Silber, *This War Ain't Over*, 77.

12. Cohen, *Depression Folk*, 131.

13. Silber, *This War Ain't Over*, 127; Robinson and Gordon, *Ballad of an American*, 102.

14. Kelley, *Hammer and Hoe*, 93.

15. Kelley, 136.

16. Kelley, 100.

17. Silber, *This War Ain't Over*, 148.

18. Robinson, *Black Marxism*, 293.

19. Makalani, *Cause of Freedom*, 76.

20. *The Struggle for Negro Emancipation* (New York: CPUSA, 1935), 1–5, 27, folder 12, United States of America Social and Political Developments Collection, International Institute of Social History, Amsterdam.

21. Erik S. McDuffie, "'No Small Amount of Change,'" in Gore, Theoharis, and Woodard, *Want to Start a Revolution?*, 35–36.

22. Kelley, *Hammer and Hoe*, 211–12.

23. Ford, *Negro and the Democratic Front*, 211; Schlesinger, *Politics of Upheaval*, 568; Kelley, *Hammer and Hoe*, 92.

24. Quoted in Smith, *Subterranean Fire*, 133.

25. Denning, *Cultural Front*, 499n32; Schlesinger, *Politics of Upheaval*, 571–72; James G. Ryan, "Communism Is the Twentieth Century Americanism,'" in Bennington et al., *The 1930s*, 111–20; Gilbert, *Our Chameleon Comrades*, 76, 83.

26. Jalloh and Falola, *United States and West Africa*, 86; Dixon, *Flaming Sword*, 371.

27. Browder, *Lincoln and the Communists*, n.p.

28. Browder, n.p.

29. Socialist Labor Party pamphlets, series 2, box 1, Arnold Petersen Papers, Wisconsin Historical Society, Madison.

30. Mills, *Ragged Revolutionaries*, 112–13.

31. Gellman, *Death Blow to Jim Crow*, 33, 173, 235, 149–51; Silber, *This War Ain't Over*, 109.

32. Andrew Zimmerman, "Second American Revolution," in Downs and Masur, *World the Civil War Made*, 325–26; Robert S. Coale, "From *Antifascistas* to PAF," in Garcia et al., *Rethinking Antifascism*, 196.

33. "Thomas Jefferson: Democracy's Rebel," series 1, box 15, Arnold Petersen Papers.

34. "Daniel De Leon: Emancipator," series 1, box 23, Arnold Petersen Papers.

35. Rosemont, *Joe Hill*, 377.

36. Brian Kelly, "Introduction," in Mandel, *Labor*, xxxii–xxxiii.

37. Cullen, *Civil War in Popular Culture*, 50–59.

38. Schwartz, *Lincoln and the Forge of National Memory*, 256–57, 304.

39. Blight, *Race and Reunion*, 393.

40. Engelhardt, *End of Victory Culture*; Hobsbawm, *Age of Extremes*, 259.

41. Smith, *Subterranean Fire*, 152.

42. Kammen, *Mystic Chords of Memory*, 416–17, 456.

43. Piketty, *Capital and Ideology*, 34.

44. Silber, *This War Ain't Over*, 164–65.

45. Glickman, *Free Enterprise*.

46. Cook, *Troubled Commemoration*, 261–69.

# Bibliography

## Unpublished Primary Sources


Amsterdam, Netherlands
International Institute of Social History
United States of America Social and Political Developments Collection
Ann Arbor, Michigan
Bentley Library, University of Michigan
David Woodman Scrapbook
George L. Yaple Scrapbook
Thomas B. Berry Scrapbooks
Joseph A. Labadie Collection, Harlan Hatcher Graduate Library, University of Michigan
Charles F. Bates Papers
John Francis Bray Papers
Labor Papers, 1878–1939
Ralph Chaplin Papers
Athens, Georgia
Hargrett Library, University of Georgia
Communist and Socialist Pamphlet Collection
Chapel Hill, North Carolina
Southern Historical Collection, Wilson Library, University of North Carolina
Cyrus Thompson Papers
Daniel L. Russell Papers
Leonidas L. Polk Papers
Marion Butler Papers
Charlottesville, Virginia
Albert and Shirley Small Special Collections Library, University of Virginia
Notebook of John Taylor Chappell and Samuel Michael Chappell

- Chicago, Illinois
  - Chicago Historical Society
    - George S. Bowen Papers
  - Newberry Library
    - Bernard J. Brommel–Eugene V. Debs Papers
    - Charles H. Kerr Company Papers
    - Franklin Rosemont Papers
- College Park, Maryland
  - George Meany Memorial AFL-CIO Archive, Hornbake Library and Special Collections, University of Maryland
    - Early Federation Records, 1881–1889
    - Samuel Gompers Scrapbook
    - United Brotherhood of Carpenters and Joiners of America Records
- Durham, North Carolina
  - Rubenstein Library, Duke University
    - Radical and Labor Pamphlets
    - William Mahone Papers, 1853–1895
- Indianapolis, Indiana
  - Indiana Historical Society
    - Eugene V. Debs Papers
    - Walter Q. Gresham Papers
  - Indiana State Library
    - Eugene V. Debs Collection
- London, United Kingdom
  - Karl Marx Memorial Library
    - Rare Books Collection
- Madison, Wisconsin
  - Wisconsin Historical Society
    - Arnold Petersen Papers
    - International Workingmen's Association Records, 1871–1877
    - Luman Hamlin Weller Papers
    - Socialist Labor Party Papers
    - Victor L. Berger Papers
- New York, New York
  - New York Historical Society
    - Independent Greenback Party Notebook, 1876
  - Tamiment Library and Robert F. Wagner Labor Archives, New York University
    - Socialist Labor Party Records
- Richmond, Virginia
  - Library of Virginia
  - Virginia Historical Society
    - George Ainsley Barksdale Scrapbook, 1861–1889
    - John Taylor Chappell Papers

Springfield, Illinois
Abraham Lincoln Presidential Library
George A. Schilling Scrapbook
Gerry Allard Papers
William F. Kruse Papers
St. Louis, Missouri
Missouri Historical Society
David R. Francis Papers
Gottlieb A. Hoehn Papers
Julius J. Goldberg Papers
Labor Collection, 1830–1935
Terre Haute, Indiana
Cunningham Library, Indiana State University
Eugene V. Debs Pamphlet Collection
Washington, D.C.
Catholic University of America Research Center and University Archives
Terence V. Powderly Papers
Gelman Library Special Collections, George Washington University
Iron Molders-Sylvis Society Collection
United Brewery Workers Records

## Labor Journals

*American Federationist*
*Anarchist: A Revolutionary Review*
*Appeal to Reason*
*Carpenter*
*Commercial Telegraphers' Journal*
*Common Cause*
*International Socialist Review*
*Iron Molders' International Journal*
*Journal of the Knights of Labor*
*Journal of United Labor*
*Mother Earth*
*National Labor Tribune*
*New Leader*
*Reconstruction*
*United Mine Workers' Journal*
*Workingman's Advocate*
*Young Socialists' Magazine*

## Newspapers and Magazines


*Abilene (KS) Weekly Reflector*
*The Alarm* (Chicago)
*Alexandria Gazette*
*American Socialist* (Chicago)
*American Whig Review*
*Anaconda (MT) Standard*
*Anti-slavery Bugle* (New Lisbon, OH)
*Arizona Republican* (Phoenix)
*Atlantic Monthly*
*Belmont Chronicle* (St. Clairsville, OH)
*Bismarck Weekly Tribune*
*Black Hills Daily Register* (Lead, SD)
*Blue-grass Blade* (Lexington, KY)
*Boston Globe*
*Brattleboro (VT) Daily Reformer*
*Breckinridge News* (Cloverport, KY)
*Butler (PA) Citizen*
*Cambria Freeman* (Ebensburg, PA)
*Carson City Daily Appeal*
*Chicago Tribune*
*Cincinnati Republikaner*
*Clayton (NM) Enterprise*
*Cleveland Leader*
*Colfax (LA) Chronicle*
*Columbus (NE) Journal*
*Comrade* (Winnfield, LA)
*Dakota Farmers' Leader* (Canton, SD)
*Davenport (IA) Daily Times*
*Day Book* (Chicago)
*Democratic Advocate* (Westminster, MD)
*Democratic Northwest* (Napoleon, OH)
*Democratic Sentinel* (Cadiz, OH)
*Detroit Free Press*
*Dodge City (KS) Globe-Republican*
*Emporia (KS) Weekly News*
*Evansville Daily Journal*
*Farmer and Mechanic* (Raleigh)
*Frankfort (KS) Bee*
*Fulton County News* (McConnellsburg, PA)
*Goodland (KS) Republic*
*Great Falls (MT) Tribune*

*Harrisburg Telegraph*
*Helena Weekly Herald*
*Hickman (KY) Courier*
*Hot Springs (SD) Weekly Star*
*Idaho Semi-Weekly World*
*Indianapolis Journal*
*Indiana Socialist*
*Indiana State Sentinel*
*Industrial Pioneer* (Chicago)
*Inter Ocean* (Chicago)
*Iron County (MO) Register*
*Jamestown (ND) Weekly Alert*
*Kansas Agitator* (Garnett)
*Kansas City Journal*
*Kansas Times* (Atwood)
*Labor Argus* (Charleston, WV)
*Labor Herald* (Richmond)
*Labor Journal* (Everett, WA)
*Labor World* (Duluth)
*Lake County Times* (Hammond, IN)
*Lexington (MO) Daily Intelligencer*
*The Liberator*
*Lincoln (NE) Commoner*
*Los Angeles Herald*
*Lucifer, the Light-Bearer* (Valley Falls, KS)
*Madison (SD) Daily Leader*
*Marion (OH) Daily Mirror*
*Marshalltown (IA) Evening Times-Republican*
*Maysville (KY) Daily Evening Bulletin*
*Maysville (KY) Evening Bulletin*
*Meridional* (Abbeville, LA)
*Mexico (MO) Daily Ledger*
*Montana News* (Lewistown)
*Morning Examiner* (Ogden, UT)
*National Democrat* (Washington, DC)
*National Era* (Washington, DC)
*National Republican* (Washington, DC)
*Nebraska Advertiser* (Brownville)
*New Iberia (LA) Enterprise and Independent Observer*
*New National Era*
*New Orleans Tribune*
*New York Age*
*New York City Sun*

*New York Herald*
*New York Times*
*New York Tribune*
*North Platte Semi-Weekly Tribune*
*Northwest Enterprise* (Anacortes, WA)
*Omaha Daily Bee*
*Ottawa Free Trader*
*Overland Monthly and Out West Magazine*
*Owasso (MI) Times*
*People's Party Paper* (Atlanta)
*People's Voice* (Wellington, KS)
*Petersburg (VA) Index*
*Petroleum Centre (PA) Daily Record*
*Philadelphia Times*
*Phillipsburg (KS) Herald*
*Pittsburgh Daily Post*
*Pittsburgh Dispatch*
*Portage Sentinel* (Ravenna, OH)
*Producers News* (Plentywood, MT)
*Progressive Farmer* (Winston, NC)
*Progressive Woman*
*Richmond Daily Dispatch*
*Richmond Dispatch*
*Roanoke Times*
*Rock Island (IL) Argus*
*Rock Island (IL) Evening Argus*
*Roseburg (OR) Review*
*Saline County Journal* (Salina, KS)
*Salt Lake City Broad Ax*
*Salt Lake Herald*
*Salt Lake Herald-Republican*
*San Francisco Call*
*Scranton Daily Times*
*Scranton Republican*
*Seattle Post-Intelligencer*
*Semi-weekly Messenger* (Wilmington, NC)
*Shenandoah Herald* (Woodstock, VA)
*Social-Democratic Herald* (Chicago)
*Spirit of Democracy* (Woodsfield, OH)
*Springfield (OH) Daily Republic*
*Stark County Democrat* (Canton, OH)
*State Chronicle* (Raleigh)
*State Journal* (Jefferson City, MO)

*Staunton (VA) Spectator*
*St. Paul Daily Globe*
*St. Tammany Farmer* (Covington, LA)
*Sumter Banner*
*Topeka Advocate*
*Topeka State Journal*
*True Southerner* (Norfolk)
*Washington Evening Star*
*Washington Herald*
*Washington Morning Times*
*Washington Sentinel*
*Washington Socialist*
*Washington Times*
*Weekly Chillicothe (MO) Crisis*
*Weekly People* (New York )
*Wenatchee (WA) Daily World*
*Wheeling (WV) Daily Intelligencer*
*Wheeling (WV) Daily Register*
*Wichita Daily Eagle*
*Wilkes-Barre (PA) Times Leader*
*Wilmington (DE) Daily Gazette*
*Workmen's Advocate* (New York)
*World's Cresset* (Fowler, MO)
*Worthington (MN) Advance*

## Published Primary Sources

Allen, Emory Adams. *The Life and Public Services of James Baird Weaver*. N.p.: W. H. Ferguson and Co., 1892.

American Federation of Labor. *Proceedings of the Forty-First Annual Convention of the American Federation of Labor, Held at Denver, Colorado, June 13 to 25*. Washington, DC: Law Reporter Printing Company, 1921.

Amter, I. *Industrial Slavery—Roosevelt's "New Deal."* New York: Workers Library Publishers, 1933.

Andreas, Alfred Theodore. *History of Chicago, Vol. III*. Chicago: A. T. Andres Co., 1886.

Basler, Roy. *The Collected Works of Abraham Lincoln*. 9 vols. New Brunswick, NJ: Rutgers University Press, 1953.

Bax, E. Belfort. *A Short History of the Paris Commune*. London: Twentieth Century Press, 1895.

Berger, Victor L. *Victor L. Berger, Hearing before the Special Committee*. Washington, DC: Government Printing Office, 1919.

Bland, T. A. *People's Party Shot and Shell*. Chicago: Charles H. Kerr and Co., 1892.

Browder, Earl. *Lincoln and the Communists*. New York: Workers Library Publishers, 1936.

Bureau of Labor and Industrial Statistics. *Second Biennial Report, 1885–1886*. Madison, WI: Democrat Printing Co., 1886.

Campbell, A. *The True Greenback; or The Way to Pay the National Debt without Taxes, and Emancipate Labor*. Chicago: Republican Book and Job Office, 1868.

Cannon, James P. *The Debs Centennial*. New York: Pioneer Publishers, 1955.

Central Intelligence Agency. *The Communist Party of the United States of America: What It Is and How It Works*. Washington, DC: United States Government Printing Office, 1956.

Claessens, August. *Eugene Victor Debs: A Tribute*. New York: Rand School Press, 1946.

Clark, Edward H. G. *People's Party Document. General Butler. A Biographical and Political Address*. N.p., 1884.

Cluseret, Gustave Paul. *Solidarity of Nations*. New York: Blackwell, 1866.

Congressional Commission on Industrial Relations. *Industrial Relations: Final Report and Testimony Submitted to Congress by the Commission on Industrial Relations, Vol. XI*. Washington, DC: Government Printing Office, 1916.

Dacunha, George W. *The Irrepressible Conflict Resumed! Address to the National Greenback Labor Party, 15th Assembly District, September 25th, 1878*. N.p., 1878.

Debs, Eugene V. *The American Movement*. Chicago: Charles H. Kerr and Co., 1904.

———. *Craft Unionism: Speech at Chicago, November 23, 1905*. Chicago: International Workers of the World, 1905.

———. *Letters of Eugene V. Debs, Vol. I, 1874–1912*. Edited by J. Robert Constantine. Urbana: University of Illinois Press, 1990.

———. "The Negro and His Nemesis." *International Socialist Review* 4, no. 7 (January 1904): 391–97.

———. *Opening Campaign Speech of Eugene V. Debs, Indianapolis, September 1, 1904*. Chicago: Socialist Party, 1904.

———. *You Railroad Men*. Chicago: Charles H. Kerr and Co., n.d.

Debs, Eugene V., and Stephen Marion Reynolds. *Debs: His Life, Writings, and Speeches*. Chicago: Charles H. Kerr, 1910.

Dixon, Thomas. *The Flaming Sword*. Atlanta: Monarch Publishing, 1939.

Donnelly, Ignatius L. *Caesar's Column: A Story of the Twentieth Century*. Chicago: F. J. Schulte and Co., 1890.

Douglass, Frederick. *Autobiographies*. New York: Library of America, 1994.

Ellyson, Moses. *The Richmond Directory and Business Advertiser, for 1856: Containing the Names, Residences, Occupations, and Places of Business of the Inhabitants of Richmond; Also a Variety of Other Useful Information*. Richmond: H. K. Ellyson, 1856.

England, George Allan. *The Wonderful Appeal Army*. Girard, KS: Appeal to Reason, 1914.

Foner, Philip S., ed. *The Autobiographies of the Haymarket Martyrs*. New York: Pathfinder, 1977.

Ford, James W. *The Negro and the Democratic Front*. New York: International Publishers, 1938.

George, Henry. *Henry George: Collected Journalistic Writings*. Vol. 1, *The Early Years, 1860–1879*. Edited by Kenneth C. Wenzer. Armonk, NY: M. E. Sharpe, 2003.

Gilbert, Dan. *Our Chameleon Comrades: The Reds Turn Yellow!* San Diego: Danielle Publishers, 1938.

Gompers, Samuel. *The Samuel Gompers Papers*. 13 vols. Edited by Stuart B. Kaufman, Peter J. Albert, and Grace Palladino. Urbana: University of Illinois Press, 1986–2013.

Hass, Eric. *The Americanism of Socialism*. New York: Labor News Company, 1954.

Hayes, Edward C. "The Horrors of Respectability." *International Socialist Review* 18, no. 4 (October 1917): 201–3.

Hervé, Gustave. *Patriotism and the Worker*. Chicago: IWW Publishing Bureau, 1912.

Hinton, Richard J. "American Labor Organizations." *North American Review* 140 (January 1885): 48–62.

———. *John Brown and His Men: With Some Account of the Roads They Traveled to Reach Harpers Ferry*. New York: Funk and Wagnalls, 1894.

Hurt, Walter. *Eugene V. Debs: An Introduction*. Williamsburg, OH: Progress Publishing Co., 1900[?].

Hyndman, H. M. *Socialism and Slavery*. London: William Reeves, 1884.

Industrial Workers of the World (IWW). *IWW Songs: To Fan the Flames of Discontent*. Chicago: IWW Publishing Bureau, 1917.

———. *Proceedings of the First Annual Convention of the Industrial Workers of the World, Founded at Chicago, June 27 to July 8, 1905*. New York: New York Labor News Company, 1905.

———. *Proceedings of the Second Annual Convention of the Industrial Workers of the World, Held at Chicago, Illinois, September 17–October 3, 1906*. Chicago: IWW, 1906.

Jackson, George. *Soledad Brother: The Prison Letters of George Jackson*. New York: Coward-McCann, 1970.

Knights of Labor. *Proceedings of the General Assembly of the Knights of Labor of America Eleventh General Session, Held at Minneapolis, Minnesota, October 4 to 19, 1887*. N.p.: The General Assembly, 1887.

Lawrence, B. M. *National Greenback Labor Songster*. New York: Liberal and Scientific Publishing House, 1878.

Le Prade, Ruth. *Debs and the Poets*. Pasadena: Upton Sinclair, 1920.

Lilienthal, Meta Stern. *Women of the Future*. New York: Rand School, 1916.

Lincoln, Abraham. *Abraham Lincoln Speeches and Writings, 1859–1865: Speeches, Letters, and Miscellaneous Writings, Presidential Messages and Proclamations*. New York: Library of America, 1989.

London, Jack. *When God Laughs and Other Short Stories*. New York: Macmillan, 1911.

Long, George. *France and Its Revolutions, 1789–1848*. London: Charles Knight, 1850.

Lum, Dyer D. *The Economics of Anarchy: A Study of the Industrial Type*. New York: Twentieth Century Publishing Co., 1890.

———. *Social Problems of Today*. Port Jervis, NY: Dyer D. Lum and Co., 1886.
Marx, Karl. *Capital*. Vol. 1. New York: Vintage Books, 1977.
———. *On America and the Civil War*. Edited by Saul K. Padover. New York: McGraw-Hill, 1972.
Marx, Karl, and Friedrich Engels. *The Civil War in the United States*. 2nd ed. Edited by Andrew Zimmerman. New York: International Publishers, 2016.
———. *Collected Works*. Vol. 19. New York: International Publishers, 2009.
McLellan, David, ed. *Karl Marx: Selected Writings*. London: Oxford University Press, 1977.
Nearing, Scott. *The New Slavery*. Chicago: Socialist Party of the United States, 1920.
Paine, William. *Shop Slavery and Emancipation*. London: P.S. King and Son, 1912.
Parsons, Lucy E. *Life of Albert R. Parsons: With Brief History of the Labor Movement in America*. Chicago: 1889.
Penn, Irvine Garland. *The Afro-American Press and Its Editors*. Springfield, MA: Willey and Co., 1891.
Petersen, Arnold. *Labor Conscription: What Does It Mean? Involuntary Servitude*. New York: Labor News Co., 1945.
Phillips, Jack. "Haywood of the I.W.W." *International Socialist Review* 18, no. 7 (January 1918): 343.
———. "Speaking of the Department of Justice." *International Socialist Review* 18, no. 8 (February 1918): 407
Pierce, Edward Lillie. *Memoir and Letters of Charles Sumner*. Vol. 4, *1860–1874*. Boston: Roberts Brothers, 1893.
Randall, J. H. *The Political Catechism and Greenback Songbook*. Washington, DC: Rufus H. Darby, 1880.
Republican Party State Convention. *Organization, Resolution, and Address of the Republican Party State Convention of Virginia, Held at Richmond, April 17, 1867*. Alexandria: Office of the Virginia State Journal, 1867.
Robertson, William Bell. *The Slavery of Labour: A Scientific Demonstration of the Identity of Free and Slave Labour*. 2nd ed. London: Sammels and Taylor, 1906.
Robinson, Earl, and Eric W. Gordon. *Ballad of an American: The Autobiography of Earl Robinson*. Lanham, MD: Scarecrow Press, 1998.
Sandburg, Carl. *Selected Poems*. Edited by George and Willene Hendrick. New York: Harcourt, 1996.
Schindler, Mary Dana. *United States Labor Greenback Song Book*. New Rochelle, NY: Geo. W. Lloyd, 1879.
Sloane, William M. "Pensions and Socialism." *Century Magazine*, June 1891, 179–88.
Socialist Labor Party. *Platform and Constitution of the Socialist Labor Party of the United States of America*. Brooklyn: SLP Press, 1890.
———. *Proceedings of the Ninth Annual Convention of the Socialist Labor Party*. New York: New York Labor News Company, 1896.
———. *Proceedings of the Tenth National Convention of the Socialist Labor Party*. New York: New York Labor News Company, 1901.

———. *They Stand for Emancipation: Abraham Lincoln and Eugene V. Debs . . . A Vote for the Socialist Party Is a Vote for Freedom*. Detroit: n.p., 1920.
Stelle, Theodore P. *People's Party Song Book*. Mt. Vernon, IL: n.p.
Stone, W. W. "The Knights of Labor on the Chinese Situation." *Overland Monthly* 7 (March 1886): 225–30.
Story, Alfred T. *Master and Slave*. London: R. Brimley Johnson, 1901.
Swinton, John. *1860—Lincoln; Debs—1905: A Remarkable Article Written in 1895 by the Great New York Journalist—John Swinton*. Terre Haute, IN: Viquesnay Printing Co., 1905.
Sylvis, William H. *The Life, Speeches, Labors, and Essays of William H. Sylvis*. Edited by James C. Sylvis. Philadelphia: Claxton, Remsen, and Haffelfinger, 1872.
Thompson, James. "Industrial Unionism: What It Is." *International Socialist Review* 18, no. 8 (February 1918): 370.
Trotsky, Leon. *Literature and Revolution*. Edited by William Keach. Chicago: Haymarket, 2005.
US Bureau of Labor. *Report on Strike of Textile Workers in Lawrence, Mass., in 1912*. Washington, DC: Government Printing Office, 1912.
Virginia Supreme Court. *Equal Suffrage: An Address from the Colored Citizens of Norfolk, Va., to the People of the United States. Also an Account of the Agitation among the Colored People of Virginia for Equal Rights. With an Appendix Concerning the Rights of Colored Witnesses before the State Courts*. New Bedford, MA: E. Anthony and Sons, 1865.
Weaver, James B. *Call to Action: An Interpretation of the Great Uprising, Its Source and Causes*. Des Moines: Iowa Printing Co., 1892.
Wentworth, Lydia G. *Patriotism*. Brookline, MA: Association to Abolish War, 1924.
Wilson, Henry. *History of the Rise and Fall of the Slave Power in America*. Vol. 2. Boston: James R. Osgood, 1875.
Woodruff, Abner. *The Advancing Proletariat*. Cleveland: IWW Publishing Bureau, 1914.
———. *The Evolution of Industrial Democracy*. Chicago: IWW Publishing Bureau, n.d.
Workingmen's Party of the United States. *Proceedings of the Union Congress, Held at Philadelphia on the 19th, 20th, 21st, and 22nd Day of July 1876*. New York: Social Democratic Printing Association, 1876.
World's Columbian Exposition. *The Columbian Exposition and World's Fair Illustrated*. Chicago: Columbian Engraving and Publishing Co., 1893.

## Secondary Sources

Adam, Anthony H., and Harold J. Gaither. *Black Populism in the United States: An Annotated Bibliography*. Westport, CT: Praeger, 2004.
Adams, Pauline, and Emma S. Thornton. *A Populist Assault: Sarah E. Van De Vort Emery on American Democracy, 1862–1895*. Bowling Green: Bowling Green State University Press, 1982.

Alexander, Adele Logan. *Homelands and Waterways: The American Journey of the Bond Family, 1846–1926.* New York: Vintage Books, 2000.
Allen, Theodore W. *The Invention of the White Race.* Vol. 1, *Racial Oppression and Social Control.* London: Verso, 1994.
Anderson, Carlotta R. *All-American Anarchist: Joseph A. Labadie and the Labor Movement.* Detroit: Wayne State University Press, 1998.
Archer, Robin. *Why Is There No Labor Party in the United States?* Princeton: Princeton University Press, 2007.
Argersinger, Peter H. *The Limits of Agrarian Radicalism: Western Populism and American Politics.* Lawrence: University Press of Kansas, 1995.
———. *Populism and Politics: William Alfred Peffer and the People's Party.* Lexington: University Press of Kentucky, 1974.
Arneson, Eric, ed. *Encyclopedia of U.S. Labor and Working-Class History.* Vol. 1. New York: Routledge, 2007.
Arnett, Alex Mathews. *The Populist Movement in Georgia.* New York: AMS Press, 1967.
Ashbaugh, Carolyn. *Lucy Parsons: American Revolutionary.* Chicago: Charles H. Kerr, 1976.
Avrich, Paul. *The Haymarket Tragedy.* Princeton: Princeton University Press, 1984.
Ayers, Edward L. *The Promise of the New South: Life after Reconstruction.* New York: Oxford University Press, 1992.
Bailey, Richard. *Neither Carpetbaggers nor Scalawags: Black Officeholders during the Reconstruction of Alabama, 1867–1878.* Montgomery: New South Books, 2010.
Baron, Ava, ed. *Work Engendered: Toward a New History of American Labor.* Ithaca: Cornell University Press, 1991.
Beckel, Deborah. *Radical Reform: Interracial Politics in Post-emancipation North Carolina.* Charlottesville: University of Virginia Press, 2011.
Beckert, Sven, and Christine Desan, eds. *American Capitalism: New Histories.* New York: Columbia University Press, 2018.
Beeby, James M. *Populism in the South Revisited: New Interpretations and New Departures.* Jackson: University Press of Mississippi, 2012.
———. *Revolt of the Tar Heels: The North Carolina Populist Movement, 1890–1901.* Jackson: University Press of Mississippi, 2008.
Bennington, J. Bret, Zenia Sacks Desilva, Michael D'Innocenzo, and Stanislao G. Pugliese, eds. *The 1930s: The Reality and the Promise.* London: Cambridge Scholars Publishing.
Bercovitch, Sacvan. *The American Jeremiad.* Madison: University of Wisconsin Press, 1978.
Billington, James H. *Fire in the Minds of Men: Origins of the Revolutionary Faith.* New Brunswick, NJ: Transaction, 1999.
Birnbaum, Jonathan, and Clarence Taylor, eds. *Civil Rights since 1787: A Reader on the Black Struggle.* New York: New York University Press, 2000.
Blackburn, Robin. *An Unfinished Revolution: Karl Marx and Abraham Lincoln.* London: Verso, 2011.

Blackmar, Frank, ed. *Kansas: A Cyclopedia of State History, Embracing Events, Institutions, Industries, Counties, Cities, Towns, Prominent Persons, Etc.* Chicago: Standard Publishing Company, 1912.

Blair, William A. *Cities of the Dead: Contesting the Memory of the Civil War in the South, 1865–1914.* Chapel Hill: University of North Carolina Press, 2004.

Blight, David W. *Race and Reunion: The Civil War in American Memory.* Cambridge, MA: Harvard University Press, 2001.

Bodnar, John, ed. *Bonds of Affection: Americans Define Their Patriotism.* Princeton: Princeton University Press, 1996.

Boris, Eileen, and Nelson Lichtenstein, eds. *Major Problems in the History of American Workers.* Lexington, MA: D. C. Heath, 1991.

Brecher, Jeremy. *Strike!* Oakland, CA: PM Press, 2014.

Brock, W. R. *An American Crisis: Congress and Reconstruction, 1865–1867.* New York: St. Martin's Press, 1963.

Brown, Jenny. *Birth Strike: The Hidden Fight over Women's Work.* Oakland, CA: PM Press, 2019.

Brundage, W. Fitzhugh. *A Socialist Utopia in the New South: The Ruskin Colonies in Tennessee and Georgia, 1894–1901.* Urbana: University of Illinois Press, 1996.

Buhle, Paul. *Marxism in the United States: A History of the American Left.* New York: Verso, 1987.

Buhle, Paul, and Dan Georgakas, eds. *The Immigrant Left in the United States.* Albany: State University of New York Press, 1996.

Callinicos, Alex. *The Revolutionary Ideas of Karl Marx.* Chicago: Haymarket Books, 2011.

Carsel, Wilford. "The Slaveholders' Indictment of Northern Wage Slavery." *Journal of Southern History* 6 (1940): 504–20.

Cecelski, David S., and Timothy B. Tyson, eds. *Democracy Betrayed: The Wilmington Race Riot of 1898 and Its Legacy.* Chapel Hill: University of North Carolina Press, 1998.

Christensen, Ron, ed. *Political Trials in History: From Antiquity to the Present.* New Brunswick, NJ: Transaction Publishers, 1991.

Clark, Robert L., Lee A. Craig, and Jack W. Wilson. *A History of Public Sector Pensions in the United States.* Philadelphia: University of Pennsylvania Press, 2003.

Cohen, Ronald D. *Depression Folk: Grassroots Music and Left-Wing Politics in 1930s America.* Chapel Hill: University of North Carolina Press, 2016.

Conlin, Joseph Robert. *Big Bill Haywood and the Radical Union Movement.* Syracuse: Syracuse University Press, 1969.

Cook, Robert J. *Civil War Memories: Contesting the Past in the United States since 1865.* Baltimore: Johns Hopkins University Press, 2017.

———. *Troubled Commemoration: The American Civil War Centennial, 1961–1965.* Baton Rouge: Louisiana State University Press, 2007.

Cornish, Dudley Taylor. *The Sable Arm: Black Troops in the Union Army, 1861–1865.* Reprint, Lawrence: University Press of Kansas, 1987.

Cott, Nancy F., ed. *History of Women in the United States*. Vol. 7, *Industrial Wage Work*. Munich, Ger.: K. G. Saur, 1993.

Crow, Jeffrey J., and Robert F. Durden. *A Maverick Republican in the Old North State: A Political Biography of Daniel L. Russell*. Baton Rouge: Louisiana State University Press, 1977.

Cullen, Jim. *The Civil War in Popular Culture: A Reusable Past*. Washington, DC: Smithsonian Institution Press, 1995.

Cunliffe, Marcus. *Chattel Slavery and Wage Slavery: The Anglo-American Context, 1830–1860*. Athens: University of Georgia Press, 1979.

Currarino, Rosanne. *The Labor Question in America: Economic Democracy in the Gilded Age*. Urbana: University of Illinois Press, 2011.

Dailey, Jane. *Before Jim Crow: The Politics of Race in Postemancipation Virginia*. Chapel Hill: University of North Carolina Press, 2000.

Davis, Cullom, Charles B. Strozier, Rebecca Monroe Veach, and Geoffrey C Ward, eds. *The Public and Private Lincoln: Contemporary Perspectives*. Carbondale: Southern Illinois University Press, 1979.

Davis, David Brion. *Inhuman Bondage: The Rise and Fall of Slavery in the New World*. New York: Oxford University Press, 2006.

Davis, Mike. *Prisoners of the American Dream: Politics and Economy in the History of the U.S. Working Class*. London: Verso, 1986.

Dawley, Alan. *Class and Community: The Industrial Revolution in Lynn*. Cambridge, MA: Harvard University Press, 1976.

Dean, Adam Wesley. *An Agrarian Republic: Farming, Antislavery Politics, and Nature Parks in the Civil War Era*. Chapel Hill: University of North Carolina Press, 2015.

Degler, Carl N. *The Other South: Southern Dissenters in the Nineteenth Century*. New York: Harper and Row, 1974.

de Man, Henry. *The Psychology of Marxian Socialism*. New Brunswick, NJ: Transaction Books, 1985.

Denning, Michael. *The Cultural Front: The Laboring of American Culture in the Twentieth Century*. New York: Verso, 1996.

DeVault, Ileen A. *United Apart: Gender and the Rise of Craft Unionism*. Ithaca: Cornell University Press, 2004.

Donald, David. "Getting Right with Lincoln." *The Atlantic*, 1956. https://www.theatlantic.com/past/docs/issues/95nov/lincoln/lincrite.htm.

Donovan, Brian. *White Slave Crusades: Race, Gender, and Anti-vice Activism, 1887–1917*. Urbana: University of Illinois Press, 2006.

Downs, Gregory P., and Kate Masur, eds. *The World the Civil War Made*. Chapel Hill: University of North Carolina Press, 2015.

Draper, Hal. *Karl Marx's Theory of Revolution*. Vol. 2, *The Politics of Social Classes*. New York: Monthly Review Press, 1978.

Draper, Theodore. *The Roots of American Communism*. New York: Viking, 1963.

Dray, Philip. *Capitol Men: The Epic Story of Reconstruction through the Lives of the First Black Congressmen*. New York: Mariner Books, 2008.

———. *There Is Power in a Union: The Epic Story of Labor in America*. New York: Anchor Books, 2010.

Dubofsky, Melvyn. *"Big Bill" Haywood*. Manchester, UK: Manchester University Press, 1987.

Du Bois, W. E. B. *Black Reconstruction*. New York: Harcourt Brace, 1935.

———. *The Souls of Black Folk*. Chicago: A. C. McClurg, 1903.

Dulles, Foster Rhea. *Labor in America: A History*. New York: Thomas Y. Crowell, 1949.

Dunlop, John T., and Walter Galenson, eds. *Labor in the Twentieth Century*. New York: Academic Press, 1978.

Eddington, Steve. *Bring Your Own God: The Spirituality of Woody Guthrie*. Bloomington, IN: Trafford Publishing, 2012.

Edmonds, Helen G. *The Negro and Fusion Politics in North Carolina, 1894–1901*. Chapel Hill: University of North Carolina Press, 1951.

Edsforth, Ronald, and Larry Bennett, eds. *Popular Culture and Political Change in Modern America*. New York: State University of New York Press, 1991.

Edwards, Rebecca. *Angels in the Machinery: Gender in American Party Politics from the Civil War to the Progressive Era*. New York: Oxford University Press, 1997.

Efford, Allison Clark. *German Immigrants, Race, and Citizenship in the Civil War Era*. New York: Cambridge University Press, 2013.

Engel, Stephen M. *American Politicians Confront the Court: Opposition Politics and Changing Responses to Judicial Power*. New York: Cambridge University Press, 2011.

Engelhardt, Tom. *The End of Victory Culture: Cold War America and the Disillusioning of a Generation*. Amherst: University of Massachusetts Press, 1995.

Engle, Stephen D. "Yankee Dutchmen: Germans, the Union, and the Construction of Wartime Identity." In *Civil War Citizens: Race, Ethnicity, and Identity in America's Bloodiest Conflict*, edited by Susannah J. Ural, 11–56. New York: New York University Press, 2010.

Fahs, Alice, and Joan Waugh, eds. *The Memory of the Civil War in American Culture*. Chapel Hill: University of North Carolina Press, 2004.

Feagin, Joe R. *Racist America: Roots, Current Realities, and Future Reparations*. New York: Routledge, 2000.

Fields, Karen E., and Barbara J. Fields. *Racecraft: The Soul of Inequality in American Life*. New York: Verso, 2012.

Fischer, David Hackett. *Liberty and Freedom: A Visual History of America's Founding Ideas*. New York: Oxford University Press, 2005.

Foner, Eric. *Free Soil, Free Labor, Free Men: The Ideology of the Republican Party before the Civil War*. New York: Oxford University Press, 1970.

———. *Reconstruction: America's Unfinished Revolution, 1863–1877*. New York: Harper and Row, 1988.

Foner, Philip S. *From the Founding of the A. F. of L. to the Emergence of American Imperialism*. Vol. 2 of *History of the Labor Movement in the United States*. New York: International Publishers, 1955.

———. *The Great Labor Uprising of 1877*. New York: Monad Press, 1977.

———. *The Industrial Workers of the World, 1905–1917.* Vol. 4 of *History of the Labor Movement in the United States.* New York: International Publishers, 1965.
———. *Labor and World War One, 1914–1918.* Vol. 7 of *History of the Labor Movement in the United States.* New York: International Publishers, 1987.
———. *Organized Labor and the Black Worker, 1619–1973.* New York: Praeger, 1974.
———. *The Policies and Practices of the American Federation of Labor, 1900–1909.* Vol. 3 of *History of the Labor Movement in the United States.* New York: International Publishers, 1964.
Foner, Philip S., and Herbert Shapiro, eds. *Northern Labor and Antislavery: A Documentary History.* Westport, CT: Greenwood Press, 1994.
Forgacs, David, ed. *The Gramsci Reader: Selected Writings, 1916–1935.* New York: New York University Press, 2000.
Fink, Leon. *The Long Gilded Age: American Capitalism and the Lessons of a New World Order.* Philadelphia: University of Pennsylvania Press, 2018.
———. *Workingmen's Democracy: The Knights of Labor and American Politics.* Urbana: University of Illinois Press, 1983.
Fitzgerald, Michael. *The Union League Movement in the Deep South: Politics and Agricultural Change during Reconstruction.* Baton Rouge: Louisiana State University Press, 1989.
Freeberg, Ernest. *Democracy's Prisoner: Eugene V. Debs, the Great War, and the Right to Dissent.* Cambridge, MA: Harvard University Press, 2008.
Gaither, Gerald H. *Blacks and the Populist Movement: Ballots and Bigotry in the New South.* Tuscaloosa: University of Alabama Press, 2005.
Garcia, Hugo, Mercedes Yusta, Xavier Tabet, and Cristina Clímaco, eds. *Rethinking Antifascism: History, Memory, and Politics, 1922 to Present.* New York: Berghahn Books, 2016.
Gellman, Erik S. *Death Blow to Jim Crow: The National Negro Congress and the Rise of Militant Civil Rights.* Chapel Hill: University of North Carolina Press, 2012.
Genovese, Eugene V. *From Rebellion to Revolution: Afro-American Slave Revolts in the Making of the Modern World.* Baton Rouge: Louisiana State University Press, 1979.
Gerteis, Joseph. *Class and the Color Line: Interracial Class Coalition in the Knights of Labor and Populist Movements.* Durham: Duke University Press, 2007.
Gilpin, R. Blakeslee. *John Brown Still Lives! America's Long Reckoning with Violence, Equality, and Change.* Chapel Hill: University of North Carolina Press, 2011.
Glickman, Lawrence B. *Free Enterprise: An American History.* New Haven: Yale University Press, 2019.
———. *A Living Wage: American Workers and the Making of Consumer Society.* Ithaca: Cornell University Press, 1997.
Goldfield, David. *Urban Growth in the Age of Sectionalism, Virginia, 1847–1861.* Baton Rouge: Louisiana State University Press, 1977.
Goodwyn, Lawrence. *The Populist Moment: A Short History of Agrarian Revolt in America.* New York: Oxford University Press, 1978.

Gore, Dayo F., Jeanne Theoharis, and Komozi Woodard, eds. *Want to Start a Revolution? Radical Women in the Black Freedom Struggle*. New York: New York University Press, 2009.

Gourevitch, Alex. *From Slavery to the Cooperative Commonwealth: Labor and Republican Liberty in the Nineteenth Century*. New York: Cambridge University Press, 2015.

Green, James R. *Death in the Haymarket: A Story of Chicago, the First Labor Movement, and the Bombing that Divided Gilded Age America*. New York: Pantheon, 2006.

———. *The World of the Worker: Labor in Twentieth-Century America*. New York: McGraw-Hill, 1980.

Greene, Julie. *Pure and Simple Politics: The American Federation of Labor and Political Activism, 1881–1917*. New York: Cambridge University Press, 1998.

Gustafson, Melanie Susan. *Women and the Republican Party, 1854–1924*. Urbana: University of Illinois Press, 2001.

Hahn, Steven. *A Nation without Borders: The United States and Its World in the Age of Civil Wars, 1830–1910*. New York: Viking, 2016.

Halbwachs, Maurice. *On Collective Memory*. Edited and translated by Lewis A. Coser. Chicago: University of Chicago Press, 1992.

Harris, M. Keith. *Across the Bloody Chasm: The Culture of Commemoration among Civil War Veterans*. Baton Rouge: Louisiana State University Press, 2014.

Hass, Eric. *The Socialist Labor Party and the Internationals*. New York: New York Labor News Company, 1949.

Heideman, Paul M., ed. *Class Struggle and the Color Line: American Socialism and the Race Question, 1900–1930*. Chicago: Haymarket, 2018.

Hicks, John D. *The Populist Revolt: A History of the Farmers' Alliance and the People's Party*. Minneapolis: University of Minnesota Press, 1931.

Hild, Matthew. *Greenbackers, Knights of Labor, and Populists: Farmer-Labor Insurgency in the Late-Nineteenth-Century South*. Athens: University of Georgia Press, 2007.

Hobsbawm, Eric. *The Age of Capital, 1848–1875*. London: Weidenfeld and Nicolson, 1975.

———. *The Age of Empire, 1875–1914*. London: Weidenfeld and Nicolson, 1987.

———. *The Age of Extremes, 1914–1991*. New York: Pantheon Books, 1995.

Hobsbawm, Eric, and Terence Ranger, eds. *The Invention of Tradition*. Cambridge: Cambridge University Press, 1993.

Hofstadter, Richard. *The Age of Reform*. New York: Vintage, 1955.

Holzer, Harold, and Norton Garfinkle. *A Just and Generous Nation: Abraham Lincoln and the Fight for American Opportunity*. New York: Basic Books, 2015.

Honeck, Mischa. *We Are the Revolutionists: German-Speaking Immigrants and American Abolitionists after 1848*. Athens: University of Georgia Press, 2011.

Horton, Carol A. *Race and the Making of American Liberalism*. New York: Oxford University Press, 2005.

Ignatiev, Noel. *How the Irish Became White*. New York: Routledge, 1995.

Jalloh, Alusine, and Toyin Falola. *The United States and West Africa: Interactions and Relations*. Rochester: University of Rochester Press, 2008.

James, C. L. R. *The Black Jacobins: Toussaint L'Ouverture and the San Domingo Revolution*. 2nd ed. New York: Vintage, 1963.

Janney, Caroline E. "'I Yield to No Man an Iota of My Conviction': Chickamauga and Chattanooga National Military Park and the Limits of Reconciliation." *Journal of the Civil War Era* 2 (September 2012): 394–420.

———. *Remembering the Civil War: Reunion and the Limits of Reconciliation*. Chapel Hill: University of North Carolina Press, 2013.

Johnpoll, Bernard, and Lillian Johnpoll. *The Impossible Dream: The Rise and Demise of Left*. Westport, CT: Greenwood Press, 1981.

Johnson, Walter. *The Broken Heart of America: St. Louis and the Violent History of the United States*. New York: Basic Books, 2020.

———. *Soul by Soul: Life inside the Antebellum Slave Market*. Cambridge, MA: Harvard University Press, 1999.

Jones, Jacqueline. *Goddess of Anarchy: The Life and Times of Lucy Parsons, American Radical*. New York: Basic Books, 2017.

Jones, William P. "'Nothing Special to Offer the Negro': Revisiting the 'Debsian View' of the Negro Question." *International Labor and Working-Class History* 74 (October 2008): 212–24.

Kammen, Michael. *Mystic Chords of Memory: The Transformation of Tradition in American Culture*. New York: Vintage, 1991.

Katz, Philip M. *From Appomattox to Montmartre: Americans and the Paris Commune*. Cambridge, MA: Harvard University Press, 1998.

Kaufman, Jason. *For the Common Good? American Civic Life and the Golden Age of Fraternity*. New York: Oxford University Press, 2002.

Kazin, Michael. *American Dreamers: How the Left Changed a Nation*. New York: Knopf, 2011.

———. *War against War: The American Fight for Peace, 1914–1918*. New York: Simon and Schuster, 2017.

Kelley, Robin D. G. *Hammer and Hoe: Alabama Communists during the Great Depression*. 2nd ed. Chapel Hill: University of North Carolina Press, 2015.

———. *Race Rebels: Culture, Politics, and the Black Working Class*. New York: Free Press, 1994.

Kendi, Ibram X. *Stamped from the Beginning: The Definitive History of Racist Ideas in America*. New York: Nation Books, 2016.

Kessler-Harris, Alice. *Gendering Labor History*. Urbana: University of Illinois Press, 2007.

Kindell, Alexandra, and Elizabeth S. Demers, eds. *Encyclopedia of Populism in America: A Historical Encyclopedia*. Vol. 1. Santa Barbara: ABC-CLIO, 2014.

Kipnis, Ira. *The American Socialist Movement, 1897–1912*. New York: Columbia University Press, 1952.

Koenig, Brigitte Anne. "American Anarchism: The Politics of Gender, Culture, and

Community from Haymarket to the First World War." PhD diss., University of California–Berkeley, 2000.
Kornbluh, Joyce L., ed. *Rebel Voices: An I.W.W. Anthology*. Ann Arbor: University of Michigan Press, 1964.
Kulikoff, Allan. *Abraham Lincoln and Karl Marx in Dialogue*. New York: Oxford University Press, 2017.
Lapides, Kenneth, ed. *Marx and Engels on Trade Unions*. New York: Praeger, 1987.
Lauck, John K. *Prairie Republic: The Political Culture of Dakota Territory, 1879–1889*. Norman: University of Oklahoma Press, 2010.
Laurie, Bruce. *Artisans into Workers: Labor in Nineteenth-Century America*. Urbana: University of Illinois Press, 1989.
Lause, Mark A. *The Civil War's Last Campaign: James B. Weaver, the Greenback-Labor Party, and the Politics of Race and Section*. Lanham, MD: University Press of America, 2001.
———. *Free Labor: The Civil War and the Making of an American Working Class*. Urbana: University of Illinois Press, 2015.
———. *A Secret Society History of the Civil War*. Urbana: University of Illinois Press, 2014.
Leikin, Steven Bernard. *The Practical Utopians: American Workers and the Cooperative Movement in the Gilded Age*. Detroit: Wayne State University Press, 2005.
Lester, Connie L. *Up from the Mudsills of Hell: The Farmers Alliance, Populism, and Progressive Agriculture in Tennessee, 1870–1915*. Athens: University of Georgia Press, 2006.
Levine, Bruce. *The Spirit of 1848: German Immigrants, Labor Conflict, and the Coming of the Civil War*. Urbana: University of Illinois Press, 1992.
Lewis, David L. *W. E. B. Du Bois: A Biography*. New York: Henry Holt, 2009.
Lewis, Ronald L. *Black Coal Miners in America: Race, Class, and Community Conflict, 1780–1980*. Lexington: University Press of Kentucky, 1987.
Litwicki, Ellen M. *America's Public Holidays, 1865–1920*. Washington, DC: Smithsonian Books, 2003.
Loughran, Trish. *The Republic in Print: Print Culture in the Age of U.S. Nation Building, 1770–1870*. New York: Columbia University Press, 2007.
Lukacs, George. *History and Class Consciousness*. Boston: MIT Press, 1972.
Makalani, Minkah. *In the Cause of Freedom: Radical Black Internationalism from Harlem to London, 1917–1939*. Chapel Hill: University of North Carolina Press, 2011.
Malin, James C. *John Brown and the Legend of Fifty-Six*. New York: Haskell House, 1942.
Mandel, Bernard. "Communications." *Science and Society* 19 (1955): 56–63.
———. *Labor, Slave and Free: Workingmen and the Anti-slavery Movement in the United States*. Reprint, Urbana: University of Illinois Press, 2007.
———. *Samuel Gompers: A Biography*. New York: Antioch Press, 1963.
Marten, James M. *Sing Not War: The Lives of Union and Confederate Veterans in Gilded Age America*. Chapel Hill: University of North Carolina Press, 2011.

Martinek, Jason D. *Socialism and Print Culture in America, 1897–1920*. New York: Routledge, 2012.
McCarthy, Timothy Patrick, and John McMillian, eds. *The Radical Reader: A Documentary History of the American Radical Tradition*. New York: New Press, 2003.
McConnell, Stuart. *Glorious Contentment: The Grand Army of the Republic, 1865–1900*. Chapel Hill: University of North Carolina Press, 1992.
McGreevy, John T. "Farmers, Nationalists, and the Origins of California Populism." *Pacific Historical Review* 58 (November 1989): 471–95.
McKillen, Elizabeth. *Making the World Safe for Workers: Labor, the Left, and Wilsonian Internationalism*. Urbana: University of Illinois Press, 2013.
McMath, Robert C., Jr. *American Populism: A Social History, 1877–1898*. New York: Hill and Wang, 1992.
McPherson, James M. *Struggle for Equality: Abolitionists and the Negro in the Civil War and Reconstruction*. Princeton: Princeton University Press, 1964.
Meier, August, and Elliot Rudwick. *Along the Color Line: Explorations in the Black Experience*. Urbana: University of Illinois Press, 1976.
Merritt, Keri Leigh. *Masterless Men: Poor Whites and Slavery in the Antebellum South*. New York: Cambridge University Press, 2017.
Messer-Kruse, Timothy. *The Haymarket Conspiracy: Transatlantic Anarchist Networks*. Urbana: University of Illinois Press, 2012.
———. *The Yankee International: Marxism and the American Reform Tradition*. Chapel Hill: University of North Carolina Press, 1998.
Miller, Julie. *Abandoned: Foundlings in Nineteenth-Century New York City*. New York: New York University Press, 2008.
Miller, Robert Worth. "Farmers and Third-Party Politics." In *The Gilded Age: Perspectives on the Origins of Modern America*, edited by Charles W. Calhoun, 283–306. Lanham, MD: Rowman and Littlefield, 2007.
———. *Populist Cartoons: An Illustrated History of the Third-Party Movement in the 1890s*. Kirksville, MO: Truman State University, 2011.
Miller, Sally M. *From Prairie to Prison: The Life of Social Activist Kate Richards*. Columbia: University of Missouri Press, 1993.
Miller, William, ed. *Men in Business: Essays in the History of Entrepreneurship*. Cambridge, MA: Harvard University Press, 1952.
Mills, Nathaniel. *Ragged Revolutionaries: The Lumpenproletariat and African American Marxism in Depression-Era Literature*. Amherst: University of Massachusetts Press, 2017.
Mitchell, Robert B. *Skirmisher: The Life, Times, and Political Career of James B. Weaver*. Roseville, MN: Edinborough Press, 2009.
Monroe, James A. *The Democratic Wish: Popular Participation and the Limits of American Government*. New York: Basic Books, 1990.
Montgomery, David. *Beyond Equality: Labor and the Radical Republicans, 1862–1872*. Urbana: University of Illinois Press, 1967.
———. *Citizen Worker: The Experience of Workers in the United States with Democ-*

*racy and the Free Market during the Nineteenth Century*. New York: Cambridge University Press, 1993.

Neff, John. *Honoring the Civil War Dead: Commemoration and the Problem of Reconciliation*. Lawrence: University Press of Kansas, 2005.

Nelson, Megan Kate. *Ruin Nation: Destruction and the American Civil War*. Athens: University of Georgia Press, 2012.

Neville, John F. *Twentieth-Century Cause Célèbre: Sacco, Vanzetti, and the Press, 1920–1927*. Westport, CT: Praeger, 2004.

Newby-Alexander, Cassandra L. *An African American History of the Civil War in Hampton Roads*. Charleston, SC: History Press, 2010.

Nimtz, August H., Jr. *Marx, Tocqueville, and Race in America: The "Absolute Democracy" or "Defiled Republic."* Lanham, MD: Lexington Books, 2003.

Norgren, Jill. *Belva Lockwood: The Woman Who Would Be President*. New York: New York University Press, 2007.

Oakes, James. "The Real Problem with White Abolitionists." *Jacobin*, August 5, 2014. https://www.jacobinmag.com/2014/08/the-real-problem-with-white-abolitionists/.

———. "Slavery Is Theft." *Jacobin*, August 13, 2015. https://www.jacobinmag.com/2015/08/slavery-abolition-lincoln-oakes-property/.

O'Conner, Richard. *Iron Wheels and Broken Men and the Plunder of the West*. New York: Putnam, 1973.

O'Donnell, Edward. *Henry George and the Crisis of Inequality: Progress and Poverty in the Gilded Age*. New York: Columbia University Press, 2015.

Olsen, James S., and Abraham O. Mendoza, eds. *American Economic History: A Dictionary and Chronology*. Santa Barbara: ABC-CLIO, 2015.

O'Malley, Michael. *Face Value: The Entwined Histories of Money and Race in America*. Chicago: University of Chicago Press, 2012.

Ostler, Jeffrey. *Prairie Populism: The Fate of Agrarian Radicalism in Kansas, Nebraska, and Iowa, 1880–1892*. Lawrence: University Press of Kansas, 1993.

Oubre, Claude F. *Forty Acres and a Mule: The Freedmen's Bureau and Black Land Ownership*. Baton Rouge: Louisiana State University Press, 1978.

Ozanne, Robert W. *The Labor Movement in Wisconsin: A History*. Madison: State Historical Society of Wisconsin, 1984.

Parramore, Thomas C. *Norfolk: The First Four Centuries*. Charlottesville: University of Virginia Press, 1994.

Pasley, Jeffrey, Andrew W. Robertson, and David Waldstreicher, eds. *Beyond the Founders: New Approaches to the Political History of the Early American Republic*. Chapel Hill: University of North Carolina Press, 2004.

Peck, Gunther. "White Slavery and Whiteness: A Transnational View of the Sources of Working-Class Radicalism and Racism." *Labor* 1 (Summer 2004): 41–64.

Perry, Jeffrey Babcock. *Hubert Harrison: The Voice of Harlem Radicalism, 1883–1918*. New York: Columbia University Press, 2009.

Peterson, Merrill D. *Abraham Lincoln in American Memory*. New York: Oxford University Press, 1994.

Peterson, Susan Carol, and Courtney Ann Vaughn-Roberson. *Women with Vision: The Presentation Sisters of South Dakota, 1880–1985*. Urbana: University of Illinois Press, 1988.

Phalen, William J. *The Democratic Soldier: The Life of General Gustave P. Cluseret*. Delhi, India: VIJ Books, 2015.

Phelan, Craig. *Grand Master Workman: Terence Powderly and the Knights of Labor*. Westport, CT: Greenwood, 2000.

Philbeam, Pamela. *French Socialists before Marx: Workers, Women, and the Social Question in France*. London: McGill-Queen's University Press, 2000.

Pietila, Anturo. *Not in My Neighborhood: How Bigotry Shaped an American City*. Chicago: Ivan R. Dee, 2010.

Piketty, Thomas. *Capital and Ideology*. Cambridge, MA: Belknap, 2020.

Pollack, Norman. *The Populist Response to Industrial America: Midwestern Populist Thought*. Cambridge, MA: Harvard University Press, 1962.

Postel, Charles. *Equality: An American Dilemma, 1866–1896*. New York: Farrar, Straus, and Giroux, 2019.

———. *The Populist Vision*. New York: Oxford University Press, 2007.

Pratt, Henry J. *Gray Agendas: Interest Groups and Public Pensions in Canada, Britain, and the United States*. Ann Arbor: University of Michigan Press, 1993.

Puette, William. *Through Jaundiced Eyes: How the Media View Organized Labor*. Ithaca: Cornell University Press, 1992.

Quarles, Benjamin. *The Negro in the Civil War*. Boston: Little, Brown, 1953.

Rabinbach, Anson. *The Human Motor: Energy, Fatigue, and the Origins of Modernity*. New York: Basic Books, 1990.

Rachleff, Peter. *Black Labor in Richmond, 1865–1890*. Urbana: University of Illinois Press, 1989.

Rehmann, Jan. *Theories of Ideology: The Powers of Alienation and Subjection*. Leden, Neth.: Koninklijke Brill NV, 2013.

Renshaw, Patrick. *The Wobblies: The Story of Syndicalism in the United States*. New York: Doubleday, 1967.

Richardson, Heather Cox. *The Death of Reconstruction: Race, Labor, and Politics in the Post–Civil War North, 1865–1901*. Cambridge, MA: Harvard University Press, 2001.

Ricker, Ralph R. *The Greenback-Labor Movement in Pennsylvania*. Bellafonte, PA: Pennsylvania Heritage, 1966.

Ritter, Gretchen. *Goldbugs and Greenbacks: The Antimonopoly Tradition and the Politics of Finance in America, 1865–1896*. New York: Cambridge University Press, 1997.

Robinson, Cedric J. *Black Marxism: The Making of the Black Radical Tradition*. London: Zed Press, 1983.

Rodgers, Daniel T. *The Work Ethic in Industrial America, 1850–1920*. Chicago: University of Chicago Press, 1978.

Rodriguez, Junius P., ed. *Slavery in the United States: A Social, Political, and Historical Encyclopedia*. Vol. 1. Santa Barbara: ABC-CLIO, 2007.

Roediger, David R. *Colored White: Transcending the Racial Past*. Berkeley: University of California Press, 2002.
———. *Seizing Freedom: Slave Emancipation and Liberty for All*. London: Verso, 2014.
———. *The Wages of Whiteness: Race and the Making of the American Working Class*. London: Verso, 1991.
———. *Working toward Whiteness: How America's Immigrants Became White*. New York: Basic Books, 2005.
Roediger, David R., and Philip S. Foner. *Our Own Time: A History of American Labor and the Working Day*. London: Verso, 1989.
Roediger, David R., and Franklin Rosemont, eds. *Haymarket Scrapbook*. Chicago: Charles H. Kerr, 1986.
Rogers, William Warren. *The One-Gallused Rebellion: Agrarianism in Alabama, 1865–1896*. Baton Rouge: Louisiana State University Press, 1970.
Rosemont, Franklin. *Joe Hill: The IWW and the Making of a Revolutionary Working Class Culture*. 2nd ed. Oakland, CA: PM Press, 2015.
Ross, Jack. *The Socialist Party of America: A Complete History*. Lincoln, NE: Potomac Books, 2015.
Ross, William G. *A Muted Fury: Populists, Progressives, and Labor Unions Confront the Courts, 1890–1937*. Princeton: Princeton University Press, 1994.
Salvatore, Nick. *Eugene V. Debs, Citizen and Socialist*. Urbana: University of Illinois Press, 1984.
Savage, Kirk. *Standing Soldiers, Kneeling Slaves: Race, War, and Monument in Nineteenth-Century America*. Princeton: Princeton University Press, 1997.
Saxton, Alexander. *The Rise and Fall of the White Republic: Class Politics and Mass Culture in Nineteenth-Century America*. New York: Verso, 1990.
Schlesinger, Arthur, Jr. *The Politics of Upheaval, 1935–1936*. Vol. 3 of *The Age of Roosevelt*. New York: Houghton-Mifflin, 1960.
Schlüter, Hermann. *Lincoln, Labor, and Slavery: A Chapter from the Social History of America*. New York: Socialist Literature Company, 1913.
Schneirov, Richard. "Chicago's Great Upheaval of 1877." *Chicago History* 9, no. 1 (Spring 1980): 2–17.
———. *Labor and Urban Politics: Class Conflict and the Origins of Modern Liberalism in Chicago, 1864–97*. Urbana: University of Illinois Press, 1998.
Schwartz, Barry. *Abraham Lincoln and the Forge of National Memory*. Chicago: University of Chicago Press, 2000.
———. *Abraham Lincoln in the Post-Heroic Era: History and Memory in Late Twentieth-Century America*. Chicago: University of Chicago Press, 2008.
———. "Collective Memory and History: How Abraham Lincoln Became a Symbol of Racial Equality." *Sociological Quarterly* 38, no. 3 (Summer 1997): 469–96.
Schwartz, Barry, and Howard Schulman. "History, Commemoration, and Belief: Abraham Lincoln in American Memory, 1945–2001." *American Sociological Review* 70, no. 2 (April 2005): 183–203.

Scipes, Kim. *AFL-CIO's Secret War against Developing Country Workers: Solidarity or Sabotage?* Lanham, MD: Lexington Books, 2010.
Secrist, Horace. "An Economic Analysis of the Constitutional Restrictions upon Public Indebtedness." PhD diss., University of Wisconsin–Madison, 1914.
Seretan, L. Glen. *Daniel DeLeon: The Odyssey of an American Marxist.* Cambridge, MA: Harvard University Press, 1979.
Shaffer, Donald R. *After the Glory: The Struggles of Black Civil War Veterans.* Lawrence: University Press of Kansas, 2004.
Shawki, Ahmed. *Socialism and Black Liberation.* Chicago: Haymarket, 2006.
Silber, Nina. *The Romance of Reunion: Northerners and the South, 1865–1900.* Chapel Hill: University of North Carolina Press, 1993.
———. *This War Ain't Over: Fighting the Civil War in New Deal America.* Chapel Hill: University of North Carolina Press.
Sklar, Martin J. *The Corporate Restructuring of American Capitalism.* New York: Cambridge University Press, 1998.
Slotkin, Richard. *The Fatal Environment: The Myth of the Frontier in the Age of Industrialization.* Norman: University of Oklahoma Press, 1994.
Smith, Sharon. *Subterranean Fire: A History of Working-Class Radicalism in the United States.* Chicago: Haymarket, 2006.
Sotheran, Charles. *Horace Greeley, and Other Pioneers of American Socialism.* 2nd ed. New York: Haskell House, 1971.
Stampp, Kenneth. *The Era of Reconstruction, 1865–1877.* New York: Vintage, 1965.
Stanley, Amy Dru. *From Bondage to Contract: Wage Labor, Marriage, and the Market in the Age of Slave Emancipation.* New York: Cambridge University Press, 1998.
Starobin, Robert S. *Industrial Slavery in the Old South.* New York: Oxford University Press, 1970.
Stauffer, John, and Henry Louis Gates Jr., eds. *The Portable Frederick Douglass.* New York: Penguin Books, 2016.
Storch, Randi. *Red Chicago: American Communism at Its Grassroots, 1928–1935.* Urbana: University of Illinois Press, 2007.
Stowell, David O. *Streets, Railroads, and the Great Strike of 1877.* Chicago: University of Chicago Press, 1999.
Stuckey, Sterling. *Slave Culture: Nationalist Theory and the Foundations of Black America.* New York: Oxford University Press, 1987.
Thompson, E. P. *The Making of the English Working Class.* New York: Pantheon, 1964.
Traverso, Enzo. *Left-Wing Melancholia: Marxism, History, and Memory.* New York: Columbia University Press, 2016.
Tuchinsky, Adam. *Horace Greeley's "New York Tribune": Civil War–Era Socialism and the Crisis of Free Labor.* Ithaca: Cornell University Press, 2009.
Tyler-McGraw, Marie. *At the Falls: Richmond, Virginia, and Its People.* Chapel Hill: University of North Carolina Press, 1994.
Van Zelm, Antoinette. "Virginia Women as Public Citizens: Emancipation Days Celebrations and Lost Cause Commemorations, 1863–1890." In *Negotiating Bound-*

*aries of Southern Womanhood: Dealing with the Powers that Be*, edited by Janet L. Coryell, 71–88. Columbia: University of Missouri Press, 2000.
Wallace, Mike. *Greater Gotham: A History of New York City from 1898 to 1919*. New York: Oxford University Press, 2017.
Warren, Robert Penn. *The Legacy of the Civil War*. New York: Random House, 1961.
Watts, Theodore F. *The First Labor Day Parade*. Silver Spring, MD: Phoenix Rising, 1983.
Weir, Robert E. *Beyond Labor's Veil: The Culture of the Knights of Labor*. University Park: Pennsylvania State University Press, 1996.
———. *Knights Unhorsed: Internal Conflict in a Gilded Age Social Movement*. Detroit: Wayne State University Press, 2000.
———. *Workers in America: A Historical Encyclopedia*. Vol. 1. Santa Barbara: ABC-CLIO, 2013.
White, Richard. *The Republic for Which It Stands: The United States during Reconstruction and the Gilded Age, 1865–1996*. New York: Oxford University Press, 2017.
Wilentz, Sean. *Chants Democratic: New York City and the Rise of the American Working Class*. New York: Oxford University Press, 1984.
———. *The Rise of American Democracy: Jefferson to Lincoln*. New York: W. W. Norton, 2005.
Woodward, C. Vann. *Origins of the New South, 1877–1913*. Baton Rouge: Louisiana State University Press, 1951.
———. *The Strange Career of Jim Crow*. New York: Oxford University Press, 1955.
Work Projects Administration. *Virginia: A Guide to the Old Dominion*. New York: Oxford University Press, 1940.
Wright, Ben, and Zachary W. Dresser, eds. *Apocalypse and the Millennium in the American Civil War Era*. Baton Rouge: Louisiana State University Press, 2013.
Wrobel, David M. *America's West: A History, 1890–1950*. New York: Cambridge University Press, 2017.
Young, Jeremy C. *The Age of Charisma: Leaders, Followers, and Emotions in American Society, 1870–1940*. New York: Cambridge University Press, 2017.
Zornow, William F. "'Bluff Ben' Wade in Kansas: The Issue of Class Conflict." *Ohio History Quarterly* 66 (January 1956): 44–52.

## Websites

http://interactive.ancestryinstitution.com
http://mapserver.lib.virginia.edu
http://www.encyclopediavirginia.org
http://www.fold3.com
https://www.jacobinmag.com
http://www.loc.gov
https://www.marxists.org

# Index

MATTHEW E. STANLEY is an associate professor of history at Albany State University. He is the author of *The Loyal West: Civil War and Reunion in Middle America*.

THE WORKING CLASS IN AMERICAN HISTORY

Worker City, Company Town: Iron and Cotton-Worker Protest in Troy and Cohoes, New York, 1855–84 *Daniel J. Walkowitz*
Life, Work, and Rebellion in the Coal Fields: The Southern West Virginia Miners, 1880–1922 *David Alan Corbin*
Women and American Socialism, 1870–1920 *Mari Jo Buhle*
Lives of Their Own: Blacks, Italians, and Poles in Pittsburgh, 1900–1960 *John Bodnar, Roger Simon, and Michael P. Weber*
Working-Class America: Essays on Labor, Community, and American Society *Edited by Michael H. Frisch and Daniel J. Walkowitz*
Eugene V. Debs: Citizen and Socialist *Nick Salvatore*
American Labor and Immigration History, 1877–1920s: Recent European Research *Edited by Dirk Hoerder*
Workingmen's Democracy: The Knights of Labor and American Politics *Leon Fink*
The Electrical Workers: A History of Labor at General Electric and Westinghouse, 1923–60 *Ronald W. Schatz*
The Mechanics of Baltimore: Workers and Politics in the Age of Revolution, 1763–1812 *Charles G. Steffen*
The Practice of Solidarity: American Hat Finishers in the Nineteenth Century *David Bensman*
The Labor History Reader *Edited by Daniel J. Leab*
Solidarity and Fragmentation: Working People and Class Consciousness in Detroit, 1875–1900 *Richard Oestreicher*
Counter Cultures: Saleswomen, Managers, and Customers in American Department Stores, 1890–1940 *Susan Porter Benson*
The New England Working Class and the New Labor History *Edited by Herbert G. Gutman and Donald H. Bell*
Labor Leaders in America *Edited by Melvyn Dubofsky and Warren Van Tine*
Barons of Labor: The San Francisco Building Trades and Union Power in the Progressive Era *Michael Kazin*
Gender at Work: The Dynamics of Job Segregation by Sex during World War II *Ruth Milkman*
Once a Cigar Maker: Men, Women, and Work Culture in American Cigar Factories, 1900–1919 *Patricia A. Cooper*
A Generation of Boomers: The Pattern of Railroad Labor Conflict in Nineteenth-Century America *Shelton Stromquist*
Work and Community in the Jungle: Chicago's Packinghouse Workers, 1894–1922 *James R. Barrett*
Workers, Managers, and Welfare Capitalism: The Shoeworkers and Tanners of Endicott Johnson, 1890–1950 *Gerald Zahavi*

Men, Women, and Work: Class, Gender, and Protest in the New England Shoe Industry, 1780–1910 *Mary Blewett*

Workers on the Waterfront: Seamen, Longshoremen, and Unionism in the 1930s *Bruce Nelson*

German Workers in Chicago: A Documentary History of Working-Class Culture from 1850 to World War I *Edited by Hartmut Keil and John B. Jentz*

On the Line: Essays in the History of Auto Work *Edited by Nelson Lichtenstein and Stephen Meyer III*

Labor's Flaming Youth: Telephone Operators and Worker Militancy, 1878–1923 *Stephen H. Norwood*

Another Civil War: Labor, Capital, and the State in the Anthracite Regions of Pennsylvania, 1840–68 *Grace Palladino*

Coal, Class, and Color: Blacks in Southern West Virginia, 1915–32 *Joe William Trotter Jr.*

For Democracy, Workers, and God: Labor Song-Poems and Labor Protest, 1865–95 *Clark D. Halker*

Dishing It Out: Waitresses and Their Unions in the Twentieth Century *Dorothy Sue Cobble*

The Spirit of 1848: German Immigrants, Labor Conflict, and the Coming of the Civil War *Bruce Levine*

Working Women of Collar City: Gender, Class, and Community in Troy, New York, 1864–86 *Carole Turbin*

Southern Labor and Black Civil Rights: Organizing Memphis Workers *Michael K. Honey*

Radicals of the Worst Sort: Laboring Women in Lawrence, Massachusetts, 1860–1912 *Ardis Cameron*

Producers, Proletarians, and Politicians: Workers and Party Politics in Evansville and New Albany, Indiana, 1850–87 *Lawrence M. Lipin*

The New Left and Labor in the 1960s *Peter B. Levy*

The Making of Western Labor Radicalism: Denver's Organized Workers, 1878–1905 *David Brundage*

In Search of the Working Class: Essays in American Labor History and Political Culture *Leon Fink*

Lawyers against Labor: From Individual Rights to Corporate Liberalism *Daniel R. Ernst*

"We Are All Leaders": The Alternative Unionism of the Early 1930s *Edited by Staughton Lynd*

The Female Economy: The Millinery and Dressmaking Trades, 1860–1930 *Wendy Gamber*

"Negro and White, Unite and Fight!": A Social History of Industrial Unionism in Meatpacking, 1930–90 *Roger Horowitz*

Power at Odds: The 1922 National Railroad Shopmen's Strike *Colin J. Davis*

The Common Ground of Womanhood: Class, Gender, and Working Girls' Clubs, 1884–1928 *Priscilla Murolo*
Marching Together: Women of the Brotherhood of Sleeping Car Porters *Melinda Chateauvert*
Down on the Killing Floor: Black and White Workers in Chicago's Packinghouses, 1904–54 *Rick Halpern*
Labor and Urban Politics: Class Conflict and the Origins of Modern Liberalism in Chicago, 1864–97 *Richard Schneirov*
All That Glitters: Class, Conflict, and Community in Cripple Creek *Elizabeth Jameson*
Waterfront Workers: New Perspectives on Race and Class *Edited by Calvin Winslow*
Labor Histories: Class, Politics, and the Working-Class Experience *Edited by Eric Arnesen, Julie Greene, and Bruce Laurie*
The Pullman Strike and the Crisis of the 1890s: Essays on Labor and Politics *Edited by Richard Schneirov, Shelton Stromquist, and Nick Salvatore*
AlabamaNorth: African-American Migrants, Community, and Working-Class Activism in Cleveland, 1914–45 *Kimberley L. Phillips*
Imagining Internationalism in American and British Labor, 1939–49 *V ictor Silverman*
William Z. Foster and the Tragedy of American Radicalism *James R. Barrett*
Colliers across the Sea: A Comparative Study of Class Formation in Scotland and the American Midwest, 1830–1924 *John H. M. Laslett*
"Rights, Not Roses": Unions and the Rise of Working-Class Feminism, 1945–80 *Dennis A. Deslippe*
Testing the New Deal: The General Textile Strike of 1934 in the American South *Janet Irons*
Hard Work: The Making of Labor History *Melvyn Dubofsky*
Southern Workers and the Search for Community: Spartanburg County, South Carolina *G. C. Waldrep III*
We Shall Be All: A History of the Industrial Workers of the World (abridged edition) *Melvyn Dubofsky, ed. Joseph A. McCartin*
Race, Class, and Power in the Alabama Coalfields, 1908–21 *Brian Kelly*
Duquesne and the Rise of Steel Unionism *James D. Rose*
Anaconda: Labor, Community, and Culture in Montana's Smelter City *Laurie Mercier*
Bridgeport's Socialist New Deal, 1915–36 *Cecelia Bucki*
Indispensable Outcasts: Hobo Workers and Community in the American Midwest, 1880–1930 *Frank Tobias Higbie*
After the Strike: A Century of Labor Struggle at Pullman *Susan Eleanor Hirsch*
Corruption and Reform in the Teamsters Union *David Witwer*
Waterfront Revolts: New York and London Dockworkers, 1946–61 *Colin J. Davis*

Black Workers' Struggle for Equality in Birmingham *Horace Huntley and David Montgomery*

The Tribe of Black Ulysses: African American Men in the Industrial South *William P. Jones*

City of Clerks: Office and Sales Workers in Philadelphia, 1870–1920 *Jerome P. Bjelopera*

Reinventing "The People": The Progressive Movement, the Class Problem, and the Origins of Modern Liberalism *Shelton Stromquist*

Radical Unionism in the Midwest, 1900–1950 *Rosemary Feurer*

Gendering Labor History *Alice Kessler-Harris*

James P. Cannon and the Origins of the American Revolutionary Left, 1890–1928 *Bryan D. Palmer*

Glass Towns: Industry, Labor, and Political Economy in Appalachia, 1890–1930s *Ken Fones-Wolf*

Workers and the Wild: Conservation, Consumerism, and Labor in Oregon, 1910–30 *Lawrence M. Lipin*

Wobblies on the Waterfront: Interracial Unionism in Progressive-Era Philadelphia *Peter Cole*

Red Chicago: American Communism at Its Grassroots, 1928–35 *Randi Storch*

Labor's Cold War: Local Politics in a Global Context *Edited by Shelton Stromquist*

Bessie Abramowitz Hillman and the Making of the Amalgamated Clothing Workers of America *Karen Pastorello*

The Great Strikes of 1877 *Edited by David O. Stowell*

Union-Free America: Workers and Antiunion Culture *Lawrence Richards*

Race against Liberalism: Black Workers and the UAW in Detroit *David M. Lewis-Colman*

Teachers and Reform: Chicago Public Education, 1929–70 *John F. Lyons*

Upheaval in the Quiet Zone: 1199/SEIU and the Politics of Healthcare Unionism *Leon Fink and Brian Greenberg*

Shadow of the Racketeer: Scandal in Organized Labor *David Witwer*

Sweet Tyranny: Migrant Labor, Industrial Agriculture, and Imperial Politics *Kathleen Mapes*

Staley: The Fight for a New American Labor Movement *Steven K. Ashby and C. J. Hawking*

On the Ground: Labor Struggles in the American Airline Industry *Liesl Miller Orenic*

NAFTA and Labor in North America *Norman Caulfield*

Making Capitalism Safe: Work Safety and Health Regulation in America, 1880–1940 *Donald W. Rogers*

Good, Reliable, White Men: Railroad Brotherhoods, 1877–1917 *Paul Michel Taillon*

Spirit of Rebellion: Labor and Religion in the New Cotton South *Jarod Roll*

The Labor Question in America: Economic Democracy in the Gilded Age *Rosanne Currarino*

Banded Together: Economic Democratization in the Brass Valley *Jeremy Brecher*

The Gospel of the Working Class: Labor's Southern Prophets in New Deal America *Erik Gellman and Jarod Roll*

Guest Workers and Resistance to U.S. Corporate Despotism *Immanuel Ness*

Gleanings of Freedom: Free and Slave Labor along the Mason-Dixon Line, 1790–1860 *Max Grivno*

Chicago in the Age of Capital: Class, Politics, and Democracy during the Civil War and Reconstruction *John B. Jentz and Richard Schneirov*

Child Care in Black and White: Working Parents and the History of Orphanages *Jessie B. Ramey*

The Haymarket Conspiracy: Transatlantic Anarchist Networks *Timothy Messer-Kruse*

Detroit's Cold War: The Origins of Postwar Conservatism *Colleen Doody*

A Renegade Union: Interracial Organizing and Labor Radicalism *Lisa Phillips*

Palomino: Clinton Jencks and Mexican-American Unionism in the American Southwest *James J. Lorence*

Latin American Migrations to the U.S. Heartland: Changing Cultural Landscapes in Middle America *Edited by Linda Allegro and Andrew Grant Wood*

Man of Fire: Selected Writings *Ernesto Galarza, ed. Armando Ibarra and Rodolfo D. Torres*

A Contest of Ideas: Capital, Politics, and Labor *Nelson Lichtenstein*

Making the World Safe for Workers: Labor, the Left, and Wilsonian Internationalism *Elizabeth McKillen*

The Rise of the Chicago Police Department: Class and Conflict, 1850–1894 *Sam Mitrani*

Workers in Hard Times: A Long View of Economic Crises *Edited by Leon Fink, Joseph A. McCartin, and Joan Sangster*

Redeeming Time: Protestantism and Chicago's Eight-Hour Movement, 1866–1912 *William A. Mirola*

Struggle for the Soul of the Postwar South: White Evangelical Protestants and Operation Dixie *Elizabeth Fones-Wolf and Ken Fones-Wolf*

Free Labor: The Civil War and the Making of an American Working Class *Mark A. Lause*

Death and Dying in the Working Class, 1865–1920 *Michael K. Rosenow*

Immigrants against the State: Yiddish and Italian Anarchism in America *Kenyon Zimmer*

Fighting for Total Person Unionism: Harold Gibbons, Ernest Calloway, and Working-Class Citizenship *Robert Bussel*

Smokestacks in the Hills: Rural-Industrial Workers in West Virginia *Louis Martin*

Disaster Citizenship: Survivors, Solidarity, and Power in the Progressive Era
*Jacob A. C. Remes*

The Pew and the Picket Line: Christianity and the American Working Class
*Edited by Christopher D. Cantwell, Heath W. Carter, and Janine Giordano Drake*

Conservative Counterrevolution: Challenging Liberalism in 1950s Milwaukee
*Tula A. Connell*

Manhood on the Line: Working-Class Masculinities in the American Heartland
*Steve Meyer*

On Gender, Labor, and Inequality *Ruth Milkman*

The Making of Working-Class Religion *Matthew Pehl*

Civic Labors: Scholar Activism and Working-Class Studies
*Edited by Dennis Deslippe, Eric Fure-Slocum, and John W. McKerley*

Victor Arnautoff and the Politics of Art *Robert W. Cherny*

Against Labor: How U.S. Employers Organized to Defeat Union Activism
*Edited by Rosemary Feurer and Chad Pearson*

Teacher Strike! Public Education and the Making of a New American Political Order *Jon Shelton*

Hillbilly Hellraisers: Federal Power and Populist Defiance in the Ozarks
*J. Blake Perkins*

Sewing the Fabric of Statehood: Garment Unions, American Labor, and the Establishment of the State of Israel *Adam Howard*

Labor and Justice across the America *Edited by Leon Fink and J uan Manuel Palacio*

Frontiers of Labor: Comparative Histories of the United States and Australia *Edited by Greg Patmore and Shelton Stromquist*

Women Have Always Worked: A Concise History, Second Edition
*Alice Kessler-Harris*

Remembering Lattimer: Labor, Migration, and Race in Pennsylvania Anthracite Country *Paul A. Shackel*

Disruption in Detroit: Autoworkers and the Elusive Postwar Boom
*Daniel J. Clark*

To Live Here, You Have to Fight: How Women Led Appalachian Movements for Social Justice *Jessica Wilkerson*

Dockworker Power: Race and Activism in Durban and the San Francisco Bay Area *Peter Cole*

Labor's Mind: A History of Working-Class Intellectual Life *Tobias Higbie*

The World in a City: Multiethnic Radicalism in Early Twentieth-Century Los Angeles *David M. Struthers*

Death to Fascism: Louis Adamic's Fight for Democracy *John P. Enyeart*

Upon the Altar of Work: Child Labor and the Rise of a New American Sectionalism *Betsy Wood*

Workers against the City: The Fight for Free Speech in *Hague v. CIO*
*Donald W. Rogers*

Union Renegades: Miners, Capitalism, and Organizing in the Gilded Age
*Dana M. Caldemeyer*

The Labor Board Crew: Remaking Worker-Employer Relations from Pearl Harbor to the Reagan Era *Ronald W. Schatz*

Grand Army of Labor: Workers, Veterans, and the Meaning of the Civil War
*Matthew E. Stanley*

The University of Illinois Press
is a founding member of the
Association of University Presses.

University of Illinois Press
1325 South Oak Street
Champaign, IL 61820-6903
www.press.uillinois.edu